The CSCE and the End of the Cold War

THE CSCE AND THE END OF THE COLD WAR

Diplomacy, Societies and Human Rights, 1972–1990

Edited by Nicolas Badalassi and Sarah B. Snyder

NEW YORK · OXFORD
www.berghahnbooks.com

First published in 2019 by
Berghahn Books
www.berghahnbooks.com

© 2019, 2020 Nicolas Badalassi and Sarah B. Snyder
First paperback edition publsihed in 2020

All rights reserved. Except for the quotation of short passages for the purposes of criticism and review, no part of this book may be reproduced in any form or by any means, electronic or mechanical, including photocopying, recording, or any information storage and retrieval system now known or to be invented, without written permission of the publisher.

Library of Congress Cataloging-in-Publication Data
Names: Badalassi, Nicolas, editor. | Snyder, Sarah B., 1977- editor.
Title: The CSCE and the end of the Cold War : diplomacy, societies and human rights, 1972-1990 / edited by Nicolas Badalassi and Sarah B. Snyder.
Description: New York : Berghahn Books, 2019. | Includes bibliographical references and index.
Identifiers: LCCN 2018026307 (print) | LCCN 2018047225 (ebook) | ISBN 9781789200270 (ebook) | ISBN 9781789200263 (hardback :¬alk. paper) |
Subjects: LCSH: Conference on Security and Cooperation in Europe--History. | Conference on Security and Cooperation in Europe (1972-1975 : Helsinki, Finland). Final Act. | Cold War. | Security, International--International cooperation.
Classification: LCC D849 (ebook) | LCC D849 .C73 2019 (print) | DDC 355/.03109409045--dc23
LC record available at https://lccn.loc.gov/2018026307

British Library Cataloguing in Publication Data
A catalogue record for this book is available from the British Library

ISBN 978-1-78920-026-3 hardback
ISBN 978-1-78920-849-8 paperback
ISBN 978-1-78920-027-0 ebook

In memory of Anne-Marie Le Gloannec (1951–2017)

Contents

Acknowledgements	ix
List of Abbreviations	x
Chronology of CSCE Meetings	xii
Introduction *Nicolas Badalassi and Sarah B. Snyder*	1

Part I. Diplomats, Diplomacies and the Making of the CSCE

Chapter 1	The Human Dimension of the CSCE, 1975–1990 *Andrei Zagorski*	17
Chapter 2	Executors or Creative Deal-Makers? The Role of the Diplomats in the Making of the Helsinki CSCE *Martin D. Brown and Angela Romano*	43
Chapter 3	From Talleyrand to Sakharov: French Diplomacy in Search of a 'Helsinki Effect' *Nicolas Badalassi*	74
Chapter 4	'Human Rights, Peace and Security Are Inseparable': Max Kampelman and the Helsinki Process *Stephan Kieninger*	97

Part II. The Transnational Promotion of Human Rights and the Role of Dissidence

Chapter 5	The Committee of Concerned Scientists and the Helsinki Final Act: 'Refusenik' Scientists, Détente and Human Rights *Elisabetta Vezzosi*	119

Chapter 6	Seeing the Value of the Helsinki Accords: Human Rights, Peace and Transnational Debates about Détente, 1981–1988 *Christian P. Peterson*	151
Chapter 7	The Importance of the Helsinki Process for the Opposition in Central and Eastern Europe and the Western Peace Movements in the 1980s *Jacek Czaputowicz*	183
Chapter 8	The Limits of Repression: Soviet Bloc Security Services vs. Transnational Helsinki Networks, 1976–1986 *Douglas Selvage*	207
Chapter 9	Helsinki at Home: NGOs, the Helsinki Final Act and Politics in the United States, 1975–1985 *Carl J. Bon Tempo*	230

Part III. The Politics of the CSCE in Europe

Chapter 10	European Détente and the CSCE: Austria and the East-Central European Theatre in the 1970s and 1980s *Maximilian Graf*	249
Chapter 11	Saving Détente: The Federal Republic of Germany and the CSCE in the 1980s *Matthias Peter*	275
Chapter 12	Transformation by Linkage? Arms Control, Human Rights and the Rift between Moscow and East Berlin in the Late 1980s *Oliver Bange*	305
Chapter 13	CSCE: Albania, the Outsider in European Political Life *Hamit Kaba*	330
Conclusion	*Nicolas Badalassi and Sarah B. Snyder*	350
Index		357

Acknowledgements

This work would not have been possible without the Program *Sociétés Plurielles*, supported by the Sorbonne Paris Cité University. We therefore first and foremost thank the professors who conceived the conference which, in December 2015 in Paris, laid the foundations for a close and regular cooperation between the various contributors to this book. In particular, we would like to thank Sophie Coeuré (University of Paris 7 – Denis Diderot), Anne de Tinguy (Sciences-Po Paris, INALCO), Anne-Marie Le Gloannec (Sciences-Po) and Frédéric Bozo (University of Paris 3 – Sorbonne Nouvelle), as well as the other members of the scientific committee: Marie-Pierre Rey (University of Paris 1 – Panthéon Sorbonne), Evguenia Obitchkina (MGIMO, Moscow) and Gottfried Niedhart (University of Mannheim).

We want to highlight particularly Anne-Marie Le Gloannec, a great specialist of contemporary Germany who left us in April 2017. Through the quality and relevance of her reflections as well as her personal investment in organizing the 2015 conference, Professor Le Gloannec's contributions guided the authors of this book for more than two years. We honour her memory by dedicating this book to her.

Thanks also to Ilaria Parisi for her efficiency and good nature in organizing the conference. More broadly, we acknowledge the international community of scholars of the CSCE and the end of the Cold War who informed our research and who offered feedback at the initial conference.

We are also grateful to all the contributors, who have cooperated to make this book a collective scientific endeavour. We also express our appreciation to our editor Chris Chappell, his editorial assistant Soyolmaa Lkhagvadorj, and the three anonymous readers for Berghahn Books. Their suggestions, feedback and support were helpful as we developed and revised the manuscript.

Finally, we acknowledge our families' support of our ongoing interest in the CSCE and all of its many consequences.

Nicolas Badalassi and Sarah B. Snyder
March 2018

Abbreviations

ABA	American Bar Association
ALP	Albania's Labor Party
BANG	Brooklyn Antinuclear Group
CBM	Confidence-Building Measures
CCS	Committee of Concerned Scientists
CDE	Conference on Confidence and Security Building Measures and Disarmament in Europe
CES	Conference on European Security
CFE	Conventional Forces in Europe
CHD	Conference on the Human Dimension
CND	Campaign for Nuclear Disarmament
CoE	Council of Europe
CPDEW	Campaign for Peace and Democracy – East and West
CPSU	Communist Party of the Soviet Union
CSBM	Confidence and Security Building Measures
CSCE	Conference on Security and Cooperation in Europe
CSSR	Czechoslovak Socialist Republic
EC	European Community
ECHR	European Court of Human Rights
EDC	European Disarmament Conference
END	European Nuclear Disarmament
ENEWD	European Network for East-West Dialogue
EPC	European Political Cooperation
EU	European Union
FDP	Free Democratic Party (FRG)
FRG	Federal Republic of Germany
GDR	German Democratic Republic
HDIM	Human Dimension Implementation Meeting
HDM	Human Dimension Mechanism
HRC	Human Rights Council
IKV	Interchurch Peace Council (Netherlands)
INF	Intermediate-Range Nuclear Forces

IPCC	International Peace Communication and Coordination Centre
KGB	Committee for State Security (USSR)
KOR	Workers' Defense Committee (Poland)
MBFR	Mutual and Balanced Force Reductions
MfS	Ministry for State Security (GDR)
MPT	Multilateral Preparatory Talks
NAACP	National Association for the Advancement of Colored People (USA)
NATO	North Atlantic Treaty Organization
NENWN	Neither East Nor West – NYC
NGO	Non-governmental organizations
NNA	Neutral and Non-Aligned Countries
NYC	New York City
ODIHR	Office for Democratic Institutions and Human Rights
OSCE	Organization for Security and Cooperation in Europe
PAEW	Peace Activists East and West
PRC	People's Republic of China
PSR	Physicians for Social Responsibility (USA)
ROPCiO	Movement to Defend Human and Civil Rights (Poland)
SALT	Strategic Arms Limitation Talks
SANE	National Committee for a Sane Nuclear Policy (USA)
SCDP	Soviet Committee for the Defense of Peace
SDI	Strategic Defense Initiative
SED	Socialist Unity Party of Germany (GDR)
SOS	Scientists for Sakharov, Orlov and Shcharansky
SPD	Social Democratic Party of Germany (FRG)
START	Strategic Arms Reduction Treaty
TNF	Theatre Nuclear Forces
UNESCO	United Nations Educational, Scientific and Cultural Organization
UNO	United Nations Organization
USA	United States of America
USHW	United States Helsinki Watch Group
USSR	Union of Soviet Socialist Republics
WGF	Western Group of Forces
WILPF	Women's International League for Peace and Freedom
WiP	Freedom and Peace Movement (Poland)
WRL	War Registers League (USA)
WTO	Warsaw Treaty Organization

Chronology of CSCE Meetings (1972–1992)

Meeting	Date	Location
Preparatory consultations	22 November 1972–8 June 1973	Dipoli (Helsinki)
CSCE – Stage I	3–7 July 1973	Helsinki
CSCE – Stage II	18 September 1973–21 July 1975	Geneva
CSCE – Stage III	30 July–1 August 1975	Helsinki
Preparatory meeting for the First Follow-up Meeting	15 June–3 August 1977	Belgrade
First Follow-up Meeting to the CSCE	4 October 1977–9 March 1978	Belgrade
Meeting of Experts to prepare the Science Forum	20 June–28 July 1978	Bonn
Meeting of Experts on the Peaceful Settlement of Disputes	31 October–11 December 1978	Montreux
Meeting of Experts on Cooperation in the Mediterranean	13 February–26 March 1979	Valletta
Science Forum	18 February–3 March 1980	Hamburg
Preparatory meeting for the Second Follow-up Meeting	9 September–10 November 1980	Madrid
Second Follow-up Meeting to the CSCE	11 November 1980–9 September 1983	Madrid
Preparatory meeting for the Conference on Confidence and Security Building Measures and Disarmament in Europe	25 October–11 November 1983	Helsinki
Conference on Confidence and Security Building Measures and Disarmament in Europe – Stage I	17 January 1984–19 September 1986	Stockholm
Meeting of Experts on the Peaceful Settlement of Disputes	21 March–30 April 1984	Athens
Seminar on Economic, Scientific and Cultural Cooperation in the Mediterranean Region	16–26 October 1984	Venice
Meeting of Experts to prepare the Culture Forum	21 November–4 December 1984	Budapest

Meeting	Date	Location
Meeting of Experts to prepare the meeting on Compliance with Human Rights and Fundamental Freedoms	7 July–17 June 1985	Ottawa
Tenth anniversary ceremony commemorating signing the Helsinki Final Act	30 July–1 August 1985	Helsinki
Culture Forum	15 October–25 November 1985	Budapest
Meeting of Experts on Human Contacts	15 April–26 May 1986	Bern
Preparatory meeting for the Third Follow-up Meeting	23 September–3 November 1986	Vienna
Third Follow-up Meeting to the CSCE	4 November 1986–19 January 1989	Vienna
Negotiations on Conventional Armed Forces in Europe	6 March 1989–19 November 1990	Vienna
Conference on Confidence and Security Building Measures and Disarmament in Europe – Stage II	9 March 1989–18 November 1990	Vienna
Information Forum	18 April 1989–12 May 1989	London
Conference on the Human Dimension of the CSCE – first meeting	30 May–23 June 1989	Paris
Meeting on the Protection of the Environment	16 October–3 November 1989	Sofia
Conference on Economic Cooperation in Europe	19 March 1990–11 April 1990	Bonn
Conference on the Human Dimension of the CSCE – second meeting	5–29 June 1990	Copenhagen
Preparatory Committee for the Summit meeting	10 July–17 November 1990	Vienna
Meeting on the Mediterranean	24 September–19 October 1990	Palma de Majorca
Paris Summit	19–21 November 1990	Paris
Meeting of Experts on the Peaceful Settlement of Disputes	15 January–8 February 1991	Valletta
Seminar on the Cultural Heritage	25 May–7 June 1991	Krakow
First Meeting of the CSCE Council of Ministers	19–20 June 1991	Berlin
Meeting of Experts on National Minorities	1–19 July 1991	Geneva
Additional Meeting of the Council of the CSCE	10 September 1991	Moscow
Conference on the Human Dimension of the CSCE – third meeting	10 September–4 October 1991	Moscow
Seminar of Experts on Democratic Institutions	4–15 November 1991	Oslo
Second Meeting of the CSCE Council of Ministers	30–31 January 1992	Prague

Meeting	Date	Location
Conference on Confidence and Security Building Measures and Disarmament in Europe – Follow-up to Stage II	9 March 1989– 4 March 1992	Vienna
Preparatory meeting for the fourth Follow-up Meeting	10–20 March 1992	Helsinki
First Additional Meeting of the Council of the CSCE	24 March 1992	Helsinki
Fourth Follow-up Meeting to the CSCE	24 March–8 July 1992	Helsinki
Helsinki Summit	9–10 July 1992	Helsinki

INTRODUCTION

Nicolas Badalassi and Sarah B. Snyder

The assumption that underlay Soviet Foreign Minister Andrei Gromyko's approach to international relations in the mid 1970s was that the sovereignty of states was paramount. In his view, the inviolability of frontiers and non-interference in internal affairs were fundamental principles for the future of peace. These issues could determine war and peace. However, having access to foreign newspapers, reunifying with a foreign spouse or having the ability to travel abroad to visit a sick relative were not seen as key questions in international relations.[1] According to the approach outlined by Gromyko in July 1974, each state should have the right to model its own society at will and protect itself against external interference. Such thinking shaped the Soviet strategy at the Conference on Security and Cooperation in Europe (CSCE), which assembled the representatives of thirty-five European and North American countries between July 1973 and August 1975.

Soviet leader Leonid Brezhnev was even more categorical when he met French president Georges Pompidou to talk about the CSCE and other East–West issues a few months before Gromyko's statement:

> First and foremost, I declare that the Soviet Union is in favour of the most extensive relations and contacts permissible in the current conditions, for the improvement of cultural exchange and so on, for all measures which favour a better understanding between peoples. But if these issues are raised with the intention to shake our social regime, our answer will be a strong 'no'.[2]

Brezhnev's remarks illustrate perfectly Moscow's desire to maintain the Westphalian system of international relations, which was based on the domination of the states and respect for frontiers in international relations and had existed in Europe since the seventeenth century. In contrast to the Kremlin's intentions, the CSCE eventually contributed to overcoming the Westphalian system. Although there are dissenters, many historians agree that the 'Helsinki process', or all of the diplomatic meetings that followed the signing of the 1975 Helsinki Final Act, influenced the events that led to the end of the East–West conflict and to the collapse of the Soviet bloc.[3] In this sense, the CSCE, its evolution and the issues it raised were at the centre of the international relations of the second part of the twentieth century. Born of Soviet willingness to freeze the European political and territorial situation in order to preserve Moscow's stranglehold over Central and Eastern Europe, the CSCE became during the 1970s the main forum of discussions between East and West and, consequently, a Western tool to observe the evolutions in the communist bloc and try to influence them.

Thus far, most accounts of the CSCE have emphasized diplomatic aspects of the Helsinki process. Scholars have examined the diplomacy that produced the Helsinki Final Act and subsequent CSCE documents from various national, regional and chronological perspectives. This book highlights instead the links among diplomacy, societies and human rights. The collected chapters analyse the broader political and societal context of the CSCE.

Negotiating the Helsinki Final Act

The CSCE negotiations did not begin favourably for North Atlantic Treaty Organization (NATO) and European Community (EC) countries. When the multilateral preparatory talks (MPT) of the CSCE started in November 1972 in Helsinki, the United States was still entangled in Vietnam, the difficulties of the dollar were harming transatlantic relations, and the Union of Soviet Socialist Republics (USSR), which had severely repressed the Prague Spring in August 1968, seemed more powerful than ever in Central and Eastern Europe. But it was precisely those elements that allowed the Western Europeans and their North American allies to shape the Soviet project of a conference on European security according to their views. On one hand, the United States' obsession with Southeast Asian issues and its relative lack of interest in Europe convinced the European members of NATO that the CSCE offered an opportunity to assert themselves against the two superpowers. In addition, the Soviet will to avoid any development inside the Eastern bloc led the same countries to think about ways to help the peoples trapped on the eastern side of the Iron Curtain. Henceforth the CSCE appeared as an ideal tool to satisfy both objectives. Between the late 1960s and the early 1970s, the West Europeans accepted the Soviet idea of a conference on European security, if the issues of respect for human rights, cultural exchange, contacts between peoples and cooperation in the field of information would be included on the agenda of the conference.

These themes reflected the priorities of Western societies during the 1960s and 1970s. In most West European and North American countries (including neutral countries like Switzerland, Sweden and Austria), young people born just after the Second World War had yearnings for the new. Sexual liberation, the augmentation of individualism, overconsumption and hedonism, the weakening of traditional values like family, work, frugality, religion, the reduction of the working class and mistrust of the state, all of which was intensified by media coverage and the omnipresence of images, redefined the populations' perceptions of their societies, their countries and the world. The Western and Neutral CSCE agenda reflected these new impulses and cannot be considered outside this broader context. Hundreds of diplomats who took part in it were immersed in the atmosphere of change that characterized those years. Even representatives of the Eastern bloc, who were exposed to the Western world at different junctures, were not cloistered from these social influences. For example, the Soviet diplomat Lev Mendelevich took advantage of his presence in Helsinki during the MPT to attend a showing of Pasolini's *Decameron*, a film forbidden in the East because of its sexual nature.[4]

One of the novelties of the CSCE stemmed from the fact that EC and NATO countries as well as the Neutral states managed to insert themes into the conference's agenda that reflected those evolutions, including cultural cooperation (opening movie theatres and reading rooms as well as eliminating barriers that prevented the circulation of cultural objects and artists), science and education (enhancing scientific exchange), diffusion of information (improving journalists' working conditions as well as distributing the press) and human contacts (reunifying families as well as facilitating bi-national marriages and tourism).[5] From 1973 onwards, these issues constituted the so-called third 'basket' of the CSCE, meaning a group of issues negotiated together.

In basket three, concrete measures complemented the principles of the 'first basket', among which respect for human rights figured prominently. The first basket also addressed inviolability of frontiers, state sovereignty and non-interference in internal affairs. The Helsinki Final Act proclaimed that the principles guiding the relations between participating states were equal and interdependent, putting respect for human rights on the same level as the Westphalian principles that were at the heart of the USSR policy aiming to freeze the European political and territorial status quo. Whereas the Soviets considered human rights as bourgeois privileges in contradiction of a communist ideal in which the collective good prevailed over the individual, the Westerners and the Neutrals managed to introduce into the Final Act some references to the non-Marxist conception of these rights by defining them as factors of peace. By including human rights among the principles guiding relations between states, the West weakened the value of sovereignty and non-interference.[6] This aspect is key to the importance of the CSCE in the history of international relations.

The CSCE's Surprising Significance

The CSCE, which brought together hundreds of diplomats during thousands of hours of meetings about diverse topics, might have failed. Yet it did not. Part of the success of the conference owes to the Western and Neutral use of traditional diplomatic methods – such as official multilateral discussions and unofficial bilateral meetings – to which the Soviets were attached. During these conversations, representatives of the European democracies tried to promote innovative themes corresponding to the realities of the European societies of the 1970s and later the 1980s. A second factor in the success of the Helsinki process was its long-term logic. The follow-up mechanism, or put differently a commitment to hold subsequent talks, was essential to understanding the impact of the conference during the last years of the Cold War. The follow-up meetings in Belgrade (1977–78), Madrid (1980–83) and Vienna (1986–89) not only evaluated the implementation of the CSCE provisions in the participating countries, but they also formed an excellent barometer of East–West relations.[7] These follow-up meetings and the parallel processes and organizations they inspired ensured that during the last decade of the Cold War, social issues were at the forefront. Especially in the socialist bloc, it was increasingly difficult for people to endure the established political and economic system and for the authorities to face protest movements in, for example, Poland and the GDR. From 1972 to 1980, the CSCE embodied a permanent link between diplomats and society, which explains why the Helsinki process and its follow-up meetings could contribute to the end of the Cold War. First, the CSCE created a set framework of negotiation and cooperation by tackling constituent issues of East–West competition, like borders, economy, science and industry, human contacts and culture. Signing the Helsinki Final Act should have meant that the leaders of each participating state accepted the legitimacy of a dialogue about human rights. In the Eastern countries such recognition was slow, which encouraged the development of independent political movements, exerting real pressure on their political authorities in favour of the implementation of the Final Act.[8] Established in Eastern Europe and across the Soviet Union, groups such as the Ukrainian Public Group of Assistance to Implementation of the Helsinki Agreements in the USSR, the Working Commission to Investigate the Use of Psychiatry for Political Purposes and Charter 77 highlighted the gap between the promises of the agreement and actual government practice.[9] They mobilized to measure implementation of the Helsinki Final Act and worked closely with sympathetic politicians, diplomats and activists to press for meaningful change.

Publication of the Helsinki Final Act in Soviet newspapers spurred non-governmental activity in the Soviet bloc.[10] Several months later, the Soviet physicist and dissident Yuri Orlov announced the creation of the 'Public Group to Promote Fulfillment of the Helsinki Accords in the USSR'. Constituted to ensure that the principle of human rights and the provisions of the third basket would be implemented in the USSR, the committee gathered numerous dissidents, including writer Alexander Ginzburg, historian Andrei Amalrik, writer and mathematician Anatoly Shcharansky, historian Lyudmila Alexeyeva and human rights activist Yelena Bonner.[11] Similar groups were launched in other Soviet republics as well as in satellite countries, the most important and the most famous being Charter 77 in Czechoslovakia. These groups soon came into contact and, in the USSR, formed a network with pre-existing religious and nationalist organizations.

The Kremlin observed with some concern a growing movement for human rights after Helsinki, beginning with the Committee for State Security (KGB) declaration that the group was illegal on 15 May 1976.[12] The main response of the KGB was to use 'psychiatric' and 'prophylactic measures' against some dissidents. The authorities progressively increased arrests and sent activists into exile. Orlov and Ginzburg were arrested, as well as other members of the committee. Suppression also occurred in Czechoslovakia against the spokespersons of Charter 77, starting with Václav Havel. The repression of Helsinki monitors spurred support in the United States and Western Europe, eventually leading to the creation of a transnational Helsinki network.

Despite crackdown and renewed East–West tensions after 1977, the struggle for human rights in Central and Eastern Europe continued, and the Helsinki Final Act had unexpected influence in the transformation of Europe. During the last fifteen years of the Cold War, diplomats and activists at the successive meetings of the CSCE tried to maintain the tie between diplomacy, society and individual rights. In addition, Western embassies to Warsaw Pact states produced numerous reports on implementation (or non-implementation) of the societal provisions of the Final Act in those countries. This synergy between diplomatic activity and societal transformation within the Helsinki process peaked in 1986 when the non-governmental organizations were authorized to attend the official CSCE discussions in Vienna. This relationship persisted amidst the transformation of Europe between 1989 and 1992 when the CSCE evolved into the Organization for Security and Cooperation in Europe.

After the end of the Cold War, the CSCE remained a player in the field of cooperative security. Due to its role in overcoming the Iron Curtain, some states have even sought to transpose the CSCE model to other regions or continents, for example to the Mediterranean or East Asia.[13]

Changing Perceptions of the CSCE

As soon as the Final Act was signed, the CSCE was disparaged by numerous Westerners who saw in the conference merely an acknowledgement of the European status quo by the leaders of the West. Suppression of the Eastern dissidents who engaged in monitoring the Helsinki Final Act also created a negative perception of the CSCE. Since the 1990s, however, many researchers have been interested in how the Helsinki process contributed to the end of the Cold War. In particular, historians in Europe and the United States have worked to challenge such a perception. They took advantage of the opening of the archives of the former East, West and Neutral member states to start a historical investigation into the CSCE. Thus, national policies towards the Helsinki process have been thoroughly studied concerning the United States, the Federal Republic of Germany (FRG), the United Kingdom, France, the EC and Neutral countries like Sweden, Austria, Finland and Switzerland.[14] Their work has led the CSCE to be regularly mentioned alongside more traditional explanations for the end of the Cold War such as Ronald Reagan's arms buildup, Mikhail Gorbachev's attempts at reform, the deterioration of the economic situation in the Eastern bloc, the role of the dissidents and the impact of Western culture on socialist societies.

A number of works, including by Daniel C. Thomas, Vojtech Mastny and Sarah B. Snyder, have sought to demonstrate the significance of the first and third basket provisions of the Helsinki Final Act.[15] The chapters collected here build upon those earlier efforts while simultaneously pushing the analysis of the social and political context into new and fruitful areas.

What Follows

This book raises the question of the relationship between European and North American diplomacies and Western and socialist societies in the framework of the Helsinki process and of the debates of the late twentieth century about human rights. The goal is to show that, far from being a closed-circuit diplomatic machine, the CSCE resulted from the diplomatic, political and societal evolutions of the 1960s, 1970s and 1980s and that, at the same time, it had an influence on those evolutions. The authors of the chapters collected here look beyond diplomatic history to highlight the ways in which leaders and diplomats who had been committed from the outset to the Helsinki process construed the CSCE and, more importantly, the societies in which its provisions had to be implemented. Essential too is the issue of reception and implementation of the Final Act as well as the influence that NGOs, intellectuals, the media, dissidents, associations, artists, political parties and movements, parliamentarians, churches etc. had on diplomatic practices. Examining these 'deep forces', to use the language of historian Pierre Renouvin, is essential to understanding international relations.[16] Analysing the 'deep forces' of the 1970s–1980s requires a focus on transnational networks committed to the defence of human rights and their involvement in the CSCE and the implementation of its provisions. The term 'transnational' refers to phenomena or histories that transcend national boundaries. Given that the nation state is not the primary unit of analysis in transnational histories, scholars focus more frequently on nonstate actors.[17] Since the 1990s, scholars have shown that transnational networks, which participated in the promotion of a model of cooperative security embodied by the CSCE, played a determining role in ending the Cold War. Such a process was linked to the intensification of globalization at that time and to the increasing contestation of state monopoly in relations with the rest of the world.[18]

This volume brings together fifteen researchers of nine nationalities, all experts in the Helsinki process. Their chapters form a coherent book that demonstrates collaboration and common reflection about the interaction between diplomacy, societies and human rights in the CSCE framework.

The book begins by analysing the role of diplomats and diplomatic machineries in the CSCE negotiations from Helsinki to Vienna and in the implementation of the Final Act as well as how these CSCE diplomats were shaped by their education, societies and generation. First, Andrei Zagorski presents the stakes and the evolutions of the CSCE human dimension, from the Helsinki negotiations to the post-Cold War period. His chapter provides an overview of the issues faced by the Western diplomats of the CSCE. Subsequent chapters by Martin D. Brown and Angela Romano, Nicolas Badalassi and Stephan Kieninger analyse British, French and American cases to show how Western diplomats committed to the Helsinki process experienced and perceived the CSCE. They highlight the ways in which the educational background of the diplomats, their career paths, their political opinions and their public commitments influenced the negotiations. The authors examine the diplomats' room to manoeuvre vis-à-vis central administrations, their personal visions of the CSCE in comparison to the official stance of their country and the influence they had on political leaders and their relations with their foreign counterparts. Particular attention is paid to the ways in which the diplomats considered the CSCE and its consequences, the themes and strategies of negotiation they favoured, their level of knowledge of the European socialist societies, their potential links with political opponents or dissidents, their insertion in intellectual networks and their relations with the defenders of human rights or the NGOs that specialized in this field.

The transnational movements that defended human rights and the role of dissidence are the focus of the book's second section. The chapters by Elisabetta Vezzosi, Christian P. Peterson and Jacek Czaputowicz analyse transnational debates on human rights stimulated by the Helsinki process. They show how networks organized on both sides of the Iron Curtain to obtain a genuine implementation of the decisions of the successive conferences from Helsinki to Vienna. They highlight how these groups perceived the CSCE and its follow-up meetings during the last fifteen years of the Cold War; they seek to evaluate the place the CSCE had in the discourse of opponents and dissidents from the East and their supporters from the West. These chapters clarify the different levels of transnational cooperation (East–West, East–East, West–West) that were central to the implementation of the CSCE provisions, via information sharing, mutual aid, international meetings or diffusion of ideas and writings.

Douglas Selvage's chapter complements this picture by tackling the attitude of the security services of the Warsaw Pact towards Helsinki groups. He gives a detailed study of measures of suppression used by the Soviet and East German authorities against defenders of human rights. In this way, he demonstrates how the socialist regimes attached to the old Westphalian order and to the principles of non-interference and sovereignty of states faced the emergence of the transnational phenomenon.

Considerable research has shown how the Final Act's liberal orientations influenced the Soviet bloc. Carl Bon Tempo takes a new approach in his chapter, showing that Western societies could also seize upon the Helsinki principles to underline the violations of human rights in the West. He analyses how the National Association for the Advancement of Colored People (NAACP), the most important US civil rights group, and several organizations and personalities struggling for the liberalization of US laws on immigration used the participation of the United States in the CSCE to push national authorities into taking more concrete measures on their respective issues.

The final section of the book consists of four case studies on the different ways in which European countries tackled the stages of the CSCE and their consequences for both European societies and international relations. Each of the chapters by Maximilian Graf, Mathias Peter, Oliver Bange and Hamit Kaba considers a type or a group of countries whose foreign policy illustrates a special relationship with the Helsinki process, including the Neutral countries, NATO and the Warsaw Pact. Specifically, the chapters examine Austria, the FRG, Hungary, Poland, the German Democratic Republic, Czechoslovakia, the Soviet Union and, finally, Albania. The inclusion of Albania is notable as it was the only European state not to take part in the CSCE.

Maximilian Graf presents the evolutions of the Central European countries towards the CSCE between 1975 and the collapse of the Berlin Wall. Subsequently, Mathias Peter demonstrates how the FRG managed to use the Helsinki process as both a tool of internal policy and a means of applying pressure on Moscow in the context of East–West tensions between 1977 and 1984. In his chapter, Peter pays particular attention to the fundamental break of Mikhail Gorbachev's ascension in 1985 and how it was reflected in the CSCE process, especially in Vienna from 1986 to 1989. Oliver Bange focuses on the shift between Moscow and East Berlin in the second part of the 1980s, when Gorbachev showed his willingness to implement all the Final Act provisions in the USSR. Hamit Kaba explains the reasons for the non-participation of Albania, which have not previously been well understood. Each chapter locates the diplomatic process of the CSCE within the social and political contexts of their specific cases.

Overall, this book seeks to show that the CSCE was more than a diplomatic process. It was first and foremost a reflection of a time, linked to empowerment of individuals on both sides of the Iron Curtain. Western diplomats understood during the 1960s that the human rights rhetoric had to be used with subtlety if they wanted to change the Eastern bloc. The CSCE and the human contacts provisions of its third basket embodied such a subtlety. Henceforth, the CSCE appeared as a rupture within the long period of the Cold War by allowing international relations during the détente years to focus on the rights and the security of peoples rather than states' prerogatives.

At the end of the Cold War, the will of the Europeans to institutionalize such a model of cooperative security explains why they sought, as early as 1989, to make the CSCE the privileged security framework within which reunification of the continent would occur.[19] Although NATO finally became the cornerstone of European security after the Cold War, the CSCE texts continued to be reinforced after the collapse of the Berlin Wall, especially via the Charter of Paris for a New Europe (1990), the CSCE Helsinki Document of 1992 and the Budapest Document of 1994. As the CSCE transitioned to the Organization for Security and Cooperation in Europe (OSCE), control instruments like the Office for Democratic Institutions and Human Rights or the High Commissioner on National Minorities were created. Under the new OSCE the human dimension prevailed over its security aspects. Most importantly, the end of the Cold War and the pace of globalization in the 1990s meant the triumph of the transnational logic on which the Helsinki process had been founded. The CSCE's progressive interaction between multilateral diplomacy, societal issues and transnational networks proves that the CSCE constitutes a fundamental step in the history of contemporary international relations.

Nicolas Badalassi is Associate Professor of Contemporary History at the Institut d'Etudes politiques d'Aix-en-Provence (Sciences-Po Aix). He holds a PhD from the University of Paris – Sorbonne Nouvelle (2011). In 2012–13, he administrated the Sorbonne Cold War Studies Project. He is the author of the award-winning *En finir avec la Guerre froide: La France, l'Europe et le processus d'Helsinki, 1965–1975* (Presses Universitaires de Rennes, 2014). He has published various articles concerning French foreign policy in the Cold War era, the Helsinki process and security in the Mediterranean. He has also co-edited with Houda

Ben Hamouda *Les pays d'Europe orientale et la Méditerranée, 1967–1989* (Les Cahiers Irice, 2013).

Sarah B. Snyder teaches at American University's School of International Service. She is the author of *From Selma to Moscow: How Human Rights Activists Transformed US Foreign Policy* (Columbia University Press, 2018) and the award-winning *Human Rights Activism and the End of the Cold War: A Transnational History of the Helsinki Network* (Cambridge University Press, 2011).

Notes

1. Conversation between Andreï Gromyko and French Foreign Minister Jean Sauvagnargues, 11 July 1974, Moscow. Archives of the French Minister of Foreign Affairs, Europe 1971–76, URSS, vol. 3726.
2. Message of Leonid Brezhnev to Georges Pompidou, 8 January 1974. National Archives of France, 5 AG 2 111, URSS, 1969–74.
3. M. Kramer, 'Editor's Note', *Journal of Cold War Studies* 18(3) (2016), 1–2. For an alternative view, see D. Selvage, 'H-Diplo Forum on "CSCE, the German Question, and the Eastern Bloc"', Retrieved 30 August 2017 from https://networks.h-net.org/system/files/contributed-files/ar701_0.pdf.
4. A. Pierret, *De la case africaine à la villa romaine: Un demi-siècle au service de l'Etat* (Paris: L'Harmattan, 2010), 144.
5. A. Romano, *From Détente in Europe to European Détente: How the West Shaped the Helsinki CSCE* (Brussels: PIE-Peter Lang, 2009).
6. D. Möckli, *European Foreign Policy during the Cold War: Heath, Brandt, Pompidou and the Dream of Political Unity, 1969–1974* (London: I.B. Tauris, 2008), 119.
7. For example, the negotiations of the Follow-up Meeting in Belgrade were difficult because of renewed East–West tensions in 1977. The Madrid meeting was suspended in 1981 after the imposition of martial law in Poland.
8. A. Roberts, 'An "Incredibly Swift Transition": Reflections on the End of the Cold War', in M.P. Leffler and O.A. Westad (eds), *The Cambridge History of the Cold War*, vol. III, *Endings* (Cambridge: Cambridge University Press, 2010), 513–34.
9. S.B. Snyder, *Human Rights Activism and the End of the Cold War: A Transnational History of the Helsinki Network* (Cambridge: Cambridge University Press, 2011), 66.
10. S. Savranskaya, 'Unintended Consequences: Soviet Interests, Expectations and Reactions to the Helsinki Final Act', in O. Bange and G. Niedhart (eds), *Helsinki 1975 and the Transformation of Europe* (New York: Berghahn Books, 2008), 183.
11. J. Andréani, *Le Piège: Helsinki et la chute du communisme* (Paris: Odile Jacob, 2005), 122.

12. According to Svetlana Savranskaya, the KGB identified, at the end of 1975, 850 political prisoners, including 261 for anti-Soviet propaganda, and 1,800 anti-Soviet groups. Besides, 68,000 persons were ordered to stop their 'unacceptable' activities. Savranskaya, 'Unintended Consequences', 185; S. Savranskaya, 'Human Rights Movement in the USSR after the Signing of the Helsinki Final Act, and the Reaction of Soviet Authorities', in L. Nuti (ed.), *The Crisis of Détente in Europe: From Helsinki to Gorbachev 1975–1985* (New York: Routledge, 2009), 29, 33–34.
13. As early as the 1970s, several Mediterranean countries sought to spread the CSCE to the whole Mediterranean. The Barcelona process, or Euromed Partnership, launched in 1995, was partly inspired by the CSCE. N. Badalassi, 'Sea and Détente in Helsinki: The Mediterranean Stake of the CSCE, 1972–1975', in E. Calandri, D. Caviglia and A. Varsori (eds), *Détente in Cold War Europe: Politics and Diplomacy in the Mediterranean and the Middle East* (London: I.B. Tauris, 2016), 61–74. In East Asia, and particularly in South Korea, some leaders and intellectuals have suggested creating a Conference on Security and Cooperation in Northeastern Asia. Connected with this effort, the Korean Society of Contemporary European Studies organized a conference in November 2015 in Seoul about *The Lessons of the Helsinki Process for the Northeast Asia Peace and Cooperation Initiative and the Trust Process on the Korean Peninsula*.
14. P. Hakkarainen, *A State of Peace in Europe: West Germany and the CSCE, 1966–1975* (New York: Berghahn Books, 2011); L. Ratti, *Britain, Ost- and Deutschlandpolitik, and the CSCE, 1955–1975* (Bern: PIE-Peter Lang, 2008); N. Badalassi, *En finir avec la Guerre froide: La France, l'Europe et le processus d'Helsinki, 1965–1975* (Rennes: Presses Universitaires de Rennes, 2014); Romano, *From Détente in Europe to European Détente*; T. Fischer, *Neutral Power in the CSCE: The N+N States and the Making of the Helsinki Accords 1975* (Baden-Baden: Nomos, 2009); B. Gilde, *Österreich im KSZE-Prozess 1969–1983: Neutraler Vermittler in humanitärer Mission* (Munich: Oldenbourg, 2013); A. Makko, *Ambassadors of Realpolitik: Sweden, the CSCE, and the Cold War* (New York: Berghahn Books, 2016). The countries of the former socialist bloc have received less attention thus far.
15. Thomas, *The Helsinki Effect*; V. Mastny, *The Helsinki Process and the Reintegration of Europe, 1986–1991: Analysis and Documentation* (New York: New York University Press, 1992); Snyder, *Human Rights Activism and the End of the Cold War*.
16. P. Renouvin, *Histoire des relations internationales*, vol. 1 (Paris: Hachette, 1953).
17. R. Keohane and J. Nye (eds), *Transnational Relations and World Politics* (Cambridge: Harvard University Press, 1970); S.B. Snyder, 'Bringing the Transnational In: Writing Human Rights into the International History of the Cold War', *Diplomacy and Statecraft* 24(1) (March 2013), 101–2.
18. M. Kaldor, *The Imaginary War: Understanding the East-West Conflict* (Oxford: Blackwell, 1990); P. Grosser, 'L'histoire des relations internationales à l'épreuve des interactions transnationales', in R. Frank (ed.), *Pour l'histoire*

des relations internationales (Paris: Presses Universitaires de France, 2012), 271–88.
19. For example, this is what Chancellor Helmut Kohl foresaw in the 'ten points plan' he presented on 28 November 1989 in view of the forthcoming German reunification.

Bibliography

Andréani, J. *Le Piège: Helsinki et la chute du communisme*. Paris: Odile Jacob, 2005.
Badalassi, N. *En finir avec la Guerre froide: La France, l'Europe et le processus d'Helsinki, 1965–1975*. Rennes: Presses Universitaires de Rennes, 2014.
Badalassi, N. 'Sea and Détente in Helsinki: The Mediterranean Stake of the CSCE, 1972–1975', in E. Calandri, D. Caviglia and A. Varsori (eds), *Détente in Cold War Europe: Politics and Diplomacy in the Mediterranean and the Middle East* (London: I.B. Tauris, 2016), 61–74.
Fischer, T. *Neutral Power in the CSCE: The N+N States and the Making of the Helsinki Accords 1975*. Baden-Baden: Nomos, 2009.
Gilde, B. *Österreich im KSZE-Prozess 1969–1983: Neutraler Vermittler in humanitärer Mission*. Munich: Oldenbourg, 2013.
Grosser, P. 'L'histoire des relations internationales à l'épreuve des interactions transnationales', in R. Frank (ed.), *Pour l'histoire des relations internationales* (Paris: Presses Universitaires de France, 2012), 271–88.
Hakkarainen, P. *A State of Peace in Europe: West Germany and the CSCE, 1966–1975*. New York: Berghahn Books, 2011.
Kaldor, M. *The Imaginary War: Understanding the East-West Conflict*. Oxford: Blackwell, 1990.
Keohane, R., and J. Nye (eds). *Transnational Relations and World Politics*. Cambridge, MA: Harvard University Press, 1970.
Kramer, M. 'Editor's Note'. *Journal of Cold War Studies* 18(3) (2016), 1–2.
Makko, A. *Ambassadors of Realpolitik: Sweden, the CSCE, and the Cold War*. New York: Berghahn Books, 2016.
Mastny, V. *The Helsinki Process and the Reintegration of Europe, 1986–1991: Analysis and Documentation*. New York: New York University Press, 1992.
Möckli, D. *European Foreign Policy during the Cold War: Heath, Brandt, Pompidou and the Dream of Political Unity, 1969–1974*. London: I.B. Tauris, 2008.
Pierret, A. *De la case africaine à la villa romaine: Un demi-siècle au service de l'Etat*. Paris: L'Harmattan, 2010.
Ratti, L. *Britain, Ost- and Deutschlandpolitik, and the CSCE, 1955–1975*. Bern: PIE-Peter Lang, 2008.
Renouvin, P. *Histoire des relations internationales*, vol. 1. Paris: Hachette, 1953.
Roberts, A. 'An "Incredibly Swift Transition": Reflections on the End of the Cold War', in M.P. Leffler and O.A. Westad (eds), *The Cambridge History of the Cold War*, vol. III, *Endings* (Cambridge: Cambridge University Press, 2010), 513–34.

Romano, A. *From Détente in Europe to European Détente: How the West Shaped the Helsinki CSCE*. Brussels: PIE-Peter Lang, 2009.

Savranskaya, S. 'Human Rights Movement in the USSR after the Signing of the Helsinki Final Act, and the Reaction of Soviet Authorities', in L. Nuti (ed.), *The Crisis of Détente in Europe: From Helsinki to Gorbachev 1975–1985* (New York: Routledge, 2009), 26–40.

Savranskaya, S. 'Unintended Consequences: Soviet Interests, Expectations and Reactions to the Helsinki Final Act', in O. Bange and G. Niedhart (eds), *Helsinki 1975 and the Transformation of Europe* (New York: Berghahn Books, 2008), 175–90.

Selvage, D. 'H-Diplo Forum on "CSCE, the German Question, and the Eastern Bloc"'. Retrieved 30 August 2017 from https://networks.h-net.org/system/files/contributed-files/ar701_0.pdf.

Snyder, S.B. 'Bringing the Transnational In: Writing Human Rights into the International History of the Cold War'. *Diplomacy and Statecraft* 24(1) (March 2013): 100–16.

Snyder, S.B. *Human Rights Activism and the End of the Cold War: A Transnational History of the Helsinki Network*. Cambridge: Cambridge University Press, 2011.

PART I

DIPLOMATS, DIPLOMACIES AND THE MAKING OF THE CSCE

 1

The Human Dimension of the CSCE, 1975–1990
Andrei Zagorski

Introduction

By introducing the respect for human rights and fundamental freedoms (principle VII) onto the agenda of East–West relations, the 1975 Final Act of the Conference on Security and Cooperation in Europe (CSCE) encouraged the consolidation and spread of human rights groups in the Eastern bloc. This development was neither desired in the East nor expected in the West at the beginning of the Helsinki process.[1] The initially anticipated effect was that of 'modest openings offered for freer movement of people and ideas', associated primarily with the 'third basket' of the Final Act (humanitarian contacts, or freer flow of people and information across the iron curtain) rather than with principle VII.[2]

While the civil society actors emerging in the East increasingly informed policies of individual Western states, the 1977 decision of the United States (US) to centre its CSCE diplomacy around human rights issues and to pursue this policy publicly challenged the initial fragile balance of the modest expectations. It served for a controversial debate over the implementation of the Helsinki commitments in the subsequent CSCE follow-up meetings in Belgrade (1977–78), Madrid (1980–83) and Vienna (1986–89), as well as in meetings of experts on human rights in Ottawa (1985) and human contacts in Bern (1986).

Communist governments continued to resist the pressure by dismissing the international discussion of the human rights performance of individual states as an intervention in internal affairs and continued to oppress the Helsinki groups in their countries. However, as the Helsinki process evolved, they gradually accepted CSCE specific practices of periodical review of the implementation of the relevant commitments. This development culminated in 1989 in the establishment of the CSCE Human Dimension Mechanism (HDM) designed to cooperatively resolve individual cases.

This chapter concentrates on the interaction between civil society and particularly human rights groups with the diplomatic framework of the Helsinki process. It explores the tools that were available for non-governmental organizations (NGOs) to provide input into the diplomatic process in the first fifteen years after the signing of the Helsinki Final Act (1975–90). More particularly, it explores whether human rights groups, at any time during this period, were granted direct access to participate in the review of the implementation of the relevant CSCE commitments and in the discussion of individual cases or rather if their access to the CSCE remained indirect.

For this purpose, the chapter begins by putting the CSCE human dimension into historical context and identifying the niche it filled among international instruments for the defence of human rights. The second part of the chapter reviews the evolution of tools that ultimately made a systematic review of the implementation of the CSCE commitments and the resolution of individual humanitarian cases possible. The third part discusses the availability of those tools to civil society actors within those frameworks. The chapter concludes by summarizing the findings and by establishing a brief connection between the 1975–90 historic experiences and the contemporary Organization for Security and Cooperation in Europe (OSCE).

Historical Context

The Helsinki Final Act was not the first international document committing states to respect human rights and fundamental freedoms. Thirty years earlier, it was the UN Charter that emphasized the member states' 'faith in fundamental human rights, in the dignity and worth of the human person, in the equal rights of men and women and of nations large and small'.[3] The 1948 Universal Declaration of Human Rights established international human rights standards, with which states are supposed to comply.[4] The 1966 International Covenant on Civil and Political Rights (International Covenant) codified these standards in a treaty.[5] Finally, the 1950 European Convention on Human Rights provided for a legally binding regional instrument for the defence of individuals' rights, subsequently amended and supplemented by additional protocols.[6]

While, generally, the implementation of international obligations in domestic law and legal practices remains the responsibility of individual states, the human rights instruments above were progressively supplemented by cooperative mechanisms that allowed the international community to engage in fact-finding, investigate alleged violations and keep states accountable for the implementation of their commitments. This was the purpose of the former UN Commission on Human Rights, now the Human Rights Council (HRC), under the Optional Protocol to the International Covenant. The Council of Europe (CoE) established an even more intrusive system of international remedies by creating, in 1959, the European Court of Human Rights (ECHR).

These developments marked the emergence of independent international institutions, which complemented national legal systems for the purpose of defence of human rights and fundamental freedoms. Despite the differences in the way the UN and the CoE-based mechanisms operate, both grant the right to communicate individual complaints to the relevant institutions.[7] In doing so, both admit a direct role to NGOs and individuals who can trigger relevant procedures and thus challenge state-centric approaches to human rights implementation.

These mechanisms were in place before the consultations on the CSCE started in 1972, although the 1966 International Covenant entered into force only in 1976. At the beginning of the CSCE, the Eastern bloc countries stayed away from any international human rights instrument. Nor would they accept any international mechanism based on individual complaints. Although they adhered to the International Covenant between 1973 and 1975, throughout the period under consideration they failed to ratify its Optional Protocol, not to speak of accepting the jurisdiction of the ECHR.[8]

Bearing in mind that, by the time the CSCE was launched, most West European nations were already parties to the European Convention on Human Rights with some of them lagging behind, this created a specific niche which the CSCE filled.[9] The ground-breaking role of the CSCE was not in introducing the principle of the respect for human rights as a norm but, rather, in including it on the agenda of East–West relations and committing the Eastern bloc countries to it. Apart from the principle itself, more specific commitments were spelled out primarily in the 'third basket' of the Final Act, which dealt, *inter alia*, with the freedom of movement of people and information across the East–West frontier.

However, committing the Eastern bloc was only part of the job. Formally accepting relevant international instruments, communist governments proceeded on the basis of understanding that the implementation of their provisions remained at the exclusive discretion of the states concerned. Any attempt to 'internationalize' the issues of the implementation of those commitments, even if simply in the form of discussing them in international fora, was rejected as interference in states' sovereign rights, including every state's 'right to determine its laws and regulations'.[10] It took the Helsinki process about a decade to bring about a change in this policy.

Review of Implementation

Respect for human rights and fundamental freedoms as well as specific commitments spelled out in the 'third basket' of the Final Act constituted the human dimension of the CSCE, although this term first appeared in the Vienna Concluding Document in 1989.[11] The Final Act further established that 'in exercising their sovereign rights, including the right to determine their laws and regulations', the participating states 'will conform with their legal obligations under international law; they will furthermore pay due regard to and implement the provisions in the Final Act'.[12] The central debate from 1975 to 1989 was whether issues of implementation of human rights provisions, being a matter of internal affairs, would remain exclusively at the discretion of individual states, as asserted by the Eastern bloc, or would become a legitimate subject for international review as a matter of common interest of participating states, as suggested by the West.

The CSCE follow-up meetings held between 1977 and 1991 played a crucial role in establishing the practice of reviewing the implementation of the relevant commitments. This became possible due to the very agreement to hold follow-up meetings, the gradual institutionalization of the implementation debate and result-oriented discussion of individual cases and further specification of relevant provisions of the Final Act. This development culminated in establishing the HDM in 1989, further improved by the Copenhagen and Moscow meetings of the CSCE Conference on the Human Dimension (CHD) in 1990 and 1991.

This progress was hardly possible without maintaining a proper balance of interest of major groups of participating states at every stage of the Helsinki process. This gradually led to the recognition of the need to ensure balanced parallel progress in different 'baskets' of the

Helsinki Final Act, most notably keeping a balance between progress in the security and the human dimensions.[13]

Follow-up to the CSCE

It was the Eastern bloc countries that initially championed the idea of an eventual follow-up to the conference or even its institutionalization in the form of a permanent Consultative Committee to be entrusted, *inter alia*, with the preparation of further pan-European conferences. A formal proposal to this effect was submitted by Czechoslovakia during the first phase of the conference in July 1973.[14] The idea of follow-up activities to the conference found support among Neutral and Non-Aligned Countries (NNA). However, in contrast to the Soviet Union, which was primarily interested in ceremonial high-level events, the NNA conceptualized follow-up activities in terms of a regular review process. As part of this process, 'the commitments the document [the Final Act] contained were to be submitted to verification at regular intervals and some sort of renewed guarantee had to be given that the guiding principles were being respected'.[15] In addition, it would 'put pressure on the participants to live up to their commitments'.[16]

NATO and European Community (EC) member states were initially reluctant to agree to any follow-up to the conference. They left it open during the negotiation of the Final Act and made their final consent conditional on actual deliverables of the CSCE. As the Final Act provisions in the 'third basket' matured, many of these states started changing their mind, while the USSR ultimately abandoned the idea of institutionalizing the CSCE. At the end of the negotiation of the Final Act, Moscow was no longer prepared even to fix dates for the first follow-up meeting. Should one take place, its terms of reference and modalities would have to be negotiated in a special preparatory meeting.[17]

The final compromise fixed the date for the opening of the preparatory meeting for the first follow-up, as well as the general mandate of the Belgrade meeting. It was expected to pursue 'a thorough exchange of views both on the implementation of the provisions of the Final Act and ... on the deepening of their mutual relations, the improvement of security and the development of co-operation in Europe, and the development of the process of détente in the future'.[18] However, while generally admitting that there would be follow-up meetings to the CSCE, decisions on holding any further meetings required the consensus of all participating states.

This implied that the continuity of the process could not be taken for granted and every subsequent follow-up meeting could become the last one, should the participating states fail to agree on the venue and the dates for the opening of the next one. The option of terminating the Helsinki process by not agreeing on a next meeting was indeed considered in Moscow in 1980.[19] It was only the third Vienna follow-up meeting (1986–89) that ultimately established the principle of holding such meetings regularly.[20] This late decision, however, lost its initial relevance after the beginning of the institutionalization of the CSCE in 1990.

Implementation Debate

General agreement to hold follow-up meetings did not yet guarantee a proper review of the implementation of the Final Act. As mentioned above, the Eastern bloc countries proceeded on the basis that their record should not be exposed to international scrutiny. Any attempt at discussing their performance during the follow-up meetings, and particularly of doing so in a public way, was rejected by them as illegitimate intervention in internal affairs.

The Final Act mandated the follow-up meeting(s) to exchange views on both the implementation of CSCE commitments and new proposals. While discussing modalities of the Belgrade meeting at a 1977 preparatory meeting, Western states sought to separate these two subjects and allocate time just for the review of implementation in plenary sessions and particularly in subsidiary working bodies arranged according to the structure of the Final Act. The review of implementation would then be followed by consideration of new proposals. They also insisted that a sufficient number of plenary sessions would be made open to the public (essentially to the press).[21] The Eastern bloc conceptualized the meeting in a different way. It was supposed to be a short consultative conference reduced to closed-door plenary sessions in order to conduct a general exchange of views on positive experiences in implementing the Final Act.[22]

After half a month of controversial deliberations, the Western approach prevailed. The 'yellow book' of the Belgrade preparatory meeting established a precedent of organizing a structured implementation debate which was of no lesser importance for shaping the Helsinki process than the 1973 'blue book' of the Helsinki consultations that prepared the CSCE.[23] However, this precedent was not appreciated by the Eastern bloc. After Belgrade, Moscow sought to avoid a repetition of the sort of implementation debate that had taken place there.[24]

The controversy over a structured review of implementation resumed at the Madrid preparatory meeting in 1980. This time it concentrated primarily on the length of the implementation debate, the possibility of returning to issues of implementation at later stages of the meeting and the number of public sessions.[25] A similar controversy repeated itself in 1985 and 1986 at the preparatory meetings defining the agenda and modalities of the CSCE meetings of experts on human rights and human contacts in Ottawa and Bern.[26]

It was only the 1986 preparatory meeting for the Vienna follow-up that accepted the Belgrade and Madrid precedents without controversy and ultimately institutionalized the practice of a structured review of implementation in subsidiary working bodies preceding the discussion of new proposals in drafting groups.[27] The Vienna meeting even recommended, while organizing subsequent follow-up activities, 'to dispense with preparatory meetings unless otherwise agreed'.[28]

Non-intervention in Internal Affairs

The legitimacy of discussing the record of implementation of the CSCE human rights provisions in other countries continued to be strongly resisted by the Eastern bloc for a long time. According to the Soviet Union, any review of implementation should be reduced to self-reports by the participating states on measures taken by them in order to meet their commitments. Such reports would not be subject to any debate, not to speak of criticism.[29] This opposition eroded, but it did so very slowly, not least due to the extremely allergic reaction to the 'naming and shaming' tactics applied by the United States first in Belgrade and then at subsequent follow-up and expert meetings. This tactic not only produced increasing frustration with the CSCE in the Eastern bloc but, furthermore, deepened divisions within individual communist countries and strengthened the voices of those who questioned the raison d'être of the OSCE.[30]

CSCE fatigue started growing in the Eastern bloc particularly with the sharp change in US policy after the election of Jimmy Carter as president. It was he who gave human rights a new prominence in US foreign policy.[31] This development had consequences for the American performance within the CSCE. It used to be a fairly low-key policy during Kissinger's tenure but changed dramatically at the Belgrade meeting in 1977–78.

Dealing with individual humanitarian cases since the 1970s was a regular practice between East and West under the umbrella of the CSCE. However, such cases were handled in a confidential manner, recognizing that any public advocacy of individual cases 'could often make matters much worse for the individuals concerned' instead of resolving such cases.³² Addressing individual cases was extremely sensitive in regard to the state of East–West relations. This was one reason why both West European participating states and the US State Department, while preparing for the Belgrade follow-up meeting, favoured a cautious approach to the review of implementation and tended to address relevant issues in a generalized way without raising individual cases in order to avoid polemics and not jeopardize the beginning Helsinki process.³³

However, this policy was abandoned by the Carter administration. Having considered the choice of 'whether or not accusations relating to specific individual human rights cases would be made public and would be handled publicly, or whether they would be raised privately with the country concerned, as was the traditional practice', the White House decided to raise specific cases publicly and to press hard on those issues in Belgrade.³⁴ This was a major change in US policy which had diverse consequences for shaping the CSCE human dimension.

It was in Belgrade that the US for the first time started explicitly and publicly raising individual cases of human rights violations in the Eastern bloc.³⁵ This change triggered a storm of objections from the Eastern participating states, claiming that it violated the principle of non-intervention. It was also extremely controversial among the Western states, most of whom preferred a more cautious approach.³⁶ The US example was followed by very few delegations in Belgrade: the Netherlands, France and Canada.³⁷

Nevertheless, the number of participating states joining the US in exercising a critique of the human rights record, and particularly of the failure by the Eastern bloc countries to implement specific provisions of the 'third basket' of the Final Act, increased from one follow-up meeting to another, including some NNA. The number of individual cases raised in this debate grew significantly between the Belgrade and the Vienna follow-up meetings, thus establishing a new practice.³⁸

For about a decade after the signing of the Final Act, the Eastern bloc countries resisted the discussion of their domestic policies at various CSCE meetings, referring to the principle of non-intervention and insisting that the implementation of the relevant provisions remained at the exclusive discretion of the states parties. However, already in Belgrade, while avoiding the discussion of individual cases brought up by the West, Eastern countries reciprocated the critique by pointing to human rights violations in the West.³⁹ The arguments raised by the East were more general and concentrated on social and economic rights. Soviet delegations never kept elaborate dossiers on the human rights performance in the West for the simple reason that they were interested in countering the critique from the West rather than in seeking resolution of particular individual cases. However, these tactics had the opposite effect. This exchange was encouraged by the Western countries at all phases of the implementation debate because it implied a *de facto* recognition of the legitimacy of discussing domestic regulations and practices pertaining to the respect for human rights in individual participating states.[40]

The situation started to change gradually after the advent of Mikhail Gorbachev as the new Soviet leader. This change first manifested itself at the 1985 CSCE Ottawa meeting of experts on human rights and fundamental freedoms. Although the Soviet delegation pursued a strictly conservative ideological perspective on the concept of human rights, it no longer hid behind the non-intervention argument and instead launched a counter-offensive accusing the West of violations particularly of social and economic rights – a move that was explicitly encouraged by Western delegations. However, in Ottawa the Soviet Union still refused to discuss individual cases raised by the West either during the sessions of the meeting or even unofficially at its margins. Neither did it seek to discuss issues it raised in response to the Western critique.[41]

The final recognition of the legitimacy of discussing human rights issues within individual states in the CSCE was signalled by Moscow at the beginning of the Vienna follow-up meeting in 1986. During the implementation debate in Vienna, some Eastern bloc countries including the Soviet Union, Hungary and Poland entirely stopped referring to the non-intervention principle (other Eastern bloc countries continued doing so although with different intensity).[42] This change was also manifested in the Soviet proposal to host a CSCE human rights conference in Moscow.

Still, it took the CSCE longer to formalize the legitimacy of the human rights implementation debate. It was ultimately the Moscow CHD meeting (September–October 1991) that 'categorically and irrevocably' declared 'that the commitments undertaken in the field of the human dimension of the CSCE are matters of direct and legitimate concern to all participating States and do not belong exclusively to the internal affairs of the State concerned'.[43] This formula drew the final line under the debate that had lasted for one and a half decades, although, more recently, its relevance is again challenged by individual CSCE states.

Human Dimension Mechanism

Establishing the practice of raising individual cases at the CSCE did not automatically lead to their resolution as long as the Eastern bloc resisted discussing them. At the same time, handling such cases bilaterally in a confidential manner was not uncommon in East–West relations, although the cooperativeness of the Eastern bloc countries depended on the atmospherics of those relations. During the high times of détente, they handled such cases more benevolently, while in the periods of growing tensions, particularly in the first half of the 1980s, their policies again became more rigid.[44]

With the beginning of the Helsinki process, lists containing names of people who were particularly denied the right to leave their country were often passed through CSCE delegations and forwarded to the capitals to be processed by competent agencies (ministries of interior and/or security services) before a decision was taken by the authorities. Often, CSCE delegations would not even know the outcome.[45] Often, particularly when the human rights record of the Eastern bloc was subject to public controversy, such requests were not followed up or responded to.[46] This *ad hoc* practice remained very fragile.

After the Belgrade meeting, the West and particularly the US initiated bilateral meetings with individual Eastern countries – Bulgaria, the GDR, Hungary, Poland and Romania – in order to discuss specific issues of the implementation of the 'third basket' provisions, most particularly related to the freedom of movement.[47] This practice was gradually institutionalized and led to the establishment of the CSCE HDM.

The 1983 Madrid Concluding Document included a modest provision committing the participating states 'to give favourable consideration to the use of bilateral round-table meetings, held on a voluntary basis, between delegations ... to discuss issues of human rights and fundamental freedoms in accordance with an agreed agenda'.[48] Romania was the first country to accept this practice by conducting a round-table meeting in Washington in 1984.[49]

At the 1985 Ottawa meeting of experts, the Western states suggested establishing a binding procedure for discussing individual cases by granting the participating states, individuals and NGOs the right to submit requests for information pertaining to individual human rights cases, which would be directed to the ministries of foreign affairs or other authorized agencies.[50] Although this proposal was rejected by the East in Ottawa, agreement on a similar procedure was reached at the Vienna follow-up meeting, which ultimately established the HDM, further improved by the CHD meetings in Copenhagen and Moscow in 1990 and 1991.

The HDM committed the participating states to respond to requests for information and to representations, including those concerning specific cases of alleged violations of human rights, forwarded to them through diplomatic channels. If not resolved at this first stage, individual cases could be further examined in bilateral and multilateral meetings of the CHD or general follow-up meetings. In order to further examine controversial cases, the participating states concerned could voluntarily invite missions of experts. Should a specific case not be resolved with the assistance of a mission of experts, the participating states (with the support of no fewer than five other states) would be able to establish a mandatory mission of rapporteurs to further address the issue.[51]

This mechanism was applied intensively and generally successfully from 1989 to 1991 almost exclusively in the context of East–West relations.[52] The intensity of invoking it declined thereafter.[53] Even without formally invoking the relevant HDM procedures, decisions of the Vienna meeting led to an unprecedented expansion of bilateral cooperation between states of the West and of the East in resolving specific individual cases. On the US side, it was operated primarily by the State Department's Bureau of Human Rights and Humanitarian Affairs with the strong involvement of the Helsinki Commission. In the Soviet Union, its counterpart was the Department for Humanitarian Cooperation and Human Rights established within the Foreign Ministry in summer 1986.

Lists of individual cases handed over to the Soviet authorities, particularly by the USA, and handled in bilateral meetings included in 1989 more than two thousand names and dealt first of all with the so-called 'refuseniks' – persons who were denied permission to emigrate or simply travel to the West – and political prisoners. Most of these cases were resolved and further applications for private travel abroad were treated more liberally even though the amendment of the relevant Soviet legislation took longer than initially anticipated.[54]

In contrast to other international instruments for the defence of human rights, the CSCE HDM did not allow for individual complaints. Nor did it establish any independent body to receive, examine and process such complaints.[55] The participating states remained the single owners of the HDM, and dealing with individual cases remained an exclusively intergovernmental business.

As long as the Eastern bloc stayed away from the CoE and UN human rights instruments, this difference did not appear too important as the CSCE remained the single available platform to address human rights in the East. The situation changed dramatically in the 1990s. Following the collapse of the communist regimes, the Eastern bloc and the USSR itself, the countries of the 'East' adhered to the European Convention on Human Rights and the Optional Protocol to the International Covenant. The examination of individual complaints then increasingly migrated to the ECHR and, in some cases related to Central Asian participating states or Belarus, to the UN HRC. This was the major, although not the single reason for the gradual decline of interest in the CSCE HDM.

After a remarkable boom in the examination of individual cases within the HDM between 1989 and 1991, the mechanism was invoked only twice thereafter – with regard to Turkmenistan in 2002 and Belarus in 2011.[56] At the same time, thousands of individual complaints go to the ECHR. As of 2017, to take only the post-Soviet states, the number of applications pending before the ECHR amounted to 1,596 from Armenia, 2,037 from Azerbaijan, 2,084 from Georgia, 1,367 from Moldova, 9,253 from Russia and 18,859 from Ukraine.[57] Based on communications from individuals, NGOs and governments, the human rights situations in Kyrgyzstan, Tajikistan, Turkmenistan and Uzbekistan (not CoE members) were repeatedly subject to review by the UN HRC under the confidential compliance procedure. In 2012 (notably after the failure of the OSCE to invoke the mandatory part of the HDM), the HRC appointed a special rapporteur on the situation of human rights in Belarus (not yet a CoE member either).[58]

CSCE and Civil Society

The CSCE was launched as an intergovernmental diplomatic process which, apart from other accomplishments, committed the Eastern bloc to international human rights standards, gradually subjected them to practices of periodical review of the implementation of the relevant commitments and, at a later stage, to result-oriented cooperative discussion of individual cases. NGOs played an important role in informing human rights policies of the Western participating states within the Helsinki process.

This was particularly true after the publication of the Final Act had inspired the occurrence of Helsinki groups in the East, for which the CSCE commitments became a major point of reference. Although these as well as other dissident, religious or national groups remained subject to repressions in the Eastern bloc throughout the collapse of the communist regimes in Europe in 1989–90, this new development remained a driver of interest extended to human rights issues in the West by both governments and non-governmental actors.

As the conference failed to establish an independent body that would receive and process individual complaints and communications from NGOs, the latter had only indirect access to the CSCE through those individual Western governments and official delegations that were interested to work with them. At the same time, while receiving the information pertaining to the implementation of the CSCE commitments, the Western states kept at their discretion whether and how to proceed with it, 'whether to cite the commitments of the Final Act, either in general approaches or in relation to the individual case'.[59]

As a result, the critique of the human rights record of individual Eastern countries was differentiated not only on the grounds of their different performance but also taking into account broader political considerations. For instance, one of the first appeals to the CSCE – an open letter to the Belgrade meeting from the Romanian dissident Paul Goma – addressed the human rights record of Bucharest.[60] However, despite the fact that the Romanian performance was an issue in the West, the country was largely spared from a targeted critique within the CSCE until the 1985 Ottawa meeting of experts.[61] One of the reasons for this was that Romania – a dissident country within the Soviet bloc in its own right – took a relatively independent stance at the conference. It often avoided aligning itself with the proposals collectively pursued by the Eastern bloc. Many (although certainly not all) Romanian proposals on various issues on the CSCE agenda went in the same direction as the proposals put forward by the Western countries.[62] This policy was honoured by the West in their decision not to ask critical questions of Bucharest for a while.

For the first time, the CSCE was confronted with the question of how to interact with non-governmental actors at the beginning of the Madrid follow-up meeting. The opening of the meeting was accompanied by 'parallel activities' (today they would be called side events) organized by Western NGOs and attended by those dissidents from the East who were expelled or allowed to emigrate from their home countries.[63]

The proper representation of the Eastern Helsinki groups at such events was impossible at that time. Although they continuously communicated with their counterparts in the West, the policies of the Soviet bloc hardened after the Belgrade meeting. Private postal communications with foreign countries were restricted; visas were denied for foreigners who were suspected of communicating with dissidents and 'refuseniks'; and foreign journalists who maintained contacts with members of the Helsinki groups were expelled. Generally, those members of the Helsinki groups who were not under arrest would not be allowed to travel abroad in order to participate in the CSCE 'parallel activities'.

This practice began to change only in 1989. After the Vienna follow-up meeting, several human rights groups from Moscow, Leningrad, Sverdlovsk and Kiev informed the Soviet Foreign Ministry that they intended to attend 'parallel activities' in conjunction with the 1989 Paris meeting of the CSCE CHD – the first of the series of three meetings scheduled in Vienna. In making their case, they referred to the Chairman's statement on the openness and access to the CSCE meetings attached to the Vienna Concluding Document (see below). The Soviet bureaucracy was shocked by this new development but, ultimately, due to intervention by the Foreign Ministry, a few dissidents, including Ludmilla Alexeeva from the Moscow Helsinki Group, Oleg Rumyantsev (then chairman of the 'Democratic Perestroika' club and coordinator of the preparatory committee for a social democratic association) and the civil rights activist Lev Timofeev, were allowed to travel to Paris.[64]

NGOs engaged in organizing 'parallel activities' in Madrid sought to deliver their messages to the meeting and the delegations.[65] The meeting was the first to be confronted with the question of how these communications were to be handled. As a result, it established a precedent followed by subsequent follow-up meetings by deciding that the CSCE would not issue any responses to communications from non-state actors, but the Secretariat would keep a file so that any delegation could get acquainted with them.[66] It would then be up to the delegations how to, or whether at all to react to those communications, whether to pursue the issues raised by NGOs within the conference or not.

At this stage, the Eastern bloc delegates avoided any contact with human rights NGOs. Nor did they attend 'parallel activities' if invited. They did not acquaint themselves with NGO communications or respond to them. They were instructed not to enter into any discussions with human rights groups. This pattern gradually started to change only in 1986 when, at the Bern meeting of experts on human contacts and particularly during the Vienna follow-up, the Soviet delegation became more responsive to invitations to NGO events.[67] However, Soviet diplomats did so not for the purpose of discussing the USSR's performance, but rather for presenting the official Soviet human rights posture.

Beginning with the Vienna follow-up meeting, the Soviet Union sought to balance the 'parallel activities' of Western NGOs with side events organized by official Soviet 'non-governmental' organizations, such as the Soviet Committee for European Security and Cooperation, the Soviet Peace Committee, the Soviet Committee of Women, the Soviet Anti-Zionist Committee and others. This new practice of promoting the

Soviet human rights discourse (in the process of change at that time) culminated in 1990 when about one hundred Soviet 'public' representatives attended 'parallel activities' organized in conjunction with the Copenhagen meeting of the CSCE HDC.[68] Most often, the Soviet-sponsored side events ran 'parallel' not only to the diplomatic conferences but also to the side events organized by Western NGOs and including émigrés from the East. However, by 1990, this dividing line started to become increasingly porous following changes in the policies of the Soviet Union and a number of other Eastern bloc countries.

With the increasing number of sessions open to the public (in Belgrade it was only the opening and the closing sessions; beginning with the Madrid meeting, an increasing number of plenary sessions were made accessible to the public), NGO representatives were also admitted to sit in the conference hall but were not given the floor. The only possibility for them to speak at CSCE meetings was if they were included on the list of official delegations of a participating state. This rare opportunity occurred when the US, beginning with the Belgrade meeting, started including 'public members' on its delegations to various CSCE meetings – individuals representing a variety of interest groups.[69] The Soviet Union reciprocated by including 'public members' on its delegations – usually members of the parliament affiliated with official Soviet NGOs – and giving them the floor at select open plenary sessions.[70]

For a short period of time during the formation of the CSCE HDM, the possibility of granting individuals and NGOs the right to request information on specific cases from the governments of the participating states was considered. This provision was part of the Western proposals for such a mechanism submitted in Ottawa in 1985 and then again in Vienna in 1987.[71] However, it was ultimately dropped, and the HDM only granted this right to the governments of the participating states.

The NGOs' input into the discussion of human rights at the CSCE was thus limited to lobbying their specific interests through the governments of interested participating states – essentially through Western governments. For most of the period under consideration, the Eastern bloc countries, as noted above, did not avail themselves of communication with either their national or the relevant foreign or international human rights groups. However, the permanent communication with Western governments and diplomats in the CSCE framework proved once again the essential role that NGOs can and do play in informing interested governments about relevant developments and specific cases, as well as in generating practical proposals to remedy the situation.

The US Department of State started to compile and analyse the relevant information soon after the signing of the Final Act. It instructed embassies in the Eastern bloc countries to regularly report on the implementation of and compliance with the CSCE provisions.[72] However, the information received from human rights NGOs turned out to be the most important source for any properly informed implementation debate at the CSCE and for the elaboration of new proposals aimed at making relevant CSCE commitments more specific and at improving their implementation.

The 1986 Bern CSCE meeting on human contacts, for instance, was addressed by many NGOs with extensive information concerning the compliance with the Final Act provisions in the Eastern bloc. The American Committee of Concerned Scientists distributed detailed documentation listing 782 Soviet Jewish scientists denied the right to reunify with their families in Israel. The West German International Society for Human Rights distributed a 122-page dossier containing details of 1,677 divided families in East Germany, Poland, Romania and the USSR. The World Federation of Free Latvians distributed a 48-page dossier on alleged Soviet violations of human contacts provisions, while the Turkish Association of Immigrants protested Bulgarian restrictions on emigration of individuals belonging to its Muslim community.[73]

The interaction between civil society and particularly the US government and diplomacy was strongly facilitated by the establishment in 1976 of a bipartisan US Helsinki Commission bringing together congressmen and government officials, as well as offering a platform for civil society to provide an input into the debate over the implementation of the CSCE commitments. The Helsinki Commission itself was represented in the US delegations to CSCE meetings beginning with Belgrade. Western diplomats, unlike their Eastern colleagues, were open to contacts with various NGOs. The USA in particular established a practice of arranging meetings for NGOs not represented among the 'public members' of its CSCE delegations in order to allow them to provide an input by briefing members of the delegations.[74]

Many civil society actors 'exhibited a certain naiveté about the realities of international politics' and 'revealed a lack of sensitivity to the wider issues at stake in the CSCE process'.[75] As a result, far from every issue raised by NGOs in this intense communication would flow into the CSCE policy of Western countries. Nevertheless, the CSCE experience has proven once again that NGOs are the single most important and efficient instrument of monitoring human rights violations. The lists of individual cases compiled by them, certainly subject to some verification process, became the basis for further examination within the procedures provided for by the CSCE HDM, although representatives of NGOs themselves were not admitted to attend the meetings organized within the HDM framework.

At the CSCE, NGOs operated in a different environment as compared to established international instruments for the defence of human rights, which assigned appropriate recipients of NGO communications – independent bodies entitled to examine and process individual complaints. In many instances, NGOs are engaged in the process of examination of such complaints, or even contribute to the review of the human rights implementation record of individual states, for instance within the framework of the UN HRC Universal Periodic Review process, despite the fact that the latter is a primarily state-driven process.[76]

While the NGOs' right to communicate messages to the CSCE was acknowledged in 1980 in Madrid, there was no body within the CSCE that could act as an appropriate recipient of those communications, not to speak of being entitled to examine them or bring them to the attention of the participating states concerned. Nor were NGOs given the possibility to contribute directly to the implementation debate.

Despite the fact that the Vienna meeting in its Concluding Document anticipated that non-governmental participants could be invited to contribute to specific meetings,[77] the mode of operation of the CSCE established in Madrid remained essentially unchanged over the years. The Chairman's statement on the openness and access to the CSCE meetings attached to the Vienna Concluding Document summarized established practices as including:

- access to the host State, to the venue and to open sessions of CSCE meetings for representatives of the media, representatives of non-governmental organizations or religious groups, and private individuals, both nationals and foreigners;
- unimpeded contacts between delegates or visitors and citizens of the host State, respect for CSCE-related activities, including the holding of peaceful gatherings, and for the freedom of journalists to report without hindrance as well as to pursue their professional activity in conformity with CSCE commitments.[78]

The purpose of the Chairman's statement was not to improve or change this mode, but rather to commit Moscow to respect those practices and particularly tolerate CSCE-related 'parallel activities' during the Moscow CHD meeting scheduled for 1991. By the time the Moscow meeting took place, the Soviet Union had survived an abortive coup d'état but found itself in the process of dissolution under the pressure of its constituent republics. This brought about a substantial change in the policies pursued by Moscow in the last months of the existence of the USSR.

In September 1991, the Soviet delegation at the Moscow CHD meeting introduced a proposal inspired by the co-chair of the delegation, one of the leaders of the Moscow Helsinki group Sergey Kovalev (at that time chairman of the Russian parliament's Committee on Human Rights). The proposal suggested improving the status and access of established human rights NGOs by granting them the status of organizations registered with and enjoying a consultative role at the CSCE. This proposal was turned down, however, by all other delegations for the simple reason that granting a special status to some NGOs would discriminate against others. As a result, the mode of interaction between the CSCE and NGOs remained unaltered.[79]

Conclusion

Serving as a point of reference, the 1975 Helsinki Final Act has played an important role in energizing and consolidating human rights groups, particularly within the Eastern bloc. The evolving network of Helsinki movements increasingly informed human rights policies of individual, particularly Western states within the CSCE. While responding to the promise of the Final Act and pushing for it to be put into practice, the emerging civil society in the East in conjunction with Western non-governmental networks became an important informal driver of change in the East and of the Helsinki process itself.

However, from 1975 to 1990, the CSCE failed to provide NGOs with any direct access to the evolving human dimension tools, including direct participation in the review of the implementation of the relevant commitments, and to give them a role in the functioning of the HDM. As a result, it failed to provide NGOs with a status similar to that they enjoy with other international human rights instruments, such as the ECHR or the UN HRC. Despite this, multiple civil society actors did influence the diplomatic CSCE process indirectly through interested Western participating states. In many Western countries they became important and influential participants in the domestic process of policy formulation, which informed instructions the respective delegations were to follow at various CSCE meetings. At the same time, final decisions whether to pursue issues raised by civil society and in which way remained at the discretion of the governments of the participating states, which consistently preserved their exclusive ownership of intergovernmental processes of negotiation, implementation review and resolution of individual cases.

The way in which the Helsinki process evolved had many underlying causes. It was not least due to the extreme sensitivity with which the participating states defined and delineated their rights and responsibilities from those of non-participants, no matter whether these were non-participating states or non-state actors.[80] Particularly in the area of human rights it was largely due to the consistent reluctance of the Eastern bloc countries to open the process for non-state actors. In their domestic policies, they continued to suppress independent non-governmental actors rather than empowering them. Giving a role to Helsinki groups at the CSCE would be the last thing to which the authorities of Eastern bloc countries would consent.

This specific history of the Helsinki process has established a path dependence, which affects the operation of the contemporary OSCE. The OSCE institutions have now become more open to bringing together representatives of participating states, experts and the NGO community in thematic meetings. Various chairs have sought to enhance diplomatic deliberations 'by bringing expert advice from NGOs, academia and think tanks into the debate'.[81] However, the full power of decision-making within the OSCE remains exclusively with the participating states, and the OCSE remains an intergovernmental business no less than the CSCE used to be.

Despite the establishment of the Warsaw-based OSCE Office for Democratic Institutions and Human Rights (ODIHR), this remains true with regard to the way in which the OSCE human dimension operates now. ODIHR has not become an independent institution entitled to receive and examine individual complaints. As regards the review of implementation of relevant OSCE commitments, it serves primarily as a clearing house and an institution through which (rather than through diplomatic channels) requests for information under the HDM and responses or comments by participating states can be processed. It can also serve as a venue for bilateral meetings under the HDM, and organizes the annual Human Dimension Implementation Meeting (HDIM) – an outgrowth of the CSCE HDC. Otherwise, it can only act upon the consensus-bound instruction from the Permanent Council or those from the Chairman-in-Office.[82]

The HDIM brings relevant NGOs together with representatives of the participating states, OSCE institutions and structures, and other relevant international actors. ODIHR forwards a summary of the discussion and proposals put forward during the meeting to the OSCE in

Vienna.[83] However, the decision whether or not to pursue those proposals within the intergovernmental negotiation process remains at the exclusive discretion of the individual participating states.

Andrei Zagorski is Head of Department at the Primakov National Research Institute of World Economy and International Relations, Russian Academy of Science (IMEMO), and Professor of International Relations at the Moscow State Institute of International Relations (MGIMO-University). He engages in European security, post-Soviet, arms control and Arctic studies. He has served as advisor to Soviet CSCE delegations (1987–91), Vice Rector of the MGIMO-University (1992–99) and Senior Vice-President of the East West Institute (2000–01). He was a Faculty Member of the Geneva Center for Security Policy (2002).

Notes

1. 'Ambassador Jacques Andréani of France', in *CSCE Testimonies. Causes and Consequences of the Helsinki Final Act. 1972–1989* (Prague: Prague Office of the OSCE Secretariat, 2013), 83–84.
2. J.J. Maresca, *Helsinki Revisited: A Key US Negotiator's Memoirs on the Development of the CSCE into the OSCE* (Stuttgart: ibidem-Verlag, 2015), 63.
3. 'Charter of the United Nations and Statute of the International Court of Justice, Preamble', *United Nations*. Retrieved 29 October 2016 from http://www.un.org/en/charter-united-nations/index.html.
4. 'The Universal Declaration of Human Rights', *United Nations*. Retrieved 29 October 2016 from http://www.un.org/Overview/rights.html.
5. 'International Covenant on Civil and Political Rights. Adopted by the General Assembly of the United Nations on 19 December 1966. Optional Protocol to the above-mentioned Covenant. Adopted by the General Assembly of the United Nations on 19 December 1966', *United Nations*. Retrieved 29 October 2016 from https://treaties.un.org/doc/Publication/UNTS/Volume%20999/volume-999-I-14668-English.pdf.
6. 'European Convention on Human Rights', *Council of Europe*. Retrieved 29 October 2016 from http://www.echr.coe.int/Documents/Convention_ENG.pdf.
7. A. Zagorski, 'Comparing Human Rights Instruments of the OSCE, United Nations and Council of Europe', in *OSCE Focus: Creating a Security Community to the Benefit of Everyone* (Geneva: DCAF, 2014), 46–47.
8. The USSR and the GDR ratified the Covenant in 1973, Hungary and Romania in 1974, Czechoslovakia in 1975. Bulgaria was the only Eastern bloc country that adhered to the Covenant before the CSCE in 1970. Hungary was the first Eastern bloc country to adhere to the Optional Protocol in

1988. The Soviet Union and Poland did so in 1991, Bulgaria in 1992 and Romania in 1993. It is fair to note here that Canada and the USA adhered to the Covenant in 1976 and 1992 respectively, while both have failed so far to adhere to the Optional Protocol. 'Status of Ratification Interactive Dashboard', *United Nations Human Rights, Office of the High Commissioner*. Retrieved 25 February 2017 from http://indicators.ohchr.org/.
9. For the dates of adherence of individual European countries to the European Convention on Human Rights, see 'Country Profiles', *Council of Europe, European Court of Human Rights*. Retrieved 25 February 2017 from http://www.echr.coe.int/Pages/home.aspx?p=press/factsheets&c=.
10. *Conference on Security and Co-operation in Europe. Final Act* (Helsinki, 1975), 4.
11. *Concluding Document of the Vienna Meeting 1986 of Representatives of Participating States of the Conference on Security and Co-operation in Europe, held on the basis of provisions of the Final Act relating to the follow-up to the Conference* (Vienna, 1989), 35–36.
12. *Final Act*, 8.
13. W. Korey, *The Promises We Keep: Human Rights, the Helsinki Process, and American Foreign Policy* (New York: St. Martin's Press, 1993), 221–26, 236–41.
14. Document CSCE/1/5, 4 July 1973. Author's archive.
15. 'Ambassador Edouard Brunner of Switzerland', in *CSCE Testimonies*, 95.
16. 'Ambassador Jaakko Iloniemi of Finland', in *CSCE Testimonies*, 31.
17. A. Zagorski, *Khelsinkskii protsess: Peregovory v ramkakh Soveshchaniya po bezopasnosti i sotrudnichestvu v Evrope 1972–1991* [The Helsinki Process: Negotiations within the Framework of the Conference on Security and Cooperation in Europe 1972–1991] (Moscow: Human Rights Publishers, 2005), 89–90.
18. *Final Act*, 57.
19. 'Ambassador Yuri Vladimirovich Dubinin of the Soviet Union', in *CSCE Testimonies*, 214–15.
20. *Concluding Document of the Vienna Meeting 1986*, 37.
21. Korey, *The Promises We Keep*, 67.
22. Zagorski, *The Helsinki Process*, 124–25.
23. *Decisions of the preparatory meeting to organize the Belgrade Meeting 1977 of Representatives of the Participating States of the Conference on Security and Co-operation in Europe, held on the basis of the provisions of the Final Act relating to the follow-up to the Conference* (Belgrade, 1977). The covers of documents adopted by each CSCE meeting differed in colour. The decisions of the Belgrade preparatory meeting became known as the 'yellow book' while the 1973 decisions of the consultations preparing for the CSCE had a blue cover and became known as the 'blue book'.
24. 'Ambassador Yuri Vladimirovich Dubinin', in *CSCE Testimonies*, 215.
25. Ibid., 217.
26. Korey, *The Promises We Keep*, 200–1.
27. Zagorski, *The Helsinki Process*, 241–42.
28. *Concluding Document of the Vienna Meeting 1986*, 37.

29. Korey, *The Promises We Keep*, 171.
30. 'Ambassador Yuri Vladimirovich Dubinin', in *CSCE Testimonies*, 215; 'Ambassador Peter Steglich of the German Democratic Republic', in *CSCE Testimonies*, 126–27.
31. J. Schissler, *The Human Rights Policy of the Carter Administration: US Policy at the Belgrade Meeting of the 'Conference on Security and Cooperation in Europe' (CSCE), October 1977–March 1978* (Frankfurt/M: HSFK, 1979).
32. Maresca, *Helsinki Revisited*, 84.
33. Ibid., 83–88; 'Spencer Oliver of the United States of America', in *CSCE Testimonies*, 223–48; G. van Well, 'Belgrad 1977: Das KSZE-Folgetreffen und seine Bedeutung für den Entspannungsprozeß', in H. Volle and W. Wagner (eds), *Das Belgrader KSZE-Folgetreffen: Der Fortgang des Entspannungsprozesses in Europa in Beiträgen und Dokumenten aus dem Europa-Archiv* (Bonn: Verlag für Internationale Politik GmbH, 1978), 9–17; P. Fischer, 'Das Ergebnis von Belgrad: Das KSZE-Folgetreffen in seiner Bedeutung für den Entspannungsprozeß', in Volle and Wagner, *Das Belgrader KSZE-Folgetreffen*, 23–32.
34. Maresca, *Helsinki Revisited*, 89–90.
35. 'Ambassador Edouard Brunner of Switzerland', in *CSCE Testimonies*, 112; Korey, *The Promises We Keep*, 81–84; 'Spencer Oliver of the United States of America', in *CSCE Testimonies*.
36. Korey, *The Promises We Keep*, 85; 'Spencer Oliver of the United States of America', in *CSCE Testimonies*.
37. V. Mastny, *Helsinki, Human Rights, and European Security: Analysis and Documentation* (Durham, NC: Duke University Press, 1986), 168; H. van der Meulen, 'Die Niederlande und das Treffen von Belgrad', in Volle and Wagner, *Das Belgrader KSZE-Folgetreffen*, 49.
38. Korey, *The Promises We Keep*, 172.
39. Fischer, 'Das Ergebnis von Belgrad', 25.
40. *Helsinki – Belgrade – Madrid: Report of the Helsinki Review Group* (London: David Davies Memorial Institute of International Studies, 1980), 6.
41. Korey, *The Promises We Keep*, 177–78.
42. Zagorski, *The Helsinki Process*, 245.
43. *Document of the Moscow Meeting of the Conference on the Human Dimension of the CSCE* (Moscow, 1991), 2.
44. In 1985, the Soviet authorities granted 6,000 permissions to leave the country for permanent residence abroad. This number grew to 108,000 in 1988 and 230,000 in 1989. See Yu. Kashlev, *Khelsinkskii protsess 1975–2005: Svet I teni glazami uchastnika* [The Helsinki Process 1975–2005: Light and Shadows through the Lens of an Eyewitness] (Moscow: Izvestiya, 2005), 148. For more, see Korey, *The Promises We Keep*, 165–66; Zagorski, *The Helsinki Process*, 154–55.
45. 'Ambassador Peter Steglich of the German Democratic Republic', in *CSCE Testimonies*, 125–26, 130–31.
46. Korey, *The Promises We Keep*, 178.
47. Ibid., 108.

48. *Concluding Document of the Madrid Meeting 1980 of Representatives of the Participating States of the Conference on Security and Co-Operation in Europe, held on the basis of the provisions of the Final Act relating to the Follow-up to the Conference* (Madrid, 1983), 7.
49. V.-Y. Ghebali, *La diplomatie de la détente: la CSCE, d'Helsinki à Vienne, 1973–1989* (Brussels: Bruylant, 1989), 108.
50. Document CSCE/OME.43, 4 June 1985. Author's archive.
51. *Compendium of OSCE Mechanisms and Procedures* (Vienna: OSCE Secretariat, 2008), 3–9.
52. A. Bloed and P. van Dijk, 'Supervisory Mechanism for the Human Dimension of the CSCE: Its Setting-Up in Vienna, Its Present Functioning and Its Possible Development towards a General Procedure for the Peaceful Settlement of CSCE Disputes', in A. Bloed and P. van Dijk (eds), *The Human Dimension of the Helsinki Process – the Vienna Follow-up Meeting and Its Aftermath* (Dordrecht, Boston and London: Martinus Nijhoff, 1991), 79.
53. A. Zagorski, 'A Contested Consensus Rule: How to Make the OSCE More Effective', *Security and Human Rights* 25(2) (2014), 185.
54. A. Zagorski, 'The Clash between Moscow and the Human Dimension of the CSCE: From Vienna to Copenhagen (1989–1990)', in *OSCE Yearbook 2005: Yearbook on the Organization for Security and Co-operation in Europe* (Baden-Baden: Nomos, 2006), 53–55.
55. Zagorski, 'Comparing Human Rights Instruments', 43–63.
56. Ibid., 52–53.
57. 'Country Profiles'.
58. Zagorski, 'Comparing Human Rights Instruments', 55.
59. Maresca, *Helsinki Revisited*, 75.
60. Mastny, *Helsinki, Human Rights, and European Security*, 195–96.
61. Ibid., 138–43.
62. Zagorski, *The Helsinki Process*.
63. *Neue Züricher Zeitung*, 26 November 1980.
64. Zagorski, 'The Clash between Moscow and the Human Dimension of the CSCE', 55–56.
65. A few of them have been documented in Mastny, *Helsinki, Human Rights, and European Security*, 196–97, 199–200.
66. Zagorski, *The Helsinki Process*, 167.
67. Kashlev, *The Helsinki Process 1975–2005*, 175–76; Korey, *The Promises We Keep*, 243.
68. Kashlev, *The Helsinki Process 1975–2005*, 164–65.
69. Mastny, *Helsinki, Human Rights, and European Security*, 198.
70. Kashlev, *The Helsinki Process 1975–2005*, 176.
71. Documents CSCE/OME.43, 4 June 1985 and CSCE/WT.19, 4 February 1987. Author's archive.
72. Mastny, *Helsinki, Human Rights, and European Security*, 116; Maresca, *Helsinki Revisited*, 73–76.
73. Korey, *The Promises We Keep*, 196.
74. Mastny, *Helsinki, Human Rights, and European Security*, 197–98.

75. Ibid., 198.
76. 'Universal Periodic Review', *Office of the UN High Commissioner on Human Rights*. Retrieved 29 October 2016 from http://www.ohchr.org/EN/HRBodies/UPR/Pages/UPRmain.aspx.
77. *Concluding Document of the Vienna Meeting 1986*, 37.
78. Ibid., 81.
79. Kashlev, *The Helsinki Process 1975–2005*, 175.
80. 'Ambassador Evarist Saliba of Malta', in *CSCE Testimonies*, 170, 173–74.
81. M. Perrin de Brichambaut, 'The OSCE in Perspective: Six Years of Service, Six Questions and a Few Answers', *Security and Human Rights* 23(1) (2012), 41.
82. *Compendium of OSCE Mechanisms and Procedures*, 10–11.
83. See for instance the summary of the most recent HDMI: OSCE ODIHR. 'Consolidated Summary. 2016 Human Dimension Implementation Meeting. Warsaw, 19–30 September 2016' (Warsaw, 2016).

Bibliography

Primary Sources

'Charter of the United Nations and Statute of the International Court of Justice, Preamble', *United Nations*. Retrieved 29 October 2016 from http://www.un.org/en/charter-united-nations/index.html.
Compendium of OSCE Mechanisms and Procedures (Vienna: OSCE Secretariat, 2008).
Concluding Document of the Madrid Meeting 1980 of Representatives of the Participating States of the Conference on Security and Co-Operation in Europe, held on the basis of the provisions of the Final Act relating to the Follow-up to the Conference (Madrid, 1983).
Concluding Document of the Vienna Meeting 1986 of Representatives of Participating States of the Conference on Security and Co-operation in Europe, held on the basis of provisions of the Final Act relating to the follow-up to the Conference (Vienna, 1989).
Conference on Security and Co-operation in Europe. Final Act (Helsinki, 1975).
'Country Profiles', *Council of Europe, European Court of Human Rights*. Retrieved 25 February 2017 from http://www.echr.coe.int/Pages/home.aspx?p=press/factsheets&c=.
CSCE Testimonies. Causes and Consequences of the Helsinki Final Act. 1972–1989 (Prague: Prague Office of the OSCE Secretariat, 2013).
Decisions of the preparatory meeting to organize the Belgrade Meeting 1977 of Representatives of the Participating States of the Conference on Security and Co-operation in Europe, held on the basis of the provisions of the Final Act relating to the follow-up to the Conference (Belgrade, 1977).
Document CSCE/1/5, 4 July 1973. Author's archive.
Document CSCE/OME.43, 4 June 1985. Author's archive.
Document CSCE/WT.19, 4 February 1987. Author's archive.

Document of the Moscow Meeting of the Conference on the Human Dimension of the CSCE (Moscow, 1991).
'European Convention on Human Rights', *Council of Europe*. Retrieved 29 October 2016 from http://www.echr.coe.int/Documents/Convention_ENG.pdf.
'International Covenant on Civil and Political Rights. Adopted by the General Assembly of the United Nations on 19 December 1966. Optional Protocol to the above-mentioned Covenant. Adopted by the General Assembly of the United Nations on 19 December 1966', *United Nations*. Retrieved 29 October 2016 from https://treaties.un.org/doc/Publication/UNTS/Volume%20999/volume-999-I-14668-English.pdf.
OSCE ODIHR. 'Consolidated Summary. 2016 Human Dimension Implementation Meeting. Warsaw, 19–30 September 2016' (Warsaw, 2016).
'Status of Ratification Interactive Dashboard', *United Nations Human Rights, Office of the High Commissioner*. Retrieved 25 February 2017 from http://indicators.ohchr.org/.
'The Universal Declaration of Human Rights', *United Nations*. Retrieved 29 October 2016 from http://www.un.org/Overview/rights.html.
'Universal Periodic Review', *Office of the UN High Commissioner on Human Rights*. Retrieved 29 October 2016 from http://www.ohchr.org/EN/HRBodies/UPR/Pages/UPRmain.aspx.

Literature

Bloed, A., and P. van Dijk. 'Supervisory Mechanism for the Human Dimension of the CSCE: Its Setting-Up in Vienna, Its Present Functioning and Its Possible Development towards a General Procedure for the Peaceful Settlement of CSCE Disputes', in A. Bloed and P. van Dijk (eds), *The Human Dimension of the Helsinki Process – the Vienna Follow-up Meeting and Its Aftermath* (Dordrecht, Boston, MA and London: Martinus Nijhoff, 1991), 74–108.
Fischer, P. 'Das Ergebnis von Belgrad: Das KSZE-Folgetreffen in seiner Bedeutung für den Entspannungsprozeß', in H. Volle and W. Wagner (eds), *Das Belgrader KSZE-Folgetreffen: Der Fortgang des Entspannungsprozesses in Europa in Beiträgen und Dokumenten aus dem Europa-Archiv* (Bonn: Verlag für Internationale Politik GmbH, 1978), 23–32.
Ghebali, V.-Y. *La diplomatie de la détente: la CSCE, d'Helsinki à Vienne, 1973–1989*. Brussels: Bruylant, 1989.
Helsinki – Belgrade – Madrid: Report of the Helsinki Review Group. London: David Davies Memorial Institute of International Studies, 1980.
Kashlev, Y. *Khelsinkskii protsess 1975–2005: Svet I teni glazami uchastnika* [The Helsinki Process 1975–2005: Light and Shadows through the Lens of an Eyewitness]. Moscow: Izvestiya, 2005.
Korey, W. *The Promises We Keep: Human Rights, the Helsinki Process, and American Foreign Policy*. New York: St. Martin's Press, 1993.
Maresca, J.J. *Helsinki Revisited: A Key US Negotiator's Memoirs on the Development of the CSCE into the OSCE*. Stuttgart: ibidem-Verlag, 2015.

Mastny, V. *Helsinki, Human Rights, and European Security: Analysis and Documentation*. Durham, NC: Duke University Press, 1986.
Perrin de Brichambaut, M. 'The OSCE in Perspective: Six Years of Service, Six Questions and a Few Answers'. *Security and Human Rights* 23(1) (2012), 31–44.
Schissler, J. *The Human Rights Policy of the Carter Administration: US Policy at the Belgrade Meeting of the 'Conference on Security and Cooperation in Europe' (CSCE), October 1977–March 1978*. Frankfurt/M: HSFK, 1979.
van der Meulen, H. 'Die Niederlande und das Treffen von Belgrad', in H. Volle and W. Wagner (eds), *Das Belgrader KSZE-Folgetreffen: Der Fortgang des Entspannungsprozesses in Europa in Beiträgen und Dokumenten aus dem Europa-Archiv* (Bonn: Verlag für Internationale Politik GmbH, 1978), 43–50.
van Well, G. 'Belgrad 1977: Das KSZE-Folgetreffen und seine Bedeutung für den Entspannungsprozeß', in H. Volle and W. Wagner (eds), *Das Belgrader KSZE-Folgetreffen: Der Fortgang des Entspannungsprozesses in Europa in Beiträgen und Dokumenten aus dem Europa-Archiv* (Bonn: Verlag für Internationale Politik GmbH, 1978), 9–17.
Zagorski, A. 'The Clash between Moscow and the Human Dimension of the CSCE: From Vienna to Copenhagen (1989–1990)', in Institute for Peace Research and Security Policy at the University of Hamburg/IFSH (ed.), *OSCE Yearbook 2005: Yearbook on the Organization for Security and Co-operation in Europe* (Baden-Baden: Nomos, 2006), 47–60.
Zagorski, A. 'Comparing Human Rights Instruments of the OSCE, United Nations and Council of Europe', in *OSCE Focus: Creating a Security Community to the Benefit of Everyone* (Geneva: DCAF, 2014), 43–63.
Zagorski, A. 'A Contested Consensus Rule: How to Make the OSCE More Effective'. *Security and Human Rights* 25(2) (2014), 180–89.
Zagorski, A. *Khelsinkskii protsess: Peregovory v ramkakh Soveshchaniya po bezopasnosti i sotrudnichestvu v Evrope 1972–1991* [The Helsinki Process: Negotiations within the Framework of the Conference on Security and Cooperation in Europe 1972–1991]. Moscow: Human Rights Publishers, 2005.

 2

Executors or Creative Deal-Makers?
The Role of the Diplomats in the Making of the Helsinki CSCE
Martin D. Brown and Angela Romano

Introduction

Over the last decade, historians have analysed the policy of numerous countries engaged in the Conference on Security and Cooperation in Europe (CSCE). This scholarship has demonstrated that the CSCE had an important role in most participating countries' Cold War policy and has revealed the amount of work that foreign ministries dedicated to its preparation and negotiations as well as the direct involvement of the highest levels of government in defining their countries' CSCE objectives. These findings stand in stark contrast with the earlier generation of literature on the CSCE, mostly produced by former diplomats engaged in the negotiations, which claimed that it was they who essentially 'invented' the Final Act.

More than six hundred diplomats were involved in the CSCE, including its preparatory phase.[1] Yet most of these participants remain anonymous, with the exception of the few who subsequently wrote memoirs or eyewitness accounts.[2] More importantly, the contribution of the vast majority of these individuals to the successful outcome of the talks remains unexamined. Scholarship has highlighted the specific role of certain diplomats only cursorily; most works tend to focus on a small cohort of senior-level personalities, a process that might be defined as the Kissingerization of the historiography of the early 1970s.[3]

The analysis presented in this chapter sprang from the consideration that the time is ripe for a better understanding of the division of labour between capitals and delegates to the negotiations, which in turn could lead to a more nuanced assessment of where exactly initiatives began. Moreover, the analysis of the interplay between governments and their diplomats on the ground would allow us to better appreciate their relative impact on the outcome of the CSCE. Such an endeavour would enrich and complement the existing historiography on national case studies and offer a more dynamic picture of the CSCE negotiations.

This chapter also attributes a wider theoretical value to the study of diplomats' role in the CSCE. The literature on global governance often depicts traditional state-centric diplomacy as struggling to adapt and maintain its continued relevance in globalized, multilateral interactions.[4] Conversely, it is here hypothesized that diplomats at the CSCE also served as vital communication channels, mediators and 'trouble shooters' with a shared *esprit de corps* that fostered relationships among the delegations of the participating states. This understanding of diplomats as forming a transnational epistemic community is reflected in the most recent literature on diplomacy, which is interested in its constitutive and mediating qualities.[5] Proponents of the English School, for example, attribute a positive international role to the diplomat.[6] The latter is not simply a representative and defender of the national interest but also a transnational agent involved in brokering international agreements and developing international organizations through changing alliances. Historical research about the League of Nations or the European Community and then European Union (EC and EU) has provided evidence to this argument.[7]

The analysis proposed in this chapter is part of a complex research project that aims to assess whether diplomats and their interactions can be counted among the factors making the CSCE 'work'. More specifically, it scrutinizes a variety of sources to appraise the contribution made by diplomats on the ground and employs prosopographical methods in order to relate CSCE diplomats' personal and career trajectories to their diplomatic action on site. Prosopography can be described as 'the investigation of the common background characteristics of a group of actors in history by means of a collective study of their lives', and its method consists in collecting various types of information about individuals of a selected group (for example, about birth and death, social origins, education, occupation, religion, experience of office and so on), then juxtaposing and combining them in order to detect correlations with behaviours and actions of these individuals.[8] It is assumed, both in this chapter and the broader research project behind it, that applying this approach to CSCE diplomats on the ground will allow for a clearer mapping of the intellectual influences and interpersonal links across national delegations, which could help to explain the success of this long-running and multifaceted diplomatic conference.⁹

Among the thirty-five countries participating in the CSCE negotiations, many could well serve as useful case studies for this exercise. There would certainly be merits in taking examples from across the Iron Curtain or from one of the neutral states. However, several practical and scientific rationales have motivated the selection of France and the United Kingdom (UK) as the case studies for this chapter. Among the former are the linguistic skills of the authors and their specific knowledge and previous analyses of the UK and French policies towards the CSCE. This earlier research underpins the scientific reasons behind these choices, which include the existence of and familiarity with the mature historiography on the UK and French CSCE experiences, the availability of diverse primary sources (archives and memoirs), and the possibility to consider countries with differing administrative and diplomatic machinery. The chapter is concerned neither with directly comparing the two systems nor with appraising the administrative aspects of diplomats' recruitment, career development and so on. Yet the nature of the relationships between the Foreign Ministry and diplomats is key to understanding the latter's background and to appraising both the latitude for action they were allowed on the ground and their ability to influence policy back home.

The authors of this chapter also contend that the UK and France represent two significant case studies within the scope of CSCE negotiations in terms of approaches and roles. Both countries belonged to the Atlantic Alliance and to the European Community (though France was a founding member of the EC and the UK had joined before the Helsinki CSCE commenced).[10] Moreover, unlike other NATO and EC members, both states were great European powers that had retained post-World War II responsibilities and rights on Berlin; they were hence directly involved in managing the European security architecture that the CSCE would be discussing.

In addition, the approaches of the UK and French governments to the CSCE and European affairs offer interesting material for inquiry into diplomats' role. The UK government had no specific goals at the CSCE, was mostly concerned with preserving the solidarity of the West, and generally in favour of promoting East–West dialogue; it was therefore inclined to coordination with NATO allies and good interactions with the Neutral or Non-Aligned countries (NNA), though alignment with EC partners would prevail. The French government was more directly concerned with shaping the European order, favouring the loosening of the Cold War straitjacket, carefully spreading the contagion of liberty in the socialist regimes and yet involving the Soviet Union in closer cooperation. More importantly, it was guided by the refusal of bloc-to-bloc negotiations, which led to being opposed to NATO-labelled initiatives and to promoting closely coordinated EC actions. We therefore have two cases in which the government's approach to European affairs indicates an inclination to broker deals with the Cold War antagonists, whatever the general goal or leading rationale behind this course of action. To what extent were UK and French diplomats aligned with governmental instructions or, on the contrary, providing inputs that influenced the latter? Did they give more substance or weaken (or even bypass) instructions from their respective capitals? At the same time, both countries' governments were acting in close relation with partners and allies; their diplomats on the ground were therefore involved in more or less close-knit groups that daily discussed negotiation tactics and proposals. Taken together, these reasons and rationales more than justify the selection of these two countries as case studies.

This chapter is organized in three sections. In the first, the case is made in favour of a new approach to CSCE study along the above-mentioned lines. In the second and third parts, two pilot studies are offered on British and French diplomats who were much involved in the CSCE negotiations. These case studies, which also comprise elements of prosopography, bring to the fore meaningful examples of diplomats' role in the negotiations and allow us to formulate some provisional considerations on a matter that warrants further exploration.

Was There Room for Diplomats' Creative Role in the CSCE?

Of the four phases of the CSCE, both the Foreign Ministers' meeting that opened the CSCE and the top-level concluding ceremony were mostly stage performances designed for a variegated audience – the press, civil societies and first and foremost the governments of the other participating countries. Statements made at both opening and concluding meetings of the CSCE were instrumental in conveying unequivocal messages about the national interpretation of the agreed rules and provisions.

By contrast, both the Multilateral Preparatory Talks (MPT) and the negotiations in Geneva were 'creative' phases, where the shaping and 'inventing' of the Final Act took place. In both cases, the diplomats on the ground were key players. But to what extent were they just executing orders from their capitals? How many initiatives did they take without, or despite, instructions from home? Did their feedback and suggestions influence or even revise the approach in the capital on specific aspects? And, finally, did they serve as midwives to compromises and/or hoped-for results? The diplomats' room for manoeuvring certainly varied across national delegations; however, the CSCE features explored below – jargon, modus operandi and socialization – suggest that diplomats had significant latitude in negotiating details and even reshaping national approaches on some specific aspects.

The Diplomats' Jargon

For nine months, delegations to the MPT held tough discussions on the agenda, the structure and the rules of the CSCE, which were eventually set out in the Final Recommendations of the Helsinki Consultations.

Jacques Andréani, the key French personality in the CSCE negotiations, wrote that in order to reconcile the goals of some delegations and the reluctance of others in a text, the MPT Recommendations adopted an allusive terminology, where each expression was perfectly understandable for negotiators, but for them only – a point also reiterated by several of the British participants.[11] This esotericism had the double effect of creating a bond among the delegates and of making the exercise almost unintelligible to the heads of departments back home, not to mention politicians, unable to decipher the 'words of the tribe'.[12] Consequently, the heads of delegations had significant autonomy in revising and refining the rules of the negotiations. The same would apply to the drafting of the Final Act, also a complex exercise of reconciling positions that were often irreconcilable. Andréani sustains that only on a few major points could politicians and ministers in capitals exercise authority.[13] Andréani's argument is quite debatable, as the situation varied remarkably across states. Indeed, his only examples in support of this view involve US National Security Adviser and Secretary of State Henry Kissinger and US President Gerald Ford, whose interest in the CSCE was fleeting to say the least. On the contrary, other countries' governments followed the negotiations closely and regularly sent detailed instructions. Yet the diplomatic jargon of these compromise agreements, with its nuances, subtleties and disputes over the placing of commas, is very seldom a matter for precise instructions from home. This aspect *per se* gave diplomats on the ground some room for autonomy and initiative in shaping CSCE rules and Final Act provisions.

The Modus Operandi

The CSCE negotiations took place within a complex, intermeshed structure of bodies. At the top was the Coordinating Committee of the thirty-five heads of delegation: it supervised and collated the documents of the commissions and sub-commissions, noted the formal approval of agreed texts, debated open and problematic issues that could not be solved in the sub-bodies and negotiated on the specific question of follow-up conferences. Below this level there were three commissions, one for each of the main agenda items (known as 'baskets'). Linked to, and dependent on, these commissions there were twelve sub-commissions in charge of editing the texts on the thematic subjects of each basket.

At each level, decisions were taken according to the rule of consensus, defined as the absence of objections presented as constituting an obstacle to decision. This rule – vigorously advocated by minor countries and Romania – assured every participating state the possibility to express its positions and protect its vital interests.[14] The rule of consensus, applied to a broad and rich agenda, contributed to making the CSCE the long negotiations we know. The phase of negotiations in Geneva eventually totalled 2,341 meetings.[15]

These were only the official ones. The necessity of reaching consensus engendered *ad hoc* alliances on different topics and continuous games of bargaining and pressure, made up alternately of connivance and arm-twisting, where the determinant elements of success were either the ability to resist or the ability to table package deals. At the same time, the intentional search for solutions that might satisfy all the participants led to reconciliation of even the most irreconcilable positions. We know that some key stalemates were unlocked during bilateral summits between Soviet and Western leaders.[16] Yet many issues that were progressing too slowly or deadlocked were solved through diplomats' negotiations in unofficial fora. Delegates of the most interested countries met in informal small working sessions, usually chaired by diplomats of the NNA. Many deals were worked out bilaterally or during (long) coffee breaks, where opposing delegations could bargain and persuade more confidentially.[17]

The Inherent Socialization

The MPT Recommendations stated that the CSCE should develop outside military alliances.[18] Nonetheless, delegations teamed up in three major caucuses – NATO, the Warsaw Pact and the NNA – each characterized by common positions and a degree of coordination.

Recent historiography has demonstrated that, though actively participating in NATO consultations, the EC member states developed a distinct collective approach and formed the most proactive and close-knit group at the CSCE.[19] Although a member of the Warsaw Pact, Romania acted independently and shared the NNA's vision of European cooperation and security beyond the blocs. The Romanian government overtly denied legitimacy to the Brezhnev Doctrine, which it had neither helped to implement nor even agreed to; consistently, and always concerned with the possibility of a Soviet punitive invasion of Romania, Bucharest clearly pushed for CSCE provisions that could offer some guarantee to or protection of the political independence and territorial integrity of all participating states (and of Romania itself).[20]

What role did the diplomats on the ground have in favouring coordinated actions by these national delegations of different kinds in fields of common interest? And how much did diplomats obey instructions from the capital? The case of the US delegation, whose contribution to the Western caucus developed in spite of (poor) instructions from Washington, is well known. A more revealing case is that of the French delegation to the MPT, which joined the NATO delegations' meetings without asking Paris for authorization. The position of the French government at the time was to avoid supporting a politics of blocs, hence it refused to participate in the NATO-labelled group; in addition, Paris invested much effort in close political cooperation with EC partners, which should not be diluted in a NATO grouping. Diplomats then argued against grudging Foreign Ministry officials that, rather than compromise French independence, their participation in the NATO caucus could help defend and further French proposals.[21] The initiative of the French diplomats on the ground did change attitudes at home and was therefore paramount in assuring a close coordination with Western allies. Moreover, it helped strengthen the unitary action of the European Community partners, as their delegations coordinated their position ahead of NATO consultations.[22]

The CSCE's diverse agenda also led to the formation of less visible *ad hoc* sub-groups: Mediterranean, Nordic, security measures-focused, economic cooperation-focused, the 'Bonn group' (West Germany plus the three allied states with special rights and responsibility on Berlin) and the German-speaking group formed in order to guarantee agreement on the German version of texts. As most diplomats were involved, often daily, in this complex set of meetings at the CSCE level, caucus level, sub-group(s), *ad hoc* contact groups and of course bilateral exchanges, they had some latitude from capitals in shaping the CSCE outcome through informal discussion and personal contacts with other delegations' opposite numbers.

According to Andréani, the length of the negotiations and the frequency of the meetings made CSCE diplomats 'a peculiar tribe, living in such a proximity that bordered promiscuity'.[23] Apart from the usual diplomatic intercourse, life during the twenty-two months in Geneva (and nine months in Helsinki for the MPT) included leisure time. As neither Helsinki nor Geneva offered the range of amenities typical of great capitals, Andréani recollects, diplomats found alternative ways to have a good time – together. Remarkably, the friendliness that characterized relations between Western and neutral diplomats gradually extended to some of the representatives of socialist countries. While the Soviets tended to keep to themselves, delegates from Poland and Hungary mingled with Western colleagues and friendships were born across the Iron Curtain.[24] These are precisely the kinds of relations we deem worth exploring and taking into account when trying to appraise the role of diplomats in the CSCE.[25]

Pilot Study: The United Kingdom

The formation of British policy towards the CSCE is well documented. The key decisions made by prime ministers, in the Cabinet and within the senior strata of the Foreign and Commonwealth Office (FCO), have all been charted and debated, as has the development and execution of these policies.[26] No mysteries surround the UK's decision-making or policy formation, or the course of the negotiations leading up to the signing of the Helsinki Final Act in August 1975.[27] However, what is less immediately apparent is the extent to which the UK diplomats can be shown to be creative deal-makers as opposed to simply executors of Whitehall's instructions.[28]

Part of the difficultly in differentiating between creative deal-makers and executors is the nature of the official documentation itself: a 'record of what one clerk said to another clerk', designed to communicate information, policy and instructions rather than reveal the nuances and cultural/social dimensions of the interactions between diplomats.[29] This is not to dismiss the documents' utility but rather to argue that these materials must be augmented with others, such as diaries and interviews, in order to illuminate the diplomats' role in the eventual success of the CSCE.[30] Unfortunately, we have few memoirs from British diplomats directly involved in these negotiations, although we do have access to interviews and oral testimonies.[31] Nevertheless, an initial survey of the available materials indicates that British diplomats at the CSCE were granted significant leeway in their ability to conduct negotiations, while liaising closely with department heads back in London.[32]

The Governmental Level

Since the late 1990s, the declassification of governmental documents and the publication of volumes of documentation by the FCO have allowed historians to reappraise the British role in the CSCE.[33] A key feature of much of the subsequent discourse has revolved around the levels of enthusiasm for the talks expressed by Whitehall.[34] It is now apparent that London was never an overly enthusiastic proponent of détente, even though it accepted the project at an early stage, and successive governments never made the talks a policy priority.[35] For example, the negotiations on Mutual and Balanced Force Reductions (MBFR) in Europe were regarded as being more important and substantive, as indicated by the seniority of the diplomatic team sent to these talks in Vienna.[36] Even the CSCE's final signing ceremony in 1975 was overshadowed by the UK referendum on EC membership and by the political crisis in Portugal.[37] So, too, opinions were expressed at senior levels in the FCO that the CSCE might be a Soviet ploy designed to undermine Western cohesion and should be treated with caution.[38] Such opinions were not universal, but they were apparent.[39] As we shall see, these reservations should not be automatically conflated with the opinions of the younger diplomats working on the ground.[40]

That said, both Harold Wilson's and Edward Heath's governments, including their foreign secretaries Michael Stewart, Alec Douglas-Home and James Callaghan, recognized that the CSCE offered opportunities to enhance and regularize the state of European security.[41] Equally, the idea was robustly supported by several of the principal allies of the United Kingdom.[42] So although Whitehall was hesitant about the CSCE and had no clear view of its potential outcomes, they were committed to the process from an early stage.[43] Nevertheless, ministers and senior civil servants exerted a relatively minor influence over what proved to be a complex, convoluted and protracted round of multilateral negotiations.

A note from Wilson to Lord Bridges in June 1974 illustrates this disconnect: 'Could you please let me know what [sic] the present state of play on the Geneva Conference on European Security. *The Economist* this week suggests that there is no progress at all. I would be grateful if you could get a full note from the Foreign Office for me to study'.[44] While excessive weight should not be attached to this anecdote, it is reasonable to suggest that in comparison to some of the other participants, such as the USSR or West Germany, high-level British political engagement with the process was at best sporadic.[45] Given these circumstances, it is demonstrable that the primary mandate for managing expectations, and the talks themselves, was delegated to the FCO.[46]

The Role of the Diplomatic Corps: On Methodological Difficulties and Tentative Arguments

Negotiations were thus conducted and directed by a relatively small group of generally younger, middle-ranking FCO diplomats based in London, Helsinki and Geneva.[47] Crispin Tickell, head of the Western Organizations Department (WOD), took the lead in fashioning the coordinating machinery required to navigate through these discussions. His department worked in conjunction with the Eastern European and Soviet Department (EESD), other ministries, as well as the embassies in Helsinki and the permanent mission to the United Nations in Geneva.[48]

However, the list remains incomplete, never mind the hundreds of other participants they may have interacted with. Neither the British documentation nor the secondary materials provide a complete record of all the attendees at the CSCE. All too often it is only the senior figures, usually the politicians, who make an appearance. Fortunately, the OSCE archive located in Prague has preserved a complete register of all delegates.[49] Moreover, we are not simply looking for names but also for details regarding diplomats' linguistic skills, prior postings, educational background, social and cultural milieus and other aspects that may help us map out networks of contacts and interactions with other delegates.[50] This information may be difficult to find: for instance, the FCO's Diplomatic Service List reveals details of earlier duties and postings, but offers no information on the languages spoken by the diplomats.[51]

With the paucity of available British memoirs, with the exception of Alexander's account, the most useful additional sources are witness testimonies and interviews.[52] It is from these materials that a more nuanced and textured picture of the diplomats' interactions with each other, as well as with their political masters, begins to emerge. The British Diplomatic Oral History Programme at Churchill College Cambridge, the OSCE itself and the Institute of Contemporary British History have all made valuable contributions here.[53] The author of this section has also interviewed a number of diplomats, journalists and politicians involved in the talks.[54] What follows is based on these materials.

First and foremost, the hesitancy and suspicions over the CSCE expressed at senior levels in Whitehall was less of an issue than is sometimes suggested in the secondary literature. Alexander, Braithwaite, Andrew Burns, Fall, Tickell, Walden and Patrick Wright have all openly expressed their enthusiasm for engaging in the process, arguing that scepticism did exist but this was to be expected and had a negligible impact on the talks.[55] As Tickell explains:

> That's partly because the people at the top didn't understand it. They regarded the CSCE as a Russian propaganda initiative that we should treat with the utmost scepticism and care. That was the prevailing view when I started. But it became clear to me after a relatively short time that we had a lot of the cards in our hands and could make quite a success of it. And we did.[56]

British diplomats were therefore doing exactly what they had been trained to do.[57]

One consequence of this hesitancy was the fact that the British delegations in Helsinki and Geneva were generally younger and more junior than those sent to the MBFR talks.[58] This fact caused some annoyance to Soviet Ambassador Valerian Zorin as well as to an anonymous Dutch ambassador, who regarded the British diplomats as 'callow and inexperienced'.[59] Such generational divides and differences in status also raise interesting questions regarding the possible advantages of experience versus youthful fervour and stamina.

Second, according to both Tickell's and Christopher Mallaby's recollections, the FCO's department heads and their subordinates enjoyed far greater leeway in decision-making than was the case with other national delegations. In particular, Douglas-Home, unlike George Brown or David Owen, exercised a very hands-off style of leadership, delegating much responsibility to his officials.[60] In his memoirs Alexander repeatedly stresses the independence of decision-making he enjoyed during discussions with the Soviets over Basket Three, and later wrote, 'Even at this range, I am surprised at the degree of discretion for the team in Geneva … I seem to have carried forward discussion of a substantial initiative, and detailed international discussion of associated texts, for at least a week before even informing the FCO'.[61] This situation allowed British diplomats to take the initiative with limited political interference or delay and was further facilitated by the lack of British public interest in the discussions.[62] Yet again, this position was not automatically an advantage in day-to-day discussions, but it is another issue to be noted.

Third is the role of language. The British delegation contained a number of French, German and Russian speakers: Sir Thomas Brimelow, Julian Bullard and Rodric Braithwaite all spoke Russian; Brian Fall both Russian and French; Beetham spoke French, German and some Finnish.[63] The British delegation does appear to have had a preponderance of Russian speakers, which may well have been advantageous, not least because it avoided reliance on translators.[64]

Finally, a genuine *esprit de corps* does appear to have emerged among the diplomats, which extended, to a certain degree, across the Iron Curtain. Beetham mentions that during preparatory talks at Dipoli in late 1972, his house was used as a meeting point as it was halfway to Helsinki. Various delegations met for lunches and drinks between sessions, including the American and Soviet ambassadors, George Vest and Lev Mendelevich.[65] Fall also recalls having after-work drinks with Vest in order to ask his advice, an occasional brandy with Prince Henry of Lichtenstein and a variety of intra-bloc dinner parties.[66] Given that all the hotels in Helsinki had been reserved for national delegations by the Finnish government for the first and third phases of the talks, there may have been plenty of opportunities for similar social interactions. The same must also have been the case in the second phase in Geneva.

These conclusions are at best tentative, and far more detailed work must be undertaken to decide whether the British diplomats were creative deal-makers or executors of Whitehall's orders, or perhaps a combination of the two. The evidence strongly suggests that British diplomats enjoyed significant autonomy of action during the talks, with minimal political interference, and that this leeway contributed to their ability to achieve UK policy objectives during the talks.

Pilot Study: France

The image of the diplomatic corps as a machinery executing orders seems particularly apt for France's Fifth Republic, where the elected president tops the foreign policy decision-making apparatus. Aided by his close entourage, he defines foreign policy's orientation; the Ministry of Foreign Affairs (MAE) refines the details and steers implementation; diplomats execute.

In fact, this is quite theoretical. The president relies on the system to form his view on major international issues: the Elysée cannot monitor all international situations and leaves considerable leeway to the Foreign Ministry, especially when it comes to long and complex negotiations.[67] Nor are diplomats on the ground mere executors: they are key informers, whose reports back home can occasionally shape policy to a large extent. They should not be seen as highly regimented either: they are not secluded from debates taking place in polity, civil society, academic and cultural milieus, and have their own views in terms of policy's course of action.

Consequently, to appraise the latitude of diplomats' role in the CSCE, it is necessary to consider the views held at the various levels of the apparatus about several aspects of French policy concerning Europe and explore their interplay. This study focuses on the pivotal issue of attitudes towards the Soviet Union.

The Elysée/MAE Level: The Moscow Constant

Two presidents supervised France's involvement in the CSCE: Georges Pompidou (up to April 1974) and Valéry Giscard d'Estaing. Pompidou, the successor of General Charles de Gaulle, continued the latter's 'détente, entente and cooperation' policy towards Moscow; he met Brezhnev five times (three times in the Soviet Union) and the two got along well.[68] Pompidou also confirmed the Gaullist principle of preserving France's independent stance vis-à-vis both superpowers.

This was also the view of his secretary-general at the Elysée, Michel Jobert, who significantly influenced the president's diplomacy. On the contrary, Foreign Minister Maurice Schumann (22 June 1969–15 March 1973) played a limited role in defining France's East–West policy. Jobert, who took over the Foreign Ministry in spring 1973, was a Gaullist more assertive than the president in pursuing France's independence from the United States' course of action and particularly concerned with resisting superpower condominium over Europe.[69] Indeed, in the speech he gave to the CSCE opening phase, he explicitly warned against the danger of Europeans' passivity in permitting their continent to be a playground for the rivalries of external forces.[70]

President Giscard was a centrist, not a Gaullist, and distinguished himself for a strong engagement with the European integration process and closer collaboration with Germany, which he considered pivotal in shaping the former. It was not by chance that the president appointed Jean Sauvagnargues, who was France's ambassador in Bonn, as foreign minister (May 1974–August 1976). Yet he also chose a chief of staff close to the Gaullist party, Maurice Ulrich, to flank Sauvagnargues.[71] More importantly, Giscard decisively exerted his prerogatives to conduct foreign policy directly. Recent scholarship has demonstrated that his approach to East–West relations was of substantial Gaullist persuasion: he constantly reached out to Moscow and often did so without informing the Foreign Ministry or in open contrast with its advice.⁷² The CSCE was no exception. At his first summit with Brezhnev (Rambouillet, December 1974), Giscard invited the Soviet leader to move from détente to entente and made the first step: he agreed to state in the summit communiqué that 'good premises' existed for convening the CSCE third phase at the top level. Acting against the advice of the foreign minister, key officials in the MAE and the French delegation to the CSCE, and without the least consultation with EC partners or Atlantic allies, Giscard removed one of the cornerstones of French (and EC) negotiation tactics at the CSCE – to withhold consent for considering a top-level final phase (a key Soviet goal) until a satisfactory deal had been secured in Basket Three.⁷³ Overall, geopolitical and Gaullist ideas dominated the French presidents' approach to the CSCE.⁷⁴

The Diplomatic Corps: Conflicting Views

Within the diplomatic apparatus, views on the Franco-Soviet relationship were diverse, with two camps clearly opposing each other since the mid 1950s: the 'Laloy school' and the 'Dejean school'.⁷⁵ The first group, comprising Sovietologists led by Jean Laloy, viewed détente as a temporary phenomenon following the Cuban missile crisis, and was suspicious about Soviet overtures. These diplomats saw the Soviet regime as animated by a subversive ideology, craving power and determined to neutralize Western Europe; hence they saw no possibility of convergence between East and West. They argued that France should adopt firmness in dealing with Soviet authorities, ask for strict reciprocity when crafting agreements and encourage local opposition.⁷⁶ Greater Western solidarity and a solid Franco-German partnership were the polestar for this Atlanticist group.

Conversely, the school of thought that developed around Ambassadors to Moscow Maurice Dejean (1955–64) and Roger Seydoux (1968–73) considered that a lasting Franco-Soviet rapprochement was both possible and desirable. These diplomats' approach to international relations was geopolitical and intentionally downplayed ideology. They saw the Soviet Union as the heirs of Russia following the latter's traditional search for status quo in Europe. They argued that a close dialogue with Moscow could allow France to be perceived as a great power, exert a pivotal role between the superpowers and hold Germany in check. Interests did converge, and Paris should actively pursue détente and cooperation with Soviet Russia. The Dejean school largely prevailed across the Quai d'Orsay under de Gaulle and Pompidou.⁷⁷

Between 1972 and 1973 the picture became more diverse, thanks to the emergence of a new generation of diplomats, such as Gabriel Robin, Bertrand Dufourcq and Jacques Andréani.[78] Robin joined the diplomatic cell at the Elysée at the age of forty-four; Dufourcq, then thirty-nine years old, was appointed deputy director of the Foreign Ministry's Western Europe department, charged with animating the French contribution to European Political Cooperation (EPC). Andréani was given a leading role in French CSCE policy. As the MPT approached, a 'CSCE cell' was created at the MAE to enable coordination among the Foreign Ministry and other ministerial departments, as well as to ensure that the overall political implications would be taken into consideration when elaborating French positions. Andréani was entrusted with the task of coordinating the CSCE cell's works. Later, he was also appointed head of the French delegation to the CSCE negotiations in Geneva, thus becoming the human link between the central administration and the CSCE delegation.

These diplomats held quite different views on East–West relations. Robin, whom Giscard maintained in the Elysée diplomatic cell, was a Gaullist and a fervent supporter of détente. Andréani, not a Gaullist, was known to be close to the *circle aronien*, and his support for détente had the more explicit goal of overcoming the Cold War system through cooperation.[79] He later defended the Final Act, presenting Basket Three as a Western 'trap' into which the Soviets had fallen, a tool for changing the socialist regimes.[80]

A Proactive French Diplomat in Basket Three

Presidents of the Republic and foreign ministers were predominantly in favour of realpolitik towards the Soviets, while Quai d'Orsay's officials close to the field of negotiation and experts of Eastern European countries appreciated the idea of freer movement of people and information.[81] This was very much Andréani's position. He monitored all discussions in Geneva but only attended the coordinating committee meeting and supervised the rest of the operations from Paris. He wrote a weekly summary telegram for the ministry and the Elysée and called for specific instructions. In actuality, most of the time he received instructions … from himself, 'because it was impossible for the department to follow!'[82] This gave diplomats on the ground some leeway for initiatives.

French diplomat Jacques Chazelle's action in Basket Three negotiations, particularly in the sub-field of information, provides a good case to elucidate the relationship between the action of diplomats on site and elaboration of policy in the capital. At the CSCE, one of Chazelle's priorities was to foster provisions that would improve citizens' access to information. Western proposals in the field, such as those improving the circulation of foreign newspapers and of journalists themselves, met with staunch opposition from the Soviets, who proved masters in the art of stonewalling. Through bilateral meetings with Yuri Dubinin, the Soviet diplomat responsible for Basket Three, Chazelle discovered a fundamental misunderstanding that pinned the Soviet position and approach to the topic: the Soviets were convinced that Western governments could influence the press. Hence they viewed these proposals as Western attempts to prepare the ground for the future dissemination of propaganda aimed at destabilizing the communist regimes.[83] Chazelle conveyed this message to both policy-makers at home and partner delegations on site. He also undertook to improve Soviet understanding of the realities of the media's role in Western society, starting with an explanation of journalists' freedom of action and independence from governments. He did so via bilateral meetings with Dubinin on the side.[84]

Chazelle also used this consolidated relationship to defuse Soviet anxieties in relation to specific Western proposals in the field of information. The German proposal on the prohibition to expel or penalize journalists because of their professional activity, for instance, met with Soviet indignation for what they saw as an assault to authorities' powers in the field of state security. Bilateral talks between Chazelle and Dubinin helped clear the air and move things forward. Chazelle explained that the provision would not create any *legal* prohibition, but only establish an agreed principle that would apply most of the time and yet allow for exceptions. Moreover, he drew Dubinin's attention to the fact that expulsions usually damaged the image of the state, and suggested that Moscow should rather consider not renewing visas for undesirable journalists rather than expel them. Dubinin agreed to give favourable consideration to the issue; he also declared readiness to make concessions on journalists' working conditions, such as the possibility to bring equipment with them, and on improving their transmission of information back home. He kept his word: in early December 1974, the Soviet delegation submitted a new text on journalists' working conditions that included these provisions. This in turn made possible a major leap forward in the negotiations in the sub-commission on information.[85]

It would seem that the merit lies indeed with the diplomats on site, especially when taking into consideration the ministerial position at the time. In reply to a note in which the French delegation recalled the main positions agreed with the EC partners on information matters, Foreign Minister Jean Sauvagnargues asked why the delegations insisted on seeking Soviet commitment to provisions that they would in any case never respect.[86] It was up to the head of the French delegation to explain the strategic benefits of this (EC-agreed) course of action. In the worst case – non-compliance and continued ideological fight – the Soviet authorities would need to implement a great propaganda effort to justify skipping the solemn engagement they had signed; this would place the regime on the defensive and reduce its room for selling the CSCE as a sort of peace treaty recording the intangibility of the 'conquests of socialism' in World War II.[87]

This specific story confirms that diplomats' continual efforts on the ground had some role in prompting agreement on the specific content of the Final Act. It also shows that exploring relations between diplomats on site may reveal interesting dynamics. A limited exercise in prosopography provides some evidence to imply that there was fertile ground for personal sympathy and intellectual understanding between Dubinin and Chazelle, which in turn may have favoured compromise on key points.

The first thing worth noticing is that Dubinin and Chazelle could talk without translators, as the Soviet diplomat spoke French fluently. According to Western diplomats, he served as a French-Russian interpreter in several high-level meetings; Claude de Kemoularia, the French representative at the UN when Dubinin was there, affirmed that Dubinin spoke 'a beautiful French' and knew French politics and French literature.[88] The latter is an interesting point of convergence with Chazelle, who was a *normalien* and held an *agrégation* in literature.[89]

The two also shared an interest in and knowledge of Asia. Chazelle had been first secretary of the French embassy in Tokyo at the end of the 1940s charged with cultural affairs and had authored three books about Indochina and the war; Dubinin's PhD thesis at the Moscow State Institute of International Relations dealt with the international politics of the Asia-Pacific region.[90]

Beyond interests and education, Dubinin's career path might have been more important in favouring a close and constructive relationship with the French diplomat. He entered the Foreign Service in 1955 as a trainee, and the next year was assigned his first mission abroad: in Paris, at the Secretariat of the United Nations Educational, Scientific and Cultural Organization (UNESCO). Dubinin spent three years in this post; it seems fair to suggest that Dubinin could indeed be more sensible and personally committed to favouring cultural exchanges. In the decade from 1960 to 1970 he alternated between increasingly responsible positions in the embassy in Paris and in the Foreign Ministry's first European Department (relations with France, Italy, the Benelux countries, Spain, Portugal and Switzerland).[91] Hence Dubinin started his career in Paris and spent several years in the French capital, being there continually during his career.

All of the above suggests that personal assets could favour Dubinin's close and constructive talks with the French. There is also room to argue that these informal discussions played an important role in unlocking stalemates and achieving compromise. At the time of the CSCE negotiations, Dubinin was neither a junior diplomat nor a lightweight one: he was the Soviet Basket Three expert and deputy-head of the Soviet delegation to the CSCE; moreover, from 1971 to 1978, he was chief of the first European Department of the Foreign Ministry. He thus had some leverage in Moscow to shift the official position on some negotiating points, though only Russian documents will tell to what extent this was the case.

Conclusion

Much of the scholarly work on the CSCE continues to be concerned with policy-makers rather than the treaty negotiators; the vast majority of the six hundred or so diplomats who negotiated and drafted the Helsinki Final Act remain nameless and faceless, and their role is overlooked. In the conviction that there is a significant 'missing human dimension' to the current study of the CSCE, this chapter has built the theoretical case in favour of exploring this human dimension in order to enhance our understanding of the CSCE process.

The limited exercise of prosopography and source analysis that this chapter has offered for the British and French cases and the ensuing findings here presented reveal a promising line of analysis that warrants further research, in particular with the view of both elucidating the division of labour between politicians and officials in capitals and diplomats on the ground and appraising their merits in allowing the CSCE to achieve a successful outcome in 1975.

The British pilot study indicates that UK diplomats at the CSCE possessed significant leeway in their ability to conduct negotiations, while liaising closely with department heads back in London. Additionally, the diplomatic team was relatively young and more junior than some of its counterparts, its members possessed a wide range of linguistic skills, particularly in Russian, and they were socially active outside the formal negotiations. Consequently, the scepticism expressed in the

Cabinet and at the higher levels of the FCO about the utility of the CSCE was counteracted by their energetic engagement on the ground. More research is required before any definitive statements can be made about their identification as 'creative deal-makers', but that balance of probability makes it likely that this was a significant factor in the UK's performance at the talks.

The French pilot study's specific story, which is more concerned with diplomats' interactions on the ground, confirms that diplomats' continual efforts to facilitate mutual understanding had some role in the successful outcome of the CSCE and the specific content of the Final Act, and thus deserve historians' attention and adequate historiographical research. It also proves that a prosopographical study may indeed help reveal diplomats' background and thinking and detect factors of convergence and understanding with specific colleagues of other delegations. In other words, research concerned with exploring relations among diplomats on site could allow us to bring to the fore and assess the 'human and socialization factor' that has been overlooked in the amazingly rich and sophisticated CSCE scholarship produced to date.

Martin D. Brown (PhD, International History, F.R.Hist.S.) is Associate Professor of International History at Richmond, the American International University in London. His research has focused on Anglo-Czechoslovak relations, the historiography of forcible population removals and Cold War diplomacy, resulting in publications in English, Czech, German and Polish. These include *Dealing with Democrats: The British Foreign Office's Relations with the Czechoslovak Émigrés in Great Britain, 1939–1945* (Peter Lang, 2006), *Slovakia in History* (Cambridge University Press, 2013, co-edited with Professors M. Teich and D. Kovác), and 'The Czechoslovak Government in Exile and the Legacy of Population Transfers: An Analysis of an English Language Discourse', in V. Smetana and K. Geaney (eds), *Exile in London: The Experience of Czechoslovakia and the Other Occupied Nations, 1938–45* (University of Chicago, 2018).

Angela Romano (PhD, International History) is Senior Research Fellow at the European University Institute (EUI) and project manager of the *PanEur1970s* project, which has received funding from the European Research Council under the European Union's Horizon 2020 research and innovation programme (Grant Agreement n. 669194). She has published extensively on the Cold War, the EC's external relations, integration and cooperation in Europe (including the CSCE) and transatlantic relations. Among her publications are *From Détente in Europe to European Détente: How the West Shaped the Helsinki CSCE* (Peter Lang, 2009), 'Untying Cold War Knots: The European Community and Eastern Europe in the Long 1970s', *Cold War History* 14(2) (2014), and 'Re-designing Military Security in Europe: Cooperation and Competition between the European Community and NATO during the Early 1980s', *European Review of History* 24(3) (2017).

Notes

1. This figure is an approximation; the OSCE Documentation Centre in Prague holds registers of all the attendees, during all phases of the negotiations.
2. L. Acimovic, *Problems of Security and Cooperation in Europe* (Alphen aan der Rijn: Springer, 1981); M. Alexander, *Managing the Cold War: A View from the Front Line* (London: Royal United Services Institute for Defence and Security Studies, 2005); L.V. Ferraris, *Report on a Negotiation: Helsinki-Geneva-Helsinki, 1972–1975* (Alphen aan der Rijn: Sijthoff & Noordhoff, 1979); J.J. Maresca, *To Helsinki* (Durham, NC: Duke University Press, 1987); J. Andréani, *Le Piège* (Paris: Odile Jacob, 2005); H.-J. Renk, *Der Weg der Schweiz nach Helsinki* (Bern: Haupt, 1996); B. von Staden, *Der Helsinki-Prozess* (Munich: Oldenbourg 1990); M. Reimaa, *Helsinki Catch: European Security Accords 1975* (Helsinki: Edita, 2008).
3. By the 'Kissingerization' of the historiography of the early 1970s we mean the overwhelming preponderance of coverage given over to the activities of Dr Henry Kissinger, and by extension to the United States of America in the secondary literature. This is not to dispute Kissinger's international significance, nor to challenge the USA's standing as *primus inter pares* in global affairs, but rather to critique the sheer volume of materials given over to these subjects to the detriment of many other personalities, nations and issues, especially with reference to the CSCE. See J.M. Hanhimäki, '"Dr. Kissinger" or "Mr. Henry"? Kissingerology, Thirty Years and Counting', *Diplomatic History* 27(5) (2003), 637–76; R. Kagan, 'The Revisionist: How Henry Kissinger Won the Cold War, or So He Thinks', *The New Republic*, 220(25) (1999), 38–48; also N. Ferguson, *Kissinger. Volume I. 1923–1968: The Idealist* (New York: Penguin Press, 2015); J. Hanhimaki, *The Flawed Architect: Henry Kissinger and American Foreign Policy* (New York: Oxford University Press, 2004); M. Del Pero, *The Eccentric Realist: Henry Kissinger and the Shaping of American Foreign Policy* (Ithaca, NY: Cornell University Press, 2009); J. Suri, *Henry Kissinger and the American Century* (Cambridge, MA: Harvard University Press, 2007). By way of comparison, historians have access to little new material or analysis about the Soviet leader Leonid Brezhnev, although two new biographies are currently in production, one in German and one in English (author's personal email correspondence, 3 and 4 June 2015).

4. A.F. Cooper, B. Hocking and W. Maley (eds), *Global Governance and Diplomacy: Worlds Apart?* (Basingstoke and New York: Palgrave Macmillan, 2008), 1–3; R.O. Keohane and J.S. Nye, Jr., 'The Club Model of Multilateral Cooperation and the World Trade Organization: Problems of Democratic Legitimacy' (Cambridge, MA: John F. Kennedy School of Government, 2001), Working Paper 4; T. Fletcher, *Naked Diplomacy: Power and Statecraft in the Digital Age* (London: William Collins, 2016), 11–22; I. Roberts (ed.), *Satow's Diplomatic Practice* (Oxford: Oxford University Press, 2009), 287–92.
5. S. Murray, 'Consolidating the Gains Made in Diplomacy Studies: A Taxonomy', *International Studies Perspectives* 9(1) (2008), 22–39; P. Sharp, 'Who Needs Diplomats? The Problem of Diplomatic Representation', *International Journal* 52(4) (1997), 624–29.
6. C. Jönsson and M. Hall, *Essence of Diplomacy* (London: Palgrave, 2005), 19–20; see also I.B. Neumann, 'The English School on Diplomacy', *Clingendael Discussion Papers in Diplomacy* no. 79 (2002).
7. A. Webster, 'The Transnational Dream: Politicians, Diplomats and Soldiers in the League of Nations' Pursuit of International Disarmament, 1920–1938', *Contemporary European History* 14(4) (2005), 493–518; N.P. Ludlow, 'Mieux que six ambassadeurs: l'émergence du COREPER durant les premières années de la CEE', in L. Badel, S. Jeannesson and N.P. Ludlow (eds), *Les administrations nationales et la construction européenne: une approche historique (1919–1975)* (Brussels: Peter Lang, 2005), 337–55.
8. L. Stone, 'Prosopography', *Daedelus Historical Studies Today* 100(1) (1971), 46. See also: 'Prosopography is a collective biography, describing the external features of a population group that the researcher has determined has something in common (profession, social origins, geographic origins, etc.). Starting from a questionnaire biographical data are collected about a well-defined group of people. On the basis of these data answers may be found to historical questions', in K. Verboven, M. Carlier and J. Dumolyn, 'A Short Manual to the Art of Prosopography', in K.S.B. Keats-Rohan (ed.), *Prosopography Approaches and Applications: A Handbook* (Oxford: Occasional Publications UPR, 2007), 39.
9. By success we mean that an agreed text was signed by all participants and considered binding, even though only politically so, by all of them.
10. France was a member of the Atlantic Alliance but had left the integrated military command structure in spring 1966 and never participated in NATO's Nuclear Planning Group. The withdrawal had been the last and most dramatic step in President Charles de Gaulle's roadmap to regain France's independence in the field of defence. The UK officially became a member of the EC on 1 January 1973, yet the government was already involved in European Political Cooperation – the mechanism for policy coordination devised by EC members – and actively participated in the preparation of common positions for the CSCE by February 1972.
11. See UK section below.
12. Andréani, *Le Piège*, 65.
13. Ibid., 65–66.

14. V.-Y. Ghebali, *La Diplomatie de la Détente: la CSCE d'Helsinki à Vienne (1973–1989)* (Brussels: Bruylant, 1989), 3–15.
15. N. Badalassi, *Adieu Yalta? La France, la détente et les origines de la Conférence sur la Sécurité et la Coopération en Europe, 1965–1975*, PhD thesis (Paris, 2011), 415.
16. In 1974, secretary of the CPSU Leonid Brezhnev met US President Richard Nixon, German Chancellor Helmut Schmidt, British Prime Minister Harold Wilson and French President Georges Pompidou. Soviet Foreign Minister Andrei Gromyko and US Secretary of State Henry Kissinger met twice in 1975 – in Geneva and Vienna – and worked out the compromise on human contacts provisions that eventually brought the conference to an end.
17. K. Holsti, 'Who Got What and How: The CSCE in Retrospection', in R. Spencer (ed.), *Canada and the Conference on Security and Cooperation in Europe* (Toronto: Centre for International Studies, University of Toronto Press, 1984), 139–40.
18. *Final Recommendation of the Helsinki Consultations*, para. 65, https://www.osce.org/it/mc/40216
19. A. Romano, *From Détente in Europe to European Détente: How the West Shaped the Helsinki CSCE* (Brussels: Peter Lang, 2009).
20. A. Romano, 'The Conference on Security and Cooperation in Europe: A Reappraisal', in A.M. Kalinovsky and C. Daigle (eds), *The Routledge Handbook of the Cold War* (London and New York: Routledge, 2014), 223–34; see also M.E. Ionescu, 'Romania: *Ostpolitik* and the CSCE, 1967–1975', in O. Bange and G. Niedhart (eds), *Helsinki 1975 and the Transformation of Europe* (New York and Oxford: Berghahn Books, 2008), 123–43.
21. Andréani, *Le Piège*, 87.
22. A. Romano, 'A Single European Voice Can Speak Louder to the World: Rationales, Ways and Means of the EPC in the CSCE Experience', in M. Rasmussen and A.-C.L. Knudsen (eds), *The Road to a United Europe: Interpretations of the Process of European Integration* (Brussels: Peter Lang, 2009), 257–70.
23. Andréani, *Le Piège*, 63.
24. Ibid.
25. Badalassi, *Adieu Yalta?* 415.
26. F.J.G. Bozek, 'Britain, European Security and Freer Movement: The Development of Britain's CSCE Policy 1969–1972', *Cold War History* 13(4) (2013), 439–61; M.D. Brown, 'A Very British Vision of Detente: The United Kingdom's Foreign Policy during the Helsinki Process, 1969–1975', in F. Bozo, M.P. Rey, B. Rother and N. Piers Ludlow (eds), *Overcoming the Iron Curtain: Visions of the End of the Cold War in Europe, 1945–1990* (Oxford: Berghahn Books, 2012), 121–27; R. Davy, 'Helsinki Myths: Setting the Record Straight on the Final Act of the CSCE, 1975', *Cold War History* 9(1) (2009), 1–22; A. Deighton, 'Ostpolitik or Westpolitik? British Foreign Policy, 1968–75', *International Affairs* 74(4) (1998), 893–901; L. Ratti, 'Britain, the German Question and the Transformation of Europe: From Ostpolitik to the Helsinki Conference, 1963–1975', in Bange and Niedhart, *Helsinki 1975*

and the Transformation of Europe, 93; P. Williams, 'Britain, Detente and the Conference on Security and Cooperation in Europe', in K. Dyson (ed.), *European Detente: Case Studies of the Politics of East-West Relations* (London: Pinter, 1986), 221 and 229; B. White, *Britain, Détente and Changing East-West Relations* (London: Routledge, 1992), 13 and 130.

27. See D.M. Anderson, 'Mau Mau in the High Court and the "Lost" British Empire Archives: Colonial Conspiracy or Bureaucratic Bungle?', *The Journal of Imperial and Commonwealth History* 39(5) (2011), 699–716.
28. The sources listed above tend to be heavily reliant on the unpublished and published documents chosen and released by the FCO. This is not a criticism but designed to highlight the limitations of these sources when analysing the interpersonal and cultural interactions of the diplomats at the CSCE.
29. K. Hamilton, 'Documenting Diplomacy, Evaluating Documents: The Case of the CSCE', in J. Kurbalija and H. Slavik (eds), *Language and Diplomacy* (Malta: DiploProjects, 2001), 207–24; Roberts, *Satow's Diplomatic Practice*, 45–60.
30. A number of interviews and recollections can be found in M.D. Kandiah and G. Staerck (eds), *The Helsinki Negotiations, the Accords and Their Impact* (University of London Institute of Historical Research, 2006), https://www.kcl.ac.uk/sspp/departments/politicaleconomy/research/british-politics-and-government/witness-seminars/index.aspx.
31. Two former Permanent Under-Secretaries (PUS) of the FCO published memoirs for this era, but neither was directly involved in the CSCE talks: P. Gore Booth, *With Great Truth and Respect* (London: Constable, 1974); D. Greenhill, *More by Accident* (York: Wilton, 1992). However, a substantial proportion of Sir Michael Alexander's memoir *Managing the Cold War* addresses his involvement with the CSCE from stage II in September 1974 until the conclusion of the Final Act.
32. On these relationships, see M.J. Hughes and R.H. Platt, 'Far Apart but Close Together: A Quantitative and Qualitative Analysis of the Career Structure and Organisational Culture of the Post-War British Diplomatic Service', *Diplomacy & Statecraft* 26(2) (2015), 266–93.
33. G. Bennett and K. Hamilton (eds), *Documents on British Policy Overseas: Britain and the Soviet Union, 1968–72*, series III, vol. I (London: Whitehall History Publishing, 1997); *The Conference of Security and Cooperation in Europe 1972–1975*, series III, vol. II (1997); and *Détente in Europe, 1972–76*, series III, vol. III (2001); K.A. Hamilton and P. Salmon (eds), *The Year of Europe: America, Europe and the Energy Crisis, 1972–1974*, series III, vol. IV (London: Routledge, 2006); and *The Southern Flank in Crisis, 1973–1976*, series III, vol. V (2006). These volumes were preceded by FCO, Miscellaneous no. 17, *Selected Documents Relating to Problems of Security and Cooperation in Europe, 1954–77* (HMSO, 1977, Cmnd. 6932). In particular, see the work of the official FCO historian K. Hamilton, *The Last Cold Warriors: Britain, Détente and the CSCE, 1972–1975* (Oxford: St Antony's College, EIRU, 1999); K. Hamilton, 'Cold War by Other Means: British Diplomacy and the Conference on Security and Cooperation in Europe, 1972–1975', in W. Loth

and G. Soutou (eds), *The Making of Detente: Eastern and Western Europe in the Cold War, 1965–1975* (Abingdon: Routledge, 2008), 168–82.
34. Bozek, 'Britain, European Security and Freer Movement', 440.
35. S. Dockrill, *Britain's Retreat from East of Suez: The Choice between Europe and the World?* (Basingstoke: Palgrave Macmillan, 2002), 198–99, 222; Greenhill, *More by Accident*, 65 and 131; D. Healey, *The Time of My Life* (London: Penguin, 1990), 358.
36. UKNA, FCO 41/1504, 'MBFR linkage with CSCE', various files, 1974; Bennett and Hamilton, *Documents on British Policy Overseas* (hereafter *DBPO*), vol. II, 43–45; *Détente in Europe, 1972–76*, vol. III, 1–53; *Foreign Relations of the United States (hereafter FRUS), 1969–76*: European Security, vol. XXXIX (Washington DC: U.S. Government Printing Office, 2008), 249–51, 258–69; E. Heath, *The Course of My Life: My Autobiography* (London: Hodder and Stoughton, 1998), 488–89.
37. HC Deb., vol. 897, cols. 230–45, 5 August 1975; T. Benn, *Against the Tide: Diaries 1973–76* (London: Hutchinson, 1989), 142–43, 385–87.
38. M. Stewart, 'Memorandum on Relations with the Soviet Union and Eastern Europe', 17 June 1969, and D. Wilson to Stewart, 'The Soviet Attitude to West Europe', 14 July 1969, *DBPO*, vol. I, 48–57, 179–87; *DBPO*, vol. I, 40–57, 229–38 and 467–71; J. Callaghan, *Time and Change* (London: Collins, 1987), 364–70; M. Stewart, *Life and Labour: An Autobiography* (London: Sigwick and Jackson, 1980), 146, 218 and 227–28.
39. Hamilton, *The Last Cold Warriors*, 3–9; Hamilton, 'Cold War by Other Means', 170–71.
40. There was something of a generational gap in the FCO's opinions, with the more senior officials being more sceptical, and the more junior officials, especially those on the ground, being slightly more optimistic of the possible outcome.
41. UKNA, PREM 15/2082, 'Visit of the Secretary of State for Foreign and Commonwealth Affairs to Helsinki for the first stage of the CSCE', 3–7 July 1973; PREM 16/392, Weston to Wright, 18 July 1975; PM's note, 23 July 1975; FCO 69/565, Wilson to Callaghan, 4 August 1975; H. Wilson, *Final Term: The Labour Government, 1974–1976* (London: Weidenfeld and Nicholson, 1979), 290–94.
42. UKNA, FCO 41/1540-44, CSCE: European political co-operation, 1974; British Diplomatic Oral History Programme (hereafter BDOHP) 34/1 M. Alexander, 13–14; *DBPO*, vol. II, 196–99; Keith A. Hamilton, 'Britain and the Conference on Security and Co-operation in Europe, 1972-77', in Kandiah and Staerck, *The Helsinki Negotiations*, 18; author's discussions with Gill Bennett at University of Belfast, May 2015.
43. The British government, although content with the wording of the final document, was still unsure of its ultimate consequences by August 1975 and had been from the outset. This was in contrast to their view of the MBFR talks, which they regarded as potentially having clearly beneficial outcomes. UKNA, Department of Trade and Industry (hereafter, BT) 241/2665, FCO minute on the CSCE, 7 July 1972, 1–10; *DBPO*, vol. II, 40–42 and 479; Romano, *From Détente in Europe to European Détente*, 95 and 195.

44. UKNA, PREM 16/392, Harold Wilson note to Lord Bridges, 1 June 1974; Thomas Edward Bridges, 2nd Baron Bridges, Private Sec. (Overseas Affairs) to Prime Minister, 1972–74.
45. Brown, 'A Very British Vision of Détente', 121–26.
46. *DBPO*, vol. II, 1–15.
47. It should be recognized that in part this division of labour was to be expected in the British system: Z. Steiner, 'Decision-Making in American and British Foreign Policy: An Open and Shut Case', *Review of International Studies* 13(1) (1987), 1–18.
48. The delegation was first led by Ambassador Anthony Elliot, then, after November 1974, by David Hildyard. Day-to-day negotiations were handled by, among others, Charles Adams, Michael Alexander, Roger Beetham, Rodric Braithwaite, Brian Fall, Michael Pakenham and David Miller.
49. For example, the British delegation for Phase II held in Geneva in September 1973 numbered fifteen diplomats plus seven administrative staff, while twenty-four were present for Phase III. The authors would like to thank Alice Němcová, Senior Assistant for Documentation and Information at the OSCE Documentation Centre in Prague, for access to these materials.
50. By way of a comparison, see the methodology outlined in M. Egeberg, Å. Gornitzka and J. Trondal, 'People Who Run the European Parliament: Staff Demography and Its Implications', *Journal of European Integration* 36(7) (2014), 659–75.
51. *The Diplomatic Service List*, H.M. Stationery Office, London, annual editions from 1972–77. Unfortunately, after the amalgamation of the Foreign and Colonial Offices in the late 1960s, the amount of detail previously provided in the list was curtailed. For example, the passing of language qualifications was omitted. In 1975 there were 182 fluent Arabists in the FCO, 159 Russian speakers and 35 with Chinese. However, it is less clear what the extent of coverage of languages used by the other CSCE participants was; G. Moorhouse, *The Diplomats: The Foreign Office Today* (London: Jonathan Cape, 1977), 78.
52. When interviewed, Sir Crispin Tickell revealed the existence of an unpublished diary of his from this era.
53. *British Diplomatic Oral History Programme* (hereafter *BDOHP*), http://www.chu.cam.ac.uk/archives/collections/BDOHP/ (accessed 3 September 2016); CSCE Oral History Project, *CSCE Testimonies: Causes and Consequences of the Helsinki Final Act, 1972–1989* (Prague: CSCE, 2013); Kandiah and Staerck, *The Helsinki Negotiations*.
54. Interviews with Roger Beetham, 8 November 2007; Christopher Mallaby, 15 November 2007; Sir Crispin Tickell, 29 November 2007; Sir Brian Fall, 12 September 2008; Sir Paul Lever, 22 June 2009; George Walden, 27 October 2009; Richard Davy, 18 June 2009; Brian Beedham, 28 June 2009; Tony Benn, 9 October 2009. Profound thanks are due to our student research assistant, Heather R. Jochens, for her sterling work transcribing some of these interviews.
55. See contributions in Kandiah and Staerck, *The Helsinki Negotiations*, 33–49; *DOHP*; Beetham, interview; Gore Booth, *With Great Truth and Respect*, 417.

56. Tickell, *DOHP*.
57. Fall interview; A.J.K. Bailes, 'Reflections on Thirty Years in the Diplomatic Service', in G. Johnson (ed.), *The Foreign Office and British Diplomacy in the Twentieth Century* (London: Routledge, 2005), 192 and 196.
58. For a comparison with the French case, see N. Badalassi's chapter in this volume, entitled 'From Talleyrand to Sakharov: French Diplomacy in Search of a "Helsinki Effect"'.
59. Fall interview; Kandiah and Staerck, *The Helsinki Negotiations*, 42–43.
60. Mallaby and Tickell interviews. See also D.R. Thorpe, *Alec Douglas-Home* (London: Sinclair Stevenson, 1996), 404–11. George Brown was foreign secretary from 11 August 1966 to 15 March 1968, David Owen from 21 February 1977 to 4 May 1979.
61. Alexander, *Managing the Cold War*, 34 and 49.
62. M.D. Brown, 'Pro-Détente versus Anti-Détente Camps: British Public Opinion, Foreign Policy and the CSCE, 1969–1975', unpublished conference paper, *International Conference on Socialism and the Cold War in Western Europe*, Queen's University Belfast, 17–18 April 2015.
63. Brimelow and Bullard were based in London but did attend the Foreign Ministers' meeting in Helsinki in 1973. Both Braithwaite and Fall were later ambassadors in Moscow.
64. Fall interview.
65. Beetham, written contribution, in Kandiah and Staerck, *The Helsinki Negotiations*, 32.
66. Fall interview.
67. See S. Cohen, 'En miettes? Fictions et fonction du discours sur "l'éclatement" de la politique extérieure', *Politique étrangère* 51(1) (1986), 143–51; M.-C. Kessler, *La politique étrangère de la France: acteurs et processus* (Paris: Les Presses de Sciences Po, 1999).
68. M. Vaïsse, *La puissance ou l'influence? La France dans le monde depuis 1958* (Paris: Fayard, 2009), 251–52.
69. Ibid., 35–37.
70. Ibid., 257.
71. M. Osmont, 'Acteurs et réseaux diplomatiques français', in C. Wenkel (ed.), *La France entre guerre froide et construction européenne (1974–1986)*, forthcoming.
72. Vaïsse, *La puissance*, 261. Also S. Cohen and M.-C. Smouts (eds), *La Politique extérieure de Valéry Giscard d'Estaing* (Paris: Presses de la FNSP, 1985).
73. Romano, *From Détente in Europe to European Détente*, 199–200. See V. Heyde, 'Nicht nur Entspannung und Menschenrechte: Die Entdeckung von Abrüstung und Rüstungskontrolle durch die französische KSZE-Politik', in M. Peter and H. Wentker (eds), *Die KSZE im Ost-West-Konflikt* (Munich: Oldenbourg Verlag, 2012), 84–85.
74. This is also the main argument of N. Badalassi, *En finir avec la guerre froide: la France, l'Europe et le processus d'Helsinki, 1965–1975* (Rennes: Presses Universitaires de Rennes, 2014).
75. See T. Gomart, *Double détente: Les relations franco-soviétiques de 1958 à 1964* (Paris: Publications de la Sorbonne, 2003).

76. Vaïsse, *La puissance*, 230–31.
77. Osmont, 'Acteurs et réseaux'. See also S. Davieau-Pousset, 'Maurice Dejean, diplomate atypique', *Relations internationales* 2015/2(162) (2015), 79–94.
78. See N. Badalassi's chapter in this book for more detail.
79. Osmont, 'Acteurs et réseaux'.
80. Andréani, *Le piège*.
81. Ibid., 48–49.
82. Badalassi, *Adieu Yalta?* 416.
83. Ibid., 571–72.
84. Ibid.
85. Ibid., 581.
86. Andréani, *Le piège*, 68.
87. A. Romano, 'The EC Nine's Vision and Attempts at Ending the Cold War', in Bozo et al., *Overcoming the Iron Curtain*, 134–46.
88. 'Man in the News; New Russian in Capital: Yuri Vladimirovich Dubinin', *The New York Times*, 21 May 1986.
89. *Normalien* refers to a graduate of the Ecole Normale Supérieure. The *agrégation* is the French state-run competitive exam for the recruitment of high school teachers and higher education academic staff for certain subjects; those who hold an *agrégation* have been successful in such a selection process.
90. J. Chazelle, *L'Indochine et la guerre* (1945); *La Paix en Extrême-Orient* (1945); and *La Guerre en Extrême-Orient* (1946), all published by Éditions du Chêne, Paris. On Chazelle's activities in Tokyo, see https://www.cairn.info/revue-relations-internationales-2008-2-page-37.htm (accessed 21 December 2016); on Dubinin's education and academic profile, see http://www.sras.org/news2.php?m=525 (accessed 21 December 2016).
91. 'Man in the News', *The New York Times*, 21 May 1986.

Bibliography

Archival Sources

British Diplomatic Oral History Programme (BDOHP). http://www.chu.cam.ac.uk/archives/collections/BDOHP/.
CSCE Oral History Project. *CSCE Testimonies: Causes and Consequences of the Helsinki Final Act, 1972–1989*. Prague: CSCE, 2013.
The Diplomatic Service List, H.M. Stationery Office, London (annual editions from 1972–77).
The National Archives of the UK, London (UKNA).

Secondary Literature

Acimovic, L. *Problems of Security and Cooperation in Europe*. Alphen aan der Rijn: Springer, 1981.

Alexander, M. *Managing the Cold War: A View from the Front Line*. London: Royal United Services Institute for Defence and Security Studies, 2005.
Anderson, D.M. 'Mau Mau in the High Court and the "Lost" British Empire Archives: Colonial Conspiracy or Bureaucratic Bungle?'. *The Journal of Imperial and Commonwealth History* 39(5) (2011), 699–716.
Andréani, J. *Le Piège*. Paris: Odile Jacob, 2005.
Badalassi, N. *Adieu Yalta? La France, la détente et les origines de la Conférence sur la Sécurité et la Coopération en Europe, 1965–1975*. PhD thesis, Paris, 2011.
Badalassi, N. *En finir avec la guerre froide: la France, l'Europe et le processus d'Helsinki, 1965–1975*. Rennes: Presses Universitaires de Rennes, 2014.
Bailes, A.J.K. 'Reflections on Thirty Years in the Diplomatic Service', in G. Johnson (ed.), *The Foreign Office and British Diplomacy in the Twentieth Century* (London: Routledge, 2005), 189–97.
Benn, T. *Against the Tide: Diaries 1973–76*. London: Hutchinson, 1989.
Bennett, G., and K. Hamilton (eds). *Documents on British Policy Overseas: Britain and the Soviet Union, 1968–72*, series III, vol. I. London: Whitehall History Publishing, 1997.
Bennett, G., and K. Hamilton (eds). *Documents on British Policy Overseas: The Conference of Security and Cooperation in Europe 1972–1975*, series III, vol. II. London: Whitehall History Publishing, 1997.
Bennett, G., and K. Hamilton (eds). *Documents on British Policy Overseas: Détente in Europe, 1972–76*, series III, vol. III. London: Whitehall History Publishing, 2001.
Bozek, F.J.G. 'Britain, European Security and Freer Movement: The Development of Britain's CSCE Policy 1969–1972'. *Cold War History* 13(4) (2013), 439–61.
Brown, M.D. 'Pro-Détente versus Anti-Détente Camps: British Public Opinion, Foreign Policy and the CSCE, 1969–1975', unpublished conference paper, *International Conference on Socialism and the Cold War in Western Europe*, Queen's University Belfast, 17–18 April 2015.
Brown, M.D. 'A Very British Vision of Detente: The United Kingdom's Foreign Policy during the Helsinki Process, 1969–1975', in F. Bozo, M.P. Rey, B. Rother and N. Piers Ludlow (eds), *Overcoming the Iron Curtain: Visions of the End of the Cold War in Europe, 1945–1990* (Oxford: Berghahn Books, 2012), 122–133.
Callaghan, J. *Time and Change*. London: Collins, 1987.
Chazelle, J. *La Guerre en Extrême-Orient*. Paris: Éditions du Chêne, 1946.
Chazelle, J. *L'Indochine et la guerre*. Paris: Éditions du Chêne, 1945.
Chazelle, J. *La Paix en Extrême-Orient*. Paris: Éditions du Chêne, 1945.
Cohen, S. 'En miettes? Fictions et fonction du discours sur "l'éclatement" de la politique extérieure'. *Politique étrangère* 51(1) (1986), 143–51.
Cohen, S., and M.-C. Smouts (eds). *La Politique extérieure de Valéry Giscard d'Estaing*. Paris: Presses de la FNSP, 1985.
Cooper, A.F., B. Hocking and W. Maley (eds). *Global Governance and Diplomacy: Worlds Apart?* Basingstoke and New York: Palgrave Macmillan, 2008.
Davieau-Pousset, S. 'Maurice Dejean, diplomate atypique'. *Relations internationales* 2015/2(162) (2015), 79–94.

Davy, R. 'Helsinki Myths: Setting the Record Straight on the Final Act of the CSCE, 1975'. *Cold War History* 9(1) (2009), 1–22.
Deighton, A. 'Ostpolitik or Westpolitik? British Foreign Policy, 1968–75'. *International Affairs* 74(4) (1998), 893–901.
Del Pero, M. *The Eccentric Realist: Henry Kissinger and the Shaping of American Foreign Policy*. Ithaca, NY: Cornell University Press, 2009.
Dockrill, S. *Britain's Retreat from East of Suez: The Choice between Europe and the World?* Basingstoke: Palgrave Macmillan, 2002.
Egeberg, M., Å. Gornitzka and J. Trondal. 'People Who Run the European Parliament: Staff Demography and Its Implications'. *Journal of European Integration* 36(7) (2014), 659–75.
FCO, Miscellaneous no. 17. *Selected Documents Relating to Problems of Security and Cooperation in Europe, 1954–77*. HMSO, 1977, Cmnd. 6932.
Ferguson, N. *Kissinger. Volume I. 1923–1968: The Idealist*. New York: Penguin Press, 2015.
Ferraris, L.V. *Report on a Negotiation: Helsinki-Geneva-Helsinki, 1972–1975*. Alphen aan der Rijn: Sijthoff & Noordhoff, 1979.
Fletcher, T. *Naked Diplomacy: Power and Statecraft in the Digital Age*. London: William Collins, 2016.
Ghebali, V.-Y. *La Diplomatie de la Détente: la CSCE d'Helsinki à Vienne (1973–1989)*. Brussels: Bruylant, 1989.
Gomart, T. *Double détente: Les relations franco-soviétiques de 1958 à 1964*. Paris: Publications de la Sorbonne, 2003.
Gore Booth, P. *With Great Truth and Respect*. London: Constable, 1974.
Greenhill, D. *More by Accident*. York: Wilton, 1992.
Hamilton, K. 'Cold War by Other Means: British Diplomacy and the Conference on Security and Cooperation in Europe, 1972–1975', in W. Loth and G. Soutou (eds), *The Making of Detente: Eastern and Western Europe in the Cold War, 1965–1975* (Abingdon: Routledge, 2008), 168–82.
Hamilton, K. 'Documenting Diplomacy, Evaluating Documents: The Case of the CSCE', in J. Kurbalija and H. Slavik (eds), *Language and Diplomacy* (Malta: DiploProjects, 2001), 207–24.
Hamilton, K. *The Last Cold Warriors: Britain, Détente and the CSCE, 1972–1975*. Oxford: St Antony's College, EIRU, 1999.
Hamilton, K.A., and P. Salmon (eds). *The Southern Flank in Crisis, 1973–1976*, series III, vol. V. London: Routledge, 2006.
Hamilton, K.A., and P. Salmon (eds). *The Year of Europe: America, Europe and the Energy Crisis, 1972–1974*, series III, vol. IV. London: Routledge, 2006.
Hanhimäki, J.M. '"Dr. Kissinger" or "Mr. Henry"? Kissingerology, Thirty Years and Counting'. *Diplomatic History* 27(5) (2003), 637–76.
Hanhimaki, J.M. *The Flawed Architect: Henry Kissinger and American Foreign Policy*. New York: Oxford University Press, 2004.
Healey, D. *The Time of My Life*. London: Penguin, 1990.
Heath, E. *The Course of My Life: My Autobiography*. London: Hodder and Stoughton, 1998.
Heyde, V. 'Nicht nur Entspannung und Menschenrechte: Die Entdeckung von Abrüstung und Rüstungskontrolle durch die französische KSZE-Politik',

in M. Peter and H. Wentker (eds), *Die KSZE im Ost-West-Konflikt* (Munich: Oldenbourg Verlag, 2012), 83–98.

Holsti, K. 'Who Got What and How: The CSCE in Retrospection', in R. Spencer (ed.), *Canada and the Conference on Security and Cooperation in Europe* (Toronto: Centre for International Studies, University of Toronto Press, 1984), 134–66.

Hughes, M.J., and R.H. Platt. 'Far Apart but Close Together: A Quantitative and Qualitative Analysis of the Career Structure and Organisational Culture of the Post-War British Diplomatic Service'. *Diplomacy & Statecraft* 26(2) (2015), 266–93.

Ionescu, M.E. 'Romania: *Ostpolitik* and the CSCE, 1967–1975', in O. Bange and G. Niedhart (eds), *Helsinki 1975 and the Transformation of Europe* (New York and Oxford: Berghahn Books, 2008), 123–43.

Jönsson, C., and M. Hall. *Essence of Diplomacy*. London: Palgrave, 2005.

Kagan, R. 'The Revisionist: How Henry Kissinger Won the Cold War, or So He Thinks'. *The New Republic* 220(25) (1999), 38–48.

Kandiah, M.D., and G. Staerck (eds). *The Helsinki Negotiations, the Accords and Their Impact*. University of London Institute of Historical Research, 2006. https://www.kcl.ac.uk/sspp/departments/politicaleconomy/research/british-politics-and-government/witness-seminars/index.aspx.

Keohane, R.O., and J.S. Nye, Jr. 'The Club Model of Multilateral Cooperation and the World Trade Organization: Problems of Democratic Legitimacy'. Cambridge, MA: John F. Kennedy School of Government, 2001, Working Paper 4.

Kessler, M.-C. *La politique étrangère de la France: acteurs et processus*. Paris: Les Presses de Sciences Po, 1999.

Ludlow, N. P. 'Mieux que six ambassadeurs. L'émergence du COREPER durant les premières années de la CEE', in L. Badel, S. Jeannesson and N.P. Ludlow (eds), *Les administrations nationales et la construction européenne: une approche historique (1919–1975)* (Brussels: Peter Lang, 2005), 337–55.

Maresca, J.J. *To Helsinki*. Durham, NC: Duke University Press, 1987.

Moorhouse, G. *The Diplomats: The Foreign Office Today*. London: Jonathan Cape, 1977.

Murray, S. 'Consolidating the Gains Made in Diplomacy Studies: A Taxonomy'. *International Studies Perspectives* 9(1) (2008), 22–39.

Neumann, I.B. 'The English School on Diplomacy'. *Clingendael Discussion Papers in Diplomacy* no. 79 (2002).

Osmont, M. 'Acteurs et réseaux diplomatiques français', in C. Wenkel (ed.), *La France entre guerre froide et construction européenne (1974–1986)*, forthcoming.

Ratti, L. 'Britain, the German Question and the Transformation of Europe: From Ostpolitik to the Helsinki Conference, 1963–1975', in O. Bange and G. Niedhart (eds), *Helsinki 1975 and the Transformation of Europe* (New York and Oxford: Berghahn Books, 2008), 83–97.

Reimaa, M. *Helsinki Catch: European Security Accords 1975*. Helsinki: Edita, 2008.

Renk, H.-J. *Der Weg der Schweiz nach Helsinki*. Bern: Haupt, 1996.

Roberts I. (ed.). *Satow's Diplomatic Practice*. Oxford: Oxford University Press, 2009.

Romano, A. 'The Conference on Security and Cooperation in Europe: A Reappraisal', in A.M. Kalinovsky and C. Daigle (eds), *The Routledge Handbook of the Cold War* (London and New York: Routledge, 2014), 223–34.

Romano, A. *From Détente in Europe to European Détente: How the West Shaped the Helsinki CSCE*. Brussels: Peter Lang, 2009.

Romano, A. 'The EC Nine's Vision and Attempts at Ending the Cold War', in F. Bozo, M.-P. Rey, N.P. Ludlow and B. Rother (eds), *Overcoming the Iron Curtain: Visions of the End of the Cold War in Europe, 1945–1990* (New York and Oxford: Berghahn Books), 134–46.

Romano, A. 'A Single European Voice Can Speak Louder to the World: Rationales, Ways and Means of the EPC in the CSCE Experience', in M. Rasmussen and A.-C.L. Knudsen (eds), *The Road to a United Europe: Interpretations of the Process of European Integration* (Brussels: Peter Lang, 2009), 257–70.

Sharp, P. 'Who Needs Diplomats? The Problem of Diplomatic Representation'. *International Journal* 52(4) (1997), 624–29.

Steiner, Z. 'Decision-Making in American and British Foreign Policy: An Open and Shut Case'. *Review of International Studies* 13(1) (1987), 1–18.

Stewart, M. *Life and Labour: An Autobiography*. London: Sigwick and Jackson, 1980.

Stone, L. 'Prosopography'. *Daedelus Historical Studies Today* 100(1) (1971), 46–79.

Suri, J. *Henry Kissinger and the American Century*. Cambridge, MA: Harvard University Press, 2007.

Thorpe, D.R. *Alec Douglas-Home*. London: Sinclair Stevenson, 1996.

Vaïsse, M. *La puissance ou l'influence? La France dans le monde depuis 1958*. Paris: Fayard, 2009.

Verboven, K., M. Carlier and J. Dumolyn. 'A Short Manual to the Art of Prosopography', in K.S.B. Keats-Rohan (ed.), *Prosopography Approaches and Applications: A Handbook* (Oxford: Occasional Publications UPR, 2007), 35–70.

von Staden, B. *Der Helsinki-Prozess*. Munich: Oldenbourg, 1990.

Webster, A. 'The Transnational Dream: Politicians, Diplomats and Soldiers in the League of Nations' Pursuit of International Disarmament, 1920–1938'. *Contemporary European History* 14(4) (2005), 493–518.

White, B. *Britain, Détente and Changing East-West Relations*. London: Routledge, 1992.

Williams, P. 'Britain, Detente and the Conference on Security and Cooperation in Europe', in K. Dyson (ed.), *European Detente: Case Studies of the Politics of East-West Relations* (London: Pinter, 1986), 221–36.

Wilson, H. *Final Term: The Labour Government, 1974–1976*. London: Weidenfeld and Nicholson, 1979.

 3

From Talleyrand to Sakharov
French Diplomacy in Search of a 'Helsinki Effect'
Nicolas Badalassi

Introduction

On 30 July 1975, the majority of European newspapers announced the news: opening in Helsinki was the greatest international conference since the Congress of Vienna in 1815. With the exception of Albania, all the countries in Europe were represented in the Finnish capital by their highest dignitaries. This concluded, in the words of the French philosopher Raymond Aron in the French newspaper *Le Figaro*, 'la foire aux diplomates' ('the diplomats' circus') that was the Conference on Security and Cooperation in Europe (CSCE); according to Aron, the heedlessness of Western leaders allowed Soviet leader Leonid Brezhnev's diplomacy to win international acclaim, obtaining the consecration of the political and territorial status quo in Europe that the Kremlin sought.[1] *Le Figaro* accompanied the statements of the prominent intellectual with a caricature that evoked an 1819 engraving on the Congress of Vienna. The West German chancellor Helmut Schmidt, the French president Valéry Giscard d'Estaing, the US president Gerald Ford and Brezhnev were all featured in poses identical to those of the powerful early nineteenth-century European representatives. The message conveyed by the conservative French paper was abundantly clear: as in 1815, in the aftermath of the fall of Napoleon I, the leaders of the two opposing sides of the Cold War, in recognizing the Soviet sphere of influence, favoured the interests of the states to the detriment of those of the people of Eastern Europe.

While such an interpretation of the Helsinki Final Act was not uncommon – the Franco-Romanian novelist Eugène Ionesco went even further, comparing it to the Munich agreements of 1938 – it revealed the perception of the event by observers, the press and public opinion.[2] *Le Figaro*'s criticism illustrated above all that the early negotiations of the CSCE went unnoticed or were perceived as complex, non-transparent or pointless. Thus, the only element the press emphasized matched Brezhnev's perception of the Final Act: the Western world recognized the European status quo and confirmed the division of the continent into two blocs. There were few press articles documenting the 'third basket' or the 'humanist' principles listed in the 'Decalogue'.

Aron and *Le Figaro*'s vision of the CSCE also proves that in the middle of the 1970s, a significant upheaval of European geopolitics was inconceivable in the short to medium term. The disappearance of the opposing blocs and the reunification of the continent were unthinkable, in light of the extent to which the two superpowers seemed inclined to grow their respective zones of influence.

Lastly, with the image of the CSCE that it transmitted, *Le Figaro* joined the denunciation, which had become common within Western societies, of the gap that had emerged between the political elite and the citizenry. The revolution of customs, the anti-establishment movements of the end of the 1960s and the development of new forces of the left proclaimed loud and clear this idea of a rupture between the apex of social order and the base, and of the necessity of rethinking the organization of society. This denunciation, which was first and foremost aimed at all the Western leaders, nonetheless did not overlook the Soviet bloc decision makers, perceived as equally conservative, as the events of Prague in August 1968 proved.

However, historical research tends to show that the Helsinki process, which remained largely misunderstood during the final years of the Cold War, contributed to the collapse of the socialist system in Central and Eastern Europe. Contrary to what may have been written about it forty years ago, it did not simply defend the exclusive interests of the states.[3] Thus, numerous Western diplomats, having taken part in the CSCE, considered the interests of Eastern European populations during the negotiations of the Helsinki Final Act between 1972 and 1975. The CSCE's genesis in this period, which is the focus of this chapter, is crucial to understanding the process that followed the signing of the Helsinki Final Act. During those years, a new generation of French diplomats became aware of the emergence of civil societies in the Soviet bloc. The Prague Spring, the multiplication of dissident writings and the growing enthusiasm for Western culture in the East were all signs that contributed to such an awareness. Therefore, the CSCE appeared for some French diplomats as a golden opportunity to forge conceptual and practical tools for the civil societies of the socialist bloc. In this way, the third basket and the principles of human rights and self-determination of peoples contained in the first basket became the official answer of the West to the suppression of the Prague Spring.

That is why, throughout the Helsinki process, French diplomacy was far from sharing the sentiment of pessimism that surrounded the CSCE and remained persuaded, just as President Georges Pompidou (1969–74) was, that the Final Act would allow the Eastern people to be inoculated with 'the virus of freedom'.[4]

In the speech that he gave during the third phase of the conference on 31 July 1975, President Valéry Giscard d'Estaing (1974–81) sought to undermine the comparison with the Congress of Vienna:

> I know that the Congress of Vienna has been quoted with regard to this. But the situations are very different. For example, some time ago, I looked at the table from the Congress of Vienna which had been kept by Talleyrand in a castle in the French countryside. It is a really small table with barely enough room for those seated in the first row of our assembly. May I remind the specialists – moreover there are a few here in this auditorium – who know only too well the Congress of Vienna that only four countries had the floor and at the end of the Conference, a fifth country, ours. All the others were invited … to be silent! There was another difference: it was the Congress which danced. More precisely, the Foreign Affairs Ministers worked and the Heads of States danced.
>
> France was represented at this Congress by its Foreign Affairs Minister Talleyrand, and I noted in the correspondence he addressed to Paris with observations about the Congress, a phrase which could serve as a reference for us: 'I will be gentle, conciliatory but positive, speaking only of principles and never differing'.
>
> The meeting which assembles us constitutes an essential human step in the long walk towards détente. We are witnessing, here in this forum, since yesterday, a change of tone in the language from the European country leaders, whether the latter are to the East or the West of our continent, and each one of us can see this.[5]

By presenting the CSCE as 'an essential human step', Giscard placed the people at the heart of the East–West dialogue. The conference thus ensured the passage to a Cold War diplomacy that was more anthropo-centred, that is, putting humans rather than states at the centre of the negotiations. Hence, this 'change of tone' in the French president's speech not only referred to the cordiality of the East–West relations that characterized détente, it particularly related to the topics broached by the negotiators during the CSCE, which would directly impact the lives of the men and women who populated the European continent. For both the head of state and the officials who had taken part in the drafting of the Final Act, this document might have considerable weight, provided it was applied correctly.

The question of the consequences of the CSCE is even more pressing with regard to the French diplomacy of General Charles de Gaulle (1958–69) and his immediate successors. The policy was based on the idea of absolute respect for the prerogatives of the nation states, which were perceived as the pillars of international relations. Therein lay the full subtlety of the French CSCE approach, which was more pragmatic than dogmatic.[6] France persisted in defending the right of each state to conduct its foreign policy as it saw fit under the cover of its full and entire sovereignty, but, in parallel, it insisted on peoples' right to self-determination. Thus, the conference appeared little by little to the French as an excellent means of refining and multilateralizing certain fundamental principles of de Gaulle's policy of détente. The CSCE provided the decision makers with the opportunity to prove that the states had effective levers to make a significant difference to the lives of people who were not necessarily dependent on them. In the 1970s, faith in the Welfare State and in the capacity of the state to influence economy and society was an almost unanimous subject in France. During the Helsinki process, the commitment of the French in favour of topics that did not necessarily match Soviet practices illustrated the willpower of one party of diplomats to show that in foreign affairs, too, a strong and diplomatic state could contribute to the happiness of peoples, or at least the improvement of their living conditions.

The aim of this chapter is to illuminate the connections between the diplomacy that produced the Helsinki Final Act and the social changes that followed. Who were the diplomats who precociously understood that East European societies were changing? How did their training, their professional experience and their political commitments play a role in this awareness? Through what means did they anticipate the CSCE could contribute to the emancipation of socialist societies? What provisions did they view as necessary to loosen the noose on individual and collective freedoms in the Eastern bloc? How did they hope to persuade the Warsaw Pact states to accept such potentially threatening norms?

A variety of elements must be considered in order to understand the frame of mind in which the French diplomats experienced the CSCE negotiations and the optimism France displayed at the outcome of these discussions. These elements stem from both the diplomats' intellectual nature, their assessment of the situation in the Soviet bloc and the strategy they adopted in the face of a USSR determined not to accept anything that might cause the Iron Curtain to waver.

The CSCE: A Result and Reflection of the 1970s

An Intellectual Framework in Support of the Criticism of the Soviet System

The drafting of the Final Act was primarily the result of human relations: the nature of relations between the states – conflicting or otherwise – was somewhat secondary throughout this negotiation. The decision-making process, the high number of participants and the significant quantity of topics prevented central administrations from following the discussions and left the agents on site a remarkable degree of flexibility. Consequently, the influence of well-known personalities in the drafting of the final document was considerable. Knowing the men from the CSCE – with the exception of the Yugoslavian delegation, almost all of the other representatives were male – is indispensable for anyone who wants to understand the positions advocated by various countries represented at Helsinki and Geneva between November 1972 and August 1975.

Regarding the French delegation, its diplomats did not stay throughout the CSCE, with the exception of Alain Pierret on the Steering Committee. The negotiators each only stayed for one year at Geneva, which was already substantial. They were young men mostly born between 1921 and 1933. Each belonged to the same generation: they had been teenagers or young adults during World War II and had only begun their professional lives during the early years of the Cold War. They witnessed the division that the East–West conflict caused in French diplomacy – among the older diplomats in particular.[7]

These officials included Jacques Andréani, François Plaisant, Alain Pierret, Gérard André, Jacques Chazelle, Robert Richard, Pierre-Henri Renard, Michel Rougagnou and even Paul Poudade. At the end of the 1960s, when the Soviets intensified their campaign aimed at convincing Westerners to accept a conference on European Security, they were the first to view this proposal positively. For them, the Prague Spring and its repression were equal indicators that the populations of Central and Eastern Europe needed to breathe.[8] The project of a conference much sought after by Moscow was the opportunity to come to their aid. Andréani, at the time at the sous-direction d'Europe orientale of the Quai d'Orsay (the 'Eastern Europe Branch'), was the main proponent of this idea, which went against the intentions of de Gaulle. The French president, deeply disappointed by the attitude of the Soviets in Prague, believed that the project of the Kremlin stemmed from pure propaganda.

However, the Andréani line ended up winning after the arrival of Georges Pompidou at the Elysée, as the new president was concerned about not remaining dependent on West German Chancellor Willy Brandt's discussions with the USSR in the framework of *Ostpolitik*.[9] Andréani was thus at the origin of the second 'C' of CSCE ('cooperation'): according to him, the West would benefit from the position of the Soviets requesting concessions from them on subjects that did not figure among their priorities, such as cultural cooperation.[10]

The role played by Andréani was therefore significant and explains why he was chosen to lead the French delegation when the conference began. His obstinacy in wanting to push the situation in the East was reflected in his intellectual and political commitments.

Andréani was a liberal and an ardent defender of democracy and human rights. As a member of the Masonic organization Grand Orient de France, Andréani had an in-depth knowledge of the theoretical and concrete implications of these principles, which were at the heart of his Masonic Lodge's work. Indeed, the Grand Orient de France, founded in 1773, is a hotbed of reflection on the fundamental values of the French Republic, whether in defence of political pluralism, the freedom of thinking and acting or equality between citizens. This unwavering commitment to democracy and to political liberalism explains in part the sensitivity of the diplomat with regard to the situation within the communist bloc.

Moreover, such a view must be placed within the specific intellectual context of the late 1960s and early 1970s. As mentioned above, the CSCE had to ensure the transition towards an anthropo-centred diplomacy of the Cold War. In other words, it was a manner of responding to the criticisms of the post-1968 society, marked by cultural revolution and challenges to conservatisms – whether they be right or left – which sought a true reconciliation between the political elite and intellectuals on the one hand and the rest of society on the other. The CSCE had to embody this reconciliation on an international scale.

More specifically, from 1973 onwards, the conference fell within an intellectual context to which Andréani was particularly partial, that of the 'Solzhenitsyn affair', that is, the French debate about the work of the Soviet dissident and, in broader terms, the totalitarian nature of the USSR. The impact of *The Gulag Archipelago* (1973) on the French intellectual world was phenomenal. According to Pierre Grémion, 'this book transcended all the philosophical and political alignments and in Paris it unleashed a crisis and an intellectual reconfiguration unprecedented since World War II'.[11]

The contradiction between the Western development of a policy of détente towards the USSR and violations of human rights there formed the heart of this debate while also raising questions about the definition of totalitarianism. The controversy took shape with the publication of several key texts such as *La Cuisinière et le Mangeur d'hommes* (The Cook and the Man-eater) by André Glucksmann which, impressed by the message of dissidents, broke with Marxism-Leninism.[12] In the journal *Esprit*, Marcel Gauchet illustrated that totalitarianism was not the prerogative of the right-wing regimes and could be applied to left-wing regimes when they claimed to establish 'a society without division' and 'a society delivered from its interior antagonism'. He argued that 'the Socialist State is the State which claims the achievement of a social unit, and that is what makes it specifically totalitarian'.[13]

In the United States the debate was going on about the 1974 Jackson-Vanik amendment regarding the emigration of Soviet Jews, and public opinion questioned the realpolitik of Secretary of State Henry Kissinger. At the same time, new political and intellectual currents appeared in France that challenged the order of French society and the place given to the communist ideology. It was from these debates that the 'new philosophers' movement emerged which, under the aegis of André Glucksmann and Bernard-Henry Lévy, undertook the denunciation of totalitarian states as dominant models of the contemporary period. Likewise, the 'deuxième gauche' ('second left'), of which Michel Rocard was the most prominent representative, fought so that the French socialists would take leave of their bias towards the USSR.[14] Moreover, Andréani was very close to Rocard, having even participated in the foundation of the Parti Socialiste Unifié (United Socialist Party) in 1960. The political justification of Andréani's actions at the CSCE was perfectly clear, even more so because a few days before the opening of the conference in Helsinki, the Soviet physicist and dissident Andrei Sakharov challenged the Westerners about the necessity of a détente that was not a duplicity. During the interview he gave to Western journalists on 21 June 1973, Sakharov warned of the effects of the dialogue between the blocs:

> A reconciliation without democratization, a reconciliation in which the West would accept the Soviet game rules, would be dangerous in the sense that it would not resolve any of the World problems and would only represent a pure and simple capitulation before the actual or supposed power of the USSR. That would be marked by an attempt to trade with the USSR, to buy its gas and petrol, whilst ignoring the other aspects. Such a development would be in my mind dangerous, because it would have serious repercussions in the USSR. It would contaminate the whole world with the anti-democratic particularities of the Soviet society. It would give the Soviet Union the possibility of by-passing the problems it cannot resolve by itself and to content itself with accumulating an even greater power.[15]

The sous-directeur d'Europe orientale took notice of this analysis. The case of Andréani is specific due to his position at the head of the French delegation, and his motivations and political orientations were not necessarily shared by all his colleagues. Nevertheless, even though political divergences could influence the way in which the diplomats considered the CSCE negotiations – Gaullists and pro-Giscard were thus numerous in the ranks of the French representation at the CSCE – all these senior officials were aware of the situation in the Eastern bloc and the difficulties to which populations under the Soviet yoke were subjected.

Concrete Solutions for Real Problems

Indeed, one of the common traits of the diplomats of the French delegation at the CSCE was their sound knowledge of the reality of socialist countries. Andréani had served in Moscow at the beginning of the 1960s; the same was true of Alain Pierret from 1969 to 1972. Paul Poudade, who participated in the third basket negotiations, achieved a certain level of proficiency in Russian and Romanian and had studied with Hélène Carrère d'Encausse, a historian specializing in Russian studies at Sciences-Po; as for François Plaisant, he knew his Soviet contacts in the first basket only too well, having rubbed shoulders with them during the quadripartite negotiations on Berlin, which resulted in the 3 September 1970 agreement. Their experience should not be disregarded when explaining their commitment in favour of the third basket and of some of the principles of the first one, especially refraining from the threat or use of force, inviolability of frontiers, non-intervention in internal affairs, cooperation among states and respect for human rights and fundamental freedoms.

These officials therefore knew what they were talking about when discussing questions of access to culture and information, the working conditions of Western businessmen and journalists in the East, reuniting of families, obtaining visas and so on at the CSCE. This is a most fundamental point: the CSCE was the result of the Cold War; it was based on a real situation, the division of Europe, which the CSCE's objective was to improve. At least that was the manner in which the French saw the conference. French diplomats based everything on tangible problems in order to propose concrete solutions. Thus, throughout the duration of the discussions in Geneva, the French multiplied the references to what they had seen in Eastern Europe. This was especially the case of the third basket. For example, when the negotiations opened on improving foreign press distribution in European countries,

Geoffroy de Courcel, General Secretary of the Quai d'Orsay, presented the problem to Anatoly Kovalev, head of the Soviet delegation at the CSCE, as follows:

> I must say that with regard to my trip to the USSR I don't have any reservations to express, except one: the only French newspaper I could find was *L'Humanité*. Clearly it's not a question of flooding the USSR market with the French, American or English press. However, we need the foreign press to be more readily accessible. Moreover, if we make decisions at the conference which indicate our desire to facilitate the circulation of newspapers, then it will be up to each State to take the necessary measures and to do so according to its own internal standards and principles.[16]

While the French were not always as direct with the Soviets, they negotiated keeping in mind their experience in the Eastern bloc. Indeed, Alain Pierret related that, during discussions about travel formalities within the states participating in the CSCE, he was constantly thinking about all the issues he had to deal with in the USSR:

> Any outing, even nearby, is more of an obstacle course than a routine and a difficult one at that. The administrative formalities are very restrictive. The diplomats cannot be more than forty kilometres from the centre of the capital at any moment, this distance is sometimes reduced to just fifteen or so kilometres. In order to go beyond this, it is necessary to submit a request two full days in advance; there is never any certainty about gaining permission.[17]

It goes without saying that from the moment the question of relations between authors and editors was broached, everyone had Solzhenitsyn in mind. But, to avoid provoking the Kremlin unnecessarily, no one made any direct reference to the famous dissident.[18]

The diplomats' personal experiences were systematically completed by numerous reports produced by different departments at the Ministry of Foreign Affairs but also, and more particularly, by those from the Ministry of Cultural Affairs. This latter party played a key role when it came to drafting French proposals for the third basket. For each of the cultural cooperation domains, the French delegation asked for a full situational analysis in order to draw up draft texts as precisely and with as much detail as possible. From September 1973 onwards, the various branches of this ministry examined the state of affairs of international cultural cooperation, in particular in the East–West context, and put forward suggested proposals.

In this way, the Direction des Fouilles et Antiquités (Excavations and Antiquities) complained about the administrative difficulties that the Eastern country researchers faced when they needed to go abroad.

The Direction de la Musique, des Arts Lyriques et de la Danse (Music, Lyrical Arts and Dance) outlined the commercial obstructions in East–West musical exchanges. The Centre National de la Cinématographie (National Centre of Cinematography) highlighted the significant cooperation that existed in this domain, on both sides of the Iron Curtain, and noted that the main problem was that the French public did not tend to appreciate Eastern European films. The Direction du Théâtre, des Maisons de la Culture et des Lettres (Theatre, Houses of Culture and Literature) evoked difficulties in terms of the circulation of theatre troops and authors' rights.[19] Based on these documents, France could propose texts including concrete measures.

Such an approach went against the Soviet method, which sought to avoid at all costs any reference to the internal situation in the socialist bloc. The USSR delegation did not waste any time going on the offensive to enforce, in the preamble of the third basket, a reminder of the strict respect of the laws, cultural mores and customs of the participating states.[20] From the beginning of the CSCE, the Soviets informed their French counterparts that respect for sovereignty and non-intervention in interior affairs constituted 'the religion' of the USSR.[21] They led a veritable offensive in the first commission to diminish the scope of the third basket by defending a concept of non-intervention in line with the Brezhnev Doctrine on limited sovereignty. The representatives of France in Geneva played a central role in defining this principle, in the sense that in parallel they had to work around the Gaullist tenet according to which sovereignty of a state could not be hampered in any way. Andréani admitted then that it was difficult for France to maintain a conciliatory position with, on the one hand, its desire to favour cultural cooperation and all nature of contacts between the East and the West and, on the other hand, its own take on the meaning of national sovereignty.[22]

Consequently, in order for the CSCE to have concrete impact in the East without colliding with the Kremlin in the process and infringing on anyone's sovereignty, the French diplomats pursued a strategy above all based on the long term.

'The Acid Which Will Corrode in the End'

For the Soviets, it was simply necessary to 'be confined to adopting some main lines' and avoid concluding firm arrangements. For France, however, it was paramount that the third basket proposals be detailed and that they could progressively become 'the acid which would corrode in the end'.²³ Hence, rather than trying to reinforce individual rights, as the UN attempted to do in several of its declarations, the delegations of the European Community (EC) felt that the key was to 'define the guidelines relating to the behaviour of the states towards their citizens, in particular by the lowering of barriers put up against cooperation and mobility in the areas where the problems [were] most severe'.²⁴

Slowly but Surely: The 'Virus of Freedom' Inoculated

If the French displayed a certain degree of optimism with regard to the expected results from the CSCE, it was partly because they were convinced that it would be relatively easy to obtain major concessions from the Soviets, and in particular from Brezhnev who had turned the conference into a personal affair. The Soviet leader perceived the CSCE as Western recognition of Soviet domination in Eastern Europe: as far as he was concerned, the signature of the Final Act had to be triumphant, even more so because the influence of Moscow continued to increase in the Third World at a time when the United States appeared to be weakened by the economic crisis due to the 1973 oil shock and discredited by the Vietnam War.²⁵

However, in wanting to showcase the absolute consecration of the political and territorial status quo in Europe on the world stage via the Helsinki summit, the USSR appeared more than ever in a claim position – the Westerners would have preferred a more discreet conclusion of the CSCE. The French felt that it was necessary to take advantage of this unexpected opportunity to gain a maximum number of concessions from the Soviets and ensure that the Final Act did not block the European situation but on the contrary constituted a first step towards reunification of the continent.²⁶

In order to reach this result, the key personalities of the French delegation in charge of the third basket negotiations – in particular Andréani and Jacques Chazelle, a graduate of the prestigious French Ecole normale supérieure in Languages and Literature who had a great interest in improving cultural cooperation between East and West²⁷ – judged that prudence was compulsory. Once again, it was not so much a radical change they were thinking about, but rather more of an improvement of the situation on particular points, in other words creating enough fissures in the Iron Curtain which, in the end, could contribute to its downfall. Consequently, the French dismissed any thoughts of launching an outright attack against the Soviet system by submitting requests that they knew in advance were inapplicable.²⁸ In their mind, in order for the CSCE to succeed, it had absolutely to favour the convergence of two politico-economical models that were predominant in Europe. This would play irredeemably in favour of the West. This point of view, very much present among French diplomats, was equally shared by Pompidou. The latter considered that differences between socialist and capitalist models were condemned to disappear 'when examining the similarities born with the technical and industrial revolution as well as the deepest needs of a modern conception of civilization'.[29] Pompidou imagined a 'decline' of the blocs 'by slow and continuous action' embodied by the process of détente.

Pompidou's commitment to the idea of convergence reflected the ambiguous attitude of the French people towards capitalism and communism. The statist and Colbertist tradition, which put the state at the heart of the regulation system, and distrust regarding capitalism remained rife in France in the early 1970s. At the same time, communism was this *'passion française'*[30] which had been deeply rooted in the country's political life since the 1920s. It even constituted a pillar of the political identity of the French during the Cold War because distinction between communists and anti-communists remained significant throughout the period.[31]

In any case, in this mindset of convergence and avoiding provocation with regard to the Warsaw Pact countries, the strategy adopted by the French delegation lay in targeting topics which it thought would facilitate dialogue with Moscow. For example, within the third basket, the French favoured the question of cultural exchanges because the Kremlin was less reticent to talk about a domain which, in the socialist countries, was subject to the state apparatus.

The French position was in reality quite perverse. By basing themselves again on a precise diagnosis, starting with a situational analysis of the bans in all areas of cultural life in the Eastern bloc, it aimed to shatter the sclerotic system that prevailed in the Soviet world. The French, who approached culture from the perspective of individual freedom, went against the Soviet views, which considered individual activities as the expression of the political collectivity to which they belonged.[32]

For Moscow, the importance of international cultural relations was linked to the 'permanent nature of the ideological battle between socialism and capitalism'.[33] Indeed, when the second phase of the CSCE in Geneva began, the official newspaper of the Communist Party of the Soviet Union (CPSU), *Pravda*, called on the USSR to make a clear distinction, among the Western third basket proposals, between what was progressive and revolutionary and what was foreign and reactionary; this came down to applying the Marxist-Leninist thesis consisting in making a choice in each culture. According to the authority of the CPSU, the socialist world was thus able to develop much-needed cultural exchanges, which already appeared as 'one of the failures of imperialism'.[34]

This reasoning explains why the Soviets embarked on a rampant campaign against one of the main texts submitted by France to the CSCE. The French proposed that the participating CSCE states would declare themselves resolved to 'favour the opening on their territory, by other interested states, individually or conjointly, of libraries and reading rooms or sections specialized in existing institutions, freely accessible to the public and administered in the conditions negotiated between the interested parties'.[35]

This proposition, ardently defended by the literary enthusiast Chazelle, poisoned French–Soviet relations at the CSCE for a period of almost two years, obliging heads of state and the governments of both countries to intervene directly in order to find a solution to the problem.[36] The affair proved to French diplomats that cultural détente was not on the agenda and that the Soviets remained guarded, including about draft texts which, at first sight, appeared secondary.

Indeed, while France managed to get the Eastern European delegations to accept a certain number of proposals which, in the long term, might turn out to be corrosive for the socialist regimes, from an early stage they thought about the means of ensuring that the terms of the Final Act would not remain unenforced.

Sovereignty Renegotiated

The accounts of former diplomats, just as the telegrams exchanged between Paris and the delegation in Geneva, bore witness to the ongoing concerns of the French to find a means of applying the Helsinki Final Act to the Eastern bloc. Amidst questioning détente, the overall defamation of the CSCE and the tension around the steadfast Soviet politics in terms of human rights, the Western representatives felt the need to prove – and to prove themselves – that their efforts would not be in vain and that the Helsinki process would be able to have a real impact on the course of the Cold War. Such a necessity forced the officials in charge of negotiations to develop an exhaustive assessment of the evolution of international relations since at least 1945 and of the reasons that had prevented it up to then from overcoming the context of the Cold War.

This reflection was led from 1969 onwards – while Georges Pompidou had barely accepted the conference – by the sous-direction d'Europe orientale of the Quai d'Orsay. It started with an observation, which moreover was that of the opponents of the CSCE: since 1945, the USSR committed itself several times in favour of respect for human rights, in particular upon signature of the Charter of the United Nations, of which one of the principles was 'defending human rights and fundamental freedom'. Yet the Charter had never been implemented in the USSR. Therefore, the French diplomats asked themselves how to ensure a different outcome. They attempted to find a balance between the need to improve the plight of populations subject to the Soviet yoke and the importance of the Gaullist tenet about state sovereignty. In the course of the 1970s, the ideas they formulated in close collaboration with their West European counterparts privileged several leads that had an impact both on the contents and the nature of the document that the conference would produce.

The sous-direction d'Europe orientale considered from the outset that the most important part of this document had to be that which defined the principles of non-use of force, inviolability of borders, sovereign equality of states and non-intervention in internal affairs.[37] Thanks to these principles, Moscow proclaimed the political and territorial status quo in Europe. Paris counted on playing on the power of words in the minds of the Soviets.

In 1969, the socialist states put forward a rigid definition of these principles, which supported the Brezhnev Doctrine on limited sovereignty.[38] For the sous-direction d'Europe orientale, their phrasing was not sufficiently explicit. The French particularly wished that infringements on national sovereignty and the independence of states be rendered, if not impossible then at the very least difficult, especially between countries belonging to the same alliance.[39] In order to proceed in this way, they suggested defining the non-use of force and non-intervention by using the definition of the aggression given by the Soviet Minister of Foreign Affairs Maxim Litvinov in 1933. This definition indicated the reasons that could not be given to justify an act of aggression: 'revolutionary or counter-revolutionary movements', 'civil war', 'troubles or strikes', 'establishment or the continuation in any State of any one political, economic or social regime'.[40] This Soviet text thus allowed a clear condemnation of the Prague Spring repression. It was a blessing for France, who wanted to indicate to the Soviets that real détente supposed the evolution of their attitude with regard to the nations of Eastern Europe subject to their influence.

Indeed, for the French, everything entered into play within the first basket, more than in any other. A clear and vigorous definition of principles – among which the Westerners had added respect for human rights and self-determination of peoples – could guarantee the application of the measures contained in the third basket. This cohesion between the two baskets was perceived by French diplomats early on as being fundamental: one incarnated the theory, the other the practice.[41] In Helsinki and Geneva, one of the French priorities resided in reinforcing this link by ensuring that all of the principles of the Decalogue were placed on equal footing. Whereas the Soviets fought for a hierarchization of principles – the one about sovereign equality was the first of the Final Act – the French and Americans managed to enforce the idea of unity and interdependence of principles.[42] Non-use of force and sovereign equality were therefore just as important as respecting human rights and self-determination of peoples.

Andréani welcomed the fact that the Decalogue was able to challenge the Westphalian Pact, which had been presiding over international relations in Europe since 1648.[43] French diplomacy thus considered that in proclaiming equality and the absence of hierarchization of principles and in enabling the prevalence of the Western definitions of sovereignty, human rights and non-intervention, the Final Act consecrated the Gaullist ideas and discredited the Brezhnev Doctrine. The first basket became the incarnation of convergence.

It was in this same spirit that France, from 1972 onwards, defended the idea of a document that would strengthen the commitment of the signatory states, something that was not done by the United Nations Charter and the Declaration of the UN about amicable relations between states in October 1970. These documents were judged to be too generalist because they did not refer to the 'concrete realities of the European situation'.[44] Thus, the Declaration of 1970 was just a solemn occasion to celebrate the twenty-fifth anniversary of the United Nations organization. However, French diplomacy considered that the document, which was to be presented at the CSCE, should be relatively versatile in order to avoid creating obstacles for the future; the Quai d'Orsay thought up, ahead of time, an act based on the model of the Congress of Vienna of 1815, a contract or set of recommendations.[45] It was crucial not to end up with a regional catalogue of principles that 'would be positioned half-way between general international law and a professed socialist international law' and which would allow the USSR to block transatlantic relations and European construction.[46]

Finally, as they intended to ensure that the CSCE would act on a long-term basis, the French diplomats who participated in the negotiations very early on thought about how to prolong the process after the signature of the Final Act and, especially, to check that the measures drawn up between 1972 and 1975 would not remain unenforced. If their judgement of the CSCE was less critical than that of their contemporaries in the summer of 1975, it was largely because their views on the continuation of the process ultimately triumphed.

The French supported the idea of an intermediate period that would follow the final conclusion of the CSCE and during which the participating states would seek to implement their commitments.[47] The interim period of a few years would be followed by a meeting of the official representatives in 1977 and would not veer towards the institutionalization of the results, as wanted by Moscow. Such an idea allowed the nine EC countries to exercise maximum control of the subsequent evolution of the multilateral process.[48] It also allowed them to combat the Soviet idea according to which the CSCE represented a final stage, the definitive consecration of the political and territorial status quo in Europe.[49]

Conclusion

In the summer of 1975, when the leaders of the two blocs found themselves in Helsinki to sign the Final Act, the French diplomats were satisfied with the result. Notwithstanding the appearances of the summit, they considered the CSCE as the complete opposite of the Congress of Vienna: the Final Act took into consideration the interests of the states in line with those of the populations, and this being on a long-term basis; it defined a framework for permanent East–West discussions about a multitude of topics; the conference made human rights a subject of discussion between the two blocs.

From 1970 to 1975, the French leaders and diplomats – although cautious in their public declarations – sincerely believed in the CSCE and the tangible impact it could have in Europe, as much in terms of security as cooperation. The French vision of the conference went beyond the simple diplomatic aspects. Paris considered that the CSCE was based on a real situation – the division of Europe – and that its aim was to improve it by allowing the Central and Eastern European countries to emancipate themselves from the Soviet yoke, by improving cultural and human exchanges or by increasing economic cooperation.

They especially considered that the Westerners had successfully turned to their advantage the steadfast importance the Soviets placed on the power of words. In light of the talent of the Russian diplomats present at the CSCE, this was no mean feat. The final aspect of the Decalogue bore witness to this. Thanks to the insistence of the Western countries, particularly France, the Decalogue proclaimed the equality of principles, placing respect for sovereignty of states and human rights on the same level. This contribution was significant in order to get to grips with the conditions of application of the Final Act. The Westphalian Pact, which had dominated European international relations since the religious wars, was in part swept aside by the CSCE. In future, the states of Europe could legitimately discuss the interior affairs of one another without infringing on their sovereignty.[50] Indeed, the contents of the Decalogue simply reinforced the sentiment of the French diplomats that the Helsinki process could have a real impact on the reality of the European situation.

If the representatives of France's vision of the CSCE went against Western opinions, it was first of all because these officials, who knew the Soviet world and diplomats as well as the international system resulting from the Cold War, did their utmost to maximize the prospects that the Helsinki process offered them. They knew how to take advantage of the goodwill of the Kremlin, at that time very much in a requesting position. They contributed to the establishment of a West European strategy based on cautiousness and non-provocation towards Moscow. They always argued in the long term, favouring the convergence of ideological systems rather than an outright attack against communism. They managed to conciliate the cornerstone principles of the Gaullist diplomacy by demanding the improvement of the situation of the populations of Central and Eastern Europe.

However, such optimism was not naive. The French negotiators knew that the Eastern bloc authorities would do everything in their power to limit the application of the Final Act. Did not the head of the KGB Yuri Andropov indicate in a speech given in June 1975 that the Kremlin would do everything it could, including in the satellite countries of the USSR, to limit the consequences of the third basket on society and the socialist systems?[51] Andréani noted thereafter that after the Helsinki summit, the party propaganda sought 'to denounce the danger of the infiltration of foreign ideas, preaching vigilance and highlighting the importance of not being mistaken about the meaning of the Helsinki document'. Furthermore, Andréani added, 'the regime intended to show dissidents that the power in place did not really have the intention of applying the measures relative to human rights'.[52]

In other words, the specialist in international relations Daniel Thomas explained, if the USSR and its allies accepted the third basket and the principles of the Decalogue relating to human rights and self-determination of peoples – norms in contradiction with the Soviet ideology, structure and practice – it was because they were convinced that the political and even economical gains of the CSCE outweighed the risks posed by the third basket and the proclamation of respect for human rights. The recognition and the legitimacy of the Eastern bloc by all of the Western countries and the neutral nations provided a new intrinsic value to the Warsaw Pact.[53]

However, as shown by the specialist in international organizations Victor-Yves Ghebali, the Helsinki Final Act 'was not a text of compromises between two ideologies, but a document full of liberated values reiterated in an oblique, ambiguous or attenuated manner'.[54] It constituted a supplementary step in the advance towards the ideological Western influence within the Soviet world. As the historian Pierre Grosser underlined, 'Helsinki corresponded with the reversal of the ideological power balance: from this moment on it was the Eastern countries who were tense about their sovereignty and feared an emancipating ideology coming from outside'.[55]

The French became fully aware of this, particularly because of the attitude of the Soviet leaders. While Brezhnev, delighted at the idea of obtaining approval from the Westerners with regard to the stronghold of the USSR over Eastern Europe, displayed a brazen triumphalism during the conclusion of the conference, a certain number of Soviet leaders were concerned about the impact that the Final Act could have. The diplomat Yuri Dubinin, in charge of the third basket within the USSR delegation in Geneva, confided in Alain Pierret on the last day of the negotiations: 'You don't know what you have won'.[56] Valerian Zorin, former ambassador in France who participated in the Helsinki talks, did not hesitate to declare to his colleagues that 'this is where all the evil will come from'.[57] Even Anatoly Kovalev, head of the Soviet delegation, was aware of the unexpected effects that the CSCE would risk having on the Eastern bloc.[58] Behind the united front and official propaganda acclaiming the Helsinki summit, the Soviet leaders were divided with regard to the overall appreciation of the Final Act.

For the French, such an attitude constituted a first victory and comforted them in their positive judgement of the CSCE, far from the Congress of Vienna and its interstate logic. In their opinion, from Talleyrand to Sakharov, there was only one step. There was no doubt that it was made in Helsinki.

Nicolas Badalassi is Associate Professor of Contemporary History at the Institut d'Etudes politiques d'Aix-en-Provence (Sciences-Po Aix). He holds a PhD from the University of Paris – Sorbonne Nouvelle (2011). In 2012–13, he administrated the *Sorbonne Cold War Studies Project*. He is the author of the award-winning *En finir avec la guerre* *froide: la France, l'Europe et le processus d'Helsinki, 1965–1975* (Presses Universitaires de Rennes, 2014). He has published various articles concerning French foreign policy in the Cold War era, the Helsinki Process and security in the Mediterranean. He has also co-edited with Houda Ben Hamouda *Les pays d'Europe orientale et la Méditerranée, 1967–1989* (Les Cahiers Irice, 2013).

Notes

1. R. Aron, 'La foire aux diplomates', *Le Figaro*, 30 July 1975.
2. E. Ionesco, 'Un nouveau Munich 1975?', *Le Figaro*, 4 August 1975.
3. See in particular D.C. Thomas, *The Helsinki Effect: International Norms, Human Rights and the Demise of Communism* (Princeton, NJ: Princeton University Press, 2001); J.M. Hanhimäki, '"They Can Write in Swahili": Kissinger, the Soviets, and the Helsinki Accords. 1973–75', *Journal of Transatlantic Studies* 1(1) (2003), 37–58; J.M. Hanhimäki, *The Flawed Architect: Henry Kissinger and American Foreign Policy* (New York: Oxford University Press, 2004); S.B. Snyder, *Human Rights Activism and the End of the Cold War: A Transnational History of the Helsinki Network* (Cambridge: Cambridge University Press, 2011); O. Bange and G. Niedhart (eds), *Helsinki 1975 and the Transformation of Europe* (New York: Berghahn Books, 2008); P. Hakkarainen, *A State of Peace in Europe: West Germany and the CSCE, 1966–1975* (New York: Berghahn Books, 2011); L. Ratti, *Britain, Ost- and Deutschlandpolitik, and the CSCE, 1955–1975* (Bern: PIE-Peter Lang, 2008); A. Romano, *From Détente in Europe to European Détente: How the West Shaped the Helsinki CSCE* (Brussels: PIE-Peter Lang, 2009).
4. Conversation Pompidou/Heath, 19 March 1972, Chequers Court, Box 5 AG 2 108, Grande-Bretagne, 1969–73, French National Archives (FNA), Pierrefitte-sur-Seine.
5. Document CSCE/III/PV.003, Book 24, Helsinki 1972–1975, OSCE Archives, Prague.
6. N. Badalassi, *En finir avec la guerre froide: la France, l'Europe et le processus d'Helsinki, 1965–1975* (Rennes: Presses Universitaires de Rennes, 2014).
7. During the 1950s, conflict developed between the supporters of Atlanticism and European integration (the 'Laloy line') and those who wanted to maintain the dialogue with Moscow (the 'Dejean line').
8. Memo by the sous-direction d'Europe orientale, 3 May 1968, Box 2034, Europe 1966–70, Organismes internationaux et grandes questions internationales, Archives of the French Ministry of Foreign Affairs (AFMFA), La Courneuve.
9. M.-P. Rey, 'Georges Pompidou, l'Union soviétique et l'Europe', in Association Georges Pompidou, *Georges Pompidou et l'Europe* (Paris: Complexe, 1995), 156.
10. Conversations with Paul Poudade and François Plaisant, December 2008.

11. P. Grémion, *Intelligence de l'anticommunisme: le Congrès pour la Liberté de la Culture à Paris. 1950–1975* (Paris: Fayard, 1995), 602.
12. M. Winock, *Le siècle des intellectuels* (Paris: Seuil, 1997).
13. M. Gauchet, 'L'expérience totalitaire et la pensée politique', *Esprit*, July–August 1976, 7.
14. J. Andréani, *Le Piège: Helsinki et la chute du communisme* (Paris: Odile Jacob, 2005), 134–35.
15. Quoted by Andréani, *Le Piège*, 117–18.
16. Conversation Kovalev/de Courcel, 11 January 1974, Paris, Box 5 AG 2 113, URSS, 1972–74, FNA.
17. A. Pierret, *De la case africaine à la villa romaine: un demi-siècle au service de l'Etat* (Paris: L'Harmattan, 2010), 123.
18. Conversation with Alain Pierret, 22 January 2011; C.G. Stefan, 'The Drafting of the Helsinki Final Act: A Personal View of the CSCE's Geneva Phase (September 1973 until July 1975)', *The Society for Historians of American Foreign Relations Newsletter* 31(2) (June 2000), 5.
19. All these reports are reunited in volume no. 15 of the series CSCE at the archives of the Quai d'Orsay.
20. Telegram n°3139/45, from Gérard André, 3 July 1973; telegram n°3285/89, from Jacques Vimont, 4 July 1973, Box 26, CSCE, AFMFA.
21. Conversation Arnaud/Dubinin, 13 September 1973, Paris, Box 33, CSCE, AFMFA.
22. Andréani, *Le Piège*, 136.
23. Conversation between Gromyko and Jobert, 26 June 1973, Box 26, CSCE, AFMFA; Conversation of the author with Pompidou's and Giscard's adviser Gabriel Robin, 17 November 2008.
24. D. Möckli, *European Foreign Policy during the Cold War: Heath, Brandt, Pompidou and the Dream of Political Unity, 1969–1974* (London: I.B. Tauris, 2008), 119.
25. Message from Brezhnev given to Giscard d'Estaing by the Ambassador Chervonenko on 11 June 1974, Box 5 AG 3 1089, URSS, 1974, FNA.
26. Memo of the sous-direction d'Europe orientale, 27 May 1971, Box 2921, Organisations internationales et grandes questions internationales, Europe 1971–76, AFMFA.
27. The Ecole normale supérieure is one of the most prestigious *grandes écoles* of France. Founded in 1794, it trains public administrators, professors and researchers. Its most famous alumni include Jean-Paul Sartre, Michel Foucault, Jean Jaurès, Aimé Césaire and Georges Pompidou.
28. Telegram n°7582/91, by Seydoux, 3 November 1972, Box 2924, Organismes internationaux et grandes questions internationales, Europe 1971–76, AFMFA.
29. Speech made at the dinner offered by Brezhnev in the Kremlin during the presidential trip in the USSR, 6 October 1970, in G. Pompidou, *Entretiens et discours*, vol. II, *1968–1974* (Paris: Plon, 1975), 175–76.
30. M. Lazar, *Le communisme, une passion française* (Paris: Perrin, 2005).
31. S. Cœuré, 'Communisme et anticommunisme', in J.-J. Becker and G. Candar (eds), *Histoire des gauches en France* (Paris: La Découverte, 2004), 499.

32. Telegram n°160, by Vimont, 6 September 1973, Box 26, CSCE, AFMFA.
33. V.-Y. Ghebali, *La diplomatie de la détente: la CSCE* (Brussels: Bruylant, 1989), 342.
34. Telegram n°160, by Vimont, 6 September 1973, Box 26, CSCE, AFMFA.
35. Note by Gabriel Robin, 19 March 1975, Box 5 AG 3 885, CSCE, FNA; Document OSCE/II/K/9, France, 21 January 1974, Book 20, Helsinki 1972–1975, OSCE Archives.
36. Conversation Pompidou/Brezhnev, 13 March 1974, Pitsunda, Box 5 AG 2 113, URSS, 1972–74, FNA; Conversation Chirac/Kossyguin, 20 March 1975, Moscow, Box 3727, URSS, Europe 1971–76, AFMFA.
37. Andréani, *Le Piège*, 48.
38. Memo by the sous-direction d'Europe orientale, 4 November 1969, Box 2692, URSS, Europe 1966–70, AFMFA.
39. Memo by the sous-direction d'Europe orientale, 2 February 1970, Box 2031, Organismes internationaux et grandes questions internationales, Europe 1966–70, AFMFA.
40. Undated memo, probably by the sous-direction d'Europe orientale, Box 2034, Organismes internationaux et grandes questions internationales, Europe 1966–70, AFMFA.
41. Memo by the direction des affaires juridiques, 24 November 1969, Box 2031, Organismes internationaux et grandes questions internationales, Europe 1966–70, AFMFA.
42. Conversation Sauvagnargues/Gromyko, 11 July 1974, Moscow, Box 3726, URSS, Europe 1971–76, AFMFA.
43. Andréani, *Le Piège*, 232.
44. Memo by the sous-direction d'Europe orientale, 21 June 1972, Box 22, CSCE, AFMFA.
45. Memo no. 246 of the direction des Affaires juridiques, 7 March 1973, Box 22, CSCE, AFMFA.
46. Ghebali, *La diplomatie de la détente*, 74–75.
47. Conversation Jobert/Gromyko, 16 February 1974, Paris, Box 5 AG 2 113, URSS, 1972–74, AFMFA.
48. Document report by the President of the CSCE sub-committee (European political cooperation), 23 May 1975, Box 18, CSCE, AFMFA.
49. Intervention of the representative of France at the follow-up working group, 14 March 1975, Box 20, CSCE, AFMFA.
50. Andréani, *Le Piège*, 232.
51. Telegram from the American Embassy to Moscow, 24 July 1975, folder 'USSR. State Department Telegrams. To SECSTATE EXDIS (7)', Box 20, National Security Advisor. Presidential Country Files for Europe and Canada, Gerald Ford Presidential Library, Ann Arbor, Michigan.
52. Andréani, *Le Piège*, 106-07.
53. Thomas, *The Helsinki Effect*, 262–64.
54. V.-Y. Ghebali, 'Les valeurs de la Grande Europe, produit du laboratoire politique de la CSCE', *Relations internationales* 73 (1993), 63.
55. P. Grosser, *Les temps de la guerre froide* (Brussels: Complexe, 1995), 284.
56. Pierret, *De la case africaine à la villa romaine*, 254.

57. Conversation with Paul Poudade, 16 December 2008.
58. S. Savranskaya, 'Unintended Consequences: Soviet Interests, Expectations and Reactions to the Helsinki Final Act', in Bange and Niedhart, *Helsinki 1975 and the Transformation of Europe*, 179.

Bibliography

Archival Material

Archives of the CSCE/OSCE (Prague)
Helsinki 1972–1975: Books 1 to 6, 8, 12 to 16, 18 to 22, 24.
Archives of the French Ministry of Foreign Affairs (La Courneuve)
Europe 1966–70:
Box 2692, URSS.
Boxes 2031 and 2034, Organismes internationaux et grandes questions internationales.
Europe 1971–76:
Boxes 15, 18, 20, 22, 26, 33, CSCE.
Boxes 2921 and 2924, Organismes internationaux et grandes questions internationales.
Boxes 3726 and 3727, URSS.
French National Archives (Pierrefitte-sur-Seine)
Presidency of Georges Pompidou: Box 5 AG 2 108, Grande-Bretagne; Box 5 AG 2 113, URSS.
Presidency of Valéry Giscard d'Estaing: Box 5 AG 3 885, CSCE; Box 5 AG 3 1089, URSS.
Gerald Ford Presidential Library (Ann Arbor, Michigan)
Folder 'USSR. State Department Telegrams. To SECSTATE EXDIS (7)', Box 20, National Security Advisor. Presidential Country Files for Europe and Canada.

Published Documents

Pompidou, G. *Entretiens et discours*, vol. II, *1968–1974*. Paris: Plon, 1975.

Published Sources

Andréani, J. *Le Piège: Helsinki et la chute du communisme*. Paris: Odile Jacob, 2005.
Badalassi, N. *En finir avec la guerre froide: la France, l'Europe et le processus d'Helsinki, 1965–1975*. Rennes: Presses Universitaires de Rennes, 2014.
Bange, O., and G. Niedhart (eds). *Helsinki 1975 and the Transformation of Europe*. New York: Berghahn Books, 2008.
Cœuré, S. 'Communisme et anticommunisme', in J.-J. Becker and G. Candar (eds), *Histoire des gauches en France* (Paris: La Découverte, 2004), 487–506.
Ghebali, V.-Y. *La diplomatie de la détente: la CSCE*. Brussels: Bruylant, 1989.

Ghebali, V.-Y. 'Les valeurs de la Grande Europe, produit du laboratoire politique de la CSCE'. *Relations internationales* 73 (1993), 63–80.
Glucksmann, A. *La Cuisinière et le Mangeur d'hommes: essai sur les rapports entre l'Etat, le marxisme et les camps de concentration*. Paris: Seuil, 1975.
Grémion, P. *Intelligence de l'anticommunisme: le Congrès pour la Liberté de la Culture à Paris. 1950–1975*. Paris: Fayard, 1995.
Grosser, P. *Les temps de la guerre froide*. Brussels: Complexe, 1995.
Hakkarainen, P. *A State of Peace in Europe: West Germany and the CSCE, 1966–1975*. New York: Berghahn Books, 2011.
Hanhimäki, J.M. *The Flawed Architect: Henry Kissinger and American Foreign Policy*. New York: Oxford University Press, 2004.
Hanhimäki, J.M. '"They Can Write in Swahili": Kissinger, the Soviets, and the Helsinki Accords. 1973–75'. *Journal of Transatlantic Studies* 1(1) (2003), 37–58.
Lazar, M. *Le communisme, une passion française*. Paris: Perrin, 2005.
Möckli, D. *European Foreign Policy during the Cold War: Heath, Brandt, Pompidou and the Dream of Political Unity, 1969–1974*. London: I.B. Tauris, 2008.
Pierret, A. *De la case africaine à la villa romaine: un demi-siècle au service de l'Etat*. Paris: L'Harmattan, 2010.
Ratti, L. *Britain, Ost- and Deutschlandpolitik, and the CSCE, 1955–1975*. Bern: PIE-Peter Lang, 2008.
Rey, M.-P. 'Georges Pompidou, l'Union soviétique et l'Europe', in Association Georges Pompidou, *Georges Pompidou et l'Europe* (Paris: Complexe, 1995), 141–70.
Romano, A. *From Détente in Europe to European Détente: How the West Shaped the Helsinki CSCE*. Brussels: PIE-Peter Lang, 2009.
Savranskaya, S. 'Unintended Consequences: Soviet Interests, Expectations and Reactions to the Helsinki Final Act', in O. Bange and G. Niedhart (eds), *Helsinki 1975 and the Transformation of Europe* (New York: Berghahn Books, 2008), 175–190.
Snyder, S.B. *Human Rights Activism and the End of the Cold War: A Transnational History of the Helsinki Network*. Cambridge: Cambridge University Press, 2011.
Solzhenitsyn, A. *The Gulag Archipelago*. New York: Collins, 1974.
Stefan, C.G. 'The Drafting of the Helsinki Final Act: A Personal View of the CSCE's Geneva Phase (September 1973 until July 1975)'. *The Society for Historians of American Foreign Relations Newsletter* 31(2) (June 2000), 7–10.
Thomas, D.C. *The Helsinki Effect: International Norms, Human Rights and the Demise of Communism*. Princeton, NJ: Princeton University Press, 2001.
Winock, M. *Le siècle des intellectuels*. Paris: Seuil, 1997.

 4

'HUMAN RIGHTS, PEACE AND SECURITY ARE INSEPARABLE'
Max Kampelman and the Helsinki Process
Stephan Kieninger

Personality and Policy: Max Kampelman and the CSCE Process

In 2013, after a remarkable career, Max Kampelman passed away at the age of ninety-two. Kampelman grew up in the Bronx as the son of immigrants from Eastern Europe. His parents came from Chernivtsi, the capital of the historical Bukovina region in the south-western part of Ukraine close to the border with Romania. His father, a butcher, died when Max was seventeen. Kampelman struggled to make it to college. He studied law at New York University, became a member of the Democratic Party and served as legislative counsel to Senator Hubert Humphrey of Minnesota. Thereafter, Kampelman began a long career in law.

This chapter sheds new light on Max Kampelman's role in the CSCE process. First, it looks into Kampelman's policy, depicting his capability to reconcile strength and diplomacy. The second section charts the path of the Helsinki process from the failure of the Belgrade follow-up to the success of the Madrid meeting. The third section highlights Kampelman's role therein, focusing on his capacity to intertwine the CSCE's arms control objectives with its human rights dimension. Finally, the last section investigates Kampelman's leadership during the concluding stages of the Madrid meeting.

In the 1980s, presidents Jimmy Carter and Ronald Reagan appointed Kampelman to lead negotiations with the Soviet Union that profoundly transformed the world. Carter named Kampelman to lead the US delegation to the Madrid CSCE follow-up meeting. The Madrid Accord of September 1983 was a breakthrough. It entailed important new commitments to the Helsinki process, including provisions dealing with human rights, trade union freedoms, religious liberties, reunification of families and the freer flow of information. It was also a novelty that East and West found agreement on incorporating additional military confidence-building measures in the CSCE process.[1] Jimmy Carter praised Kampelman as 'an eloquent voice for human rights'.[2] In 1985, Ronald Reagan appointed Kampelman to lead the US–Soviet arms control negotiations in Geneva that culminated in the conclusion of the START I Treaty in 1991. In 1989, Reagan hailed him in a letter, emphasizing that 'your success there will benefit generations to come'.[3] In a nutshell, Kampelman's career is a model of bipartisanship in US foreign policy.

Kampelman perceived himself as a 'private man in public life'. His memoirs carry this subtitle,[4] and indeed, as a private citizen, he was proud to serve his country. In 1981, he underlined his dedication and his determination to continue under the Reagan administration in a letter to Lawrence Eagleburger, the Assistant Secretary of State for European Affairs. Kampelman emphasized that 'I do fit the fundamental requirements for this role and would do it well … But I am not looking for a job. I have a good one that pays better and has better hours. I enjoy the Madrid experience and I am a patriot'.[5] This was typical of Kampelman. He never asked for a government post or for an ambassadorship. He had strong views and firm convictions. He was often characterized as a hard-nosed pacifist, and there is some basis to this opinion of him. Kampelman was a conscientious objector during World War II. He claimed the right to refuse to perform military service on the grounds of his pacifism. In his memoirs, Kampelman pointed out that 'my pacifism grew out of my education and family training and had deep roots in my understanding of the Jewish belief that I had been taught, strengthened by my exposure to the Quakers'.[6] At the same time, there was a hard-nosed side to him: Kampelman was a member of the Committee on the Present Danger, and he was critical of Nixon's and Kissinger's policy towards the Soviet Union.[7]

Kampelman's strategy was to emphasize soft power, which made him a good fit for the CSCE. In the 1970s, the Helsinki process had many ups and downs. There was no script for the process, and the CSCE negotiations always benefitted from innovation and creativity. Max Kampelman had the talents and the leadership capabilities to navigate the Madrid meeting to a successful conclusion. One of Kampelman's assets was his ability to garner support in different communities. He had close ties to the evolving US Helsinki network,[8] and direct access to President Ronald Reagan, Vice President George Bush and Secretary of State George Shultz. Kampelman trusted the policy advice of the State Department's Bureau of European Affairs, and worked closely with its directors, George Vest and Lawrence Eagleburger. He picked the able Warren Zimmermann as his deputy in Madrid. Kampelman listened to his European partners, and last but not least, due to his own heritage, he had a personal interest in East European affairs. Kampelman viewed Richard Nixon's and Henry Kissinger's foreign policy with criticism. In the mid 1970s, he established close ties with the members of the US Helsinki Commission. As Kampelman put it, 'Kissinger's emphasis on realpolitik led many House members to believe he would sell out human rights considerations if he saw them as adversely affecting American security interests, as he defined those interests'.[9] Domestic opposition to détente emerged in the United States for two major reasons. In the aftermath of Watergate, the most imminent source of criticism was the reproach that Kissinger had sacrificed morality in America's foreign policy. Against the background of the Soviet Union's tremendous strategic build-up, the second central point of criticism was the argument that Nixon, Kissinger and Ford had sold off America's position of power in the arms race.[10]

In the 1970s, Max Kampelman joined the Committee on the Present Danger, whose mission was to 'alert the public on the growing Soviet threat'.[11] However, unlike many members of the committee, Kampelman pursued a different approach. He opposed communism and he opposed the Cold War. He believed that patience and hard-nosed diplomacy were essential in US–Soviet relations. Prior to the resumption of the arms control negotiations in Geneva in 1985, Kampelman said of the Soviet Union: 'We cannot wish it away. It is here and it is militarily powerful. We share the same globe. We must try to find a formula under which we can live together in dignity. We must engage in that pursuit of peace without illusion but with persistence, regardless of provocation'.[12] This, in a nutshell, was Kampelman's strategy of peace.

Early on, Kampelman wanted the Reagan administration to reverse the arms race and to highlight America's soft power. In November 1982, Kampelman wrote a remarkable letter to his old friend Eugene Rostow. He reiterated that 'you and I have for years joined in the advocacy of adequate military power for the United States. We both agree upon its urgency, but I think we would also both agree to its inadequacy. Our military power, which is great but no longer superior, must be directed by a political strategy of superior quality'. Kampelman continued: 'my emphasis on the battlefield of the mind does not at all mean that I ignore the reality of the guns and the realpolitik of geography. ... What I am urging is that we now exploit the ideological disarray in which the Soviets find themselves. ... We are making plans to counter their military adventurism, but that is not enough. We must engage them more actively in the political struggle as well'.[13] Last but not least, Kampelman strongly supported Reagan's nuclear abolitionism and the vision for a world free of nuclear weapons. He wrote to Rostow that 'to get to the point, on the top of our agenda we should have a US proposal for complete nuclear disarmament of all nation states of the world'.[14]

Dialogue with the Soviet Union was part of Kampelman's hard-nosed diplomacy. He believed that strength and diplomacy went together. US–Soviet relations were in crisis, and President Carter froze relations after the Soviet intervention in Afghanistan.[15] Kampelman believed that the lack of communication between the US and Soviet leaders could result in misunderstanding and unpredictability. The CSCE negotiations were one of the few opportunities for US–Soviet talks about the general state of bilateral relations, and Kampelman was eager to seize this opportunity. In March 1981, Kampelman turned to Assistant Secretary of State for European Affairs Lawrence Eagleburger, arguing that 'the first and primary objective should be clarity and understanding. Our own chief objective should not be negotiation. We must understand one another's position and come to judge on another's national interest as we perceive it'. Kampelman reiterated that 'the clarity may well produce nothing more in many areas than a growing awareness that the differences of national interest or of perception are very real, not subject to easy solution. That too would be an important advance, even if it should not produce immediate negotiation and agreement'.[16] In his response, Eagleburger readily agreed, pointing out that 'dialogue unfortunately tends to wane when the bilateral relationship is strained'. He emphasized that 'as you suggest, it should be the other way around – higher tension should bring a more intensive dialogue'.[17]

Kampelman managed to combine public diplomacy and top-secret backchannel talks with the Soviets. Early on, Kampelman anticipated that Sergej Kondrashev of the Soviet CSCE delegation was in fact a KGB General with close ties to the Soviet leadership. In December 1980, Kampelman approached Kondrashev in an attempt to start a confidential dialogue and to turn over to him a list of 'Israeli cases' consisting of the names of Soviet citizens who had been denied permission to leave the Soviet Union and go to Israel.[18] Like President Reagan, Kampelman sympathized with the victims of communist repression. Kampelman told Kondrashev that 'the release of a few hundred political prisoners, the relaxation of barriers in the family reunification area and the reopening of emigration opportunities to Soviet Jews were all steps that could be taken with significantly positive results without weakening the fabric of their society'.[19]

As things turned out, the Kampelman–Kondrashev conversation of December 1980 was the start of a confidential dialogue between them that finally enabled them to negotiate the release of the members of two Pentacostal families in 1983. Ronald Reagan was particularly interested in the fate of the Vashchenko and Chmykhalov families who had been seeking asylum in the US Embassy in Moscow back in 1978.[20] In January 1982, when two of the Pentacostals undertook a hunger strike, Reagan sent a private letter to Brezhnev, pressing him to grant exit visas for the Pentacostal families, citing the Helsinki Final Act in support of their right to leave the Soviet Union.[21] In February 1983, Reagan met Soviet Ambassador Anatoli Dobrynin and asked that the two families be allowed to emigrate as a sign of goodwill to the United States. Reagan promised that he would not draw public attention to the case; he pledged 'no crowing'.[22]

In effect, Kampelman's policy and the success of the Madrid meeting underpinned the fact that US–Soviet cooperation and East–West contacts remained an influential factor in Ronald Reagan's foreign policy. The CSCE was essential in this endeavour. The Helsinki process decisively helped to stabilize the emerging crisis of détente in the early 1980s by providing both superpowers with a framework in which they could sort out the manifold strains in their relations. The Madrid follow-up was decisive for the 'long détente' in Europe. It epitomized the efforts to protect the peace-maintaining framework and the gains of East–West cooperation against the background of the Euromissile crisis and the escalation of the global Cold War.[23] Like the CSCE process, Kampelman's policy was multidimensional. Time and again, he pointed out that the 'genius of the Final Act is its recognition that true security depends upon a balance of progress on security, on human rights and on economic cooperation'.[24] In a nutshell, Kampelman used the breadth of the Helsinki process to reach package solutions and to foster both arms control and human rights.

From Crisis to Opportunity: The CSCE Process between the Follow-Up Meetings in Belgrade and Madrid

The Madrid meeting helped to reconcile the competing West European and American policies, and Max Kampelman had a decisive role in this endeavour. In the second half of the 1970s, the Carter White House and the West Europeans had pursued contrasting concepts for détente.[25] The problem at the Belgrade CSCE follow-up was not that the Carter administration attacked the Soviet Union in terms of human rights, but that Carter did it without allied consensus. The West Europeans perceived Carter's public human rights diplomacy as a threat to their efforts to build bridges of increased human contacts across the Iron Curtain. In 1977, West Germany's Foreign Minister Hans Dietrich Genscher told Carter's National Security Adviser Zbigniew Brzezinski that the West Germans were eager to conduct quiet diplomacy and 'to keep Eastern Europe engaged in a multilateral process'.[26] The Schmidt-Genscher administration wanted the authorities in the Warsaw Pact states to allow as many citizens of German origin as possible to emigrate to the West.[27] Helmut Schmidt emphasized that 'we cannot talk in abstract terms about human rights'.[28] The West German policy was to try to achieve 'the greatest happiness for the greatest number'.[29]

The State Department shared the West European point of view. After the failure and collapse of the Belgrade follow-up meeting, Warren Zimmermann and John Maresca pointed out that 'the CSCE will – and should – become less important as a forum for the achievement of human rights objectives (since the Soviets won't knuckle under to our pressure there) and more important as an umbrella permitting the expansion of contacts between East and West'.[30] Marshall Shulman, the special advisor on Soviet affairs to Secretary of State Cyrus R. Vance, came to the conclusion that 'it should be clear that the effort to compel changes in Soviet institutions and practices by frontal demands is likely to be counterproductive'.[31]

At the time, Arthur Goldberg led the US delegation at the Belgrade meeting. In 1979, Goldberg wrote to Willy Brandt, claiming that the West German delegation in Belgrade 'took the lead in urging that it would be deleterious to speak forthrightly about human rights'.[32] Brandt responded that 'social democrats all over the world have always been committed to human rights. They are more than a basic element of our common ideals'. Brandt cautioned that 'all this ... will not guide us into reducing the discussion on human rights to an instrument for other purposes'. Brandt believed that 'it has proved judicious in certain cases to refrain from public action. In doing so we could help many people in Eastern Europe to claim their rights'.[33]

The West Germans envisaged détente as the means to transform Europe and to heal Germany's division.[34] The Brandt, Schmidt and Kohl administrations pursued an open-ended strategy for unification that was not primarily focused on the 'classical reunification approach'. Rather, reunification was conceived as a distant objective. For the time being, it was important to retain a sense of 'Germanness' and to expand human contacts. The concept was that the two Germanies would come closer in economic, cultural and social ways, in movement of people. Thus, it was imperative for the Germans to 'keep détente alive'.[35] After all, Ostpolitik had over time resulted in 'Soviet tolerance for closer FRG-GDR relations and for greater reunification with ethnic Germans in Eastern Europe'.[36] Since the emergence of détente in Europe in the 1960s and 1970s, the West Europeans were eager to perforate the Iron Curtain and to open up the way to direct encounter and competition between the societies of East and West.[37] In the 1980s, America's allies grew increasingly concerned that US–Soviet confrontation could jeopardize the benefits of East–West cooperation in Europe.[38] As things turned out, Max Kampelman came to play a pivotal role in the effort to keep détente alive and to balance US and West European interests.

The Helsinki Final Act meant that the communist regimes in Eastern Europe accepted for the first time that relations between peoples – and therefore the attitudes of governments to their own citizens – should be the subject of multilateral discussions. The CSCE gave East and West the opportunity to pursue détente on a broad basis, yet with competing objectives. The two sides differed over the question of how the gap left by the Cold War would be filled. The Soviets envisaged détente as a 'certain amount of official co-operation between two groupings of countries with different concepts'. In addition, the Western proponents of a dynamic détente wanted a 'gradual overcoming of the barriers separating the people involved'.[39]

The follow-up in Madrid was a breakthrough as it intertwined human rights and arms control. In September 1981, John Greenwald of the US CSCE delegation outlined the aims in a memorandum to Max Kampelman, writing that 'my suggestion is that we talk ourselves, and encourage others to talk, about the shape of a new human rights protective structure that we would aim to build within CSCE over the next ten years or so. The idea can – and at this stage must – be general and long-range'. Greenwald emphasized that 'we have spoken frequently at Madrid of the confidence-building aspect of human rights, of the interrelationship between the human and the military aspects of security'.[40]

These results were all the more remarkable as détente was in crisis, and the conference was on the verge of collapse. There was a nine-month recess between March and November 1982 in the wake of the declaration of martial law in Poland in December 1981. In addition, the Madrid follow-up was an essential exercise for NATO to find a 'new consensus' over its East–West policy.[41] Initially, in the aftermath of the declaration of martial law in Poland, Ronald Reagan considered the Helsinki process 'null and void'.⁴² In contrast, the West Europeans saw the CSCE as an excellent opportunity for NATO to sustain public attention on Poland and to 'breathe fresh air into Eastern Europe'.⁴³ The Reagan administration was hesitant to go for a substantial CSCE document as long as the Polish authorities maintained martial law. The lifting of martial law in July 1983 helped Reagan to justify the conclusion of the Madrid meeting domestically. Moreover, Reagan was only prepared to sign an agreement with the USSR if the Soviet leaders brought the kind of concessions the West had long sought.⁴⁴ Finally, Max Kampelman and his colleagues managed to achieve a good concluding document entailing significant improvement of the humanitarian provisions of the Helsinki Final Act and its provisions on human rights as well as Soviet consent to the convocation of an expert meeting on human contacts. Moreover, the Warsaw Pact countries agreed to hold the first stage of a European Disarmament Conference (EDC) dealing with confidence-building measures and to reduce the risk of surprise military attack.

The West Europeans needed the success of the Madrid follow-up and the convocation of a conference on confidence- and security-building measures in order to maintain East–West dialogue and to counter domestic protest after the envisaged missile deployment.⁴⁵ In April 1983, West German Chancellor Helmut Kohl told Denmark's Prime Minister Schlüter that the Reagan administration had not emphasized the interconnection between the CSCE and the decision for deployment. As Kohl put it, the Americans had put the Madrid follow-up and the Euromissile issue in 'different drawers'. But Kohl was confident that Secretary of State George Shultz had come to appreciate the virtue of emphasizing the interconnection.⁴⁶

The substantive results of the CSCE follow-up in Madrid were an asset for the Kohl administration in their efforts to continue Brandt's and Schmidt's Ostpolitik.⁴⁷ West Germany's Foreign Minister Hans Dietrich Genscher believed that it was beneficial for the confidence-building process to tell the Warsaw Pact leaders right away that the envisaged changes should not be brought about 'through crusades or Trojan horses, or through coercion and pressure'. The changes should evolve from the CSCE process, and the Warsaw Pact countries should be given the opportunity to play their part and to contribute.⁴⁸ The Madrid follow-up strengthened NATO's cohesion. In 1984, Ronald Reagan and Helmut Kohl were in agreement that 'time is not working to the Soviet advantage' and that 'the idea of Communism has lost much of its force'. Reagan and Kohl were united in their assumption that the citizens of the Soviet Union needed 'better information regarding the West'. Kohl thought 'that we should not forget what it means to live in a country sealed from the outside. Distortions are great, and thirst for information is great'.[49]

The success in Madrid made it possible for Reagan and Kohl to think aloud together and to pursue a common policy to perforate the Iron Curtain. Like the West Europeans, the Reagan administration began to conceive human rights 'in the collective way'. The Madrid Accord underlined that NATO managed to achieve two important policy objectives at the same time. It was possible to name the names of imprisoned dissidents and to demand individual human rights improvements and to help as many citizens in Eastern Europe as possible to claim their rights. In January 1984, Shultz used his opening speech at the Stockholm conference on confidence-building measures in Europe in order to emphasize that 'human rights were central to any discussion of European security. ... An artificial barrier has cruelly divided this continent – and indeed heartlessly divided one of its great nations. ... This division is the essence of Europe's security and human rights problem, and we all know it'.[50]

Intertwining Arms Control and Human Rights: Max Kampelman and NATO's Agenda

The Belgrade meeting failed to produce a substantive concluding document. Thus, in 1978, the Giscard administration brought up the idea to strengthen the CSCE's arms control dimension. In January 1978, the French Foreign Ministry went public with the idea for the convocation of a European Disarmament Conference (EDC) in order to give the CSCE process new life by injecting additional confidence-building measures (CBMs) that had hitherto been discussed in the East–West negotiations on Mutual and Balanced Forces Reductions (MBFR).[51] The Schmidt and Giscard governments were in agreement that one major task of the Madrid CSCE follow-up was to establish a mandate for such a conference with the objective to expand the CBMs area up to the Ural Mountains, expanding the 250-kilometre band that had originally been agreed upon in Helsinki in 1975.[52] Moreover, from 1979 onwards, the EDC proposal was conceived to accompany NATO's dual-track decision, to protect it against public criticism and to embed it within a broad framework of arms control policy.[53] The EDC initiative was seen as a lever for NATO to stay on the offensive in the disarmament field and to continue military détente.[54]

In the late 1970s, there were competing American approaches towards the EDC idea. Zbigniew Brzezinski wanted to avoid such a project while Soviet troops were still in Afghanistan. Secretary of State Cyrus Vance, however, backed the French idea. In 1979, on Genscher's behalf, Vance even solicited NATO's support for the EDC project as it was aimed at expanding the CBMs area to all of Europe, thereby helping to avoid a special military status for West Germany.[55] Finally, Brzezinski gave Kampelman the latitude to make the decision on the French proposal.[56] In 1981, Kampelman wanted the newly elected Reagan administration to support the plan to convoke an EDC after the Madrid meeting. He made the point that 'our NATO allies all strongly support EDC and hope that we will, not only as a way of maintaining NATO unity, but also because they think the French initiative is extremely helpful as a propaganda weapon against the left in Europe'.[57] In the end, the Reagan administration backed the French proposal.[58]

In February 1981, Kampelman vigorously supported the EDC idea in a CSCE plenary session, arguing that 'we have the opportunity starting here in Madrid and within our CSCE process to explore the new and promising field of confidence-building measures'. He warned the Soviet side that 'we will absolutely not lend our support in this meeting to a cosmetic and meaningless negotiation'.[59] Last but not least, Kampelman linked the CSCE's security aspects with its human dimension. He made the point that 'the CSCE cannot survive in the future solely as a security negotiation. The genius of the Final Act is its recognition that true security depends upon a balance of progress on security, on human rights and on economic cooperation'.[60] His objective was to link US support for the French idea with West European endorsement for a public Western human rights policy.

The Soviet Union's interest in the convocation of a disarmament conference gave Kampelman additional leverage to pursue a tough human rights approach. Early on, Kampelman named the names of imprisoned Soviet dissidents. On 12 May 1981, for instance, he highlighted the fifth birthday of the Moscow Helsinki Watch Group. He warned the Soviet authorities that the members of the Helsinki Group faced 'repression, exile, arrest, imprisonment and ostracism'.[61] On 19 May 1981, Kampelman reminded the CSCE's plenary session of Andrei Sakharov's sixtieth birthday. He expressed 'the abhorrence we feel at his continued exile and at the harassment and petty punishments that accompany his exile'. He added: 'the care of human life and happiness, and not their destruction, is the first and only legitimate object of good government'.[62]

Kampelman approached the Soviets several times to facilitate the release of Juri Orlov, the imprisoned chairman of the Moscow Helsinki Group. In June 1981, Orlov's wife turned to Kampelman. She wrote that 'they are gradually killing my husband, torturing him, destroying his health, turning him into an invalid'.[63] In November 1982, Kampelman wrote a letter to Kovalev, the head of the Soviet delegation. He reiterated that 'on behalf of many in the West concerned about Dr. Orlov's plight, we urge a compassionate response to these concerns so that he and his wife and two boys may emigrate'.[64] In 1983, Kampelman was determined to bring the Soviets to grant Orlov and his family exit visas when he negotiated with Kondrashev over the release of the Pentacostal families.[65]

In 1981, the debates in Madrid grew harsh. The USSR adopted maximalist positions when the CPSU's General Secretary Leonid Brezhnev tried to pressure the Western countries to agree to a westward extension of the CBMs zone and to deliver an appropriate proposal in due time.[66] The NATO countries responded in July 1981 with demands for Soviet concessions, including the convocation of an expert meeting on human rights and family reunification, improved protection for the Helsinki Monitor Groups, free practice of religion and a cessation of radio jamming.[67]

In September 1981, the Reagan administration made its support for the EDC idea and the westward expansion of the CBMs area dependent on the convocation of a CSCE expert meeting on human rights. Reagan was in search of a visible way to maintain domestic support for the Helsinki process.[68] However, the West European NATO allies feared that too much public pressure could be counterproductive. Hans-Dietrich Genscher argued that 'there was no reason for pessimism'. It was imperative for the West not to throw in the towel or walk away from the bargaining table.[69]

Max Kampelman and the Final Phase of the Madrid Meeting, 1982–83

The declaration of martial law in Poland in December 1981 had produced even more pressure to abrogate the Madrid meeting. In January 1982, Kampelman assessed the new situation with Kondrashev. He reported to Eagleburger, writing that the Soviets still approached the negotiations with confidence and that 'their confidence is based on the belief that a number of Western states consider the continuity of the Helsinki process more important than the immediate Polish crisis'. Kampelman wrote that 'the Soviets will emphasize that the meeting is close to being finished. They will urge completion without delay. They expressed strong disagreement to a Belgrade type concluding document or to any document which was an agreement to disagree. They do not want to end Madrid without a substantive result'.[70]

The Madrid meeting turned into a waiting game. In November 1982, it was finally continued after a nine-month recess. There were changes in the Reagan administration's leadership as well. Alexander Haig resigned as Secretary of State and praised Kampelman as a 'great patriot, a wise adviser, and a trusted friend'.[71] George Shultz took over and asked Max Kampelman to stay. Shultz was well aware that Kampelman's absence from his prominent Washington law firm was burdensome. In fact, Kampelman flew back to Washington at weekends. Shultz wrote that, 'in asking you to continue, I am well aware of the personal, professional and financial costs which your service entails. No one could reasonably require you to make those sacrifices, and your decision not to continue would be totally justified. Nevertheless, for our country's sake, I hope that you will be able to return to Madrid as the head of our team'.[72] Kampelman was determined to continue. In his response to Shultz, he wrote that 'it is in the best interest of the Helsinki process for our meeting to come to an end by Christmas, but I do not believe our national interests require that decision. I am, therefore, quite likely to recommend that we return to Madrid for a reconvened meeting, should we be unable to complete our work in 1982'.[73]

Initially, Kampelman's view was challenged by Richard Burt, who succeeded Lawrence Eagleburger as director of the State Department's European Bureau. Burt feared that NATO's solidarity might break apart if the Madrid meeting went on for another extension. Thus, he believed that 'our objective ... should be the early conclusion of the Madrid meeting with a non-substantive document which would preserve the CSCE process by setting the date and place for the next review conference'.[74] George Shultz did not share Burt's judgement. Shultz wrote to Reagan that 'at the moment, our Allies are not prepared to agree to such an early conclusion, and the Germans in particular will be reluctant to do so any time before their elections planned for next March'.[75] Kampelman wanted an extension and a substantial document. In October 1982, he increased the stakes and informed his allies that the Reagan administration needed more visible results.[76]

At the same time, Kampelman made a great effort to educate the Reagan administration about the virtues of the Helsinki process. In November 1982, he told his West German counterpart Jörg Kastl in confidence that he and Secretary Shultz ran the CSCE business: both the National Security Council as well as the European Bureau were kept out. In fact, its new director, Richard Burt, broke with the tradition of the European Bureau, which was to let the Europeans decide what they primarily needed from the Helsinki process. Kampelman told Kastl that Shultz did not forward Burt's policy recommendation to the president.[77] Finally, Shultz and Kampelman prevailed, and Burt came to support their approach. In January 1983, Burt noted that 'for our part, in accordance with the President's guidance we will continue to pursue agreement on a full, balanced and substantive final document which furthers Eastern compliance with CSCE obligations, particularly on human rights'.[78]

Reagan, Shultz and Kampelman were prepared to support the West Europeans to achieve a substantial concluding document. Kampelman knew that Reagan needed the release of the Pentacostals as a sign of Soviet goodwill. Finally, in May 1983, Kondrashev indicated that the Soviet leadership was prepared to grant twenty-three Pentacostals exit visas, three Helsinki monitors would be released and allowed to emigrate, and there would be possible movement on Sharansky and five other prominent cases.[79] Kampelman informed Shultz that 'we are at the "end game"' and that 'we have every reason to be pleased with the results'.[80] He managed to secure the promise that the members of the Vashchenko and Chmykhalov families could leave the Soviet Union for Israel.

Finally, the foreign ministers of the participating states signed the concluding document on 8 September 1983.[81] The Madrid Accord was a breakthrough. There was a considerable change in Reagan's position. He came to appreciate the benefits of the CSCE process and went public to defend the Madrid Accord. He made the point that 'in an ideal world, agreements such as this would not be necessary. But we believe it is the best agreement attainable, one which significantly improves on the Helsinki Final Act and advances the efforts of the West to hold out a beacon of hope for those in the East who seek a more free, just and secure life'.[82] Equally important, the Madrid Accord established mandates for subsequent interim meetings. Madrid achieved mandates for the convocation of a meeting in Ottawa on human rights and fundamental freedoms and in Bern on human contacts. And it achieved a clear-cut mandate for a specific conference on CBMs that started in Stockholm in January 1984.[83] Moreover, it set the date for the next follow-up meeting, which was to start in Vienna in October 1986, leading to significantly improved human rights practices in Eastern Europe.[84]

Looking back at the Madrid experience in his memoirs, Kampelman emphasized that the meeting 'was a major stage-setter for the East-West progress that followed'.[85] The Madrid meeting produced a more thorough and candid review of implementation than was achieved at Belgrade, with a greater range of NATO and even neutral and non-aligned delegations criticizing aspects of Eastern compliance. Max Kampelman helped to make human rights a part of a combined and coordinated Western policy.

Stephan Kieninger is a historian who specializes in the history of the Cold War with related interests in modern US history and the history of international relations. He is the author of *The Diplomacy of Détente: Cooperative Security Policies from Helmut Schmidt to George Shultz* (Routledge, 2018), which explains how pan-European trade and the Helsinki process kept détente alive despite recurring crisis in international relations. His first book, *Dynamic Détente: The United States and Europe, 1964–1975* (Rowman and Littlefield, 2016) looks into the emergence of détente and its ramifications for the transformation of Europe. He received his PhD from Mannheim University.

Notes

1. See 'Concluding Document of the Second Follow-up Meeting, Madrid, 11 November 1980 to 9 September 1983', at https://www.osce.org/mc/40871?download=true (accessed 11 June 2018).
2. Letter from Carter to Kampelman, 25 February 1983, Minnesota Historical Society, Minneapolis (hereafter referred to as MHS), Max M. Kampelman Papers, Box 13.
3. Letter from Reagan to Kampelman, 19 January 1989, MHS, Kampelman Papers, Box 13.
4. See M.M. Kampelman, *Entering New Worlds: The Memoirs of a Private Man in Public Life* (New York: Harper Collins, 1991).
5. Letter from Kampelman to Eagleburger, 12 March 1981, MHS, Kampelman Papers, Box 13.
6. Kampelman, *Entering New Worlds*, 40.
7. Author interview with Kampelman, November 2008.
8. As a case in point, Kampelman supported Helsinki Watch in its efforts to capture attention for the cause of human rights during the negotiations in Madrid. See S.B. Snyder, *Human Rights Activism and the End of the Cold War: A Transnational History of the Helsinki Network* (Cambridge: Cambridge University Press, 2011), 151–54.
9. Kampelman, *Entering New Worlds*, 224. Eventually, Kissinger supported the dynamic elements in the Helsinki Final Act, and he followed his West European partners and the advice from the State Department's Bureau of European Affairs. For a recent account on Kissinger's détente policy, see S. Kieninger, *Dynamic Détente: The United States and Europe, 1964–1975* (Lanham, MD: Rowman and Littlefield, 2016).

10. Mario Del Pero distinguishes between the 'strategic dimension' and the 'moral dimension' of the neoconservative critique of détente. See M. Del Pero, *The Eccentric Realist: Henry Kissinger and the Shaping of America's Foreign Policy* (Ithaca, NY: Cornell University Press, 2009), 121, 130.
11. See A. Hessing Cahn, *Killing Détente: The Right Attacks the CIA* (University Park, PA: Penn State University Press, 1998).
12. See 'Max Kampelman, Who Led Arms Talks, Dies at 92', *The New York Times*, 28 January 2013, http://www.nytimes.com/2013/01/29/world/europe/max-kampelman-who-led-arms-talks-with-soviet-union-dies-at-92.html?_r=0.
13. Letter from Kampelman to Rostow, 18 November 1982, MHS, Kampelman Papers, Box 14.
14. Ibid.
15. For the background, see Stephan Kieninger, *The Diplomacy of Détente: Cooperative Security Policies from Helmut Schmidt to George Shultz* (London: Routledge, 2018).
16. Letter from Kampelman to Eagleburger, 12 March 1981, MHS, Kampelman Papers, Box 13.
17. Letter from Eagleburger to Kampelman, no date, MHS, Kampelman Papers, Box 13.
18. Memorandum by Kampelman on his meeting with Kondrashev, 18 December 1981, MHS, Kampelman Papers, Box 13.
19. Ibid.
20. See Telegram from the US Embassy in Moscow to the Department of State (Nr. 15174), 29 June 1978, Department of State Declassification Project, Telegrams, 1973–1979, https://aad.archives.gov/aad/createpdf?rid=144108&dt=2694&dl=2009URL (accessed 11 June 2018).
21. Message from President Reagan to Soviet General Secretary Brezhnev, 14 January 1982, in: Foreign Relations of the United States, 1981–1988, Vol. III (Soviet Union, January 1981–January 1983), U.S. Government Printing Office, Washington, DC 2016, 415-416. For the context, see Snyder, *Human Rights Activism and the End of the Cold War*.
22. See A. Dobrynin, *In Confidence: Moscow's Ambassador to America's Six Cold War Presidents* (New York: Random House, 1995), 518.
23. See S. Kieninger, 'Between Power Politics and Morality: The United States, the Long Détente, and the Transformation of Europe, 1969–1985', in O. Bange and P. Villaume (eds), *The Long Détente: Changing Concepts of Security and Cooperation in Europe, 1950s–1980s* (Budapest: Central European University Press, 2017), 281–313.
24. Remarks by Max M. Kampelman, Plenary Session CSCE, 16 February 1981, MHS, Kampelman Papers, Box 15.
25. See B. Walker, '"Neither Shy nor Demagogic": The Carter Administration Goes to Belgrade', in V. Bilandzic, D. Dahlmann and M. Kosanovic (eds), *From Helsinki to Belgrade: The First CSCE Follow-Up Meeting and the Crisis of Détente* (Bonn: Vandenhoeck and Ruprecht, 2012), 185–204.
26. Memorandum of Conversation between Brzezinski and Genscher, 14 March 1977, Jimmy Carter Presidential Library, Atlanta (GA), National Security Affairs 7, Box 33.

27. Genscher reiterated that the authorities in Poland and the Soviet Union had granted exit visas for 120,000 ethnic Germans to leave for the West since the conclusion of the Helsinki Final Act in August 1975. Ibid.
28. Memorandum of Conversation between Schmidt and Vance, 31 March 1977, Akten zur Auswärtigen Politik der Bundesrepublik Deutschland (AAPD), Vol.1977, Doc. 82, 413–31.
29. See O. Bange, '"The Greatest Happiness for the Greatest Number": The FRG and the GDR at the Belgrade CSCE Conference (1977–78)', in Bilandzic, Dahlmann and Kosanovic, *From Helsinki to Belgrade*, 225–54.
30. Memorandum from Zimmermann and Maresca, 'Europe's Future: The Ghost of Christmas Yet to Come', Georgetown University Library, Walter Stoessel Papers, Box 1.
31. See M.M. Shulman, 'On Learning to Live with Authoritarian Regimes', *Foreign Affairs* 55(1) (1977), 325–38.
32. Letter from Goldberg to Brandt, 16 March 1979, Archiv des sozialen Demokratie, Willy-Brandt-Archiv, A 11.1. (Personal Correspondence 1968–1980), vol. 89.
33. See Letter from Brandt to Goldberg, 25 May 1979, Archiv des sozialen Demokratie, Willy-Brandt-Archiv, A 11.1. (Personal Correspondence 1968–1980), vol. 89.
34. See O. Bange and G. Niedhart (eds), *Helsinki 1975 and the Transformation of Europe* (New York and Oxford: Berghahn Books, 2008).
35. See O. Bange, '"Keeping Détente Alive": Inner-German Relations under Helmut Schmidt and Erich Honecker, 1974–1982', in L. Nuti (ed.), *The Crisis of Détente in Europe: From Helsinki to Gorbachev 1975–1985* (London: Routledge, 2009), 230–43.
36. Memorandum from Vladimir Lehovich, 'Some Thoughts on Europe and the US', no date, Georgetown University Library, Stoessel Papers, Box 1. Lehovich served as Political Counselor at the US Embassy in Bonn during the second half of the 1970s.
37. See P. Villaume and O.A. Westad (eds), *Perforating the Iron Curtain: European Détente, Transatlantic Relations, and the Cold War 1965–1985* (Copenhagen: Museum Tusculanum Press, 2010).
38. For a succinct contemporary account and an appeal for more understanding and improved consultations in NATO, see H.D. Genscher, 'Toward an Overall Western Strategy for Peace, Freedom and Progress', *Foreign Affairs* 61(1) (1982), 42–66.
39. Remarks by Rijnhard van Lynden, then Dutch Ambassador in Washington, during a session of the North Atlantic Council, 13 March 1974, NATO Archives, Brussels, Minutes of the North Atlantic Council, 1969–1974 (C-R), (74)-11. For a distinction between 'détente statique' and 'détente dynamique', see J. Andréani, *Le Piège: Helsinki et la Chute du Communisme* (Paris: Odile Jacob, 2005), 41. See also N. Badalassi, *En Finir avec la Guerre Froide: La France, l'Europe at le Processus d'Helsinki, 1965–1975* (Rennes: Presses Universitaires de Rennes, 2014); Kieninger, *Dynamic Détente*.
40. Memorandum from Jonathan Greenwald to Kampelman, 'One for the Road', 21 September 1981, MHS, Kampelman Papers, Box 14.

41. See S.B. Snyder, 'The CSCE and the Atlantic Alliance: Forging a new Consensus in Madrid', *Journal of Transatlantic Studies* 8(1) (2010), 56–68; D. Selvage, 'The Superpowers and the Conference on Security and Cooperation in Europe, 1977–1983: Human Rights, Nuclear Weapons, and Western Europe', in M. Peter and H. Wentker (eds), *Die KSZE im Ost-West-Konflikt: Internationale Politik und gesellschaftliche Transformation 1975–1990* (Munich: Oldenbourg Publishers, 2012), 15–58.
42. Secretary of State Alexander Haig objected on the spot, arguing that 'Europe will go bonkers if we do that'. See US National Security Council Minutes, 22 December 1981, at http://www.margaretthatcher.org/document/110968.
43. Memorandum of Conversation between Genscher and Bush, 9 March 1982, AAPD 1982, Doc. 78, 390–94.
44. Memorandum of Conversation between Genscher and Kampelman, 2 July 1983, AAPD 1983, Doc. 196, 1015–21.
45. Memorandum of Conversation between Kohl, Genscher and Shultz, 15 April 1983, AAPD 1983, Doc. 101, 517–23.
46. Memorandum of Conversation between Kohl, Genscher, Schlüter and Ellemann-Jensen, 19 April 1983, AAPD 1983, Doc. 106, 545–58.
47. For an in-depth study on West Germany's CSCE policy, see M. Peter, *Die Bundesrepublik Deutschland im KSZE-Prozess 1975–1983: Die Umkehrung der Diplomatie* (Munich: Oldenbourg Publishers, 2015).
48. See Letter from Genscher to von Staden, 20 December 1983, AAPD 1983, Doc. 388, 1925. For a comprehensive account on Genscher's policy, see A. Bresselau von Bressensdorf, *Frieden durch Kommunikation: Das System Genscher und die Entspannungspolitik im Zweiten Kalten Krieg 1979–1982/83* (Munich: Oldenbourg Publishers, 2015).
49. Memorandum of Conversation between Reagan and Kohl, 5 March 1984, in 'The Euromissiles Crisis and the End of the Cold War: 1977–1987', at https://www.wilsoncenter.org/publication/the-euromissiles-crisis-and-the-end-of-the-cold-war-1977-1987. For the German record, see AAPD 1984, Doc. 71, 355–60.
50. See G.P. Shultz, *Turmoil and Triumph: Diplomacy, Power, and the Victory of the American Ideal* (New York: Simon and Schuster, 1993), 467–68.
51. For an assessment of the French initiative, see Memorandum by Blech, 1 February 1978, AAPD 1978, Doc. 27, 163–71.
52. See Blech's Summary of the NATO Ministerial Meeting's session of 15 December 1979, AAPD 1979, 1909–13.
53. See Peter, *Die Bundesrepublik Deutschland im KSZE-Prozess*, 349–55.
54. See Telegram from Pauls, then Bonn's NATO Ambassador, to the Foreign Office, 13 December 1979, AAPD 1979, 1899–1902.
55. See Blech's Report to the Foreign Office, 30 May 1979, AAPD 1979, 731–36.
56. See Kampelman, *Entering New Worlds*, 244–45.
57. Memorandum by Kampelman, 'French CDE Proposal at Madrid CSCE Meeting', 9 January 1981, MHS, Kampelman Papers, Box 15.
58. Memorandum of Conversation between Genscher and Haig, 9 March 1981, AAPD 1981, Doc. 62, 333–47.

59. Remarks by Max M. Kampelman, Plenary Session CSCE, 16 February 1981, MHS, Kampelman Papers, Box 15.
60. Ibid.
61. Remarks by Max M. Kampelman, Plenary Session CSCE, 12 May 1981, MHS, Kampelman Papers, Box 15.
62. Remarks by Max M. Kampelman, Chairman, US Delegation, Plenary Session CSCE, 19 May 1981, MHS, Kampelman Papers, Box 15.
63. Letter from Irina Valitova Orlov to Kampelman, 23 June 1981, MHS, Kampelman Papers, Box 13.
64. See Letter from Kampelman to Kovalev, 23 November 1982, MHS, Kampelman Papers, Box 13.
65. See Memorandum from Kampelman to Shultz, 7 May 1983, MHS, Kampelman Papers, Box 15.
66. See Peter, *Die Bundesrepublik Deutschland im KSZE-Prozess*, 456–62.
67. See ibid., 464.
68. See Memorandum of Conversation between Genscher, Cheysson, Carrington and Haig, 23 September 1981, AAPD 1981, Doc. 271, 1427–40.
69. Report from Ambassador Wieck to the Foreign Office, 10 December 1981, AAPD 1981, Doc. 358, 1919–22.
70. Memorandum from Kampelman to Eagleburger, 20 January 1982, MHS, Kampelman Papers, Box 13.
71. Letter from Haig to Kampelman, 2 August 1982, MHS, Kampelman Papers, Box 14.
72. Letter from Shultz to Kampelman, 4 September 1982, MHS, Kampelman Papers, Box 14.
73. Letter from Kampelman to Shultz, 1 October 1982, MHS, Kampelman Papers, Box 14.
74. Memorandum from Burt to Eagleburger and Shultz, 'CSCE: Memorandum for the President on our Approach to the Madrid Meeting', 14 September 1982, MHS, Kampelman Papers, Box 15.
75. Memorandum from Shultz to Reagan, 'CSCE: US Approach to the Resumed Madrid Review Conference', no date, MHS, Kampelman Papers, Box 15.
76. Memorandum by Pfeffer, 'Madrider KSZE-Folgetreffen', 13 October 1982, AAPD 1982, Doc. 270, 1403–7.
77. Kastl to the Foreign Office, 'Madrider KSZE-Folgetreffen, hier: Gespräch mit US-Del Kampelman', 11 November 1982, AAPD 1982, Doc. 300, 1561–64.
78. Memorandum from Burt to Shultz, 'CSCE: Status of Madrid Meeting', Draft, 3 January 1983, MHS, Kampelman Papers, Box 15.
79. Memorandum from Kampelman to Shultz, 7 May 1983, MHS, Kampelman Papers, Box 15.
80. Memorandum from Kampelman to Burt, 12 May 1983, MHS, Kampelman Papers, Box 15.
81. However, the meeting was overshadowed by the shootdown of Korean Airlines flight 007 by the USSR. The Soviet Union first denied the shootdown, then claimed it was a spy plane and, at last, a provocation by the United States. The hardliners in the Reagan administration did not want

Secretary Shultz to attend the meeting. Finally, Shultz barely prevailed, convincing Reagan to let him go by promising to discuss only KAL 007 and the failure of the Soviets to release Sharansky. See Shultz, *Turmoil and Triumph*, 364–70.
82. Statement by the President, for immediate release, 15 July 1983, MHS, Kampelman Papers, Box 16.
83. The preparatory meeting started in October 1983.
84. See S.B. Snyder, 'The Foundation for Vienna: A Reassessment of the CSCE in the mid 1980s', *Cold War History* 10(4) (2010), 493–512.
85. Kampelman, *Entering New Worlds*, 279.

Bibliography

Andréani, J. *Le Piège: Helsinki et la Chute du Communisme*. Paris: Odile Jacob, 2005.

Badalassi, N. *En Finir avec la Guerre Froide: La France, l'Europe at le Processus d'Helsinki, 1965–1975*. Rennes: Presses Universitaires de Rennes, 2014.

Bange, O. '"The Greatest Happiness for the Greatest Number": The FRG and the GDR at the Belgrade CSCE Conference (1977–78)', in V. Bilandzic, D. Dahlmann and M. Kosanovic (eds), *From Helsinki to Belgrade: The First CSCE Follow-Up Meeting and the Crisis of Détente* (Bonn: Vandenhoeck and Ruprecht, 2012), 225–54.

Bange, O. '"Keeping Détente Alive": Inner-German Relations under Helmut Schmidt and Erich Honecker, 1974–1982', in L. Nuti (ed.), *The Crisis of Détente in Europe: From Helsinki to Gorbachev 1975–1985* (London: Routledge, 2009), 230–43.

Bange, O., and G. Niedhart (eds). *Helsinki 1975 and the Transformation of Europe*. New York and Oxford: Berghahn Books, 2008.

Bresselau von Bressensdorf, A. *Frieden durch Kommunikation: Das System Genscher und die Entspannungspolitik im Zweiten Kalten Krieg 1979–1982/83*. Munich: Oldenbourg Publishers, 2015.

Del Pero, M. *The Eccentric Realist: Henry Kissinger and the Shaping of America's Foreign Policy*. Ithaca, NY: Cornell University Press, 2009.

Dobrynin, A. *In Confidence: Moscow's Ambassador to America's Six Cold War Presidents*. New York: Random House, 1995.

Genscher, H.D. 'Toward an Overall Western Strategy for Peace, Freedom and Progress'. *Foreign Affairs* 61(1) (1982), 42–66.

Hessing Cahn, A. *Killing Détente: The Right Attacks the CIA*. University Park, PA: Penn State University Press, 1998.

Kampelman, M.M. *Entering New Worlds: The Memoirs of a Private Man in Public Life*. New York: Harper Collins, 1991.

Kieninger, S. 'Between Power Politics and Morality: The United States, the Long Détente, and the Transformation of Europe, 1969–1985', in O. Bange and P. Villaume (eds), *The Long Détente: Changing Concepts of Security and Cooperation in Europe, 1950s–1980s* (Budapest: Central European University Press, 2017), 281–313.

Kieninger, S. *The Diplomacy of Détente: Cooperative Security Policies from Helmut Schmidt to George Shultz*. London: Routledge, 2018.

Kieninger, S. *Dynamic Détente: The United States and Europe, 1964–1975*. Lanham, MD: Rowman and Littlefield, 2016.

Peter, M. *Die Bundesrepublik Deutschland im KSZE-Prozess 1975–1983: Die Umkehrung der Diplomatie*. Munich: Oldenbourg Publishers, 2015.

Selvage, D. 'The Superpowers and the Conference on Security and Cooperation in Europe, 1977–1983: Human Rights, Nuclear Weapons, and Western Europe', in M. Peter and H. Wentker (eds), *Die KSZE im Ost-West-Konflikt: Internationale Politik und gesellschaftliche Transformation 1975–1990* (Munich: Oldenbourg Publishers, 2012), 15–58.

Shulman, M.M. 'On Learning to Live with Authoritarian Regimes'. *Foreign Affairs* 55(1) (1977), 325–38.

Shultz, G.P. *Turmoil and Triumph: Diplomacy, Power, and the Victory of the American Ideal*. New York: Simon and Schuster, 1993.

Snyder, S.B. 'The CSCE and the Atlantic Alliance: Forging a New Consensus in Madrid'. *Journal of Transatlantic Studies* 8(1) (2010), 56–68.

Snyder, S.B. 'The Foundation for Vienna: A Reassessment of the CSCE in the mid 1980s'. *Cold War History* 10(4) (2010), 493–512.

Snyder, S.B. *Human Rights Activism and the End of the Cold War: A Transnational History of the Helsinki Network*. Cambridge: Cambridge University Press, 2011.

Villaume, P., and O.A. Westad (eds). *Perforating the Iron Curtain: European Détente, Transatlantic Relations, and the Cold War 1965–1985* (Copenhagen: Museum Tusculanum Press, 2010).

Walker, B. '"Neither Shy nor Demagogic": The Carter Administration Goes to Belgrade', in V. Bilandzic, D. Dahlmann and M. Kosanovic (eds), *From Helsinki to Belgrade: The First CSCE Follow-Up Meeting and the Crisis of Détente* (Bonn: Vandenhoeck and Ruprecht, 2012), 185–204.

PART II

THE TRANSNATIONAL PROMOTION OF HUMAN RIGHTS AND THE ROLE OF DISSIDENCE

5

THE COMMITTEE OF CONCERNED SCIENTISTS AND THE HELSINKI FINAL ACT
'Refusenik' Scientists, Détente and Human Rights
Elisabetta Vezzosi

Introduction

In his interesting essay on the relationship between scientific internationalism, human rights and the Cold War, historian Paul Rubinson seems to agree with historian Joseph Manzione's assertion that 'bipolar scientific internationalism' existed that would unite the scientific community with an anti-communist and pro-Western ideology.[1] Scientific internationalism, therefore, although it engaged with human rights in many different ways, would be driven mainly by the strength of scientific values, preferring not to be overly involved in the dynamics of international politics. Over time, scientists would abandon their concern for human rights in the belief that 'science would be international, but noncontroversial'.[2]

These contentions and this conclusion did not match the experience of the Committee of Concerned Scientists (CCS), an independent national organization that had begun its work as an ad hoc committee in Washington, DC and New York City in September 1972 when a group of American scientists recognized the need to translate into constructive action the deep concern that they felt for their Soviet, and in particular Jewish, colleagues who were being denied basic scientific and personal rights because of their wish to emigrate and their view of human rights. Within a short space of time, as a result of petitions, official denunciations, public meetings and publications, the Committee had grown in terms of members and objectives to such an extent that it established itself formally in 1973 with a leadership of forty executive members and an advisory board of fifteen national sponsors. Its membership rose to four thousand in 1974. A central role was attributed to the executive directors, mostly women, about whom we still have only precious little information. Ruth Levine (1973–74), Lilli S. Chertoff (1974–76) and Dorothy Hirsch (1977–2003) played a key role in building national and international networks.

The universal principles that the CCS embraced were very clear: freedom for scientists and scholars; freedom to exchange personal and scientific information and data; freedom of research, publication and travel for scientific encounters, lectures and conferences; freedom of association, emigration and preservation of individual and collective human rights without distinction of race, language, religion, age, sex or social background. The objective of the Committee, which had been formed specifically to protect the human rights of scientists, was to create a national and international network with other organizations – not necessarily professional organizations – that shared the same aims.

The Committee supported international scientific exchanges, especially between the United States and the Soviet Union, and insisted that the protection of human rights should in no way be conditioned by détente, the period of improved relations between the United States and the Soviet Union during the 1970s. During the Annual Conference of 1973, the CCS dealt with the topic of the recognition, implementation and preservation of individual and collective human rights, stating:

> We fully support international scientific exchange and collaboration, especially between the United States and Soviet Union. But it is our firm conviction that mankind will not reap the benefits of scientific progress if those basic human rights and freedoms, which are the essence of science, are thwarted or subverted in any nation, against any person. These human rights are not negotiable; they must not be sacrificed in the name of 'détente', because no true world détente is possible without their preservation.[3]

This position on détente evidences the determination of the CCS to oppose, when necessary, the US government's policies if they threatened to jeopardize scientific transnationalism, in which scientific and human rights should be inseparable.

The CCS insisted on the importance of the 1975 Helsinki Final Act and especially the second and third baskets, respectively 'Cooperation in the Field of Economics, of Science and Technology and of the Environment' and 'Cooperation in Humanitarian and other Fields', but did not hesitate to condemn the violation of scientists' rights in the Eastern European Helsinki nations and especially in the Soviet Union. The Commission never refrained from criticism of US foreign policy, and even if it did not have a significant role in the preparatory phase of the Conference on Security and Cooperation in Europe (CSCE), it worked vigorously to assure compliance with the Helsinki Final Act. From 1975 onwards, in fact, it monitored violations of the Act and publicly denounced them. At the same time, it sought to maintain constant exchange and consultation relations with the US government, and especially with Guyford Stever, Science Adviser to President Gerald Ford; Matthew Nimetz, Counselor of the Department of State since 1977 and Under Secretary of State for Security Assistance, Science and Technology since December 1979; and Frank Press, appointed by President Jimmy Carter as Science Adviser and Director of the Office of Science and Technology Policy in 1977.

Over the years, the CCS continued its efforts to use the Helsinki Final Act to aid oppressed colleagues, maintaining contact with the Commission on Security and Cooperation in Europe and providing it with information on violations of the Act's provisions and new proposals. The CCS showed great skill in dealing with the relationship between political power and scientific and human rights, and it had a significant role in the government's decisions during the preparation of the two CSCE follow-up meetings: the Belgrade follow-up meeting (from 4 October 1977 to 9 March 1978) and the Madrid meeting (from 11 November 1980 to 9 September 1983).

Indirect support for the action of the Committee of Concerned Scientists was provided by the English physicist John Ziman, whose writings focused especially on the nature of open science and the importance of scientific cooperation and worldwide network, possible only in a climate of freedom guaranteed by the observance of human rights. Ziman wrote as follows:

> The Scientific Community has responded weakly and ineffectually to the oppression of individual scientists, and to the inhuman misuse of scientific technique in a number of countries. There has been little recognition of the inseparable connection between the traditional norms of basic science and the political and legal liberties embodied in the international and national Codes of Human Rights. In many cases, the natural sympathy of individuals and learned societies for the plight of scientific colleagues has been inhibited by appeals to the supposed traditions of apolitical transnationalism.[4]

The Committee of Concerned Scientists rejected any form of 'apolitical transnationalism', gaining credibility and increasingly becoming the reference point to which scientists all over the United States (and even abroad) turned for consultation, information materials and help in promoting scientific and human rights.

The Refusenik Scientists and the International Scientific Community

In 1972, Benjamin Levich, a world-renowned authority in the field of physicochemical hydrodynamics and a corresponding member of the Soviet Academy of Sciences, asked the Soviet authorities for a visa to emigrate to Israel with his wife Tanya. Under the false pretext that he was in possession of nuclear secrets, Soviet authorities turned down his request and immediately afterwards deprived him of his chair at the University of Moscow, removing him from his position as director of the Hydrodynamics Institute. His name was removed from textbooks, from lists of citations and university courses, and his mail was intercepted. Even opportunities to meet or collaborate with colleagues in and outside the Soviet Union were denied him, so much so that some years later he wrote in an open letter:

> My name was removed from textbooks and university courses; all efforts are being made to make me a non-person in Soviet physical chemistry, where I have been active for 40 years. I and my family are subject to police threats, intimidation, surveillance and persecution. Several times I have been held under home arrest, detained by the KGB for questioning ... I wish to stress here that my case, as well as the whole problem of emigration of scientists, can by no means be considered a political one. I am not persecuted for being an opponent of the Soviet regime which I have never been, not for being a Jew, nor for my desire to emigrate from the USSR, but for the very fact of being a scientist ... A well-known thesis of the Soviet authorities, supported by the USSR Academy of Sciences, is that a scientist has a special responsibility to the State and, as a result, his freedom of movement should be a subject of special control by the State. This claim of the State to have a right to specifically restrict scientists' personal freedom, as compared to the freedom that other people have, is the root of the whole problem of emigration of scientists.[5]

Again in 1977, the *Literaturnaia Gazeta* (*Literary Gazette*), the official weekly publication of the Soviet Writers' Union, directed personal attacks against Levich for his ties with Western scientists and criticized the International Scientific Conference on Physicochemical and Hydrodynamics held at Oxford University in July 1977, in his honour, to celebrate his sixtieth birthday. Although 150 scientists, including nineteen Nobel Prize winners, had taken part in the conference, not only did the Soviet authorities refuse Levich permission to attend it, but they defined it as 'an organized anti-Soviet action' and a 'pro-Israel-smelling plot'.[6] In August 1973, the same authorities had forbidden five important Soviet scientists – the physicians Mark Azbel, Moshe Gitterman and Alexander Voronel (who in April 1972 organized the first International Seminar on Collective Phenomena), the mathematician Alexander Lundts and the electronic engineer Victor Brailovsky – from attending the International Conference on Magnetism that was due to be held in Moscow. They had taken part in June in a hunger strike against the denial of their right to emigrate, and in September they would publicly condemn the repressive measures taken against Andrei Sakharov.

In protest at the exclusion of their colleagues from the conference, about forty Western scientists who had attended it gathered at Voronel's house for the first of a series of informal meetings later known as the Sunday Seminars, which became an outright form of resistance for the so-called Soviet Jewish 'refuseniks', a term that identified those who were asking to emigrate but were being denied visas.[7] Forced to stay in the Soviet Union, they lost their jobs, were banned from the official Soviet scientific community and could not publish or be quoted. In some cases, they even had their degrees revoked and only with great difficulty managed to find unqualified work. Having become 'non-persons', in many cases they were arrested as 'parasites' on the grounds that they had no 'acceptable' means of support. Although these continual violations of their rights were less serious than those of the Stalinist regime, the persecution was particularly severe in the scientific and academic community and actually worsened with the establishment of détente. The political scientist Vladimir (Ze'ev) Khanin defines refusenik association in Moscow and in some other places as a 'community in the making' that experienced the transition from a semi-structured to a more institutionalized structure.[8]

The Sunday Seminars were not supported by all the refusenik scientists, some of whom preferred to attract international attention by other means such as demonstrations and petitions. However, they constituted for many scientists fundamental opportunities for scientific exchanges, vital to maintaining their professional level and to cultivating contacts with the international scientific community. In 1974, the Sunday Seminars came under attack by the Committee for State Security of the Soviet Union (KGB), which denied access to the apartment of Alexander Voronel – accused of 'parasitism' – in which the seminars were usually held. In January of the same year, Azbel, Voronel and Brailovsky began to plan an international symposium on the application of physics and mathematics to other branches of science to be held in Moscow from 1 to 5 July 1974, and in March an international organizing committee was created. With the support of many foreign scientific organizations, the Committee received 150 reports, thirty from Soviet scientists (including Andrei Sakharov) and over 120 from the United States, the UK, France and Israel. In June–July, on the same days that President Nixon visited Moscow (27 June–3 July), the police arrested the seminar organizers and their families, holding them in jail without trial. In addition, the Soviet authorities confiscated the scientific materials and cancelled the seminar.[9]

When Voronel and his wife Nina obtained their exit visa at the end of 1974, Voronel told reporters at Tel Aviv airport that the seminars were part of the struggle for emigration and had proved effective: 'Instead of us fearing the KGB it was the KGB that feared the activities of Jewish scientists'.[10] The Sunday Seminars, the International Seminars on Collective Phenomena (headed by Azbel after Voronel's departure) and the seminars on control systems and the application of mathematical methods to medicine and biology organized for the first time in 1972 by Aleksandr Lerner, the humanities seminar headed by Vitalii Rubin and the engineering seminar organized by Yuli Kosharovsky, by 1973 were a fundamental forum for the exchange of ideas. They continued with the participation of foreign, in large part American, scientists and became a lifeline for the community of refusenik scientists.[11] During the CCS annual conference of 1974, Myrna Shinbaum – member and assistant director of the National Conference on Soviet Jewry and organizer of the Second and Third World Conference on Soviet Jewry in Brussels 1976 and Jerusalem 1983 – witnessed the success of the Sunday Seminars. She described the presence of as many as twenty scientists and the indescribable excitement aroused after they took part in the seminar held on 17 November 1974 by Greg Dash of the University of Washington in Seattle at the house of Victor Brailovsky who, less than a month after the signing of the Helsinki Final Act, was prevented from attending the Fourth International Joint Conference on Artificial Intelligence in Tbilisi, Georgia.[12]

Benjamin Levich, Mark Azbel, Moshe Gitterman and Alexander Voronel are only some of the refusenik scientists for whom the Committee of Concerned Scientists unconditionally mobilized, initiating a complex debate on the choices made by the different US administrations and in particular by Secretary of State Henry Kissinger, in that those choices were dictated by the climate of détente and were resistant to any course of action that might compromise it.

Détente was at the centre of the Committee's attention and discussions to the extent that 'Scientific Exchange and Détente' and 'Secrecy and National Security' were the two themes on which the annual meeting of 1974 hinged. Richard E. Pipes, historian, Polish Jew, professor at Harvard University and expert in Russian history, was invited to the meeting to analyse the Soviet view of détente in relation to the significance attributed to 'secrecy'. A staunch opponent of détente, Pipes insisted that every time a Soviet scientist requested permission to leave the country, the level of 'secrecy' would rise. In his view, détente for the Soviets was an instrument to favour and develop commerce, access to import-export banks, technology and science, while scientific exchanges would play a significant role especially for their effect on public opinion in the world. For this reason, he advised the Committee to concentrate on the condition of certain Soviet scientists by denouncing and publicizing the violation of basic human rights, by boycotting international conferences scheduled to take place in the Soviet Union and transferring them to another venue. Pipes also urged the Committee to extend its objectives to include the 'right to emigrate' in addition to the 'right to be free'.[13]

It is difficult to determine whether Pipes' position was shared by the Committee of Concerned Scientists, which was very heterogeneous in political terms. But its activity was certainly centred on systematic denunciation of repression and the attacks on the refuseniks' seminars carried out by the KGB, the official press agency TASS and the Soviet *Literary Gazette* as acts incompatible with détente and a betrayal of the traditional standards of scientific freedom:[14]

> There is speculation that this latest Soviet attack on a seminar that has been conducted peacefully each week for three years is linked to Soviet frustration over congressional reluctance to grant 'most favored nation' status. If this is so, it would appear that the Soviet government is prepared to sacrifice even internationally accepted standards of scientific freedom to its own doctrinaire conception of détente.
>
> The charges in the Tass commentary against the Moscow scientists are known to be absurd by all Western scientists who have visited them. The reduction of Professor Voronel's possessions to bare essentials is patent refutation of the charge that he finds 'anti-Soviet activity' more profitable than work. The charges of 'parasitism' against those who were dismissed from their jobs and are prevented from taking other work in their fields is monstrous.[15]

The officials in the Committee of Concerned Scientists and the United States Department of State shared a preoccupation regarding a lack of reciprocity, equality and mutual benefit because, while cooperation in the field of science and technology was an effective tool with which to develop normal relations and lessen tensions, it would be a mistake for the United States to take part in an unequal exchange at the technological level 'in the name of détente'.[16] Their overall attitudes, however, were very different: that of the Department of State was much more cautious, while that of the CCS was, at times, more radical: 'we are having détente with uncivilized people', remarked the mathematician Mark Kac in the course of the CCS annual conference of 1975.

While the CCS considered it essential to establish a network of scientific organizations with the same goals – thanks to the efforts and urging of the executive director Mark Mellman, the International Council of Scientific Unions had modified its 'Resolution on the Free Circulation of Scientists' to include the issue of emigration and had created within it a Committee on the Safeguard of the Pursuits of Scientists – equally important for pursuit of its objectives was the continuity of relations with the Department of State, whose members were often invited to CCS meetings.

The Soviet dissidents challenged the premises of détente – cooperation between the United States and the USSR presupposed abstention on both sides from interference in the other's internal policies – maintaining that it was impossible to have relations with a government that not only systematically violated human rights but also threatened global security. The scientists who adhered to the CCS wanted instead to safeguard that policy and force the USSR to measure up to Western values, first and foremost among which was respect for basic human rights. The reference was to the International Covenant on Economic, Social and Cultural Rights and to the International Covenant on Civil and Political Rights subscribed to by the USSR in 1966 and which legally bound the signatories to respect the right of every citizen to privacy, freedom of religion, and freedom to leave his/her own country.

Moreover, the 1948 UN Universal Declaration of Human Rights was constantly cited in the struggle in favour of the refuseniks in the 1970s by the majority of the scientific associations at work in the United States, and many international scientific organizations established internal commissions dedicated to the defence of human rights.[17] The American Mathematical Society, the American Psychiatric Association, the American Physical Society, the Association for Computing Machinery and the American Society of Civil Engineers were only some of the principal organizations that included the protection of human rights among their objectives. In addition to the CCS, the American Physical Society had a very active Committee on the International Freedom of Scientists, while the American Association for the Advancement of Science and the United States National Academy of Sciences created in

1976 the Committee on Scientific Freedom and Responsibility and the Committee on Human Rights, respectively.[18] The CCS created temporary partnerships with many scientific and non-scientific societies, university departments and international organizations.[19] Furthermore, the CCS collaborated with Jewish societies: the National Conference for Soviet Jewry, an organization that coordinated the main national Jewish organizations and local Jewish community groups working to stimulate and heighten interest in the problems of the Soviet Jews; the American Jewish Committee; the Medical and Scientific Committee for Soviet Jewry of the United Kingdom; the French Scientific Committee for the Protection of Rights of Jews; the Belgian Committee in Support of the Jews in the Soviet Union; and some others.[20]

It was precisely the visible mobilization of scientists at an international level that induced the US government to acknowledge the central importance of the issue of the rights of scientists and the strength of the bond between science and domestic and foreign policy.[21] According to the CCS, science and politics were 'inexorably intertwined', even though in the warped Soviet view, science was part of 'partisan politics': 'Those scientists who fail to subordinate their work to the implementation of communism or who are not active fighters for their country (as interpreted by its political leadership) are not worthy of being scientists'.[22] It was the Jackson-Vanik Amendment to the Trade Act of 1974 – which denied most favoured nation status to some non-market economies that restricted emigration by their citizens and other human rights – that made the first move in this direction, threatening détente with its determination to interfere in the internal policy of the Soviet Union. But, as the refusenik Benjamin Levich wrote, noninterference was not an option when the rights of scientists were at risk:

> Noninterference turns out to be collaboration with the political bureaucrats in their confrontation with scientists. If science is to be preserved, we must side, instead, with the scientists when those bureaucrats force a confrontation.[23]

Scientists' Rights and Détente: The Jackson-Vanik Amendment

Starting in 1972, Democratic senator Henry M. Jackson, a Cold War liberal and committed anti-communist, had embraced the language of humanitarianism and human rights as part of an anti-communist drive alongside the American Jewish groups and the Soviet dissident movement that used the deliberations of the United Nations as means to attract world attention to their preoccupations, not least of which was the imposition of the 'Diploma tax', one of the instruments invented by the Soviet authorities to stop the 'brain drain'. In an editorial of September 1973 in *The New York Times*, Jackson pressed for a 'Human détente',[24] more than once making reference to Article 13 of the Declaration on Human Rights relating to the 'Right to freedom of movement', while Andrei Sakharov, the great dissident physicist who had led the Committee on Human Rights in the Soviet Union, supported the approval of the Jackson-Vanik Amendment in an open letter to the American Congress in 1973:

> I am appealing to the Congress of the United States to give its support to the Jackson Amendment, which represents in my view and in the view of its sponsors an attempt to protect the right of emigration of citizens in countries that are entering into new and friendlier relations with the United States. The Jackson Amendment is made even more significant by the fact that the world is only just entering on a new course of détente and it is therefore essential that the proper direction be followed [from] the outset. This is a fundamental issue, extending far beyond the question of emigration ... Adoption of the amendment therefore cannot be a threat to Soviet-American relations. All the more, it would not imperil international détente.[25]

The proponents, Jackson and Democratic congressman Charles A. Vanik, were well aware that Kissinger, who continued to see the Amendment as a serious threat to détente, opposed it, but Jackson insisted that the Amendment was in alignment with an entire tradition of America as a 'nation of immigrants' and that the right to emigrate was 'an American issue'.[26] The concern of the United States for the Russian Jews was considered a longstanding one, since in the last century at least ten American presidents, from Ulysses S. Grant to Richard Nixon, had intervened directly or indirectly in their favour.[27]

It was in support of the Jackson-Vanik Amendment to the Trade Act that once again the CCS allied itself with the National Conference for Soviet Jewry. Within the context of the World Conference of Jewish Communities on Soviet Jewry (the first took place in 1971), and especially the second, which was held in Brussels in February 1976 with the participation of 1,200 delegates from thirty-two countries, the situation of Soviet Jews was discussed in five workshops, one of which was dedicated to the CSCE – 'The Helsinki and Other International Understandings' – and another to the refuseniks – 'Prisoners of Conscience and Refuseniks'. A delegation from the CCS also took part in the conference, including the co-chairman Jack Cohen and other members of the board, some of whom delivered papers in the plenary sessions.[28]

The intense activity of the National Conference for Soviet Jewry was flanked by that of the National Interreligious Task Force on Soviet Jewry, which managed to mobilize millions of non-Jewish Americans on behalf of the Soviet Jews and met Jackson on Capitol Hill in 1972. After the meeting, Jackson affirmed that the cause of Soviet Jewry was not just their problem but 'a matter of Christian conscience and American conscience',[29] and that the organization aligned itself with the National Conference on Soviet Jewry – sometimes internally divided on tactics and strategies – in support of the protection of human rights in the USSR.[30] The two organizations, in fact, took part in the mobilization in support of the Jackson-Vanik Amendment to the Trade Act, passed in 1974 and signed by President Gerald Ford in 1975.[31] It made freedom of emigration a condition of the normalization of trade relations between the United States and countries with non-market economies, including the Soviet Union.

Leonid Brezhnev, General Secretary of the Central Committee of the Communist Party of the Soviet Union, reacted by declaring in a letter to President Ford that the new trade legislation was 'fundamentally unacceptable' and maintained that there were no laws in the USSR that denied the right to emigrate to citizens who were justified to do so and did not pose a threat to national security.[32] On the other hand, dissidents, American Jewish organizations and scientists argued that the denial of the right to emigrate had nothing to do with those considerations. 'How could it apply to the cases of many scientists who had never been connected with security matters, or had severed such connections years ago?' wrote William Korey, who was invited to a CCS meeting in 1973.[33] Director of the Illinois-Missouri office of the Anti-Defamation League (ADL) in 1954 and then of the ADL regional office in Washington, DC, Korey became involved in the Soviet Jewry Movement in 1960 when he headed the B'nai B'rith International of New York City and later the B'nai B'rith's International Council and its department of research on international politics, whose main concern was discrimination against Soviet Jews and their desire to emigrate. Korey supported approval of the Jackson-Vanik Amendment, just as in 1975 he would defend the Helsinki Final Act: 'Jackson-Mills-Vanik is deeply rooted in the American tradition, which has displayed a continuing concern for oppressed minorities abroad'.[34]

Senator Jackson, aware of the complicated nature of the discussions, argued that he would withdraw his amendment only if Kissinger managed to arrange the granting of visas to sixty thousand emigrants with the Soviet authorities. The USSR increased the number of visas in anticipation of the success of the Amendment, reducing it as soon as it had been approved. It expanded the number again in the run-up to the Strategic Arms Limitation Talks (SALT) II accord of 1979, which was not ratified because of Afghanistan's occupation in the same year. Détente was not interrupted because of the Amendment, whose power of persuasion had become somewhat weakened. Kissinger seemed to convert himself to the cause of human rights, for tactical purposes, in order to counter the perception that détente ignored the moral dimension of anti-communism and weakened it. In fact, however, as historian Daniel Sargent wrote, 'Only in the face of sustained pressure from US allies and domestic proponents did he concede space for human rights in East-West relations'.[35]

Discussion of the Jackson-Vanik Amendment accompanied the first years of activity of the CCS, which devoted debates, papers and reflections to it. Moshe Gitterman, a refusenik who had recently emigrated from the USSR, delivered a paper in October 1973 at a conference organized by the CCS entitled 'Scientific Cooperation, Human Rights and Emigration; Impact on Soviet Jewish Scientists' to express his strong support for the Amendment, which in his opinion would support the rights of Soviet scientists:

> The time is ripe. Passage of the Jackson-Mills-Vanik bill is impending. After the Middle East war both the US and the USSR are anxious to return to good terms and are willing to pay some price for it. Perhaps we can obtain the freedom of Azbel, Voronel, Levich and others at this critical moment.[36]

Despite the favourable opinion of the Committee on the aims of the Amendment, it seemed much more cautious about the concrete support for its approval. The CCS therefore decided that it would reserve its final opinion until Kissinger explained to the country the agreements reached on Soviet emigration and the USSR officially committed itself to the number of visas to be issued annually (informal agreements mentioned around fifty-five thousand visas a year).[37] This indefinite position was to become one of full consent following the insertion of the Amendment in the Trade Reform Act on 18 October 1974, so much so that Fred Pollack and Mel Pomerantz, co-chairmen of the CCS, wrote thus in the official communication of the Committee:

> We applaud the successful efforts of the Administration and the Legislative sponsors of the Jackson amendment to the Trade Reform Act, in reaching an agreement that will facilitate the free flow of people and ideas so ardently desired by the American public.

> The scientific community eagerly awaits implementation of those measures in the agreement which apply to its colleagues in the USSR. However it remains alert to possible abuses, among them, misapplication of the secrecy classification as a means of preventing individuals who so desire from leaving the Soviet Union, and any attempts to prevent scientists from continuing their productive scientific research during their waiting period.
> The good faith of the Soviet Union will be judged by the speed with which 'unreasonable impediments' are removed from the path of those who now qualify for emigration.[38]

From that moment on, the future activity of the CCS was to become a subject that required 'careful consideration and planning',[39] especially because within the area of the Jackson Amendment scientists seemed particularly unprotected and vulnerable in regard to the presumed 'secrecy' of their work, something that gave rise to concern, as in the case of the Soviet biochemist Alexander Goldfarb.[40] The question of scientific exchanges between the United States and the USSR continued to be an extremely awkward issue. It often happened that, when Soviet scientists were invited to give lectures abroad, Soviet authorities replaced them with other speakers who were, more often than not, less qualified scientists or unknown party officials who gravely compromised the standing of science in international conferences. If the American scientific organizations agreed that 'bad practices of the Russians are making détente difficult',[41] at the same time some scientists indeed considered détente dangerous for their freedom. Edward Stern wrote thus to the editor of *Physics Today* in May 1974: 'It is well documented that the repression in the Soviet Union against scientists and intellectuals in general has increased with the growth of détente'.[42] According to the CCS, no true world détente was possible without the preservation of human and scientific rights and it was unacceptable that the Soviet government sacrificed internationally accepted standards of scientific freedom to its own 'doctrinaire conception' of détente.

The Helsinki Final Act: Doubts on Soviet Implementation

In the second half of the 1970s, the attention of the Committee of Concerned Scientists focused on the Helsinki Final Act. Of the baskets into which the final document was divided, those of most interest to scientists were the second – 'Cooperation in the Field of Economics, of Science and Technology and of the Environment' – and the third – 'Cooperation in Humanitarian and other Fields', the most innovative part of the act in that it dealt with the 'human dimension'. While there were numerous denunciations of the unequal reciprocity between the United States and the Soviet Union, especially with regard to the third basket, and while President Ford gave interviews in which he complained about the 'limited progress' in the agreements with Eastern bloc countries and announced a forthcoming report and the creation of a Congressional Commission to monitor the Helsinki Final Act,[43] the CCS made it clear from the outset that it doubted the effectiveness of the agreements. In the course of the annual meeting of 1975, the physicist and CCS member Joe Birman was the first to express doubts and reservations:

> The general principles subscribed by both sides in Helsinki having to do with the free flow of information and people which I think is a broad political objective that the US has stood for in world affairs. So I would like to raise the question as to whether in our scientific and technological exchange programs sufficient intention has been put on the side of the broad political objectives that the US has had in world affairs and particularly toward moving the governments, in this case the Soviet government, towards some commonality on the general issue of human rights, individual freedom, etc.[44]

It once again became vitally important for the CCS to reinforce relations with the government agencies competent in the matter of scientific exchange programmes also because the Department of State had hitherto usually adopted a policy designed to discourage participants in scientific exchanges from discussing the situation of the ostracized Soviet scientists. In September 1976, CCS representatives met with Guyford Stever – director of the National Science Foundation, Science Advisor to President Ford and US Chairman of the joint commission which had jurisdiction over inter-government exchanges – and the intense exchange of opinion changed the Department of State's stance. Stever appeared to accept the CCS's position that 'secrecy' was a mere pretext used by Soviet authorities to prevent emigration and that numbers were not more important than the lives of individual people.[45] The meeting, as well as many other in-depth discussions on this issue, led the Department of State 'to drop their objections',[46] thus reversing the attitude hitherto adopted. In December 1976, the CCS invited as one of the main speakers at its annual meeting Zbigniew Brzezinski, at that time director of the Research Institute on International Change at Columbia University and shortly afterwards Counselor for National Security in the Carter administration, who had been asked to deliver a paper on 'the new administration's approach to détente and human rights', with special reference to his views on the role of science and scientific exchange as part of the détente process.[47]

According to the CCS, scientific and technological cooperation made an important contribution to security and cooperation among the participating states, and it could be used to promote the development of scientific and human rights. At the same time, government agencies began to turn to the CCS for information and 'guidance' on matters that fell within its competence. In 1976, the Congressional Research Service asked the Committee to provide an analysis of scientific exchanges and human rights, which would be incorporated into a report. The CCS also prepared an analysis of the scientific rights section of the Helsinki Final Act and violations thereof for the Commission on Security and Cooperation in Europe to be incorporated in their briefing books.[48]

The Committee's assessment of the Final Act's results was harshly critical of the USSR: 'The evidence would indicate that the USSR has failed to implement the Final Act thus far ... What we see here is a conscious attempt by the Soviet government to scientifically kill those people that apply for permission to emigrate or attempt to defend the civil rights of others ... The lack of free international collaboration among scientists is detrimental to scientific progress'.[49]

The Helsinki Final Act did not alter Soviet practice in the field of scientific exchanges. Many American scholars complained that exchanges with the USSR were difficult if not impossible, because Soviet authorities often did not allow their scientists to attend conferences abroad and restricted access to US scientists visiting the USSR. This constituted a serious limitation to the IREX (International Research and Exchanges Board) programme, established in 1968 by the American Council of Learned Societies and the Social Science Research Council to administer academic exchange programmes between scholars in the United States and the countries of East Central and Southeast Europe and the Soviet Union. During the academic year 1975–76, 164 Americans and 168 Soviet and East European scholars and scientists participated in these exchange programmes and the organization supported directly or indirectly some 1,000 scholars involved in various forms of East–West cooperation. Allen H. Kassof, executive director of the IREX programme, stated in front of the Commission on Security and Cooperation in Europe on 24 May 1977:

> The Helsinki document – and compliance with its provisions – is, therefore, of fundamental concern to us. The Final Act both codifies and further stimulates the gradual but significant opening of East–West communication which has now been taking place for a number of years. Very difficult and complex problems characterize the exchange of scholars, researchers, and scientists with Eastern Europe and Soviet Union – and will continue to do so for the foreseeable future.[50]

It is not surprising if, based on these problems, the University of Maryland decided to suspend the IREX programme:

> We realize that this is an unusual action which we are taking. We believe, however, that it is in the spirit of the Helsinki agreements to which our country and the Soviet Union are signatories. We also believe that this action may assist the many scientists throughout the world who are trying to achieve a true, free exchange of science and scientists. Specifically, it may permit Professor Levich to resume a full scientific career in a free atmosphere and to be reunited with his family, a humanitarian goal consistent with the Helsinki agreement and the UN Covenant on Civil and Political Rights (1966).[51]

While the CCS could claim credit for having been one of the first organizations to recognize the importance of the Helsinki Final Act in challenging the Soviet denial of scientific rights, its limits were discussed between the Committee and the staff of the Congressional Commission on Security and Cooperation in Europe in the course of special auditions on the issue. It was the co-chairman of the CCS, Bob Adelstein, who testified in front of the Commission with the purpose of reviewing 'Soviet implementation' of the provisions contained in the second basket on scientific and technological cooperation:

> In some sense Soviet implementation of these provisions is a litmus test of compliance with the free flow of people and ideas sections of the Final Act. If the Soviets reject the free flow of scientists and scientific information, an area in which benefits certainly accrue to them, it is highly unlikely that they would permit the free flow of people and ideas in areas from which they derive non direct benefits... Unfortunately, the international scientific community is suffering the loss of the talents of several hundred Soviet scientists. Because these people have applied to rejoin members of their families abroad, they are dismissed from their academic and research posts and subjected to cruel harassments. An intensive effort is made by the Soviet authorities to ostracize and isolate these scientists. Without access to libraries, conferences and colleagues they cannot keep abreast of current development. Such circumstances inevitably lead to the scientific death of these refuseniks ... We hope that the leadership of the USSR will, in the coming years, implement the Final Act in its entirety so that security and cooperation in Europe become a concrete reality rather than a lofty ideal.[52]

CCS Role at Follow-up Meetings: From Belgrade to Madrid

Adelstein's testimony was at the roots of the discussions on the theme of the Belgrade meeting, the first follow-up meeting of the CSCE, which took place between 4 October 1977 and 9 March 1978.[53] Before the meeting, the CCS participated in a series of encounters with congressmen and officials of the Department of State to make sure that issues of concern to it would be fully and properly debated in Belgrade, while Mark Azbel (who had just received his emigration visa) and Bob Adelstein met with the Science Adviser Frank Press, considered 'very responsive': 'He had some familiarity with the issues that concern us and was sympathetic. We discussed the general situation of refusenik scientists and the ways scientific exchange can be used to aid them. Dr Press was also asked to intervene on specific cases'.[54]

While from the start of the Belgrade meeting the CCS had provided studies, analyses and papers to support the United States delegation, it was Matthew Nimetz who constantly engaged with interested groups and organizations, including the CCS, for the duration of the conference, thus allowing them to have a voice in the final deliberations.[55] The CCS pointed out to Nimetz the general and specific failures on the part of the USSR to implement the Helsinki Final Act fully,[56] and Bob Adelstein declared that 'if the Soviets want to have a scientific exchange, they must treat their scientists like human beings even if they undertake to defend human rights and the Helsinki Accords'.[57] According to Nimetz, the Soviets had no definite idea of what kind of concluding documents they were prepared to endorse in Belgrade. They had difficulties adopting significant elements of US human rights and humanitarian proposals, while the United States had little interest in accepting 'seemingly anodyne but potentially troublesome Soviet ideas'.[58]

The Belgrade meeting devoted much of the time to reviewing the implementation record achieved in the period between Helsinki and Belgrade and to negotiating a concluding document that would sum up the review experience and include agreed proposals for improved implementation and further cooperation between the thirty-five participant states. The final document stressed the importance of developing détente; the need for implementation of all provisions of the Final Act fully, unilaterally, bilaterally and multilaterally; and the commitment to organize a new meeting in Madrid on 11 November 1980 and a series of experts' meetings, including a scientific one to be held in Bonn on 20 June 1978. It was highly controversial because it did not add anything to the text of the Final Act with regard to human rights and did not even reiterate any of the human rights principles included in that document.

After the Belgrade meeting, the Department of State intended to continue discussions with scientists and scientific organizations, believing that the CSCE would continue to be an important element of European policy. The existence of the Helsinki Final Act's commitments could provide inspiration and encouragement to those seeking improvements in their individual lives and in East–West relations; it constituted a public reference point for reminding the Soviets and the nations of Eastern Europe of their international obligations and responsibilities. On 20 June 1978, the experts' meeting in Bonn also discussed the organization of a possible scientific forum, an occasion to debate governmental restrictions on scientists and how they affected their work and personal freedom.[59]

The CCS continued to denounce the denial of rights to the refusenik scientists, whose situation was becoming worse in 1978 after the trials of Anatoly Sharansky – 'a living symbol of Soviet human-rights abuses in the post-Helsinki era'[60] – and Yuri Orlov, a soviet nuclear physicist, dissident and refusenik, human rights leader, founder and first chairman of the Moscow Helsinki Monitoring Group established on 12 May 1976.[61] The latter, an active member of the Sunday Seminars, was accused of treason and passing classified information, including scientific material, to intelligence agents in the West.[62] The Department of State denounced his arrest, declaring that President Carter and Secretary of State Cyrus Vance would express their concern to the Soviet government. Many scientists from cities other than Moscow were prevented from taking part in the refuseniks' seminars or publishing in Western scientific journals, while KGB interrogations continued without interruption, as did the searches of homes and the application of restrictions that represented downright 'scientific death' for many.

In July 1978, during Sharansky's trial in Moscow, the ad hoc organization 'Scientists for Sakharov, Orlov and Shcharansky' (SOS) invited his wife Avital, then living in Israel, to meet American scientists around the country to obtain support for her husband. They then embarked on a moratorium on scientific exchanges between individual American scientists and the Soviet Union. Owen Chamberlain, Nobel Prize winner for Physics in 1959 and professor at Berkeley, protested bitterly about the trial of the scientists in testimony given before the Sub-Commission on Science and Technology in July 1978: some four hundred scientists had signed a 'Statement of Conscience' in which they expressed their desire to withdraw cooperation with the Soviet Union until the scientists were released from prison, and they reiterated that it should be American and Soviet scientists, and not governments, that defined the form of the exchanges: 'In summary, American scientists are becoming more demonstrative in their opposition to Soviet strictures on human rights'.[63] The next year, in March 1979, about 2,400 American scientists decided to suspend, as individuals, all professional cooperation with Soviet colleagues, and in 1980 the 'Scientists for Sakharov, Orlov and Shcharansky' organized a mass campaign which collected the signatures of 7,900 scientists from forty-four countries for a six-month moratorium on scientific cooperation with Soviet scientists from May to November 1980.[64]

The CCS, albeit with deep internal divisions, was always opposed to the SOS's position in support of a blanket boycott of all forms of scientific cooperation with the Soviet Union. Mark Kac, an internationally renowned mathematician and member of the CCS Board, wrote to one of the leaders of the SOS, Paul J. Flory, on the subject. While the CCS was in complete agreement with the sense of outrage that prompted the SOS's action, it found itself 'in an unfortunate disagreement with SOS as to the tactical value of the action it took' because a blanket boycott was considered a 'one shot affair making the much-needed repetitive protests ineffective'.[65] Furthermore, the CCS opposed the suspension of the relations with refusenik colleagues which exchanges and meetings greatly facilitated. Although Kac wrote to Flory that 'it would be most unfortunate if trying to reach the same goals we would find ourselves divided by tactical differences and lack of coordination',[66] two years later, in July 1981, Paul J. Flory reiterated his position: 'In conclusion, advocacy of relaxation of restrictions on US-Soviet scientific cooperation at present would have disastrous consequences. We should redouble our efforts, not relax them'.[67]

After the Helsinki Final Act and above all after the Belgrade follow-up meeting, there was an increase in the number of Soviet Jews who emigrated – 20,509 from June 1977 to May 1979 – but the number of refuseniks remained the same. So, in this regard, the commitment of the organizations of scientists did not waver. The Soviet Union's refusal to respect the Helsinki agreements was denounced in no uncertain terms in the *Bulletin of the Atomic Scientists*, in which it was stressed that transnational scientific cooperation – 'An International Republic of Science' – was the only real basis for the advancement of science:

> It is only in a transnational sphere that a clear political orientation for science can be seen. The ideal of an international Republic of Science can never be set aside, for it embodies the fundamental norm of universalism that is the only guarantee of the reliability and objectivity of scientific knowledge... In the last few years the call for the protection of the human rights of scientists and others has become a significant factor in world politics.[68]

During 1980, the Department of State and the CCS were involved in the preparation of the CSCE second follow-up meeting in Madrid, which was held from 11 November 1980 to 9 September 1983. The Department suggested that the meeting authorize a committee to meet before the review conference and formulate guidelines on the definition of the relationship between national security and scientific inquiry and time limitations in restrictions imposed upon scientists for security reasons.[69] It was the CCS's fervent hope that in Madrid the signatories of the Final Act would make substantial progress towards eliminating these restrictions for the benefit of all.[70]

The Madrid meeting, however, did not respond to the great expectations concerning a substantial change in the Soviet attitude. The refusenik mathematician Naum Meiman, one of the scientists in which the CCS was very strongly interested, wrote after the conference:

> I have no idea at all what decisions will eventually be made at the Madrid Conference on the implementation of the Helsinki Accords. I don't know whether its participants will succeed in coming to terms as was the case of Belgrade, ostensibly not to see the naked King. But I do know only far too well that my own personal rights which were proclaimed and guaranteed in Helsinki have been harshly and cynically violated for about six years now.[71]

Conclusion

In 1978, Benjamin Levich and his wife Tanya succeeded in emigrating after six years of repeated requests and refusals. Levich was the only member of the Soviet Academy of Sciences who was allowed to leave the country; after a brief stay in Israel, he settled in the United States, where he accepted the position of Albert Einstein Professor of Science at City College of the City University of New York.[72] The success of Levich's request to emigrate, though belated, was due to Senator Edward Kennedy's interest in the case and to the untiring efforts of the Committee of Concerned Scientists, one of the first organizations to make public its support of Sakharov and the emigration of minorities from the Soviet Union.[73] The CCS denounced the obstructionism of the Soviet authorities in implementing scientific exchanges and allowing scientists to emigrate. Robert Adelstein wrote in his report on the Belgrade meeting that the CCS's intention was not to end scientific exchanges with the USSR, but only on condition that the Soviets treated their scientists as human beings and respected the Helsinki Accords.[74]

To put pressure on the Soviet authorities, the mobilization of the international scientists' community was crucial. The Committee's efforts in urging an intensification of the activities of their European colleagues were therefore unceasing.[75] It was convinced that scientists should act by creating pressure groups to lobby not only their governments but also the Soviet authorities, who feared action in favour of human rights by any creditable organization in the public eye. Brezhnev complained in 1978 that human rights constituted 'the main line of ideological attack against socialist countries'.[76]

A partial balance of the Committee's activity was drawn up by Mark Mellman at the end of 1976:

> We can say confidently that the year has been a good one. While our colleagues abroad are still in peril, we have no doubt made progress. Some leading refusenik scientists have been permitted to emigrate and are now leading productive lives. Others still in the Soviet Union have been aided in their struggle to maintain their viability as scientists. The persecution of some of their colleagues in other parts of the world has been eased as well. Perhaps we are never aware of the most important result of our efforts, the persecution that is not leveled at a scientist because his government fears a condemnatory reaction.[77]

The CCS organized endless initiatives to support refusenik scientists in the United States and elsewhere. Two of the most significant were the Tbilisi Artificial Intelligence Conference (fruit above all of Jack Minker's work), 'the most spectacular and successful of 1975'[78] because the refuseniks Alexander Lerner and the Goldstein brothers were allowed to attend, and a conference on the occasion of the fifth anniversary of the establishment of the International Seminar on Collective Phenomena (closed in 1981 by the KGB) chaired by Mark Azbel and held in Moscow between 17 and 20 April 1977 with huge international participation (ten American scientists). These occasions were of vital importance given continued Soviet repression of informal seminars organized by scientists, including those outside of Moscow: Naum Salansky in Vilnius, Vladimir Kislik in Kiev and many others are cases in point. Threatened with arrest in 1977, Azbel received his exit visa in the same year, and after his departure Brailovsky guided the seminar. When he was arrested in 1980 and then sent into exile, the seminars tirelessly continued in his apartment or in the apartments of Yakov Alpert and Alik Yoffe.

Within a few years, the CCS had become one of the most significant points of reference for American and foreign scientists' associations on the question of scientists' human rights, and its credibility was recognized at an international level: 'We have established a reputation for credibility and have been meticulous in checking and double checking the information we circulate. We have received requests for assistance in setting up similar organizations from several foreign countries and have provided help and guidance wherever possible'.[79]

Cautious in its approach to the possible success of the Jackson-Vanik Amendment and the outcome of the Helsinki Final Act – which could, nonetheless, boast two important moments in its affirmation of human rights at an international level – the Committee of Concerned Scientists advanced proposals that shunned an acritical attitude to détente if the cause of fundamental human rights was marginalized in its name. The CCS was fully aware of the importance of maintaining continuous relations with the US Department of State in the conviction that safeguarding human rights was a core element in international relations, but it was only prior to and during the Conference of Belgrade that it became an actual point of reference for representatives of the American government.

The CCS was very active in preparation of the first scientific forum – planned for 18–29 February 1980 in Hamburg – called by the Helsinki Final Act to discuss 'current and future developments in science and to promote the expansion of contacts, communications and exchange of information between scientific institutions and scientists'.[80] In its view, the US delegation should focus its interest primarily on free international exchanges of scientists and scientific information and human rights because the scientific forum was intended to follow up on the implementation of Basket Two of the Final Act concerning scientific and technological cooperation:

> The forum should begin to formulate proposals designed to break down harmful intrusions on free interchange. For example, national security considerations have been invoked by both East and West to limit cooperation at various times and on various projects. At the forum, scientists could begin to formulate guidelines limiting the impingement of security interests on international scientific cooperation.[81]

Scientists, like the majority of American citizens, were deeply disturbed by the Soviet invasion of Afghanistan in 1979. According to the CCS, it was very important to send a clear message to the Soviet Union that the world regarded the aggression as reprehensible, but the actions taken to demonstrate the resistance to Soviet aggression could not lead irreversibly to military conflict between the two countries. The US administration had to draw a distinction between restricting the sale of high technology to the Soviets and restricting scientific exchanges that could erroneously deny the Soviets access to American scientific advances.[82] While détente entered a period of irreversible crisis, the indefatigable work of the Committee of Concerned Scientists led to the indisputable conviction that 'Concern for Human Rights is firmly in place on the personal and institutional agendas of the American scientific community'.[83]

Elisabetta Vezzosi, PhD (Genova-Minneapolis), is Professor of United States History and Women's and Gender History at Università di Trieste. A former President of the Italian Society of Women Historians, she is currently President of the Italian Association for North American Studies. Her main research fields are Italian immigration in the United States, history of the Welfare State, women's and gender history, American scientists during the Cold War, African American women and international relations. Her latest book is *Discourses of Emancipation and the Boundaries of Freedom* (Edizioni Università di Trieste, 2015, ed. with Leonardo Buonomo). Forthcoming in 2019 is *African American Women, Panafricanism and Human Rights: A Transnational Vision, 1893–1960*.

Notes

1. P. Rubinson, '"For Our Soviet Colleagues": Scientific Internationalism, Human Rights, and the Cold War', in A. Iriye, P. Goedde and W.I. Hitchcock (eds), *The Human Rights Revolution: An International History* (New York: Oxford University Press, 2012), 245–64; J. Manzione, '"Amusing and Amazing and Practical and Military": The Legacy of Scientific Internationalism in American Foreign Policy, 1945–63', *Diplomatic History* 24(1) (2000), 49–55.
2. Rubinson, '"For Our Soviet Colleagues"', 260.
3. Committee of Concerned Scientists, Annual Conference, 28 October 1973, 'Scientific Cooperation, Human Rights and Emigration; Impact on Soviet Jewish Scientists', Chairman Dr Melvin Pomerantz, Committee of Concerned Scientists Records (CCSR), Series I: Administrative Files, 1973–2006, Box 1, Folder Annual Meeting 1973, 2–3, Rare Books and Manuscript Library, Columbia University Libraries (RBML – CUL), HR#0004. See also E. Callen and E.A. Stern, 'Abuses of Scientific Exchanges: Détente Ought Not to Be a Shield for Soviet Tactics', *The Bulletin of the Atomic Scientists* 31(2) (1975), 32–35.
4. J. Ziman, *Of One Mind: The Collectivization of Science* (Dordrecht: Springer Science & Business Media, 1997), 261. See also J. Ziman, P. Sieghart and J. Humphrey, *The World of Science and the Rule of Law: A Study of the Observance and Violations of the Human Rights of Scientists in the Participating States of the Helsinki Accords* (New York: Oxford University Press, 1986).
5. CCS, An open letter from Prof. Benjamin Levich (but Veniamin Levich), Moscow, October 1976, CCSR, Series I: Administrative Files, 1973–2006, Box 1, Folder Annual Meeting 1975, RBML – CUL.

6. On the importance of the conference, labelled 'provocative' by the Soviet *Literary Gazette*, see B. Spalding, 'Protest by Conference', *New Scientist* 78(1101) (1978), 288–89. See also G. Beckerman, *When They Come for Us, We'll Be Gone: The Epic Struggle to Save Soviet Jewry* (Boston and New York: Houghton Mifflin Harcourt, 2010).
7. The term 'refusenik' was coined in 1971 by the Soviet Jewry human rights activist Michael Sherbourne, who translated it from the Russian 'otkaznik', and it was internationally recognized. For the genesis of the term, see M. Hurst, *British Human Rights Organizations and Soviet Dissent, 1965–1985* (London and Oxford: Bloomsbury Publishing, 2016), 105. See also P. Buwalda, *They Did Not Dwell Alone: Jewish Emigration from the Soviet Union, 1967–1990* (Washington, DC: The Woodrow Wilson Center Press, 1997), 62; and M. Azbel, *Refusenik, Trapped in the Soviet Union* (New York: Paragon House Publishers, 1981). See also Y. Kosharovsky, "We Are Jews Again". Jewish Activism in the Soviet Union (Syracuse NY: Syracuse University Press, 2017)
8. V.Z. Khanin, 'The Refusenik Community in Moscow: Social Networks and Models of Identification', *East European Jewish Affairs* 41(1–2) (2011), 77–88.
9. 'Memorandum from I. Andropov to the CPSU Central Committee Moscow, 18 April 1974 n. 1024-A', in B. Mozorov, *Documents on Soviet Jewish Emigration* (Oxford: Routledge, 2013), 197.
10. Y. Shargil, 'Voronel and Wife in Israel', *Jewish Telegraphic Agency. Daily News Bulletin* 41(57) (30 December 1974), 1.
11. Myrna Shinbaum, National Conference on Soviet Jewry, Report from the USSR, Committee of Concerned Scientists, Minutes of Annual Conference, 1 December 1974, CCSR, Series I: Administrative Files, 1973–2006, Box 1, Folder Annual Meeting 1974, RBML – CUL, 5.
12. M. Shinbaum, 'Mobilizing America: The National Conference on Soviet Jewry', in M. Friedman and A.D. Chernin (eds), *A Second Exodus: The American Movement to Free Soviet Jews* (Hanover, NH: Brandeis University Press, 1999), 173–80.
13. Committee of Concerned Scientists, Minutes of Annual Conference, 1 December 1974, Background Papers Prof. Richard E. Pipes, Harvard University, CCSR, Series I: Administrative Files, 1973–2006, Box 1, Folder Annual Meeting 1974, RBML – CUL, 3.
14. Lilli S. Chertoff to Dr Edward A. Stern, 11 August 1975, CCSR, Series I: Administrative Files, 1973–2006, Box 1, Folder Annual Meeting 1975, RBML – CUL.
15. CCS, Press release – For immediate release, Lilli S. Chertoff, New York, 16 October 1974, CCSR, Series I: Administrative Files, 1973–2006, Box 1, Folder Annual Meeting 1974, RBML – CUL.
16. Committee of Concerned Scientists, US-USSR Scientific and Technological Exchange Programs, Speech by William A. Root, Department of State, at the Annual Conference of the Committee of Concerned Scientists at Automation House, 14 December 1975, Draft 12/9/1975, CCSR, Series I: Administrative Files, 1973–2006, Box 1, Folder Annual Meeting 1975, RBML – CUL.

17. C. Corillon, 'The Role of Science and Scientists in Human Rights', *Annals of the American Academy of Political and Social Science* 506(1) (1989), 129–40; R.P. Claude, *Science in the Service of Human Rights* (Philadelphia: University of Pennsylvania Press, 2002); J. Minker, *Scientific Freedom and Human Rights: Scientists of Conscience during the Cold War* (Los Alamitos, CA: IEEE CS Press, 2012). See also C.P. Peterson, *Globalizing Human Rights: Private Citizens, the Soviet Union, and the West* (New York: Routledge, 2012).
18. See also B.J. Keys, *Reclaiming American Virtue: The Human Rights Revolution of the 1970s* (Cambridge, MA: Harvard University Press, 2014), 220.
19. The Centre de Physique Théorique at Palaiseau, France; the Institute of Theoretical Physics at Trondheim; the Norwegian Physical Society; the Institute of Physics in Oslo, Norway; the Jerusalem Institute for Scientific Research and Development; the Société Française de Physique, sponsor of the International Seminar on Collective Phenomena; the Canadian Committee of Scientists and Scholars for Soviet Dissidents; the Canadian Science for Peace; the International Council of Scientific Union; the International Union of Pure and Applied Chemistry Scientists for the Release of Soviet Refuseniks in London; the UNESCO Committee on Conventions and Recommendations; the Center for Human Rights; and the Secretary General of the United Nations organization (UN).
20. See M.R. Sanua, *Let Us Prove Strong: The American Jewish Committee, 1945–2006* (Waltham, MA: Brandeis University Press, 2007), 288; G.M. Riegner, *Never Despair: Sixty Years in the Service of the Jewish People and Human Rights* (Chicago: Ivan R. Dee, 2006); M. Galchinsky, *Jews and Human Rights: Dancing at Three Weddings* (Lanham, MD: Rowman & Littlefield Publishing Group, Inc., 2008); Friedman and Chernin, *A Second Exodus*; H.L. Feingold, *'Silent No More': Saving the Jews of Russia, the American Jewish Effort, 1967–1989* (Syracuse, NY: Syracuse University Press, 2007); P. Peretz, *Let My People Go: The Transnational Politics of Soviet Jewish Emigration during the Cold War* (New York: Routledge, 2017).
21. L.L. Lubrano, 'National and International Politics in US-USSR Scientific Cooperation', *Social Studies of Science* 11(4) (1981), 451–80.
22. M. Mellman (executive director of the Committee of Concerned Scientists Inc.), 'Human Rights: A Different Perspective', *The Bulletin of the Atomic Scientists* 34(9) (1978), 60–61.
23. CCS, An open letter from Prof. Benjamin Levich, Moscow, October 1976, CCSR, Series I: Administrative Files, 1973–2006, Box 1, Folder Annual Meeting 1975, RBML – CUL.
24. H.M. Jackson, 'First, Human Détente', *The New York Times*, 9 September 1973.
25. A. Sakharov, 'Open Letter to the United States Congress', 14 September 1973, *The Congressional Record*, 13 December 1974. See also C. Rhéaume, 'Western Scientists' Reaction to Andrei Sakharov's Human Rights Struggle in the Soviet Union, 1968–1989', *Human Rights Quarterly* 30(1) (2008), 1–20.
26. Quoted in W.D. Korey, 'The Struggle over Jackson-Mills-Vanik', *American Jewish Year Book* 75 (1974–75), 201.
27. Ibid.

28. CCS, Brussels Conference, CCSR, Series I: Administrative Files, 1973–2006, Box 1, Folder Annual Meeting 1976, RBML – CUL.
29. Quoted in Sanua, *Let Us Prove Strong*, 288.
30. S. Altshuler, *From Exodus to Freedom: A History of the Soviet Jewry Movement* (Lanham, MD: Rowman & Littlefield Publishers, 2005), 29.
31. Section 401, Title IV of the Trade Act of 1974, P.L. 93-618.
32. Quoted in J.M. Hanhimäki, *The Rise and Fall of Détente: American Foreign Policy and the Transformation of the Cold War* (Washington, DC: Potomac Books, 2012).
33. Korey, 'The Struggle over Jackson-Mills-Vanik', 222.
34. 'The Right to Leave', text of the speech delivered by Dr William Korey, director of B'nai B'rith UN control office, at a recent American Israel Public Affairs Committee policy conference, n.d., CCSR, Series I: Administrative Files, 1973–2006, Box 1, Folder Annual Meeting 1973, RBML – CUL.
35. D.J. Sargent, *A Superpower Transformed: The Remaking of American Foreign Relations in the 1970s* (Oxford and New York: Oxford University Press, 2015), 210. See also Barbara Keys, 'Congress, Kissinger, and the Origins of Human Rights Diplomacy', *Diplomatic History* 34(5) (2010), 823–51.
36. Manuscript, text of the conference of Gitterman, n.d., CCSR, Series I: Administrative Files, 1973–2006, Box 1, Folder Annual Meeting 1973, RBML – CUL.
37. Typewritten text, n.d., 'The Jackson Amendment', CCSR, Series I: Administrative Files, 1973–2006, Box 1, Folder Annual Meeting 1974, RBML – CUL.
38. CCS News release, For immediate release, 21 October 1974, CCSR, Series I: Administrative Files, 1973–2006, Box 1, Folder Annual Meeting 1974, RBML – CUL.
39. Lilli S. Chertoff, executive director, to Dear Colleague, 4 November 1974, CCSR, Series I: Administrative Files, 1973–2006, Box 1, Folder Annual Meeting 1974, RBML – CUL.
40. Lilli S. Chertoff to Prof. Morrel H. Cohen, James Franck Institute, University of Chicago, 29 October 1974, CCSR, Series I: Administrative Files, 1973–2006, Box 1, Folder Annual Meeting 1974, RBML – CUL.
41. Committee of Concerned Scientists, Minutes of Annual Conference, 1 December 1974, Separate typewritten, CCSR, Series I: Administrative Files, 1973–2006, Box 1, Folder Annual Meeting 1974, RBML – CUL, 1.
42. Edward Stern to Editor of *Physics Today*, 15 May 1974, CCSR, Series V: Subject Files, 1970–2002, Box 107, Folder Scientific Exchange Programs, 1974, RBML – CUL.
43. D. Binder, 'Ford Sees Some Gains under Helsinki Pact', *The New York Times*, 9 December 1976.
44. Joe Birman, intervention, Annual Meeting 1975 – discussion – tape 1, CCSR, Series I: Administrative Files, 1973–2006, Box 1, Folder Annual Meeting 1975, RBML – CUL. In 2006, Joe Birman was awarded 'The Heinz R. Pagels Human Rights of Scientists Award'.

45. Mark S. Mellman, Meeting with Dr H. Guyford Stever, 9 September 1976, CCSR, Series V: Subject Files, 1970–2002, Box 107, Folder Scientific Exchange Programs 1974–1976, RBML – CUL.
46. CCS, Annual Report, December 1976, CCSR, Series I: Administrative Files, 1973–2006, Box 1, Folder Annual Meeting 1976, RBML – CUL, 5.
47. Letter from Jack Cohen (National Co-Chairman) and H. Eugene Stanley (National Co-Chairman) to Dr Zbigniew Brzezinski, Research Institute on International Change, New York, 16 November 1976, CCSR, Series I: Administrative Files, 1973–2006, Box 1, Folder Annual Meeting 1976, RBML – CUL.
48. CCS, Annual Report, December 1976, CCSR, Series I: Administrative Files, 1973–2006, Box 1, Folder Annual Meeting 1976, RBML – CUL, 6.
49. Mark Mellman to Robert Rand, 27 October 1976, CCSR, Series IV: Organizations and Conferences, 1973–2005, Box 91, Folder CSCE – Belgrade 1977, RBML – CUL.
50. 'Statement of Dr. Allen H. Kassof, Executive Director, IREX', in *Hearings before the Commission on Security and Cooperation in Europe, Ninety-Fifth Congress, First Session on Implementation of the Helsinki Accords*, Vol. III, *Information Flow, and Cultural and Educational Exchange, 19, 24 and 25 May 1977* (Washington, DC: US Government Printing Office, 1977), 76 and 78.
51. Letter from some scientists of the Maryland University, Department of Computer Science, 8 June 1976, to Dr Allen H. Kassof, Executive Director International Research & Exchange Board, New York, CCSR, Series IV: Organizations and Conferences, 1973–2005, Box 91, Folder CSCE – Belgrade 1977, RBML – CUL.
52. 'Statement of Dr. Robert Adelstein, Co-chairman, Committee of Concerned Scientists', in *Basket Three: Implementation of the Helsinki Accords. Hearings before the Commission on Security and Cooperation in Europe, Ninety-Fifth Congress, First Session on Implementation of the Helsinki Accords*, Vol. III, *Information Flow, and Cultural and Educational Exchange, 19, 24 and 25 May 1977* (Washington, DC: US Government Printing Office, 1977), 99 and 103. See also Committee of Concerned Scientists, Inc., Annual Report, December 1977, CCSR, Series IV: Organizations and Conferences, 1973–2005, Box 91, Folder Annual Meeting 1977, RBML – CUL, 7.
53. V. Bilandžić, D. Dahlmann and M. Kosanović (eds), *From Helsinki to Belgrade: The First CSCE Follow-up Meeting and the Crisis of Détente* (Göttingen: V&R Unipress, 2012). See also S.B. Snyder, 'Follow-up at Belgrade: How Human Rights Activists Shaped the Helsinki Process', paper presented at the conference 'From Helsinki to Belgrade. The First CSCE Follow-up Meeting in Belgrade 1977/78', Belgrade, 9 March 2008.
54. Committee of Concerned Scientists, Inc., Annual Report, December 1977, CCSR, Series I: Administrative Files, 1973–2006, Box 1, Folder Annual Meeting 1976, RBML – CUL.
55. S.B. Snyder, *Human Rights Activism and the End of the Cold War: A Transnational History of the Helsinki Network* (New York: Cambridge University Press, 2011), 98; U. Tulli, *Tra diritti umani e distensione: L'amministrazione Carter e il dissenso in URSS* (Milan: Franco Angeli, 2013), 142; D.B. Fascell, 'The

Helsinki Accord: A Case Study', *Annals of the American Academy of Political and Social Science* 442(1) (1979), 76; D.C. Thomas, *The Helsinki Effect: International Norms, Human Rights, and the Demise of Communism* (Princeton, NJ: Princeton University Press, 2001).
56. Mark Mellman to Matthew Nimetz, Counselor Department of State, 9 June 1977, CCSR, Series IV: Organizations and Conferences, 1973–2005, Box 91, Folder CSCE – Belgrade 1977, RBML – CUL.
57. Report on trip to Belgrade by Dr Robert S. Adelstein, n.d., CCSR, Series IV: Organizations and Conferences, 1973–2005, Box 91, Folder CSCE – Belgrade 1977, RBML – CUL.
58. Update on Belgrade Conference, 9 January 1978, CCSR, Series IV: Organizations and Conferences, 1973–2005, Box 91, Folder CSCE – Belgrade 1977, RBML – CUL.
59. Department of State, Matthew Nimetz to Mark Mellman, 30 June 1978, CCSR, Series IV: Organizations and Conferences, 1973–2005, Box 91, Folder CSCE – Belgrade 1977, RBML – CUL.
60. T.M. Magstadt, 'Emigration and Citizenship: Implication for Soviet-American Relations', *Policy Analysis* 70 (1986), https://www.cato.org/publications/policy-analysis/emigration-citizenship-implications-sovieta-merican-relations.
61. Yuri Orlov was released from his exile in Siberia in 1986 and deported to the United States, where he became Professor of Physics and Government at Cornell University. See Y. Orlov, *Dangerous Thoughts: Memoirs of a Russian Life* (New York: William Morrow & Co., 1991). On the Moscow Helsinki Group, see L. Alexeeva, 'The Moscow Helsinki Group: The Seed from which the Helsinki Movement Grew', *OCSE Magazine* 7(3) (2010), 9–10, http://www.osce.org/secretariat/73223?download=true.
62. CCS, Annual Report, December 1978, CCSR, Series I: Administrative Files, 1973–2006, Box 1, Folder Annual Meeting 1979, RBML – CUL.
63. O. Chamberlain, 'Scientists Protest Trials in USSR', *The Bulletin of the Atomic Scientists* 34(8) (1978), 9.
64. R.L. Merritt and E.C. Hanson, *Science, Politics, and International Conferences: A Functional Analysis of the Moscow Political Science Congress* (Boulder and London: Lynne Rienner Publishers, 1989), 55.
65. Mark Kac – co-chairman CCS – to Professor Paul J. Flory, Stanford University, 23 March 1979, CCSR, Series V: Subject Files, 1970–2002, Box 107, Folder Scientific Exchange Programs 1978–1979, RBML – CUL.
66. Ibid.
67. Paul J. Flory, US Soviet Scientific Relations, 15 July 1981, CCSR, Series V: Subject Files, 1970–2002, Box 107, Folder Scientific Programs 1979–1991, RBML – CUL. On the contrast between the SOS and the CCS, see G. Sonnert (with assistance of G. Holton), *Ivory Bridges, Connecting Science and Society* (Cambridge, MA: MIT Press, 2002). About Paul J. Flory, see G.D. Patterson et al., *Paul John Flory: A Life of Science and Friends* (Boca Raton, FL: CRC Press, 2015).
68. J. Ziman, 'Human Rights and the Polity of Science', *The Bulletin of the Atomic Scientists* 34(8) (1978), 20–22.

69. Matthew Nimetz to Mark Mellman, 17 December 1979, CCSR, Series IV: Organizations and Conferences, 1973–2005, Box 91, Folder CSCE Helsinki 78/79, RBML – CUL.
70. CCS, Briefing Material for the United States delegation to the Madrid CSCE Review Conference, 1 August 1980, CCSR, Series IV: Organizations and Conferences, 1973–2005, Box 91, Folder CSCE Helsinki 78/79, RBML – CUL.
71. Professor Naum Meiman, Press Statement, Moscow, 6 May 1981, CCSR, Series II: Refusenik Closed Files, 1973–2001, Box 28, Folder Naum Meiman 1980–1981, RBML – CUL.
72. T.W. Ennis, 'Dr. Benjamin G. Levich Dies: Scientist and Soviet Émigré', *The New York Times*, 21 January 1987.
73. Lilli S. Chertoff to Prof. Hans Bethe, Department of Physics, Cornell University, 12 September 1974, CCSR, Series I: Administrative Files, 1973–2006, Box 1, Folder Annual Meeting 1974, RBML – CUL.
74. Report on trip to Belgrade by Dr Robert S. Adelstein, n.d., CCSR, Series IV: Organizations and Conferences, 1973–2005, Box 91, Folder CSCE – Belgrade 1977, RBML – CUL, 8.
75. CCS, Annual Board and Program Meeting, 19 December 1976, CCSR, Series I: Administrative Files, 1973–2006, Box 1, Folder Annual Meeting 1976, RBML – CUL.
76. Quoted in Keys, *Reclaiming American Virtue*, 264.
77. CCS Annual Report, December 1976, CCSR, Series I: Administrative Files, 1973–2006, Box 1, Folder Annual Meeting 1976, RBML – CUL.
78. Annual Report, December 1975 from Lilli S. Chertoff, 14 December 1975, CCSR, Series I: Administrative Files, 1973–2006, Box 1, Folder Annual Meeting 1974, RBML – CUL, 4.
79. Ibid., 5–6.
80. CCS, Position paper in the Scientific Forum, n.d., CCSR, Series V: Subject Files, 1970–2002, Box 103, Folder Helsinki Final Act, RBML – CUL.
81. M. Gottesman, M. Kac and M. Mellman (CCS), 'Helsinki Final Act', *Science* 207(4427) (1980), 137.
82. CCS, Testimony submitted to the Commission on Security and Cooperation in Europe, Subcommittee in Science, Research and Technology and Subcommittee on International Security and Scientific Affairs, US House of Representatives, 31 January 1980, by Dr Max Gottesman – Co-chairman CCS – and Mrs Dorothy Hirsh, Executive Director, CCS. Inc., CCSR, Series V: Subject Files, 1970–2002, Box 103, Folder Helsinki Final Act, RBML – CUL.
83. CCS, Annual Report, December 1978, CCSR, Series I: Administrative Files, 1973–2006, Box 1, Folder Annual Meeting 1979, RBML – CUL.

Bibliography

Alexeeva, L. 'The Moscow Helsinki Group: The Seed from which the Helsinki Movement Grew'. *OCSE Magazine* 7(3) (2010), 9–13. http://www.osce.org/secretariat/73223?download=true.

Altshuler, S. *From Exodus to Freedom: A History of the Soviet Jewry Movement*. Lanham, MD: Rowman & Littlefield Publishers, 2005.

Azbel, M. *Refusenik, Trapped in the Soviet Union*. New York: Paragon House Publishers, 1981.

Beckerman, G. *When They Come for Us, We'll Be Gone: The Epic Struggle to Save Soviet Jewry*. Boston, MA and New York: Houghton Mifflin Harcourt, 2010.

Bilandžić, V., D. Dahlmann and M. Kosanović (eds). *From Helsinki to Belgrade: The First CSCE Follow-up Meeting and the Crisis of Détente*. Göttingen: V&R Unipress, 2012.

Binder, D. 'Ford Sees Some Gains under Helsinki Pact'. *The New York Times*, 9 December 1976.

Buwalda, P. *They Did Not Dwell Alone: Jewish Emigration from the Soviet Union, 1967–1990*. Washington, DC: The Woodrow Wilson Center Press, 1997.

Callen, E., and E.A. Stern. 'Abuses of Scientific Exchanges: Détente Ought Not to Be a Shield for Soviet Tactics'. *The Bulletin of the Atomic Scientists* 31(2) (1975), 32–35.

Chamberlain, O. 'Scientists Protest Trials in USSR'. *The Bulletin of the Atomic Scientists* 34(8) (1978), 9–50.

Claude, R.P. *Science in the Service of Human Rights*. Philadelphia, PA: University of Pennsylvania Press, 2002.

Corillon, C. 'The Role of Science and Scientists in Human Rights'. *Annals of the American Academy of Political and Social Science* 506(1) (1989), 129–40.

Ennis, T.W. 'Dr. Benjamin G. Levich Dies: Scientist and Soviet Émigré'. *The New York Times*, 21 January 1987.

Fascell, D.B. 'The Helsinki Accord: A Case Study'. *Annals of the American Academy of Political and Social Science* 442(1) (1979), 69–76.

Feingold, H.L. *'Silent No More': Saving the Jews of Russia, the American Jewish Effort, 1967–1989*. Syracuse, NY: Syracuse University Press, 2007.

Friedman, M., and A.D. Chernin (eds). *A Second Exodus: The American Movement to Free Soviet Jews*. Hanover, NH: Brandeis University Press, 1999.

Galchinsky, M. *Jews and Human Rights: Dancing at Three Weddings*. Lanham, MD: The Rowman & Littlefield Publishing Group, Inc., 2008.

Gottesman, M., M. Kac and M. Mellman. 'Helsinki Final Act'. *Science* 207(4427) (1980): 137.

Hanhimäki, J.M. *The Rise and Fall of Détente: American Foreign Policy and the Transformation of the Cold War*. Washington, DC: Potomac Books, 2012.

Hurst, M. *British Human Rights Organizations and Soviet Dissent, 1965–1985*. London and Oxford: Bloomsbury Publishing, 2016.

Jackson, H.M. 'First, Human Détente'. *The New York Times*, 9 September 1973.

Keys, B. 'Congress, Kissinger, and the Origins of Human Rights Diplomacy'. *Diplomatic History* 34(5) (2010), 823–851.

Keys, B.J. *Reclaiming American Virtue: The Human Rights Revolution of the 1970s*. Cambridge, MA: Harvard University Press, 2014.

Khanin, V.Z. 'The Refusenik Community in Moscow: Social Networks and Models of Identification'. *East European Jewish Affairs* 41(1–2) (2011), 77–88.

Korey, W.D. 'The Struggle over Jackson-Mills-Vanik'. *American Jewish Year Book* 75 (1974–75), 199–234.

Kosharovsky, Y., *'We Are Jews Again': Jewish Activism in the Soviet Union*. Syracuse, N.Y.: Syracuse University Press, 2017.

Lubrano, L.L. 'National and International Politics in US-USSR Scientific Cooperation'. *Social Studies of Science* 11(4) (1981), 451–80.

Magstadt, T.M. 'Emigration and Citizenship: Implication for Soviet-American Relations'. *Policy Analysis* 70 (1986). https://www.cato.org/publications/pol icy-analysis/emigration-citizenship-implications-sovietamerican-relations

Manzione, J. '"Amusing and Amazing and Practical and Military": The Legacy of Scientific Internationalism in American Foreign Policy, 1945–63'. *Diplomatic History* 24(1) (2000), 49–55.

Mellman, M. 'Human Rights: A Different Perspective'. *The Bulletin of the Atomic Scientists* 34(9) (1978), 60–61.

Merritt, R.L., and E.C. Hanson. *Science, Politics, and International Conferences: A Functional Analysis of the Moscow Political Science Congress*. Boulder and London: Lynne Rienner Publishers, 1989.

Minker, J. *Scientific Freedom and Human Rights: Scientists of Conscience during the Cold War*. Los Alamitos, CA: IEEE CS Press, 2012.

Mozorov, B. *Documents on Soviet Jewish Emigration*. Oxford: Routledge, 2013.

Orlov, Y. *Dangerous Thoughts: Memoirs of a Russian Life*. New York: William Morrow & Co., 1991.

Patterson, G.D., et al. *Paul John Flory: A Life of Science and Friends*. Boca Raton, FL: CRC Press, 2015.

Peretz, P. *Let My People Go: The Transnational Politics of Soviet Jewish Emigration during the Cold War*. New York: Routledge, 2017.

Peterson, C.P. *Globalizing Human Rights: Private Citizens, the Soviet Union, and the West*. New York: Routledge, 2012.

Rhéaume, C. 'Western Scientists' Reaction to Andrei Sakharov's Human Rights Struggle in the Soviet Union, 1968–1989'. *Human Rights Quarterly* 30(1) (2008), 1–20.

Riegner, G.M. *Never Despair: Sixty Years in the Service of the Jewish People and Human Rights*. Chicago, IL: Ivan R. Dee, 2006.

Rubinson, P. '"For Our Soviet Colleagues": Scientific Internationalism, Human Rights, and the Cold War', in A. Iriye, P. Goedde and W.I. Hitchcock (eds), *The Human Rights Revolution: An International History* (New York: Oxford University Press, 2012), 245–64.

Sakharov, A. 'Open Letter to the United States Congress', 14 September 1973. *The Congressional Record*, 13 December 1974.

Sanua, M.R. *Let Us Prove Strong: The American Jewish Committee, 1945–2006*. Waltham, MA: Brandeis University Press, 2007.

Sargent, D.J. *A Superpower Transformed: The Remaking of American Foreign Relations in the 1970s*. Oxford and New York: Oxford University Press, 2015.

Shargil, Y. 'Voronel and Wife in Israel'. *Jewish Telegraphic Agency. Daily News Bulletin* 41(57) (30 December 1974), 1.

Shinbaum, M. 'Mobilizing America: The National Conference on Soviet Jewry', in M. Friedman and A.D. Chernin (eds), *A Second Exodus: The American Movement to Free Soviet Jews* (Hanover, NH: Brandeis University Press, 1999), 173–80.

Snyder, S.B. *Human Rights Activism and the End of the Cold War: A Transnational History of the Helsinki Network*. New York: Cambridge University Press, 2011.

Sonnert, G., with assistance of G. Holton. *Ivory Bridges, Connecting Science and Society*. Cambridge, MA: MIT Press, 2002.

Spalding, B. 'Protest by Conference'. *New Scientist* 78(1101) (1978), 288–89.

'Statement of Dr. Allen H. Kassof, Executive Director, IREX', in *Hearings before the Commission on Security and Cooperation in Europe, Ninety-Fifth Congress, First Session on Implementation of the Helsinki Accords*, Vol. III, *Information Flow, and Cultural and Educational Exchange, 19, 24 and 25 May 1977*. Washington, DC: US Government Printing Office, 1977.

'Statement of Dr. Robert Adelstein, Co-chairman, Committee of Concerned Scientists', in *Basket Three: Implementation of the Helsinki Accords. Hearings before the Commission on Security and Cooperation in Europe, Ninety-Fifth Congress, First Session on Implementation of the Helsinki Accords*, Vol. III, *Information Flow, and Cultural and Educational Exchange, 19, 24 and 25 May 1977*. Washington, DC: US Government Printing Office, 1997.

Thomas, D.C. *The Helsinki Effect: International Norms, Human Rights, and the Demise of Communism*. Princeton, NJ: Princeton University Press, 2001.

Tulli, U. *Tra diritti umani e distensione: L'amministrazione Carter e il dissenso in URSS*. Milan: Franco Angeli, 2013.

Ziman, J. 'Human Rights and the Polity of Science'. *The Bulletin of the Atomic Scientists* 34(8) (1978), 20–22.

Ziman, J. *Of One Mind: The Collectivization of Science*. Dordrecht: Springer Science & Business Media, 1997.

Ziman, J., P. Sieghart and J. Humphrey. *The World of Science and the Rule of Law: A Study of the Observance and Violations of the Human Rights of Scientists in the Participating States of the Helsinki Accords*. New York: Oxford University Press, 1986.

 6

SEEING THE VALUE OF THE HELSINKI ACCORDS
Human Rights, Peace and Transnational Debates about Détente, 1981–1988

Christian P. Peterson

In 1987, representatives of the Czechoslovakian non-governmental organization (NGO) Charter 77 sent a letter to the European Nuclear Disarmament (END) Convention in Coventry, England that challenged Western peace activists to do even more to challenge the 'status quo' in Europe.[1] In defence of this position, the authors explained that even the best treaties that governments signed would easily become 'discarded' pieces of paper if private citizens failed to lay the foundations of our shared 'European home'. Hoping to further this goal, the authors urged the conference attendees to act in ways consistent with the Helsinki process and forge the transnational contacts necessary to bring about a united, peaceful Europe.[2] Following their own advice, the authors also invited the attendees to visit Prague during the following year and attend peace seminars. Such a move, the document noted, would give private citizens on both sides of the Iron Curtain a chance to discuss the best ways to advance the 'new détente [from below]' and link the causes of peace and human rights.[3]

The arguments articulated above raise important questions about how private citizens understood the interconnections among the issues of human rights violations, the struggle for peace, the provisions of the Helsinki Final Act and the process of détente during the 1980s. Several scholars have addressed parts of these subjects, including some who argue that the steps private citizens took on behalf of peace and/or human rights deserve most of the credit for ending the Cold War and bringing about the collapse of the Soviet Bloc.[4] While these works have different points of emphasis, they make a strong case that Central-Eastern European activists exchanged information with each other related to the subjects of human rights, peace and the environment.⁵ They also reveal how private citizens in Western Europe and the Soviet Bloc worked to communicate with each other and engaged in arguments about how best to balance the goals of human rights and peace promotion. Several authors recount how the Helsinki Accords played an important role in helping Central-Eastern European dissenters convince some Western peace activists to link the causes of peace and human rights.⁶ Some of these works also address the subject of how transnational actors worked to promote a 'détente' or 'Helsinki' from below, designed to ease Cold War tensions and produce regular contacts across the Iron Curtain.⁷

This chapter will build on these previous studies in several ways. First it will provide a more in-depth analysis of how debates during the 1980s about human rights, peace and the meaning of the Helsinki Accords fit into larger arguments about how best to further the process of détente.⁸ Such an approach will help demonstrate the limitations of suggesting that all Central-Eastern European dissenters refused to identify with the concept of détente or that all Western peace activists hesitated to see a connection between the Helsinki process and the forging of a 'détente from below'.⁹ It will also reveal the limitations of defining the process of détente only as a 'top-down' phenomenon that encompassed the ways in which governmental elites worked to reduce Cold War tensions through negotiations and agreements.¹⁰ Instead of deferring to elites, a wide array of activists articulated broader conceptions of détente (i.e. détente from below) that linked the tasks of curbing human rights violations, promoting peace, opening borders and reducing military armaments.

Third, to help illustrate the arguments described above, this chapter will devote more attention to the contributions of understudied transnational peace groups like the Moscow Trust Group, the Brooklyn Antinuclear Group (BANG) and the Campaign for Peace and Democracy – East and West (CPDEW) than many works do. As part of this process, it will widen the lens beyond the experience of groups like END and examine how transnational debates about peace and human rights promotion influenced the behaviour of US peace groups. To accomplish this task, it will recount the story of how groups like the US Helsinki Watch Group (USHW) and CPDEW challenged US peace activists to defend the activities of the Moscow Trust Group and link the causes of peace and human rights.¹¹

The debates about the linkages between pursuing détente, challenging human rights violations and promoting peace during the 1980s did not appear out of nowhere. In many ways, they reflected a growing unease with the top-down approaches to détente that emerged during the 1970s. Without belabouring the point, the Nixon administration and Soviet leaders on the whole preferred a Kissinger-style détente that avoided the issue of human rights to facilitate the signing of agreements that eased Cold War tensions and served each side's interests. For all of their differences, Western European policymakers tended to prefer a multilateral or dynamic version of détente that utilized ever-increasing levels of East–West trade, personal contacts and exchanges to 'liberalize' the Soviet Bloc.[12] Despite emphasizing the importance of human rights as a legitimate issue of international concern, many of these Western European policymakers feared that pressing this issue too forcefully in practice would undermine the forces of liberalization capable of one day bringing democratic government to their Eastern neighbours.[13]

The language of the Final Act includes elements of Kissinger-style détente and the European Community's multilateral or dynamic counterpart.[14] Signed by the United States, Canada, the Soviet Union and thirty-two other European nations in August 1975, this agreement pledged each signatory to respect the existing boundaries of the others (i.e. territorial sovereignty), save the possibility of peaceful change in the future. It also called on the signatories to settle their disputes without war, reduce their military armaments and negotiate 'confidence-building measures' to promote peace. Overcoming the resistance of the Nixon administration, members of the EC succeeded in including language that called on signatories not to violate their citizens' basic 'civil, political, economic, social, [and] cultural ... rights, as well as other "freedoms"'. They also helped include language in the agreement that encouraged signatories to increase the level of contacts among private citizens through mechanisms as diverse as person-to-person exchanges, cultural agreements and scientific conferences.[15]

As several authors have pointed out in recent works, the language of the Final Act did not necessarily endorse the status quo in superpower relations or the Cold War divisions in Europe.[16] For example, as mentioned above, the signatories reserved the right to change the political status quo in Europe by negotiating peaceful boundary changes. The signatories even linked the causes of peace and human rights in Principle VII of Basket One. 'The Participating States', the document observes, recognize that governmental 'respect' for 'human rights' ensures the 'peace ... [and] justice' required to have stable and productive relations with each other. Instead of treating these pledges as mere words on paper, Principle VII also confirmed the right of each individual to 'know and act upon his rights' as outlined in the Final Act.

This stipulation gave private citizens the ability to cite this agreement when attacking their governments' human rights abuses or defending the interrelationship between the causes of human rights and peace.[17] When viewed from this angle, the Final Act did not so much confirm the status quo as link the advancement of security, peace, human rights, trade and human contacts in an interrelated negotiating framework best defined as the Helsinki process. This framework proved difficult to ignore because the language of Basket Four resulted in a wide array of follow-up meetings beginning in 1977 that allowed signatories to discuss their implementation records and undertake new commitments.

Even though arguments over the exact parameters of détente appeared moot during the early 1980s in the wake of the Soviet invasion of Afghanistan, private citizens played an important role in resurrecting these debates. To understand why this happened, we first need to turn our attention to the growth of peace activism that took place in Europe and the United States during the late 1970s and 1980s. Distrustful of bureaucratic discretion and authority, hundreds of thousands of US and Western European citizens challenged the 'dual track' decision of NATO as well as the Reagan administration's nuclear modernization policies and harsh anti-Soviet rhetoric.[18] In the case of the United States, groups like the War Resisters League (WRL), Women's International League for Peace and Freedom (WILPF), Physicians for Social Responsibility (PSR) and SANE (National Committee for a Sane Nuclear Policy) saw their memberships grow as they participated in a wide variety of demonstrations aimed at stopping the Reagan administration's nuclear modernization programmes. A large number of peace groups and hundreds of thousands of private citizens also worked on behalf on the Nuclear Weapons Freeze Campaign, which hoped to bring about a freeze and eventual reduction in the superpowers' nuclear arsenals. The appeal of a nuclear freeze and the idea of peace manifested itself in June 1982 when somewhere between 500,000 and one million people from a broad array of groups attended a rally in New York's Central Park.[19]

Fearful that the world bordered on the precipice of nuclear annihilation, a diverse array of Western European private citizens and peace groups with many different agendas also worked to stop the dual track decision (i.e. Euromissiles) and challenge the Reagan administration's nuclear weapons policies. For example, in November 1981, as many as 500,000 people gathered in Amsterdam to protest the Dutch government's decision to accept Euromissiles and the Reagan administration's 'zero option' arms control proposal.[20] In the United Kingdom, the British group Campaign for Nuclear Disarmament (CND) organized a series of protests during the early to mid 1980s designed to prevent London's acceptance of Euromissiles and abolish British nuclear weapons, including one in 1983 that 'drew an estimated 400,000 participants'.[21] While this group worked to organize visible and well-attended demonstrations, it saw its membership rise from about four thousand in 1979 to over one hundred thousand by 1984.[22]

As for West Germany, a wide variety of religious organizations, churches, environmental groups, political parties, unions and pacifists urged their government not to accept the dual track missiles and begin the process of winding down the nuclear arms race – positions outlined in the Krefeld Appeal of November 1980. Committed to accomplishing these goals, roughly 250,000 private citizens staged a demonstration in Bonn in October 1981. During the peak of Western European antinuclear protests in 1983, more than a million people staged protests across West Germany on a 'single day' in October as part of an unsuccessful effort to stop the dual track deployment from taking place. Similar demonstrations involving hundreds of thousands of people also took place in Belgium, Scandinavia and Italy during the early to mid 1980s.[23]

The rise of peace activism in Western Europe and the United States did not take place in a vacuum. A wide variety of peace groups formed in the Soviet Union and Central-Eastern Europe that hoped to forge enduring and meaningful connections with their Western counterparts. For example, in the Soviet Union, a small number of scientists and other intellectuals formed the 'Group to Establish Trust between the USSR and USA' (better known as the Moscow Trust Group) in June 1982, which aimed to halt the nuclear arms race and promote peace between the superpowers by breaking down the Cold War barriers that separated private citizens.[24] Well aware that Solidarity did not place much emphasis on promoting peace, a small group of Polish private citizens formed an underground group called KOS (Committee of Social Resistance) after the imposition of martial law in December 1981. While KOS hoped to forge transnational links with Western activists designed to promote peace, it struggled to find partners in light of the fact that it blamed the totalitarianism of the Soviet Bloc nations for the arms race and continuation of the Cold War. In the spring of 1985, a group called Freedom and Peace (WiP) came into existence to challenge the repression of Poles who refused to take their nation's military oath and perform compulsory military service for two years. From its inception, WiP members worked in the open to make alternative military service a universal right and forge links with Westerners in ways that promoted peace all over the world.[25]

The extensive repression that peace activists in the Soviet Bloc faced on a regular basis raised some uncomfortable questions for many peace activists in the United States and Western Europe given the positions they tended to take. While generalizing about the views of diverse actors with many different policy preferences necessitates simplification, this chapter will nevertheless carry out such an undertaking for one simple reason: it helps explain why some unofficial Soviet Bloc peace activists and participants in groups such as CPDEW pursued the policies that they did. Even if some (many did not) Western activists criticized Soviet internal repression and deployment of weapons such as the SS-20 missile, most hesitated to champion the link between peace and human rights. This position grew out of the assumption that dealing with the dangers of nuclear weapons had to take precedence over every other issue given the catastrophic consequences of any nuclear exchange.[26] It also reflected a general belief that raising the subject of human rights violations in the Soviet Bloc would either impede the task of promoting peace or raise Cold War tensions in ways that made a nuclear exchange more likely.[27] Given the prevalence of these views, most Western peace actors privileged the goal of convincing their own governments to take unilateral steps to curb the nuclear arms race, such as rejecting participation in the dual track decision. Many also hesitated to identify themselves with or work to forge transnational contacts with peace activists in the Soviet Bloc.[28] Instead of pursuing such a goal, many saw more value in reducing Cold War tensions by engaging in dialogue with the representatives of official Eastern Bloc peace groups like the Soviet Committee for the Defense of Peace (SCDP).[29]

Perhaps not surprisingly in light of these positions, evidence suggests that most Western peace activists did not view the Helsinki process as a natural ally in their efforts to create a more peaceful world. On one level, this tendency grew out of the erroneous perception that the provisions of the Final Act had little to do with promoting peace and mainly worked to strengthen the Cold War status quo in Europe.[30] Many Western activists also acted on the assumption that abolishing nuclear weapons had precedence over working to democratize the Soviet Bloc. According to this view, the existence of weapons, rather than the profound political, ideological and economic differences between the Western and Eastern Blocs, best explained the continuation of the Cold War.[31]

As several scholars have pointed out, some peace groups do not fit the generalizations offered above, such as the Dutch group Interchurch Peace Council (IKV), END and the Moscow Trust Group. Unwilling to rely on the 'expertise' of elites to ease Cold War tensions, each of these groups embraced the argument that private citizens and government officials needed to take matters into their own hands and cultivate a détente from below.[32] While this concept defies a simple definition, it in effect refers to the belief that private citizens needed to take an internationalist, non-aligned view of the Cold War and work towards creating a more democratic world order without nuclear weapons. For example, during the late 1970s, IKV worked to forge enduring transnational contacts with other Western European peace groups so it could build a broad international movement for peace committed to bringing about nuclear disarmament. Because of these efforts, IKV played an important role in helping West German peace groups organize the peace demonstration in Bonn mentioned above.[33]

Inspired by the efforts of the IKV to build an international movement for peace, British historian and activist E.P. Thompson played a key role in creating the END Appeal of April 1980. Employing language that in effect advocated the cultivation of a détente from below, this document urged private citizens 'not to wait upon governments' to create a more peaceful world. To 'enforce détente' on policymakers, especially those in the United States and Soviet Union, private citizens needed to find the most efficacious ways of abolishing nuclear weapons in their own individual nations, which might include steps such as the creation of nuclear-free zones. At the same time, Europeans needed to do everything in their power to increase the level of personal contacts and exchanges that took place between private citizens on both sides of the Iron Curtain. If Europeans interacted with each other on a regular basis and challenged the assumptions that fuelled the nuclear arms race, they could build a non-aligned, peaceful and democratic continent devoid of nuclear armaments.[34]

The Moscow Trust Group offered an even more compelling definition of détente from below in a letter addressed to the Second END Convention that took place in West Berlin (1983). The process of détente 'can only be viable', the authors argued, when 'it is not restricted to [the] formal agendas' of policymakers wedded to preserving the status quo. Instead of waiting for the world to change by itself, private citizens on both sides of the Iron Curtain needed to make the Cold War obsolete by breaking down the barriers that prevented them from getting to know and trust each other. While such a notion may appear naive, the authors continued, 'humanizing international relations' through regular contacts across the Cold War divide represented the only real way to 'destroy the roots of the arms race in the very place of its origin – human consciousness', an argument that some activists in Czechoslovakia and Poland also shared.[35]

The groups mentioned above took a wide variety of steps to further the process of détente from below. For example, E.P. Thompson published numerous books and articles that urged private citizens to forge the transnational contacts needed to destroy the Cold War barriers that perpetuated the conflict and bring about nuclear disarmament. As part of a larger effort to support peace activism in the Soviet Bloc, he also held meetings with peace activists in Hungary and activists in Czechoslovakia in 1982 and 1983.[36] Along with distributing bulletins, magazines and pamphlets, members of British END strove to convince members of CND to take a more vocal stance against the efforts of Soviet Bloc governments to repress independent peace activities. Committed to building a broad international movement for peace, supporters of the END Appeal in Great Britain worked with other Western Europeans to create the END Convention/Liaison Committee, which helped organize the END Conventions that took place in Europe from 1982 to 1990. These conventions became important transnational forums where a diverse array of peace activists, trade union members, representatives of political parties and other interested individuals from different nations discussed the best ways to further the goals of the END Appeal.[37]

The Moscow Trust Group encouraged Soviet and American citizens to create a 'four-sided' dialogue between politicians and private citizens by participating in activities like pen-pal programmes and exchanges that included the children of politicians. Trust Group members also sent a wide array of documents abroad that requested Western peace activists to support their efforts and join them in carrying out transnational protests designed to further the cause of peace. To draw attention to their cause, members worked to obtain signatures for their peace petitions, put on public exhibitions and held seminars aimed at highlighting the danger of nuclear war.[38]

The harsh repression that dissenters in the Soviet Union and Central-Eastern Europe faced on a regular basis for their work to promote peace raised an obvious point: the cultivation of a détente from below could not take place unless private citizens had the freedom to forge transnational contacts and hold government officials accountable for their behaviour. This reality shaped the behaviour of IKV. In comparison to Moscow Trust Group or supporters of the END Appeal like E.P. Thompson, members of this group made a greater effort to build a détente from below by linking the causes of peace and human rights during the first half of the 1980s. To cite a few examples, the General Secretary of IKV Mient Jan Faber published documents that he had received from Central-Eastern European peace activists, including

Hungarians, East Germans and Poles, that outlined the repression they faced for working to promote peace.[39] Not afraid to raise 'Cold War tensions', some members of IKV mentioned the subject of Soviet human rights violations at a Church Peace Committee meeting in Moscow (1983).[40]

The importance of linking peace and human rights came naturally to many activists in the Soviet Bloc. Over and over again, supporters of Charter 77 and members of WiP endorsed the argument that governments could not be trusted to act in peaceful ways without first respecting basic human rights and subjecting themselves to meaningful public oversight.[41] Despite the efforts of IKV, a wide variety of activists in Poland and Czechoslovakia continued to criticize Western peace activists, including END supports like E.P. Thompson, for their seeming preoccupation with facilitating the signing of an arms control agreement rather than helping to end the Cold War by promoting democracy and human rights in the Soviet Bloc, a point the Czech activist Vaclav Havel made clear in his essay, 'Anatomy of a Reticence', in 1985.[42] To put this insight another way, many activists in the Soviet Bloc disliked how Western European peace activists seemed willing to settle for a temporary 'ceasefire' instead of helping them to bring about the democratization of their nations required to end the nuclear arms race once and for all and forge a permanent peace in Europe.

The prevalence of the arguments described above helps to account for why a wide variety of transnational actors on both sides of the Cold War began to turn to the Final Act in ways that in effect linked the causes of peace promotion, human rights and the forging of a détente from below. This process began to gather some traction when Charter 77 issued a statement urging members of Western European peace movements to embrace the Helsinki process during the winter of 1981. Such a course of action would bear fruit, the authors insisted, because the Final Act recognized the close links between government respect for human rights, the development of détente and the creation of an enduring peace in Europe.[43] A short time later, some supporters of END sent an open letter to the SCDP Chairman Yuri Zhukov that advanced similar arguments.[44]

In the United States, a group called Campaign for Peace and Democracy – East and West (CPDEW) made the provisions of the Final Act an important part of its campaign to link the causes of peace promotion, human rights and détente. This group formed in 1982 when a small number of US Social Democrats decided to challenge the pathologies of US liberal-democratic capitalism and Soviet-style socialism that fuelled the Cold War and inhibited global economic development.

Eventually consisting of feminists, trade unionists, peace activists and environmentalists, CPDEW urged Western peace activists to exploit the Helsinki process in ways that furthered a 'dynamic' conception of détente and produced a 'democratic peace'.[45]

To make sure that politicians carried out 'fundamental change', CPDEW publicized the activities of imprisoned and/or harassed activists in less developed countries and the Eastern Bloc. Members of CPDEW encouraged Western European peace activists to criticize Soviet repression of peace activities. In the summer of 1982, founding members and co-directors Joanne Landy and Gail Danecker sent General Secretary Brezhnev a letter that accused the Soviet government of 'hypocrisy' for persecuting Moscow Trust Group members like Sergei Batrovin. On several occasions, members of CPDEW met with officials of the Polish Embassy to protest the trials of Solidarity and KOR (Workers' Defense Committee) activists. They also signed a protest letter located on the *New York Times* op-ed page that condemned the Polish government's carrying out of such trials.[46]

Other groups followed paths similar to that of CPDEW. During the summer of 1985, a small number of US peace activists formed a group called Peace Activists East and West (PAEW). Committed to linking the causes of peace and human rights, this organization defined its task as bringing the Cold War to an end by facilitating dialogue between Western peace activists and private citizens in the Eastern Bloc, especially members of the Moscow Trust Group. Much like CPDEW, it hoped to break down the Cold War divisions and convince the US government to stop backing 'right-wing' dictatorships across the globe. To further these causes, PAEW issued a wide variety of publications urging American peace activists to carry out direct protests such as picketing to help free imprisoned activists in the East; it also encouraged people to travel abroad and meet with Central-Eastern activists in their own country.[47] The PAEW even held conferences in which exiled Central-Eastern dissenters such as Zdena Tomin of Charter 77 delivered speeches imploring Western peace activists to link the causes of peace, human rights and the forging of a détente from below.[48]

Across the ocean, several Western European peace groups selected IKV to serve as the 'communication and coordination centre' of a new entity called the International Peace Communication and Coordination Centre (IPCC). Once up and running in 1981, this clearinghouse strove to help non-aligned Western European peace groups better coordinate their activities, although some North Americans also attended this forum as representatives of affiliated organizations such as the Nuclear Weapons Freeze Campaign. As IKV International Secretary and IPCC

Coordinator Wim Bartels later explained, this clearinghouse viewed the Helsinki Accords as legitimating its efforts to forge more transnational contacts with peace activists in the Soviet Bloc. Yet, as he also later admitted, the IPCC mostly focused on stopping the dual track deployments than using the Helsinki process to build a détente from below as described above during its first five years of existence.[49]

While groups affiliated with the IPCC focused on preventing the dual track deployments, the USHW undertook its own effort to use the Final Act in ways that linked the causes of peace, human rights and détente. Defending the right of private citizens to carry out unofficial peace activities in the Eastern Bloc, it sent letters to members of the US Congress urging them to support the behaviour of Central-Eastern European peace activists by citing the provisions of the Helsinki Accords.[50] It also lobbied American delegations at the various Final Act follow-up meetings to address the mistreatment of Eastern Bloc peace activists, a campaign that bore fruit.[51] In addition to carrying out the actions described above, members asked peace activists to sign petitions in defence of persecuted groups like the Moscow Trust Group and Charter 77.[52] The USHW also published a wide array of documents and pamphlets that linked the causes of governmental respect for human rights, peace and the forging of a legitimate détente in Europe, including editorials in *The New York Times*.[53]

Working for the USHW as lead researcher on the Soviet Union and Eastern Europe, Catherine A. Fitzpatrick went out of her way to help exiled members of the Trust Group enhance their efforts to forge a détente from below. Undertaking such a campaign came naturally to Fitzpatrick. As a volunteer with Amnesty International, she had made contacts with a number of US peace groups, including WRL. She also consulted with Trust Group members on several occasions when visiting the Soviet Union during the early 1980s, including the time she posed as Sergei Batrovin's cousin to visit him during his confinement in a psychiatric hospital. This background helps account for why she helped members of the Moscow Trust Group to organize a 'silent vigil' in New York on 1 January 1983 that asked the general public to think about the best ways to reduce tensions among nations and bring about disarmament. She also exchanged letters with exiled members of the Trust Group on a regular basis. In one of these letters, she pledged to help Batrovin make US peace activists less hostile to his group. These critics, she wrote, would better grasp the enduring link between peace and freedom once they internalized the fact that the Soviets put Trust Group members in mental wards just for 'standing in front of the [Soviet] Academy of Sciences with a sign'.[54]

Acting on her belief in making Western peace groups 'better than they were', Fitzpatrick and other members of the USHW challenged American and Western European activists to expand their focus beyond the narrow horizons of disarmament and defend members of the Moscow Trust Group.[55] For example, Fitzpatrick and USHW Executive Director Aryeh Neier sent hundreds of appeals and personal letters to Western peace activists asking them to support the independent peace activities in the USSR by citing the provisions of the Final Act.[56] During the June 1982 disarmament rally that took place in New York, Fitzpatrick and other supporters walked around with signs urging Western peace activists to support persecuted members of the Trust Group. Fitzpatrick also helped put together an information clearinghouse known as the Moscow Trust Group Network. This loosely affiliated network consisted of individuals interested in receiving information about the plight of the Trust Group, including exiled members, some US peace activists and members of anarchist groups like BANG (see below). Instead of faulting the Trust Group for receiving support from US 'right-wing' groups or calling members 'CIA dupes', Fitzpatrick wrote in one Network memorandum, Western peace activists should concentrate on helping it form a broad transnational movement committed to cultivating a détente from below.[57]

The efforts of Fitzpatrick helped convince some mainstream US peace groups to show more support for peace activists in the Soviet Bloc. To cite a few examples, members of WRL and SANE signed letters on behalf of the Trust Group that were sent to Soviet government officials, including General Secretary Yuri Andropov, and attended press conferences to publicize this group's plight.[58] Furthermore, Fitzpatrick and members of US peace groups such as WRL lobbied on behalf of the Moscow Trust Group during a private meeting with the First Soviet Secretary to the UN Mission Leonid Bindy that took place in the spring of 1983. Several months later, the USHW publicized a demonstration in New York and several European cities in which a wide array of peace activists released balloons carrying the pictures of imprisoned Trust Group members.[59]

The cause of linking peace promotion, human rights and forging a détente from below did not just influence the behaviour of 'left-wing' circles in the West. A very small number of anarchists and libertarians in New York formed the Brooklyn Anti-Nuclear Group (BANG) and Neither East Nor West – NYC (NENWN). The former group started in 1979 and published a newsletter on a regular basis that devoted considerable attention to the activities of Soviet and Central-Eastern European peace activists. As part of this coverage, it challenged Western peace activists to link the causes of peace and human rights. In defence of this position, a BANG publication observed that the disinterest or contempt that many Westerners had for independent peace activists in the East ignored the reality that linking human rights and peace represents the only real way to create a better world. After all, did not Westerners see the exercise of basic freedoms as the necessary precondition for promoting positive historical change? Why should the same standard not hold for those in the East? Along with outlining the repressive nature of Soviet-style socialism, this document also asked Western peace activists to think of Poland, Afghanistan and the plight of the Baltic Republics before referring to the military buildup of the Warsaw Pact as a necessary 'defensive measure'.[60]

After BANG disbanded, the anarchist Bob McGlynn put a new group together in 1986 called Neither East Nor West – NYC (NENWN). Committed to undermining existing Cold War structures, this anarchist group defended the close link between governmental respect for basic human rights and peace. It also supported using the Helsinki process to cultivate a détente from below on the grounds that US and Soviet policymakers had no genuine interest in a 'real détente' that would undermine their ability to 'dominate small, weak countries'.[61] To further this agenda, members forged a working relationship with exiled members of the Moscow Trust Group and WiP to raise public awareness about the human rights violations taking place in the Eastern Bloc. It also carried out grassroots activities like picketing the Soviet and East German consulates in New York.[62]

Despite the best efforts of CPDEW, Fitzpatrick and groups like BANG, many US peace activists hesitated to embrace the Helsinki process or link the causes of human rights and peace. This ambivalence or hostility spurred Fitzpatrick to attend a wide array of peace forums to raise awareness about the links between human rights, peace and the Helsinki Final Act.[63] To cite one example, she headed a panel at an American Friends Service Committee (AFSC) conference, near the end of 1984, in which pro-Soviet peace activists tried to shout her down and discredit the Trust Group as a CIA front. To avoid a shouting match, Fitzpatrick patiently outlined Soviet violations of the Final Act and defended the 'organic link between peace and human rights'.[64]

The transnational debates about the interconnections among the issues of human rights, peace, the Helsinki process and détente played out at the Third Annual END Convention in Perugia, Italy (1984). Bowing to the pressure of activists who favoured the forging of a real détente from below, the END Convention/Liaison Committee invited more than one hundred unofficial peace activists from East-Central

Europe and the Soviet Union to attend the convention.⁶⁵ This decision caught the attention of the attendee Dr Richard Falk, a well-known US peace activist, human rights advocate and international law scholar. Such a development, he later wrote, represented an important victory for those who favoured forging a détente from below over 'traditionalists' who privileged the goal of negotiating with official Soviet Bloc peace representatives.⁶⁶

Hoping to build on this achievement, a group of European activists committed to linking the causes of peace and human rights formed the European Network for East-West Dialogue (ENEWD) just before the Perugia meeting concluded. This group recommended that activists use the Helsinki Accords to defend the close connection between governmental respect for basic human rights and the cause of peace. It also advocated using the language of the Helsinki Accords to forge a 'dynamic détente from below' that linked the people of the 'East and West' in the cause of peace.⁶⁷

The rise of ENEWD did not take place in a vacuum. In March 1985, representatives of Charter 77 issued the 'Prague Appeal'. While this document may not have used the term 'détente', it in effect took the position that private citizens on both sides of the Iron Curtain should use the Helsinki process to forge the détente from below needed to wind down the Cold War.⁶⁸ While not as novel as one author suggests, the idea of using the Helsinki process to promote peace appears to have gained more support in the mid 1980s after the appearance of the Prague Appeal.⁶⁹ For example, in a candid official response to the appearance of this document, British END admitted its previous 'ignorance' of the Helsinki process and vowed to make greater use of it in the future to further the goals of the END Appeal.⁷⁰

In what one scholar has called an unprecedented 'transnational creative process', ENEWD worked with groups and individuals from over a dozen countries, including some from Central and Eastern Europe, to produce a peace platform called *Giving Real Life to the Helsinki Accords: A Memorandum to European Peoples and Governments*. After undergoing a series of revisions based on the input from Central-Eastern European activists, ENEWD sent this document (with over five thousand signatures) to the delegations attending the Final Act follow-up meeting in Vienna (November 1986 to January 1989). Its contents offered an in-depth explanation of why the Helsinki process linked the causes of human rights and peace in ways that built the détente from below needed to transform the Cold War status quo. If the process of détente was to be successful, the appeal argued, private citizens from different nations needed to interact with each other to build the 'mutual trust' necessary to create a more peaceful world. Although government agreements had their place in forging a more peaceful world, they could not replace 'the grassroots contacts and common activities between ... individuals across frontiers' required to 'dissolve the structure of the Cold War'.[71] Impressed with this document, Wim Bartels helped organize a five-day conference that took place just before the convening of the Vienna follow-up meeting on 4 November whose agenda explored how IPCC affiliated groups could use the provisions of the Final Act to promote peace more effectively. Instead of focusing on challenging the nuclear weapons themselves as its members had tended to do in the past, he advised, the IPCC should use the Helsinki process to build the governmental and public support necessary to overcome the Cold War divisions that legitimated the building of weapons in the first place.[72] Bartels himself acted on this advice when he and other Western European peace activists discussed the future of peace promotion with their American counterparts, including how they might better use the Helsinki process to further their goals, when touring the United States in December 1988.[73]

The relaxation of Cold War tensions and cracks in the 'monolithic' Eastern Bloc that appeared during the late 1980s only increased the determination of many activists to use the Helsinki process in ways designed to cultivate a détente from below. In May 1988, Fitzpatrick delivered a speech before the Fellowship of Reconciliation Conference in New York. Not averse to raising uncomfortable issues, she critiqued how many US peace activists continued to deny the direct link between governmental respect for basic human rights and peace just as they had during the 1970s and the first half of the 1980s. How could the activists who continued to deny this relationship, she wondered, account for the reality that even the SCDP had begun to sponsor public forums aimed at examining the links between peace and human rights? Such a turn of events, she mused, now meant that US peace activists who continued to avoid the subject of Soviet human rights violations or ignored the Final Act had become 'less progressive than Soviet officials'. When viewed in this light, Fitzpatrick concluded, the US peace movement needed a 'de-Stalinization' programme just as much, if not more, than the Soviet Union.[74]

A wide variety of transnational actors also worked to forge an enduring and influential transnational peace network. Working with exiled members of the Moscow Trust Group and US peace groups such as Fellowship of Reconciliation, CPDEW organized a conference titled 'Détente from Below' that at least in part addressed the question of how the Helsinki Final Act could be used to promote peace and human rights in Europe.[75] The co-director of CPDEW, Joanne Landy, accepted the invitation from WiP to attend a seminar in Warsaw titled 'International Peace and the Helsinki Agreement'. Even though the Polish government employed a mixture of arrests and visa denials to prevent this meeting from taking place, Landy and the representatives of peace groups from thirteen Western countries still managed to meet and debate a wide variety of issues in working groups, such as 'peace and human rights' and how to implement a 'new détente'. The attendees may not have been able to reach a consensus on the best way to move towards disarmament or the sincerity of Mikhail Gorbachev's reform programme, but they nevertheless released a statement endorsing the view that 'cooperation between peace and human rights movements East and West' represents the 'fundamental basis for détente'.[76]

During the next two years, activists staged similar meetings in Budapest (November 1987), Moscow (1987) and Cracow (August 1988). The expulsions and arrests that the Czechoslovakian authorities used to break up two meetings that were scheduled to take place in Prague during the summer (June) and autumn (November) of 1988 did not prevent some transnational contacts from taking place. Based on her meetings with members of the Czechoslovakian group Independent Peace Association and participants from other countries, Joanne Landy praised the increased willingness of US peace activists to further the process of détente from below by travelling abroad to meet their counterparts in the Eastern Bloc. The time that she spent in Czechoslovakia also led her to applaud Western peace activists for becoming more receptive to the ideas of forging a 'democratic peace' and the 'indivisible' link between the causes of 'peace and human rights'.[77]

Landy's observations raise the question of just what private citizens accomplished during the 1980s when they participated in debates about how human rights, peace and the process of détente related to each other. This chapter has shown how activists on both sides of the Iron Curtain came to see the Helsinki process as an integral element of forging the détente from below needed to end the Cold War on peaceful terms. While scholars need to devote more attention to this subject, this chapter also confirms the argument that Central and Eastern European dissenters helped some Western peace activists better appreciate the enduring links between the causes of peace and human rights. On the other hand, it has also shown that US groups USHW and CPDEW needed little prodding from Europeans to defend the links between peace and human rights, as well as publicize the value of the Helsinki process.

Even though some Western peace activists became more sensitive to the links between peace and human rights, evidence suggests that invoking the Final Act could not always overcome the differences that divided private citizens.[78] To cite a few examples, some members of WiP called Landy naive about possible Soviet aggression when she argued that the United States could best further the cause of détente from below by withdrawing all military forces from Europe.[79] Many US peace activists also continued to favour a top-down version of détente that placed more emphasis on signing arms control agreements than addressing Soviet and Central-Eastern European human rights violations. This point of view comes across in Pam Solo's inside account of her leadership role in the US nuclear freeze movement. Reflecting on her experience as an American delegate to the IPCC, she retrospectively took US freeze advocates to task for lacking an 'international perspective'. Instead of using the Helsinki process to promote a détente from below, most remained preoccupied with securing arms control agreements that would have done little to challenge the underlying structures of the 'Cold War status quo'.[80]

For all of these shortcomings, the transnational activists described in this chapter deserve credit for a number of accomplishments. Grasping how the Final Act linked the causes of peace and human rights, they used this agreement to unite activists on both sides of the Iron Curtain in the common project of building a détente from below. More to the point, the activists described above played an important role in articulating broader conceptions of détente that linked the tasks of curbing human right violations, promoting peace, opening borders and reducing military armaments. The existence of such behaviour reveals the limitations of only explaining the process of détente as a function of interstate relations or what policymakers said on the subject, as many authors currently do.[81] It also helps show why scholars cannot write a full, convincing international history of détente unless they pay close attention to how private citizens defined and worked to further this process 'from below'.

This chapter also serves as a useful reminder that the story of how communism collapsed in the Soviet Bloc involves far more than recounting systemic economic failures or the unintended consequences of Mikhail Gorbachev's reform programme.[82] In their own way, the activists described in this chapter helped private citizens see the value of drawing on 'liberal' and non-violent ideas when they pressed their leaders to abandon Soviet-style socialism, a reality that helped make the 1989 'revolutions' as peaceful as they were, apart from in Romania.[83] They also made it increasingly difficult for Western peace activists and the 'progressive' left in Western Europe to paint the continuation of the Cold War as a function of the US government's aggressive military policies and unwillingness to reconcile itself to Soviet-style socialism. After all, how could the Soviet Union be a peaceful, progressive nation if its leaders sent peace activists to psychiatric hospitals and repressed grassroots protest? How could the 'master narrative' of socialism's eventual triumph be true if the forging of a more peaceful Europe could not take place without more respect for 'bourgeois' civil liberties in the Soviet Bloc?[84]

The efforts to promote peace described in this chapter also reinforce another important point: top-down governmental agreements in areas like arms control and the liberalization strategies described above can only go so far in furthering the cause of peace. Instead of waiting for words on paper to change the world by themselves, private citizens made the Final Act their own and explained why the tensions that fuelled the Cold War would continue as long as governments in the Soviet Bloc denied their citizens basic human rights in the name of ideological correctness or historic inevitability.[85] They then used the Helsinki process as a weapon of peace to begin the task of building democratic institutions, well-functioning civil societies and transnational connections needed to make the Iron Curtain an obsolete relic – a development that many politicians during the 1980s had a hard time envisioning.[86]

Christian P. Peterson teaches history at Ferris State University (USA). As well as winning several teaching awards, he has written book chapters and articles for publications such as *Diplomatic History*. He has authored two books, including *Globalizing Human Rights: Private Citizens, the Soviet Union, and the West* (Routledge, 2012). His co-edited *The Routledge History of World Peace since 1750* currently has a release date of August 2018. During the summer of 2016, Christian co-directed a National Endowment for the Humanities institute for US high school teachers titled 'War, Revolution, and Empire: US-Russian/Soviet Relations since 1776'.

Notes

1. The British group END came into existence after the appearance of the END Appeal in April 1980. In effect, END urged private citizens across the world to take an internationalist, non-aligned view of the Cold War and work towards creating a more democratic European continent devoid of nuclear

weapons. Technically speaking, British END created the END Liaison Committee, which met for the first time in December 1981. This small group originally assumed the task of organizing the END Conventions, which began in Brussels in July 1982. A new group called the END Convention/Liaison Committee began to take shape in 1981. This committee consisted of representatives from a wide range of Western European peace groups, including British END. It also assumed the primary role in organizing the conventions. In 1985, British END became an official 'membership organization' of about six hundred people. For an excellent description of these developments, including an analysis of divisions within the END Convention/Liaison Committee, see P. Burke, 'END Transnational Peace Campaigning in the 1980s', in E. Conze et al. (eds), *Nuclear Threats, Nuclear Fear, and the Cold War of the 1980s* (Cambridge: Cambridge University Press, 2017), especially 231 and 239.

2. This chapter will define 'transnational' as the 'contacts, exchanges, discourses' and information flows that 'cut across or permeate at least two nation-states'. I employ a definition of 'transnational' derived from the writings of Robert Brier. See 'Entangled Protest: Dissent and the Transnational History of the 1970s and 1980s', in R. Brier (ed.), *Entangled Protest: Transnational Approaches to the History of Dissent in Eastern Europe and the Soviet Union* (Osnabrück: Fibre Verlag, 2013), 11–28; and P. Kenney, 'Electromagnetic Forces and Radio Waves *or* Does Transnational History Actually Happen?' in Brier, *Entangled Protest*, 43–52. See also A. Iriye, *Global and Transnational History: The Past, Present, and Future* (Basingstoke and New York: Palgrave Macmillan, 2013).

3. 'Charter 77 Document No 46/87: Letter to the END Convention in Coventry', Series III, Cathy Fitzpatrick Files (CFF), Box 1, Folder: Charter 77, 1982–1988, Human Rights Watch Records: Helsinki Watch, 1952–2003 (HRWR), Columbia University Rare Book & Manuscript Library, New York City.

4. For example, see M. Kaldor, 'Who Killed the Cold War', *The Bulletin of Atomic Scientists* 51(4) (1995), 57; Kaldor, *Bringing Peace and Human Rights Together* (London: Centre for the Study of Global Governance, London School of Economics, 1999); J. Tirman, 'How We Ended the Cold War', *The Nation*, 14 October 1999, http://www.thenation.com/article/how-we-ended-cold-war/; and D. Cortright, *Peace Works: The Citizen's Role in Ending the Cold War* (Boulder, CO: Westview Press, 1993).

5. For example, see H. Nehring, 'The Politics of Security across the "Iron Curtain": Peace Movements in East and West Germany in the 1980s', in Brier, *Entangled Protest*, 229–47; K. Szulecki, 'Hijacked Ideas: Human Rights, Peace, and Environmentalism in Czechoslovak and Polish Dissident Discourses', *East European Politics and Societies* 25(2) (2011), 272–95; and T. Vilimek, 'Oppositionists in the CSSR and the GDR: Mutual Awareness, Exchanges of Ideas and Cooperation, 1968–1989', in Brier, *Entangled Protest*, 55–85.

6. K. Szulecki, '"Freedom and Peace Are Indivisible": On the Czechoslovak and Polish Dissident Input to the European Peace Movement, 1985–1989',

in Brier, *Entangled Protest*, 199–227; P. Burke, 'A Transnational Movement of Citizens' Strategic Debates in the 1980s Western Peace Movement', in G. Horn and P. Kenney (eds), *Transnational Moments of Change: Europe 1945, 1968, and 1989* (Lanham, MD: Rowman & Littlefield Publishers, Inc., 2004), 189–206; and P. Kenney, *A Carnival of Revolution: Central Europe 1989* (Princeton, NJ: Princeton University Press, 2002), especially Chapter 3.

7. See H. Fedorowicz, *East-West Dialogue: Detente from Below* (Dundas, ON: Peace Research Institute-Dundas, 1991); M. Kaldor, G. Holden, and R. Falk (eds), *The New Detente: Rethinking East-West Relations* (London: Verso, 1989); M. Kaldor, *Europe from Below: An East-West Dialogue* (London and New York: Verso, 1991); and J. Rupnik, 'The Legacy of Charter 77 and the Emergence of a European Public Space', in J. Suk, T. Oldřich and M. Devátá (eds), *Charter 77: From the Assertion of Human Rights to a Democratic Revolution, 1977–1989: The Proceedings of the Conference to Mark the 30th Anniversary of Charter 77, Prague, 21–23 March 2007* (Prague: Ústavpro Soudobé Dějiny AV ČR, 2007), 17–28.

8. For all their strengths, these works do not really address this issue: S. Snyder, *Human Rights Activism and the End of the Cold War* (New York: Cambridge University Press, 2011); C. Peterson, *Globalizing Human Rights: Private Citizens, the Soviet Union, and the West* (New York: Routledge, 2011); W. Korey, *The Promises We Keep: Human Rights, the Helsinki Process, and American Foreign Policy* (New York: St. Martin's Press, 1993); and D. Thomas, *The Helsinki Effect: International Norms, Human Rights, and the Demise of Communism* (Princeton, NJ: Princeton University Press, 2001).

9. K. Szulecki argues that Central/Eastern European dissenters would not use the term 'détente' and the Western concept of 'détente from below' did not include the 'component' of the Helsinki Accords. This chapter will take issue with both these statements. See Szulecki, 'Freedom and Peace Are Indivisible', 219. See also Kenney, *A Carnival of Revolution*, Chapter 3.

10. Just like the term 'transnational', détente has no simple definition. For the difficulties involved in defining the term détente, see 'Détente and Its Legacy', Special Issue of *Cold War History* 8(4) (November 2008), http://h-diplo.org/roundtables/PDF/Roundtable-X-26.pdf; and K. Nelson, *The Making of Détente: Soviet-American Relations in the Shadow of Vietnam* (Baltimore and London: The Johns Hopkins University Press, 1995), notes on 152–53. Many works treat détente as a top-down phenomenon and privilege how nation-states worked to reduce Cold War tensions. For examples of this tendency, see J. Hanhimaki, *The Rise and Fall of Détente: American Foreign Policy and the Transformation of the Cold War* (Washington, DC: Potomac Books, 2013); and R. Garthoff, *Detente and Confrontation: American-Soviet Relations from Nixon to Reagan*, 2nd ed. (Washington, DC: Brookings Institution, 1994).

11. American private citizens created US Helsinki Watch Group (USHW) in 1979. This organization worked to coordinate their activities with and show visible support for Final Act monitors. Members also decided to publish and distribute accurate, up-to-date reports about human rights

conditions in all signatory states and travel to Warsaw Pact nations whenever feasible to speak with dissenters.
12. See D. Mockli, 'The EC Nine, the CSCE, and the Changing Pattern of European Security', in A. Wenger, V. Mastny and C. Nuenlist (eds), *Origins of the European Security System: The Helsinki Process Revisited, 1965–1975* (New York: Routledge, 2008), 148; and A. Romano, *From Détente in Europe to European Détente* (Bern: P.I.E. Peter Lang, 2009), especially 195. S. Kieninger essentially advances the argument that the Johnson administration and 'bridge builders' in the Nixon administration also favoured this gradual liberalization policy, a process that he refers to as 'dynamic détente'. While an important point, he does not really explain how much liberalization could take place if Eastern Bloc regimes continued to violate the basic civil and political rights of their citizens on a systematic basis. Although not his intention, he also recounts how private citizens would actually do their part in forging such a 'dynamic détente'. See S. Kieninger, *Dynamic Détente: The United States and Europe, 1964–1975* (Lanham, MD: Lexington Books, 2016).
13. For an excellent description of why many Western European Social Democrats shied away from challenging the human rights violations of the Soviet Bloc regimes in a public fashion, see R. Brier, 'The Helsinki Final Act, the Second Stage of *Ostpolitik*, and Human Rights in Eastern Europe: The Case of Poland', in R. Mariager et al. (eds), *Human Rights in Europe during the Cold War* (London and New York: Routledge, 2014), 75–94. For a broad, nuanced approach to this subject, see B. Boel, 'Western European Social Democrats and Dissidence in the Soviet Bloc during the Cold War', in Brier, *Entangled Protest*, 151–69.
14. Daniel J. Sargent makes a similar argument. See his new book, *A Superpower Transformed: The Remaking of American Foreign Relations in the 1970s* (New York: Oxford University Press, 2015), 216.
15. 'Appendix: Extract from the Final Act of the Conference on Security and Cooperation in Europe', in D. Kommers and G. Loescher (eds), *Human Rights and American Foreign Policy* (Notre Dame: University of Notre Dame Press, 1979), 145–46. Also see the electronic copy of the Helsinki Accords located at http://www.hri.org/docs/Helsinki75.html (accessed 10 December 2015).
16. To cite two examples, see Kieninger, *Dynamic Détente*; and Snyder, *Human Rights Activism*.
17. See note 15.
18. In response to the Soviet decision to deploy the SS-20 missile, NATO agreed to the 'dual track' decision in 1979, which pledged the United States and several Western European countries to deploy 572 Pershing II and ground-launched cruise missiles (i.e. 'Euromissiles') in 1983 should negotiations to reduce nuclear weapons in the European theatre fail. The term 'zero option' refers to the US offer not to carry out the dual track decision if the Soviets removed their intermediate-range nuclear missiles aimed at Western Europe.
19. As Lawrence S. Wittner describes, 'antinuclear agitation reached new heights' in the United States and Western Europe during the early to mid

1980s. See L. Wittner, *Confronting the Bomb: A Short History of the World Nuclear Disarmament Movement* (Stanford, CA: Stanford University Press, 2009), 152. To cite an example of this growth in the United States, the membership of SANE grew from 17,000 in March 1982 to 150,000 by September 1986. See Swarthmore College Peace Collection, 'SANE Inc. Records, 1957–1987', retrieved 10 December 2015 from https://www.swarthmore.edu/library/peace/DG051-099/dg058sane.htm/dg058saneintr.htm. See also Cortright, *Peace Works*, 5–26. For an excellent account of US anti-nuclear activism, see K. Harvey, *American Anti-Nuclear Activism, 1975–1990* (New York: Palgrave Macmillan, 2014).
20. Cortright, *Peace Works*, 123.
21. Wittner, *Confronting the Bomb*, 144.
22. See Burke, 'END Transnational Peace Campaigning in the 1980s', 231.
23. For an account of these developments, see Cortright, *Peace Works*, 115–21; Wittner, *Confronting the Bomb*, Chapter 7; and T. Rochon, *Mobilizing for Peace: The Antinuclear Movements in Western Europe* (Princeton, NJ: Princeton University Press, 1988), Chapter 1. The 'single day' quote comes from page 6.
24. For a description of the Trust Group's founding and evolution, see C. Fitzpatrick and J. Fleischman, *From Below: Independent Peace and Environmental Movements in Eastern Europe and the Soviet Union* (New York: The Helsinki Watch Committee, 1987), 107–34; and E. Kuznetsov, 'The Independent Peace Movement in the USSR', in V. Tismaneanu (ed.), *In Search of Civil Society: Independent Peace Movements in the Soviet Bloc* (London: Routledge, 1990), 70.
25. For information on KOS, see G. Wylie, 'Social Movements and International Change: The Case of "Detente from Below"', *The International Journal of Peace Studies* 4(2) 1999, https://www.gmu.edu/programs/icar/ijps/vol4_2/wylie.htm. For information on WiP and KOS, see C. Lazarski, 'The Polish Independent Peace Movement', in Tismaneanu, *In Search of Civil Society*, 118–34; and Fitzpatrick and Fleischman, *From Below*, 77–90.
26. For an example of such a view, see P. Monks' editorial in *END: Journal of European Nuclear Disarmament* (August/September 1983). See also C. Peterson, *Ronald Reagan and Antinuclear Movements in the United States and Western Europe, 1981–1987* (Lewiston, NY: Edwin Mellen Press, 2003), especially Chapter 2.
27. During a meeting with representatives of the Soviet government in Moscow in the summer of 1984, SANE Executive Director David Cortright agreed when a fellow participant said 'let's stick to peace and disarmament' instead of raising the issue of Soviet human rights violations. After all, he reasoned, the cause of 'peace and disarmament would suffer' if Westerners told the Soviets how to run their 'own internal system'. See 'Images of the Soviet Union', August 1984, SANE, Series G, Files of David Cortright, Box 75, Folder: Activities & Projects: SANE Material, Swarthmore College Peace Collection (SCPC), Swarthmore, PA. During a skype interview with the author on 15 July 2016, David Cortright confirmed that during much of the 1980s, he saw human rights as a 'political wedge' issue that 'right-wing'

forces used to undermine the cause of peace and justify the building of nuclear weapons.
28. For commentary on why US freeze advocates tended to shy away from forging contacts with Soviet Bloc unofficial peace activists, see P. Solo, *From Protest to Policy: Beyond the Freeze to Common Security* (Cambridge, MA: Ballinger Publishing Company, 1988), 111–14; D. Cortright and R. Pagnucco, 'Transnational Activism in the Nuclear Weapons Freeze Campaign', in T. Rochon and D. Meyer (eds), *Coalitions and Political Movements: The Lessons of the Nuclear Freeze* (Boulder, CO: Lynne Rienner, 1997), 81–96.
29. To cite one example, the leadership of WILPF refused to acknowledge the existence of the Moscow Trust Group on the grounds that such a move would only succeed in dividing the 'anti-war cause' and help 'Reaganites who are trying to keep the peace movement divided'. See WILPF, 'Policy Committee Report on Independent Peace Groups, National Board Meeting, 23–25 September 1983', PART III: US SECTION SERIES A,2: BOARD, OFFICER AND MEMBER MEETINGS/CONFERENCES AND PAPERS OF NON-STAFF LEADERS, Box 28, Folder DG 043 Biennial national meeting (& board meeting), Harverford (PA): Board meeting, Philadelphia (PA), Sept. 23–25, 1983, 4, SCPC.
30. David McReynolds (DM) of WRL made a similar point in 1986 when he observed in a letter that placing too much emphasis on monitoring Soviet compliance with the Final Act would probably undermine the larger goal of creating a more peaceful world. See Letter, DM to Cathy Fitzpatrick (CF), 12 August 1986, Series III, CFF, Box 25, Folder: McReynolds, David, 1982–1988, HRWR. David Cortright confirmed to this author that he did not see the Helsinki process as a mechanism to promote peace until the late 1980s (Cortright, skype interview, 15 July 2016).
31. In the report that he wrote about his 1984 trip to the Soviet Union, SANE Executive Director David Cortright stressed the need to reduce nuclear arsenals and Soviet citizens' desire for peace. He even went so far as to argue that the United States would never have 'peace and improved relations' with the USSR unless Americans recognized the Soviets' right to 'their own internal system'. See 'Images of the Soviet Union', August 1984, SCPC.
32. For a description of the growing distrust of Cold War elites, see P. Kelly, 'The European Peace Movement: Conversation with Petra Kelly and Gert Bastian – Emergence of the Peace Movement', 23 October 1984, http://globetrotter.berkeley.edu/conversations/KellyBastian/kelly-bastian3.html; and John Mason, 'Interview with Mary Kaldor', *Telos* 51 (20 March 1982), 88–96, especially 91.
33. S. Kalden, 'A Case of "Hollanditis": The Interchurch Peace Council in the Netherlands and the Christian Peace Movement in Western Europe', in Conze et al., *Nuclear Threats, Nuclear Fear, and the Cold War of the 1980s*, 258–59.
34. See P. Baehr, 'E.P. Thompson and European Nuclear Disarmament (END): A Critical Retrospective', *Online Journal for Peace and Conflict Resolution* 2.5/3.1 (March 2000), www.trinstitute.org/ojpcr/3_1baehr.htm. For a copy

of the END Appeal, see 'A Nuclear Free Europe', in E. Thompson, *Protest and Survive* (Nottingham, UK: Russell Press, 1981), 16ff.
35. 'Moscow Trust Group to Establish Trust between the USSR and USA, Statement to Second European Nuclear Disarmament Conference, West Berlin, 1983', Series III, CFF, Box 31, Folder: Correspondence, 1983–1986, HRWR. For examples of Czech and Polish support, see Letter, Jaroslav Sabata to E.P. Thompson, 'The Struggle for Peace and Eastern Europe', *Across Frontiers* (Spring 1984). WiP participant Jacek Czaputowicz supported the concept of détente during the 1980s despite the refusal of many Central-Eastern European activists to endorse the concept (Jacek Czaputowicz, skype interview with author, 9 May 2016).
36. See E. Thompson and F. Koszegi, *The New Hungarian Peace Movement: END Special Report* (London: European Nuclear Disarmament, 1983). See also Thompson, *Beyond the Cold War* (London: Pantheon, 1982).
37. See Burke, 'END Transnational Peace Campaigning in the 1980s', 231–37.
38. US Helsinki Commission, *Documents of the Soviet Groups to Establish Trust between the US and USSR* (Washington, DC: US Government Printing Office, 1984), especially 1–15; and Memorandum (Memo), Sergei Batrovin (SB) and Mikhail Ostrovosky (MO) to US, Canadian, and European Peace Groups, September 1983, Series III, CFF, Box 34, Folder: October 1 Demonstrations, 1983, HRWR. This author is well aware that Moscow Trust Group members were not due paying members of a hierarchical organization. For groups like the Moscow Trust Group, BANG, PAEW (Peace Activists East and West) and CPDEW, I use the term 'member' to denote someone who identified with and actively worked for a specific group.
39. Czaputowicz interview with author. See also Kenney, *A Carnival of Revolution*, 94–95.
40. 'The Politics of the Dutch Missile Decision: A CPD/EW Interview with Wim Bartels', *Peace and Democracy News* (Winter 1984–85); and Letter, IKV to Jacek Kuron, January 1985, Series III, CFF, Box 1, Folder: Poland: Movement – Disarmament, 1982–1988, HRWR. See also 'Underground Solidarity and the Western Peace Movement', *Across Frontiers* (Summer 1984).
41. For example, see J. Kavan and Z. Tomin (eds), *Voices from Prague: Documents on Czechoslovakia and the Peace Movement* (London: END and Palach Press, 1983), 15–16; 'An Open Letter from Charter 77 to the Western European Peace Movement', *Peace and Democracy News* (Winter 1984–85); and '"Freedom and Peace" Declaration of Principles', Series III, CFF, Box 37, Folder: *Peace and Democracy News* (magazine), 1984–1990, HRWR.
42. 'A Dialogue in the Defense of Peace', Series III, CFF, Box 1, Folder: Poland: Movement – Disarmament, 1982–1988, HRWR; 'Underground Solidarity and the Western Peace Movement', *Across Frontiers* (Summer 1984). For a copy of Havel's essay 'Anatomy of a Reticence', see P. Wilson (ed.), *Open Letters: Selected Writings, 1965–1990* (New York: Alfred A. Knopf, 1991), 291–322. See also Kavan and Tomin, *Voices from Prague*. It took time for supporters of END, including E.P. Thompson, to figure out how to reconcile the tasks of peace and human rights promotion. For a nice account

of Thompson's conflicted attitude towards human rights during the early 1980s, see Thompson's *Zero Option* (London: Merlin Press, 1982), 100.
43. Kavan and Tomin, *Voices from Prague*, 23; and US Helsinki Commission, *Human Rights in Czechoslovakia: The Documents of Charter 77, 1982–1987* (Washington, DC: US Government Printing Office, 1988), 196. For another account of this development, see Jacek Czaputowicz's contribution to this volume, 'The Importance of the Helsinki Process for the Opposition in Central and Eastern Europe and the Western Peace Movements in the 1980s'.
44. 'An Open Letter to Soviet Peace Committee', Series III, CFF, Box 28, Folder: Background, 1982–1986, HRWR.
45. J. Landy, 'Disarmament and Democracy', Series III, CFF, Box 1, Folder: Hungary (General), 1984–1988, HRWR.
46. 'Welcome to our Readers' and 'Highlights of Recent Campaign Activities', in *Peace & Democracy News* (Spring 1984); Letter, CPDEW (known at the time as West/East Peace and Democracy Project) to Soviet General Secretary Leonid Brezhnev, 10 August 1982, Series III, CFF, Box 28, Folder: Background, 1982–1986, HRWR; and 'Peace, Labor & Religious Meet with Polish Embassy Officials to Protest Trial of Solidarity Leaders', *Peace and Democracy News* (Spring 1984).
47. 'New Peace Group Promotes East-West Grassroots Ties', *Peace & Democracy News* (Summer/Fall) 1986; and Memo, PAEWCC, 'Urgent Action', Series III, CFF, Box 37, Folder: Peace Activists East and West (PAEW), 1985–1988, HRWR.
48. PAEW, 'Peace and Human Rights – Making the Connection', Series III, CFF, Box 37, Folder: Peace Activists East and West (PAEW), 1985–1988, HRWR.
49. W. Bartels, 'IPCC Leader', interview, 1990, http://russianpeaceanddemocracy.com/wim-bartels-1990. See also Kalden, 'A Case of "Hollanditis"', 259–60.
50. Letter, CF to Dante Fascell, 19 March 1984, Series III, CFF, Box 5, Folder: Batovrin, Sergei: Testimony, 1982–1988, HRWR; and Letter, CF to Edward Markey, 19 March 1984, Series III, CFF, Box 5, Folder: Batovrin, Sergei: Testimony, 1982–1988, HRWR.
51. For example, see M. Kampelman, *Three Years at the East-West Divide: The Words of US Ambassador Max Kampelman at the Madrid Conference on Security and Human Rights* (New York: Freedom House, 1983), 123–25.
52. For example, see Aryeh Neier, 'Rights: Bulwark of Peace', Series III, CFF, Box 5, Folder: Helsinki Watch Defense, 1982–1985, HRWR. For an example of a petition, see 'Signers of letter to Leonid I. Brezhnev', Series III, Box 31, Folder: Correspondence, 1983–1986, HRWR.
53. Open Letter in defense of Moscow Trust Group, Series III, CFF, Box 5, Folder: Helsinki Watch Defense, 1982–1985, HRWR.
54. Memo, 'New Year's Day Actions', CFF, Box 5, Folder: Helsinki Watch Defense, 1982–1985, HRWR; and Letter, CF to SB, ND, CFF, Box 5, Folder: Batavian, Sergei: Testimony, 1982–1988, HRWR.
55. Catherine A. (Cathy) Fitzpatrick, skype interview with author, 10 September 2015.

56. Letter, David McReynolds (DM) to CF, 19 February 1987, Series III, CFF, Box 25, Folder: McReynolds, David, 1982–1988, HRWR.
57. Cathy Fitzpatrick, 'The Trust Group and the Western Peace Movement: The Hard Questions', Series III, CFF, Box 31, Folder: Documents, 1985–1986, 20–25, HRWR.
58. Memo, 'Independent Moscow Peace Group', Series III, CFF, Box 31, Folder: Defense of group in the US, 1985–1987, HRWR; 'Statement by Mikhail Ostrovsky', Series III, CFF, Box 31, Folder: Defense of group in the US, 1985–1987, HRWR; and 'Letter to Yuri Andropov', Series III, Box 31, Folder: Correspondence, 1983–1986, HRWR.
59. Meeting with Leonid Bindy, First Secretary, Soviet Mission to UN, 1 March 1983, Series III, CFF, Box 37, Folder: Peace Issues, 1980–1985, HRWR; and 'North American and European Peace Activists Call for October 1 Demonstrations in Solidarity with Harassed Soviet Peace Group', Series III, CFF, Box 31, Folder: Defense of group in the US, 1985–1987, HRWR.
60. 'An Appeal to US Disarmament Activists', *BANG Notes* (Winter 1984/85), Series III, CFF, Box 31, Folder: Defense of Group (Moscow Trust Group) in the US, 1985–1987, HRWR; and Bob McGlynn, skype interview with author, 1 August 2016. While NENWN numbered thirty to forty people, NENWN branches formed in cities across the country, including San Francisco and Kansas City. Future researchers need to determine how many people actively participated in these groups.
61. C. Bobson, 'Some Thoughts on Détente and Human Rights', Series III, CFF, Box 1, Folder: Movement – Disarmament, 1982–1987, HRWR.
62. 'Détente from Below: Polish Activists Meet Westerners and Draft Statement against Pentagon/superpower intervention and police riot/gentrification in NYC', *On Gogol Boulevard* (Fall 1988), Series III, CFF, Box 34, Folder: McGlynn, Bob (Peace movements in Soviet Bloc), 1986–1988, HRWR; McGlynn, skype interview with author.
63. This point comes across in Fitzpatrick's correspondence with David McReynolds of WRL. For example, see Letter, DM to CF, 12 August 1986, Series III, CFF, Box 25, Folder: McReynolds, David, 1982–1988, HRWR.
64. Untitled Document, Series III, CFF, Box 22, Folder: Lectures by Cathy Fitzpatrick: Correspondence, 1983–1988, HRWR.
65. Dieter Esche et al. to members of Liaison Committee, 'Some Remarks about the Controversy Concerning the East-West Dialogue', 27 February 1984, 1–3, Series III, CFF, Box 38, Folder: Perugia (Soviet delegations to the Third European Convention for Nuclear Disarmament) 1984, HRWR.
66. R. Falk, 'An American View of the Perugia Conference', *Peace & Democracy News* (Winter 1984/85); and 'Euronukes Opponents thrive on Disagreement', Series III, CFF, Box 38, Folder: Perugia (Soviet delegations to the Third European Convention for Nuclear Disarmament) 1984, HRWR.
67. For an example of such views, see 'On Peace in Europe', *Across Frontiers* (Winter/Spring 1985).
68. Fitzpatrick and Fleischman, *From Below*, 207–12.
69. When analysing the Prague Appeal and the appearance of *Giving Real Life to the Helsinki Accords* (see below), Szulecki overstates the novelty of using

the Helsinki process to end the Cold War. See 'Freedom and Peace Are Indivisible'.
70. 'END's Response to Prague Appeal', Campaign for Peace and Democracy Records (CPDR), Box 2, Folder: CPDEW #24, The Tammiment Library & Labor Archives (TLLA), New York University, New York City.
71. Fitzpatrick and Fleischman, *From Below*, 239–49. The 'transnational creative process' quotes come from Szulecki, 'Freedom and Peace Are Indivisible', 223 and 221–27. For examples of the transnational debates that shaped this process, see 'Letter to the Milan Forum on Helsinki: 16–18 May', *East European Reporter* 2(1) (1986); and 'A Statement of Views of some Signatories of Charter 77 Submitted to the Milan Forum', *East European Reporter* 2(1) (1986). See also Czaputowicz's contribution to this volume.
72. Letter, IPCC to CF, 28 June 1986, Series X, International Federation for Human Rights Files, 1975–1996, Box 7, Folder: Nader, Gerald – Correspondence, HRWR; and Bartels, 'IPCC Leader'.
73. 'Calendar', *Nuclear Times* (Nov/Dec 1988); and Bartels, 'IPCC Leader'.
74. Cathy Fitzpatrick, 'Speech before Fellowship of Reconciliation Conference, 6–7 May 1988, Nyak, New York', Series III, CFF, Box 32, Folder: Lectures and Manuscripts, HRWR.
75. 'Highlights of CPD/EW Activities', *Peace & Democracy News* (Winter/Spring 1985).
76. 'Freedom and Peace Seminar: "International Peace and the Helsinki Agreement"', Warsaw, 7–9 May 1987, Series III, CFF, Box 1, Folder: Freedom and Peace, 1985–1988, HRWR. See also 'With Satisfaction We Hereby Present to You A First Set of Documents from the Independent Seminar "International Peace and the Helsinki Agreements, Warsaw, 7, 8, 9 May 1987"', Series III, CFF, Box 1, Folder: Freedom and Peace, 1985–1988, HRWR; and 'The Program of the Peace Seminar in Warsaw', CPDR, Box 3, Folder: Freedom and Peace Seminar, May 1987, TLLA; and Piotr Niemczyk, 'The Peace Race', *East European Reporter* 3(1) (1988).
77. 'Worth Every Disrupted Minute: Interview', *East European Reporter* 3(3) (1988), 22–24.
78. E.P. Thompson became more sensitive to the issue of Soviet Bloc human rights violations. See Burke, 'A Transnational Movement of Citizens' Strategic Debates'; and Szulecki, 'Freedom and Peace Are Indivisible'. Robert Brier also mentions this development in his article 'From Dissidence to Neoliberalism? Reflections on the Human Rights Legacy of 1989', European Network Remembrance and Solidarity, 8 September 2015, http://enrs.eu/en/articles/1575-from-dissidence-to-neoliberalism-reflections-on-the-human-rights-legacy-of-1989.
79. Letter, Joanne Landy to Piotr Niemczyk, 25 July 1987, Series III, CFF, Box 1, Folder: Freedom and Peace, 1987–1988, HRWR. To view some of the critical letters that members of WiP addressed and/or sent to Joanne Landy, see Series III, CFF, Box 1, Folder: Freedom and Peace, 1987–1988, HRWR. For a deeper discussion of the divisions among Western and Central and Eastern European peace activists, see Czaputowicz's contribution to this volume.

80. Solo, *From Protest to Policy*, 111–14. For a similar view, see Cortright, *Peace Works*, 212–13.
81. See note 10.
82. For more on this view, see V. Tismaneanu and B. Jacob (eds), *The End and the Beginning: The Revolutions of 1989 and the Resurgence of History* (Budapest: Central European University Press, 2012).
83. For example, see J. Rupnik, 'The Legacies of Dissent: Charter 77, the Helsinki Effect, and the Emergence of a European Public Space', in F. Kind-Kovács and J. Labov (eds), *Samizdat, Tamizdat, and Beyond: Transnational Media during and after Socialism* (New York: Berghahn Books, 2013), 320–28. See also selected essays in Tismaneanu and Jacob, *The End and the Beginning*.
84. The idea of a 'master narrative' comes from Tony Judt. He also makes a strong case that critiques of Soviet-style socialism began to undermine the European (French in particular) 'progressive left's' faith in the welfare state, centralized planning and socialism. See his work *Postwar: A History of Europe since 1945* (New York: Penguin Press, 2005), Chapter 18.
85. For more detailed analyses of these topics, see P. Blokker, 'Dissidence, Republicanism, and Democratic Change', *East European Politics and Societies* 25(2) (2011), 219–43. See also V. Tismaneanu, *Reinventing Politics: Eastern Europe from Stalin to Havel* (New York: The Free Press, 1992), Chapters 4 and 5.
86. For debates about the meaning of the term civil society, see John Keane, *Global Civil Society?* (London: Cambridge University Press, 2003), 175–76. For works that deal with the role that 'civil society' played in the ending of the Cold War, see B. Falk, 'Resistance and Dissent in Central and Eastern Europe: An Emerging Historiography', *East European Politics and Societies* 25(2) (2011), 336–38; Falk, *The Dilemmas of Dissidence in East-Central Europe: Citizen Intellectuals and Philosopher Kings* (Budapest and New York: Central European University Press, 2003), Chapter 8; Rupnik, 'The Legacies of Dissent', 320–28; M. Kaldor, *Global Civil Society: An Answer to War* (London: Blackwell Press, 2003). When discussing the revolutions in 'Eastern Europe', Sarah Snyder makes reference to the concept of 'second society'. See Snyder, *Human Rights Activism*, 228.

Bibliography

Archives

Columbia University Rare Book & Manuscript Library, New York City.
Swarthmore College Peace Collection, Swarthmore, Pennsylvania.
The Tammiment Library & Labor Archives (TLLA), New York University, New York City.

Periodicals

Across Frontiers
East European Reporter

END: *Journal of European Nuclear Disarmament*
Peace and Democracy News

Secondary Sources

'Appendix: Extract from the Final Act of the Conference on Security and Cooperation in Europe', in D. Kommers and G. Loescher (eds), *Human Rights and American Foreign Policy* (Notre Dame, IN: University of Notre Dame Press, 1979), 145–46.

Baehr, P. 'E.P. Thompson and European Nuclear Disarmament (END): A Critical Retrospective'. *Online Journal for Peace and Conflict Resolution* 2.5/3.1 (March 2000). www.trinstitute.org/ojpcr/3_1baehr.htm.

Bartels, W. 'IPCC Leader'. Interview. 1990. http://russianpeaceanddemocracy.com/wim-bartels-1990.

Blokker, P. 'Dissidence, Republicanism, and Democratic Change'. *East European Politics and Societies* 25(2) (2011), 219–43.

Boel, B. 'Western European Social Democrats and Dissidence in the Soviet Bloc during the Cold War', in R. Brier (ed.), *Entangled Protest: Transnational Approaches to the History of Dissent in Eastern Europe and the Soviet Union* (Osnabrück: Fibre Verlag, 2013), 151–69.

Brier, R. 'Entangled Protest: Dissent and the Transnational History of the 1970s and 1980s', in R. Brier (ed.), *Entangled Protest: Transnational Approaches to the History of Dissent in Eastern Europe and the Soviet Union* (Osnabrück: Fibre Verlag, 2013), 11–28.

Brier, R. 'From Dissidence to Neoliberalism? Reflections on the Human Rights Legacy of 1989'. European Network Remembrance and Solidarity, 8 September 2015. http://enrs.eu/en/articles/1575-from-dissidence-to-neoliberalism-reflections-on-the-human-rights-legacy-of-1989.

Brier, R. 'The Helsinki Final Act, the Second Stage of *Ostpolitik*, and Human Rights in Eastern Europe: The Case of Poland', in R. Mariager et al. (eds), *Human Rights in Europe during the Cold War* (London and New York: Routledge, 2014), 75–94.

Burke, P. 'END Transnational Peace Campaigning in the 1980s', in E. Conze et al. (eds), *Nuclear Threats, Nuclear Fear, and the Cold War of the 1980s* (Cambridge: Cambridge University Press, 2017), 227–50.

Burke, P. 'A Transnational Movement of Citizens' Strategic Debates in the 1980s Western Peace Movement', in G. Horn and P. Kenney (eds), *Transnational Moments of Change: Europe 1945, 1968, and 1989* (Lanham, MD: Rowman & Littlefield Publishers, Inc., 2004), 189–206.

Cortright, D. *Peace Works: The Citizen's Role in Ending the Cold War*. Boulder, CO: Westview Press, 1993.

Cortright, D., and R. Pagnucco. 'Transnational Activism in the Nuclear Weapons Freeze Campaign', in T. Rochon and D. Meyer (eds), *Coalitions and Political Movements: The Lessons of the Nuclear Freeze* (Boulder, CO: Lynne Rienner, 1997), 81–96.

'Détente and Its Legacy', Special Issue of *Cold War History* 8 (4) (2008). http://h-diplo.org/roundtables/PDF/Roundtable-X-26.pdf.

Falk, B. *The Dilemmas of Dissidence in East-Central Europe: Citizen Intellectuals and Philosopher Kings*. Budapest and New York: Central European University Press, 2003.

Falk, B. 'Resistance and Dissent in Central and Eastern Europe: An Emerging Historiography'. *East European Politics and Societies* 25(2) (2011), 318–60.

Fedorowicz, H. *East-West Dialogue: Detente from Below*. Dundas, ON: Peace Research Institute-Dundas, 1991.

Fitzpatrick, C. and J. Fleischman, *From Below: Independent Peace and Environmental Movements in Eastern Europe and the Soviet Union*. New York: The Helsinki Watch Committee, 1987.

Garthoff, R. *Detente and Confrontation: American-Soviet Relations from Nixon to Reagan*. 2nd ed. Washington, DC: Brookings Institution, 1994.

Hanhimaki, J. *The Rise and Fall of Détente: American Foreign Policy and the Transformation of the Cold War*. Washington, DC: Potomac Books, 2013.

Harvey, K. *American Anti-Nuclear Activism, 1975–1990*. New York: Palgrave Macmillan, 2014.

'Interview with Mary Kaldor'. *Telos* 51 (1982), 88–96.

Iriye, A. *Global and Transnational History: The Past, Present, and Future*. Basingstoke and New York: Palgrave Macmillan, 2013.

Judt, T. *Postwar: A History of Europe since 1945*. New York: Penguin Press, 2005.

Kalden, S. 'A Case of "Hollanditis": The Interchurch Peace Council in the Netherlands and the Christian Peace Movement in Western Europe', in E. Conze et al. (eds), *Nuclear Threats, Nuclear Fear, and the Cold War of the 1980s* (Cambridge: Cambridge University Press, 2016), 251–68.

Kaldor, M. *Bringing Peace and Human Rights Together*. London: Centre for the Study of Global Governance, London School of Economics, 1999.

Kaldor, M. *Global Civil Society: An Answer to War*. London: Blackwell Press, 2003.

Kaldor, M. 'Who Killed the Cold War'. *The Bulletin of Atomic Scientists* 51(4) (1995), 57.

Kaldor, M. (ed.). *Europe from Below: An East-West Dialogue*. London and New York: Verso, 1991.

Kaldor, M., G. Holden, and R. Falk (eds). *The New Detente: Rethinking East-West Relations*. London: Verso, 1989.

Kampelman, M. *Three Years at the East-West Divide: The Words of US Ambassador Max Kampelman at the Madrid Conference on Security and Human Rights*. New York: Freedom House, 1983.

Kavan, J., and Z. Tomin (eds). *Voices from Prague: Documents on Czechoslovakia and the Peace Movement*. London: END and Palach Press, 1983.

Keane, J. *Global Civil Society?* London: Cambridge University Press, 2003.

Kelly, P. 'The European Peace Movement: Conversation with Petra Kelly and Gert Bastian – Emergence of the Peace Movement'. 23 October 1984. http://globetrotter.berkeley.edu/conversations/KellyBastian/kelly-bastian3.html.

Kenney, P. *A Carnival of Revolution: Central Europe 1989*. Princeton, NJ: Princeton University Press, 2002.

Kenney, P. 'Electromagnetic Forces and Radio Waves *or* Does Transnational History Actually Happen?' in R. Brier (ed.), *Entangled Protest: Transnational Approaches to the History of Dissent in Eastern Europe and the Soviet Union* (Osnabrück: Fibre Verlag, 2013), 43–52.

Kieninger, S. *Dynamic Détente: The United States and Europe, 1964–1975.* Lanham, MD: Lexington Books, 2016.

Korey, W. *The Promises We Keep: Human Rights, the Helsinki Process, and American Foreign Policy.* New York: St. Martin's Press, 1993.

Kuznetsov, E. 'The Independent Peace Movement in the USSR', in V. Tismaneanu (ed.), *In Search of Civil Society: Independent Peace Movements in the Soviet Bloc* (London: Routledge, 1990), 54–70.

Lazarski, C. 'The Polish Independent Peace Movement', in V. Tismaneanu (ed.), *In Search of Civil Society: Independent Peace Movements in the Soviet Bloc* (London: Routledge, 1990), 118–34.

Mockli, D. 'The EC Nine, the CSCE, and the Changing Pattern of European Security', in A. Wenger, V. Mastny and C. Nuenlist (eds), *Origins of the European Security System: The Helsinki Process Revisited, 1965–1975* (New York: Routledge, 2008), 145–63.

Nehring, H. 'The Politics of Security across the "Iron Curtain": Peace Movements in East and West Germany in the 1980s', in R. Brier (ed.), *Entangled Protest: Transnational Approaches to the History of Dissent in Eastern Europe and the Soviet Union* (Osnabrück: Fibre Verlag, 2013), 229–47.

Nelson, K. *The Making of Détente: Soviet-American Relations in the Shadow of Vietnam.* Baltimore, MD and London: The Johns Hopkins University Press, 1995.

Peterson, C. *Globalizing Human Rights: Private Citizens, the Soviet Union, and the West.* New York: Routledge, 2011.

Peterson, C. *Ronald Reagan and Antinuclear Movements in the United States and Western Europe, 1981–1987.* Lewiston, NY: Edwin Mellen Press, 2003.

Rochon, T. *Mobilizing for Peace: The Antinuclear Movements in Western Europe.* Princeton, NJ: Princeton University Press, 1988.

Romano, A. *From Détente in Europe to European Détente.* Bern: P.I.E. Peter Lang, 2009.

Rupnik, J. 'The Legacies of Dissent: Charter 77, the Helsinki Effect, and the Emergence of a European Public Space', in F. Kind-Kovács and J. Labov (eds), *Samizdat, Tamizdat, and Beyond: Transnational Media during and after Socialism* (New York: Berghahn Books, 2013), 320–28.

Rupnik, J. 'The Legacy of Charter 77 and the Emergence of a European Public Space', in J. Suk, T. Oldřich and M. Devátá (eds), *Charter 77: From the Assertion of Human Rights to a Democratic Revolution, 1977–1989: The Proceedings of the Conference to Mark the 30th Anniversary of Charter 77, Prague, 21–23 March 2007* (Prague: Ústavpro Soudobé Dějiny AV ČR, 2007), 17–28.

Sargent, D. *A Superpower Transformed: The Remaking of American Foreign Relations in the 1970s.* New York: Oxford University Press, 2015.

Snyder, S. *Human Rights Activism and the End of the Cold War.* New York: Cambridge University Press, 2011.

Solo, P. *From Protest to Policy: Beyond the Freeze to Common Security*. Cambridge, MA: Ballinger Publishing Company, 1988.

Swarthmore College Peace Collection. 'SANE Inc. Records, 1957–1987'. Retrieved 10 December 2016 from https://www.swarthmore.edu/library/peace/DG051-099/dg058sane.htm/dg058saneintr.htm.

Szulecki, K. '"Freedom and Peace Are Indivisible": On the Czechoslovak and Polish Dissident Input to the European Peace Movement, 1985–1989', in R. Brier (ed.), *Entangled Protest: Transnational Approaches to the History of Dissent in Eastern Europe and the Soviet Union* (Osnabrück: Fibre Verlag, 2013), 199–227.

Szulecki, K. 'Hijacked Ideas: Human Rights, Peace, and Environmentalism in Czechoslovak and Polish Dissident Discourses'. *East European Politics and Societies* 25(2) (2011), 272–95.

Thomas, D. *The Helsinki Effect: International Norms, Human Rights, and the Demise of Communism*. Princeton, NJ: Princeton University Press, 2001.

Thompson, E.P. *Protest and Survive*. Nottingham, UK: Russell Press, 1981.

Thompson, E.P. *Beyond the Cold War*. London: Pantheon, 1982.

Thompson, E.P. *Zero Option*. London: Merlin Press, 1982.

Thompson, E.P., and F. Koszegi. *The New Hungarian Peace Movement: END Special Report*. London: European Nuclear Disarmament, 1983.

Tirman, J. 'How We Ended the Cold War'. *The Nation*, 14 October 1999. http://www.thenation.com/article/how-we-ended-cold-war/.

Tismaneanu, V. *Reinventing Politics: Eastern Europe from Stalin to Havel*. New York: The Free Press, 1992.

Tismaneanu, V., and B. Jacob (eds). *The End and the Beginning: The Revolutions of 1989 and the Resurgence of History*. Budapest: Central European University Press, 2012.

US Helsinki Commission. *Documents of the Soviet Groups to Establish Trust between the US and USSR*. Washington, DC: US Government Printing Office, 1984.

US Helsinki Commission. *Human Rights in Czechoslovakia: The Documents of Charter 77, 1982–1987*. Washington, DC: US Government Printing Office, 1988.

Vilimek, T. 'Oppositionists in the CSSR and the GDR: Mutual Awareness, Exchanges of Ideas and Cooperation, 1968–1989', in R. Brier (ed.), *Entangled Protest: Transnational Approaches to the History of Dissent in Eastern Europe and the Soviet Union* (Osnabrück: Fibre Verlag, 2013), 55–85.

Wilson, P. (ed.). *Open Letters: Selected Writings, 1965–1990*. New York: Alfred A. Knopf, 1991.

Wittner, L. *Confronting the Bomb: A Short History of the World Nuclear Disarmament Movement*. Stanford, CA: Stanford University Press, 2009.

Wylie, G. 'Social Movements and International Change: The Case of "Detente from Below"'. *The International Journal of Peace Studies* 4(2) (1999). https://www.gmu.edu/programs/icar/ijps/vol4_2/wylie.htm.

 7

The Importance of the Helsinki Process for the Opposition in Central and Eastern Europe and the Western Peace Movements in the 1980s

Jacek Czaputowicz

Introduction

The Final Act of the Conference on Security and Cooperation in Europe (CSCE) held in Helsinki was perceived as an instrument to bring about a change in the countries of the Eastern Bloc. Signing the Final Act, the countries of Central and Eastern Europe committed to observing 'human rights and fundamental freedoms, including the freedom of thought, conscience, religion or belief' and to supporting the movement of people and ideas between the East and the West. In return, they expected détente and development of cooperation. The value of the Helsinki Final Act was for them that it confirmed borders in Europe and consolidated the territorial status quo. At the same time, they opposed any interpretation of the Helsinki process that would give Western countries the right to interfere with their internal affairs.

The 'third basket', which concerned the observance of human rights, was treated by communist authorities as a potential instrument that could be used by the West to undermine the legitimacy of those holding power. Indeed, diplomats from Western countries, including US Ambassador Arthur Goldberg, protested at the CSCE against repressions and arrests of dissidents. The Polish participant of the CSCE follow-up meeting held in Belgrade in 1977 wrote that Western countries attempted to 'legitimise on an international plane the minority opposition and dissidence in socialist countries and to put forward a whole catalogue of unrealistic postulates concerning contacts between people and the flow of information'.[1]

Communist and Western countries differed in the direction of causal relations between human rights and international relations. Countries of the Eastern Bloc maintained that détente led to better observance of human rights, while Western countries believed that it was rather human rights that led to détente.[2]

The aim of this chapter is to show the importance of the Helsinki Final Act for the cooperation between dissident groups in Central and Eastern Europe and peace movements in the West. How the CSCE process was used to pursue goals of democratization of the communist system as well as the transnational cooperation regarding diffusion of ideas between the East and the West will also be discussed. The first part focuses on the process of establishing cooperation between Central and Eastern European opposition groups and Western peace movements, with special focus on the significance of Charter 77's Prague Appeal and the Helsinki Memorandum. The second part is dedicated to the international peace seminar, 'International Peace and the Helsinki Accords', organized by the 'Freedom and Peace' Movement in Warsaw in May 1987, and on the 'Jaruzelski Plan', put forward at the CSCE. The third part concentrates on the discussions held in 1987 and 1988 between dissidents from Central and Eastern Europe and peace and human rights activists from the West in Budapest, Moscow, Prague and Krakow.

Transnational Dialogue and the Helsinki Memorandum

For opposition movements in Central and Eastern Europe, the Helsinki Final Act constituted a convenient starting point for demanding political and civil freedoms, a source of legitimacy for their demands in the area of human rights. From their point of view, 'the Helsinki agreement contained the seeds of the destruction of the Soviet system, either because of the cooperative nature of the process set in train by Helsinki, or because of the normative effect of human rights provisions written into the Final Act'.[3]

The Helsinki Final Act contributed to the consolidation of democratic opposition in Central European countries, including the establishment of the Workers' Defence Committee (Komitet Obrony Robotników) in Poland and Charter 77 (Charta 77) in Czechoslovakia. The culminating point was the formation of the Solidarity movement in August 1980, which, however, was deemed illegal after martial law had been declared in Poland on 13 December 1981. In the mid 1980s, the CSCE process was the point of reference for the debate between the opposition groups in

Central and Eastern Europe and the Western peace-oriented movement on rapprochement between the societies of the East and the West and on overcoming the continent's division into opposing blocs.

In December 1979, NATO decided to deploy American cruise and Pershing missiles in Europe, which raised a sense of insecurity in the Western European societies. This, in turn, gave rise to peace movements aimed at nuclear disarmament. They were divided into those who supported détente from above, with contacts with authorities and official peace movements in communist countries, and those who preferred détente from below, with contacts with dissidents and independent peace groups in the East. The second group included European Nuclear Disarmament (END), established in response to NATO's decision to deploy nuclear missiles in Western Europe as a reaction to a Soviet deployment of such missiles in Eastern Europe. In 1980, END issued an appeal demanding that Europe, from Poland to Portugal, be freed of nuclear weapons and that the right of people on both sides of the Iron Curtain to participate in the common movement of social organizations, labour unions, churches and citizens be protected.[4] In 1982–91, END organized yearly peace conventions attended by peace activists from both the West and the East.

After the declaration of martial law, when the Western peace movement wanted to establish contacts with the Polish opposition, it turned out that their potential interlocutors were either in internment camps or underground. In 1982 and 1983, activists focused on combating the regime, and thus showed little interest in developing dialogue and international cooperation.[5] For this reason, the first contacts established by the Western peace movement were with human rights activists in Czechoslovakia, East Germany and Hungary.

Initially, communist authorities perceived the peace movement as a political ally in the struggle against 'American imperialism', or at least a propaganda tool useful in criticizing NATO and the Western governments.[6] Mass protests organized by Western peace movements were widely reported in official media. For this reason, the peace movement was initially approached with suspicion by dissidents and opposition activists from Central and Eastern Europe. However, the mistrust was gradually overcome and this perception started to change. The year 1985 was key in the development of cooperation. It was then that a qualitative change took place in the exchange of views between activists on both sides of the Iron Curtain. As one researcher says, 'a combination of Perestroika, the end of the Western peace struggle and the emergence of a Polish peace group stimulated the East West dialogue "from below"'.[7] The cooperation was, however, initiated by the Prague

Appeal addressed to Western peace movements by the Czechoslovakian Charter 77 on 11 March 1985.

The Appeal introduced the notion of indivisibility of peace. In the view of its authors, only peace within states themselves, between their governments and societies, could bring lasting international peace. The political division of Europe was seen as the source of tensions that threatened the entire world. The CSCE process not only consolidated the territorial status quo (as stressed by communists) but also raised the issue of observance of human rights (which was emphasized by Western countries and dissident movements within the bloc). As a pan-European process, it could contribute to ensuring peace in accordance with human rights and without a division into antagonist blocs. NATO and the Warsaw Pact should be dissolved, US and Soviet troops should be withdrawn to their homelands, and the armed forces of European countries should be reduced. The long-term goal, in turn, should be to overcome the division of Europe and unify the continent, starting with the unification of Germany.[8] The Polish Underground Committee for Social Resistance (KOS) supported the Appeal with reservations, claiming that the Helsinki process did not overcome but strengthened the logic of division of Europe into blocs.[9]

The initiatives developed simultaneously. On 17 March 1985, a week after the Prague Appeal was issued, a week-long hunger strike started in Podkowa Leśna, a town near Warsaw, as a protest against the imprisonment of Marek Adamkiewicz, sentenced to two and a half years in prison for refusing to take the military oath. Polish soldiers were forced to take an oath in which they committed to defend the country from imperialism and protect peace in a brotherly alliance with the Soviet army. The strike was accompanied by seminars on peace and human rights issues, inspired by John Paul II's New Year's addresses on peace. During the hunger strike, the participants discussed cooperation between the Polish opposition and the Western peace movement, the same issues that had been addressed in the Prague Appeal.[10]

An important factor for the establishment of cooperation with Poland were visits of Mient Jan Faber, secretary of the Dutch Interchurch Peace Council (IKV), who met with prominent Solidarity leaders Lech Wałęsa and Jacek Kuroń in April 1985 to invite them to the 1986 peace congress in Amsterdam. However, IKV's cooperation with the 'Freedom and Peace' Movement (in Polish 'Ruch Wolność i Pokój' or WiP) proved even more fruitful. Both organizations were involved in discussions on the role of the Helsinki process in disarmament talks and in rapprochement between Western and Eastern states.[11]

The 'Freedom and Peace' Movement maintained contacts with dissidents from other countries of Central and Eastern Europe, particularly East Germany, Czechoslovakia, Hungary and the Soviet Union.[12] Western observers claim that by placing new problems on the political agenda and using new methods of activity, the 'Freedom and Peace' Movement contributed to the democratic transformation of the Polish society.[13] WiP members employed new methods of civil disobedience, they refused to take the military oath and do military service, returned their military ID cards and organized hunger protests, demonstrations, sit-ins, petitions and international seminars. They demanded the introduction of alternative military service, a reform of the military, the withdrawal of Soviet troops from Poland and the dissolution of the Warsaw Pact. Dozens of WiP members were sentenced to two to three years in prison.[14]

In the Western peace movement, there was a growing conviction that the 1980 END appeal's focus on disarmament was largely no longer sufficient. Work began on a new document, one for which the starting point was the suggestion contained in the Prague Appeal that the Helsinki process could provide a good basis for the cooperation of independent groups from the East and West.

This led to the drafting of the Helsinki Memorandum, *Giving Real Life to the Helsinki Accords*, the content of which was the result of a compromise following a written exchange of opinions between Western peace activists and dissidents from Central and Eastern Europe. The participation of Jan Minkiewicz and Jan Kavan, representatives of the 'Freedom and Peace' Movement and of Charter 77 in the West, in the editorial committee, ensured that the position of activists from Poland and Czechoslovakia was taken into account.[15] The draft document reflected the structure of the Helsinki Final Act itself, its three parts corresponding to three 'baskets': European security; cooperation in economy, ecology, science and culture; as well as human rights and the self-determination of peoples.

Another draft was discussed during a seminar that took place on 16–18 May 1986 in Milan.[16] However, Central and East European activists met in Ljubljana and sent their remarks. In their opinion, the Memorandum was unbalanced, lacked a logical line of argumentation and expressed a position presented during official diplomatic talks rather than a point of view of independent social movements. The authors proposed to reverse the main line of argument: instead of 'disarmament first – the rest will follow', it should be 'human rights are a pre-condition – the rest is the result'.[17] In the document's new introduction the authors underlined that many governmental commitments to the Helsinki Final Act had not been observed and that the militarization of societies on both sides of the Iron Curtain contributed to the creation of an enemy image. To change this situation, it was necessary to guarantee the freedoms of conscience, assembly, organization and information, which would lead to democratization and self-determination of societies. The Helsinki process was a useful pan-European platform but social pressure from independent groups was necessary to revive it.[18]

Charter 77 activists also expressed an opinion on the Memorandum. In their view, transforming the Soviet Union into a democratic federation was still possible in the framework of economic and political integration engulfing the whole continent. However, Europe could not be neutral as long as Soviet and American troops were stationed on its territory. The main problem omitted in the document was German unification. Chartists understood that in order to guarantee grounds for stable peace in Europe, the German state should be allowed to reunify.[19]

The influence of the signatories from the East can be seen when comparing the initial version of the Memorandum, written mainly by peace activists from the West, with the final version, produced after consultations with activists from the East. While the title of both versions is the same – *Giving Real Life to the Helsinki Accords* – they have different subtitles: *A Memorandum to the European Peoples and Governments* (draft) and *A Memorandum, Drawn Up in Common by Independent Groups and Individuals in Eastern and Western Europe* (final version). The final adopted version emphasizes the participation of people from the East in the drafting of the document. Human rights were moved from last place slightly towards the front. The final order of the parts was then as follows: Introduction, Détente from below (including human contacts), European security, Human rights, Economic and ecological cooperation, Cultural cooperation and the Europe we envisage.

Many passages of the draft did not make it into the final document. The draft blamed both the Soviet Union and the United States for the confrontation policy, arms race, militarization of societies and violating 'human rights and the right of self-determination of peoples in their respective spheres of influence'.[20] The idea conveyed by the draft that lasting disarmament could not be 'bought' at the expense of human rights was further strengthened by opposing the idea 'to play off peace against freedom or vice versa'.[21] In the final version there was also no longer any reference to the END Appeal for a Nuclear Weapons Free Europe of 1980 and to specific disarmament initiatives such as the Palme Corridor or the Rapacki Plan. Some of the removed sentences included those stating that trade sanctions imposed against Poland after the state of emergency had been counterproductive because they consolidated the positions of proponents of a hardline approach among the authorities.[22]

Furthermore, the language of fear and emotion in the draft – for example, 'increasingly irrational levels of horror are reached' – was toned down. The fear of a militarily strong Europe, as manifested in the following: 'Western Europe as a third superpower would only increase the dangers threatening our continent', was overcome as well.[23] Under the influence of signatories from Central and Eastern Europe, the message conveyed by the Memorandum became more measured and less anti-American.

The Memorandum was issued on 3 November 1986, the day before the CSCE review meeting in Vienna. The signatories decided that the CSCE Final Act could provide the basis for the unification of Europe. The division of the continent into two blocs could be overcome by giving Europe a constitution that would ensure full observance of the principles declared in the Helsinki Final Act. Establishing direct contacts between societies on both sides of the Iron Curtain would contribute to erosion of the Cold War structure of international relations.[24]

The signatories demanded that European nations have the right to solve political and economic problems in a democratic manner. Overcoming the division of the continent required solving the German issue.[25] They called for a reduction followed by complete withdrawal of foreign troops and weaponry from the territories of European states, closing down of foreign military bases, dissolution of the North Atlantic Treaty Organization and the Warsaw Pact, as well as the cancellation of the military treaties between CSCE countries. A peaceful Europe should be built on the basis of full respect for the right to self-determination and of the observance of the principles proclaimed in the Helsinki Accords, guaranteed under international law.[26]

The Helsinki Memorandum played a crucial role in the development of dialogue between Central European dissidents and Western peace movements. It led to the initiation of independent peace seminars in Warsaw and Budapest and establishment of the Helsinki Citizens' Assembly in 1990.[27] Some renowned activists of the Polish opposition, such as Lech Wałęsa, Tadeusz Mazowiecki, Jacek Kuroń and Adam Michnik, did not participate in these activities. None of these names can be found as signatories of the Helsinki Memorandum. It seems that Solidarity deliberately avoided taking a stand on foreign policy, international security, military service and the shape of the future political order in Europe, leaving space for the political initiatives of the 'Freedom and Peace' Movement.[28]

There were significant programme differences between activists from Central Europe and Western peace activists. For example, Western activists and the Polish 'Freedom and Peace' Movement 'endorsed different readings of the Superpowers and thus differing assessments of the wisdom of unilateral disarmament'.[29] These differences are shown in a joint declaration signed by the 'Freedom and Peace' Movement and the German Green Party. Poles opposed the idea of unilateral disarmament of Western countries, they had a different perception of the nature of Soviet totalitarianism, and they did not acknowledge threats to Poland's security from NATO. There were differences of opinion in the analyses of the nature of the Western military alliance and the threat it posed to Poles as well as regards the possible consequences of unilateral disarmament.[30] The cooperation was based on the recognition that disarmament and the struggle against totalitarian systems were to be considered equally important.

The principles defined in the Helsinki Memorandum were subsequently developed in letters addressed to the CPSU First Secretary Mikhail Gorbachev by the 'Freedom and Peace' Movement and Charter 77. In a letter of 10 April 1987, the Krakow division of the 'Freedom and Peace' Movement demanded withdrawal of Soviet troops from Poland and other Central European countries and of American troops from Western Europe, dissolution of the military blocs – the Warsaw Pact and NATO – as well as actions towards integration of the divided Europe. The letter stated that the Warsaw Pact did not operate as an actual military alliance but rather as an instrument of the USSR's foreign policy.[31]

In an open letter to Gorbachev half a year later, Charter 77 demanded withdrawal of Soviet troops and nuclear missiles from Czechoslovakia, which was to contribute to the success of disarmament negotiations and convince Czechs and Slovaks that democracy, openness and respect for human rights were more than empty slogans. Charter 77 activists stressed that freedom, democracy and universal values were indivisible, defended the idea of 'democratic peace' and the link between peace and human rights.[32] As might be expected, neither 'Freedom and Peace' nor Charter 77 received answers to their letters. Nevertheless, these letters prove that some opposition groups in Central and Eastern Europe put forward far-reaching objectives that materialized only a few years later.

International Peace Seminar in Warsaw

A debate on the programme proposed in the Helsinki Memorandum was the purpose of the independent international seminar 'International Peace and the Helsinki Accords', held on 7–9 May 1987 in the Divine Mercy Church in Warsaw. The authorities arrested more than twenty members of the 'Freedom and Peace' Movement and denied visas to foreign participants, but they were still unable to prevent the seminar from taking place.[33] The seminar was attended by fifty foreigners from sixteen countries and two hundred participants from Poland. A representative of the US-based Helsinki Watch observed: 'the Polish authorities appear to have been surprised at the number of Westerners who came for the seminar, and perhaps in the interests of public relations, they made no further attempts to obstruct it'.[34]

The meetings were held in four thematic areas: on the new stage of disarmament policy; the relations between peace and human rights; personal responsibility for peace; and environmental issues. During the opening session, Dieter Esche from the European Network for East-West Dialogue stressed that signatories of the Memorandum were often able to modify their initial position and accept the arguments of the other side. However, as one Western activist argued, there should be no 'illusion that we have a common movement. In the Helsinki Memorandum we came to a position of saying *both* [peace and human rights concerns] are important. That does not mean that for Poles in their immediate situation human rights don't have a priority'.[35]

One of the leading advisors of Solidarity, Bronisław Geremek, stated in his speech that the Western peace movement formed after World War II supported the *pax sovietica*. By becoming unilaterally involved in political conflicts, it contributed to the depreciation of the notion of peace in the social consciousness of many Europeans. He believed that in the international dimension, the peace movement should not accept the imperial order but instead advocate freedom and sovereignty of nations. In the internal dimension, the movement could not accept totalitarianism and should adopt democratic internal order as the prerequisite of peaceful existence and development of nations. In the moral dimension, the movement should adopt respect for human and civil rights as the foundation of the coexistence of people and nations.[36]

Some of those who were unable to attend nonetheless managed to deliver their positions. The Initiative for Peace and Human Rights from East Germany sent a draft declaration on conscientious objection, which was adopted as the position of the seminar's attendees. The declaration called disarmament proposals alone insufficient and indicated that grassroots work towards peace and human rights was needed. Apart from recognizing the right to conscientious objection and alternative military service, it also proposed that the Warsaw Pact be prohibited from exerting pressure on member states.[37] In a letter addressed to the participants of the seminar, Janos Kis, who was denied a passport, wrote that although the distance between Paris and Warsaw or between Vienna and Budapest had decreased, the distance between Warsaw and Budapest had not. In other words, contacts between two parts of the divided Europe became easier than contacts between societies on the same side of the Iron Curtain in Central and Eastern Europe. In his opinion, Central and Eastern European countries would not be satisfied with just the elimination of nuclear weapons. They would not feel secure until Soviet troops left their territories. This, however, could be done only within some kind of system of balance between the East and the West.[38]

The seminar constituted a breakthrough in the methods of cooperation between Central European opposition and Western peace movements. Even though many people were denied visas or detained at the border, many others attended nonetheless, including Jiri Vančura from Charter 77, the representative of Charter 77 in the West Jan Kavan and Tomas Mastnak from Ljubljana. The spokesman for foreign policy of the German Sozialdemokratische Partei Deutschlands (SPD), Karsten Voigt, highlighted in his letter to the seminar that the CSCE Final Act could become the basis of the future peace order in Europe. He believed that the arms race needed to be halted while taking into account human rights and that the focus should be on striving to establish an international order in which Europe would be united.[39]

Jackson Diehl wrote in *The Washington Post* that the conference was the first of its kind to be organized in the communist bloc. Diehl quoted Janet Fleischman, a representative of the New York-based Helsinki Watch, who stressed that the fact that the conference had been organized and held in the centre of Warsaw was an astounding success. At the same time, she reminded readers that the government called this event an international-scale provocation that would adversely affect the atmosphere before the visit of John Paul II to Poland planned for the following month. The participants also discussed the relations between peace movements from the East and the West. 'Freedom and Peace' as well as Charter 77 and other groups from the Eastern Bloc sometimes accused Western activists of lacking sensitivity to human rights problems in countries governed by communists.[40]

The seminar was held on the eve of the announcement of the 'Jaruzelski Plan' at the 2nd Congress of Patriotic Movement for

National Rebirth held on 9–10 May 1987. The Plan was based on a specific interpretation of the Helsinki process as mainly concerned with security issues. It provided for gradual withdrawal of tactical and operational types of nuclear and conventional weapons, for a change of the nature of military doctrines to strictly defensive, and for the introduction of new means of trust building.[41] On 12 May 1987, the Plan was presented at the CSCE by Polish Minister of Foreign Affairs Marian Orzechowski. On 28–29 May it was backed by the Warsaw Pact's Political Consultative Committee in Berlin and became a part of the common disarmament plan. It concerned nine countries: East Germany, Poland, Czechoslovakia and Hungary as well as West Germany, Denmark, Belgium, the Netherlands and Luxembourg. Later, this was to be expanded to the entirety of Europe from the Atlantic all the way to the Urals.

At a press conference, government spokesman Jerzy Urban accused the 'Freedom and Peace' Movement of actively working against Poland's defensive capabilities and torpedoing official disarmament initiatives. In his opinion, the plan presented by General Wojciech Jaruzelski was an important regional concept that was congruent with Soviet proposals of nuclear disarmament and reducing military potentials. Instead, 'Freedom and Peace', the government spokesman stated, promoted something entirely different, that is unilateral disarmament aimed at weakening the socialist countries, thus showing that it was not a peace movement but a group acting objectively on behalf of those powers that boycotted the numerous peaceful initiatives of socialist countries.[42]

The 'Freedom and Peace' Movement maintained that the return to disarmament negotiations between the United States and the Soviet Union in the second half of the 1980s created a chance for a reduction of the nuclear potentials. The changes taking place in the USSR had to be taken advantage of to improve Poland's geopolitical situation. Gorbachev's peace policy was affecting the countries of the bloc. Paradoxically, however, societies started fearing a reduction of the missile arsenals. In the West, this was because of the risk of upsetting the balance of power and weakening security, while in the East it was because, without changes in the political system, weapons reduction would create the risk of cementing the geopolitical status quo.[43]

One of the arguments used in discussion with Western partners was that technical disarmament – focusing on the number of weapons, deadlines of their withdrawal, means of control and so on – was insufficient and that what was additionally required was the participation and co-responsibility of societies. Technical disarmament alone would simply cement the division into opposing political blocs and would not eliminate the key threat to peace – the lack of democracy. The arms reduction was to be only a step on the path towards establishing a lasting foundation for peace: freedom, democracy, human rights and international cooperation. What should be sought instead was the so-called political disarmament through eliminating the sources of threats to peace rather than the effects. Political disarmament should include withdrawal of foreign armies to their own territories, dissolution of both military pacts – the Warsaw Pact and NATO – as well as integration and unification of the divided Europe.[44]

Seminars in Budapest, Moscow, Prague and Krakow

The Warsaw seminar of the 'Freedom and Peace' Movement provided inspiration to opposition activists from other countries of the region. It proved that direct contacts between Eastern dissidents and Western peace and human rights activists above the Iron Curtain were possible. Meetings similar to the one in Warsaw were organized in other capitals of the region, namely in Budapest, Moscow and Prague, as well as in Krakow. This cooperation led to the establishment of the Helsinki Citizens Assembly in 1990.

On 21–22 November 1986, the European Network for East-West Dialogue and students of the Bibó College organized another seminar in Budapest, similar to the one in Warsaw, which was attended by 150 activists from seventeen countries, including the leading representatives of the Hungarian opposition. In the opening address, a representative of the College, Victor Orban, said that the seminar reclaimed the next piece of the empire of official policy: the field of détente, of East–West contacts.[45]

Debates held at the seminar concerned the prospects of Gorbachev's reforms, the chances of establishing a pan-European democratic movement as well as conscientious objection to military service. In a common declaration, the participants undertook to engage in cooperation for disarmament that was to contribute to initiating a withdrawal of foreign troops from Eastern and Western Europe, overcoming the division of the continent and creating an independent, democratic and peaceful Europe.[46]

On 10–16 December 1987, a seminar on the observance of human rights was held in Moscow, organized by Leo Timofeyev of the Glasnost Press Club. The aim of the seminar was to create effective mechanisms for international monitoring of the USSR's compliance with international agreements on humanitarian issues and to do this before the scheduled CSCE review meeting in Moscow. Debates held in private apartments concerned international trust and disarmament, freedom of the press, freedom of religion, interpersonal contacts and ethnic problems. They were attended by some 300–400 people from all over the Soviet Union, including Larisa Bogoraz, Father Gleb Yakunin and the founder of the Georgian Helsinki Group Zviad Gamsachurdia as well as Jan Urban from the Czechoslovakian Charter 77 and representatives of Western organizations, including the American and Swedish Helsinki Committees.[47] Timofeyev was allowed to speak at the meeting of Soviet officials with the delegates of the International Helsinki Federation. Later, the federation started a support campaign for the Russian proposal within CSCE to hold a human rights conference in Moscow. The conference ultimately took place in 1991, already in different geopolitical circumstances.[48]

Charter 77 and the newly established Independent Peace Association planned to hold a seminar on the role of human rights in ensuring democratic peace, overcoming militarist ideology and conscientious objection in Prague on 17–19 June 1988. Apart from being a platform for discussing important political matters, the seminar was aimed at showing the communist authorities that the dissidents involved in the peace dialogue were supported by foreign partners. However, the police detained the organizers, and participants from abroad.[49] A week later, Czechoslovakian Prime Minister Lubomir Strougal said at a press conference in Vienna that the actions of the police 'shouldn't have to be repeated'.[50]

The meeting in Prague scheduled for 11–13 November 1988 did not take place either. Even before the arrival of twenty activists from the West coordinated by the International Helsinki Federation, the police arrested twenty-five Czechoslovakian activists who intended to participate in the meeting. Václav Havel of Charter 77 avoided arrest because he went into hiding a couple of days earlier. He even managed to open the seminar, but was detained a few moments later. The peace activists from the West went to the police station to demand the release of the detainees, but this took place only after the former had already left the country.[51]

This was already a period of increased social activity. After the demonstration to commemorate the anniversary of the 1968 Soviet invasion, Václav Havel, Jana Petrova from the Independent Peace Association and Ota Veverka from the John Lennon Peace Club were sentenced to nine to twelve months of imprisonment.[52] This shows that Czechoslovak communists did not intend to pursue the path of reform chosen by Mikhail Gorbachev.

On 25–28 August 1988, the 'Freedom and Peace' Movement and Solidarity's Commission for the Rule of Law held a conference on human rights in Krakow. It was attended by some one thousand people, including four hundred from abroad.[53] The conference was attended by representatives of institutions that supported the opposition in Central and Eastern Europe. Jan Rokita, a 'Freedom and Peace' leader from Krakow, criticized the doctrine of sovereignty for allowing violations of human rights by authoritarian regimes, citing the US's removal of the regime in Grenada as a positive example.[54] His words were criticized by Western peace activists as acceptance of the use of force in international relations by Reagan's administration.[55] From the perspective of the communist states, however, the use of force in order to stop grave violations of human rights might be sometimes justified and in line with the responsibility to protect doctrine proclaimed a decade later.

In a resolution on European integration, the participants stated that the societies of Central and Eastern Europe should have the opportunity to appoint observers at the European Parliament, which would bring the problems from beyond the Iron Curtain closer to Western societies and the workings of the European Parliament to the Eastern ones. These observers should be chosen in free and democratic elections, and if this was not possible, they should be nominated by independent social movements. The common objective was defined as overcoming the post-Yalta division of Europe and its unification.[56]

Conclusion

Opposition groups from Central and Eastern Europe demanded that political and civil freedoms guaranteed in CSCE documents (freedom of thought, of conscience, of assembly and of information) be observed in the countries that signed these documents. The development and announcement of the Helsinki Memorandum was a visible sign that a critical mass was achieved, that activists from the East and West became involved with the aim to consolidate the CSCE norms. Without these bottom-up movements, which strived to change the system, the Helsinki process would be defunct. One of the major initiatives in this regard was the memorandum issued in 1986 – *Giving Real Life to the Helsinki Accords*. The Helsinki Memorandum was the subject of an independent peace seminar organized in Warsaw in May 1987 by the 'Freedom and Peace' Movement, which prompted the organization of similar meetings in Budapest, Moscow, Prague and Krakow.

The subject of the debate between dissidents and Western peace activists were issues related to the definition of peace, disarmament and withdrawal of foreign troops from the territories of Central European countries. Human and civil rights, especially the freedom of belief, assembly and association, were considered the prerequisites of unhindered development of societies and international stability. East European activists helped their Western partners to understand the link between peace, freedom and human rights.[57] An important role in this context was played by the idea of overcoming the division of Europe into two antagonist blocs.

The propaganda of the communist authorities attempted to take advantage of the Western peace movement's anti-American sentiments. When, however, the movement started demanding the observance of human rights and freedom for prisoners of conscience in Central and Eastern Europe, it was no longer considered a useful tool. Central European dissidents took the initiative in defining the idea of peace. They convinced a significant share of Western public opinion that freedom and human rights were its integral part. They transformed Western peace movements into important allies in pursuing the common goal.[58]

In the second half of the 1980s, the authorities of Central European countries intended to use the Helsinki process to increase their legitimacy. This was the aim of the 'Jaruzelski Plan', put forward at the CSCE in 1987. However, the activities of opposition groups from Central and Eastern Europe, including hosting an independent seminar on 'International Peace and the Helsinki Accords' in May 1987 in Warsaw and reaction to it by the authorities, showed very clearly that this initiative of the authorities was but a façade.

Independent peace activists from Central and Eastern Europe believed that 'technical' disarmament focusing on the number of weapons, deadlines for their withdrawal and means of control, but taking place without the participation and co-responsibility of societies, was insufficient. This kind of disarmament would consolidate the division into antagonist political blocs. Instead, political disarmament was advocated, which would consist in eliminating the sources rather than just the consequences of threats to peace. Reducing armaments was perceived as only one step on the path to creating lasting foundations of peace: freedom, democracy, human rights and international cooperation. As was written by the 'Freedom and Peace' Movement and Charter 77 in letters to Mikhail Gorbachev, foreign troops should be withdrawn to their homelands and the divided Europe should be integrated. This programme was seen as radical, but it expressed the aspirations of Central and Eastern European societies. The programme materialized as early as 1989, with the electoral victory of Solidarity and the velvet revolutions in Central and East Europe.

Jacek Czaputowicz is a professor at the University of Warsaw and Head of the Methodology of European Studies Unit at the Faculty of Political Sciences and International Studies. In 1970 and 1980 he was active in political opposition in Poland. After 1989 he worked in the Polish Foreign Ministry and other public administration institutions. Prof. Czaputowicz has authored a number of academic publications, including *Theories of International Relations: Criticism and Systematisation* (WN PWN, 2008); *International Security: Contemporary Concepts* (2012), *Sovereignty* (PISM, 2013) and *Theories of European Integration* (WN PWN, 2018).

Notes

1. J. Nowak, 'An East European Perspective', in N. Andren and K.E. Birnbaum (eds), *Belgrade and Beyond: The CSCE in Perspectives* (Alphen aan den Rijn: Sijthoff & Noordhoff, 1980), 41–42. See also W. Jarząbek, 'Hope and Reality: Poland and the Conference on Security and Cooperation in Europe, 1964–1989', Working Paper of the Woodrow Wilson International Center for Scholars 56 (May 2008).
2. In the words of US Ambassador Richard Schifter at a CSCE conference in 1985, 'respect for human rights in individual states contributes to the improvement of international relations … disrespect for human rights contributes to the deterioration of international relations'. *CSCE Public Statements*, 284–85, as cited in J. Fry, *The Helsinki Process: Negotiating Security and Cooperation in Europe* (Washington, DC: National Defense University Press, 1993), 96.
3. P. Chilton, 'Mechanics of Change: Social Movements, Transnational Coalitions, and the Transformation Processes in Eastern Europe', in Th. Risse-Kappen (ed.), *Bringing Transnational Relations Back In* (Cambridge: Cambridge University Press, 1995), 200–1.
4. Appeal for European Nuclear Disarmament launched on 28 April 1980, in E.P. Thompson and D. Smith (eds), *Protest and Survive* (Harmondsworth: Penguin Books, 1980), 223–26.
5. K. Szulecki, 'Freedom and Peace Are Indivisible', in R. Brier (ed.), *Entangled Protest: Transnational Approaches to the History of Dissent in Eastern Europe and the Soviet Union* (Osnabrück: Fibre Verlag, 2013), 208–27.
6. V. Bukovsky, 'The Peace Movements and the Soviet Union', *Commentary* (May 1982), 25–41, https://www.commentarymagazine.com/articles/the-peace-movement-the-soviet-union/.

7. Ch. Miedema, 'A Transnational Movement Breaking Down the Blocs? The "Alliance" between the Western Peace Movement and the Polish Opposition in the 1980s', Paper prepared for the Conference *New Perspectives in the Transnational History of Communism in East-Central Europe*, Institute of National Remembrance, Poznań, October 2014, 18. On 9 May 1983, the Polish Underground Committee for Social Resistance (KOS) sent an open 'Letter to the Peace and Anti-Nuclear Movement in Western Europe', in which it pointed out that demanding the freezing of the arms race from NATO without demanding the same from the Warsaw Pact did not contribute to peace. END answered that it was protesting as much against the cruise missiles as against SS-20. See 'Polish Underground and European Nuclear Disarmament: An Exchange on Peace, Human Rights and the Cold War', *Peace and Democracy News* (Spring 1984), 8–9.
8. 'The Prague Appeal', *East European Reporter* 1(1) (1985), 27–28. See also K. Szulecki, 'Heretical Geopolitics of Central Europe: Dissidents, Intellectuals and an Alternative European Order', *Geoforum* 65 (2015), 25–36.
9. 'Introduction', *Palach Press Bulletin* 26 (1985), 5.
10. A. Smółka-Gnauck, *Między Wolnością a Pokojem: Zarys historii Ruchu 'Wolność i Pokój'* [Between Freedom and Peace: An Outline of the History of the 'Freedom and Peace' Movement] (Warsaw: IPN, 2012), 36–44, 281–86.
11. Ch. Miedema, 'The Transnationality of Dutch Solidarity with the Polish Opposition 1980–1989', *Revue Belge de Philologie et d'Histoire* 89 (2011), 1307–30; Miedema, 'Struggling Against the Bomb or Against the Bloc Divide? The Dutch Peace Movement and Eastern Europe', *Dutch Crossing* 39(3) (2015), 261–74.
12. Smółka-Gnauck, *Między Wolnością a Pokojem*, 244. See also I.-S. Kowalczuk and A. Polzin (eds), *Fasse Dich kurz! Der grenzüberschreitende Telefonverkehr der Opposition in den 1980er Jahren und das Ministerium für Staatssicherheit*, Analysen und Dokumente 41 (Göttingen: Vandenhoeck & Ruprecht, 2014), 362–64.
13. L. Jones, *The Process of Engagement in Non-Violent Collective Action*, PhD dissertation, University of Bath, 1995, 238.
14. Ch. Lazarski, 'The Polish Independent Peace Movement', in V. Tismaneanu (ed.), *In Search of Civil Society: Independent Peace Movement in the Soviet Bloc* (New York and London: Routledge, 1990), 125–26.
15. See Szulecki, 'Freedom and Peace Are Indivisible', 223. The editorial committee of the Memorandum was composed of Wolfgang Müller and Mient Jan Faber, both from the IKV, Dieter Esche from Alternative Liste – West from Berlin, Christian Semler, advisor to the Green Party, as well as Georg Breuer, an Austrian peace activist. See Miedema, 'A Transnational Movement'. The initial draft, in turn, bears the signatures of Georg Breuer, Dieter Esche, Silvie Mantrand, and Christian Semler, while Wim Bartels and Wolfgang Müller were observers in the discussion. *Giving Real Life to the Helsinki Accords: A Memorandum to the European Peoples and Governments*, typescript, courtesy of Padraic Kenney.
16. *Giving Real Life to the Helsinki Accords: A Memorandum to the European Peoples and Government* (second draft), Instytut Pamięci Narodowej BU 514/32/6, k.

153–56. It was signed by Georg Breuer, Dieter Esche, Mient Jan Faber, Jan Minkiewicz, Wolfgang Müller and Christian Semler.
17. *Comments* [signed by Ljubljana Peace Group, Roland Jahn and Jan Minkiewicz], IPN BU 514/32/6, k. 141. Cf. M. Hauner, 'Anti-militarism and the Independent Peace Movement in Czechoslovakia', in Tismaneanu, *In Search of Civil Society*, 109.
18. *Introduction*, IPN BU 514/32/6, k. 149.
19. 'Charter 77 Document 12/86', *East European Reporter* 2(1) (1986), 24–27; Hauner, 'Anti-militarism', 109. See also 'Commentaries on the Memorandum from the END German-German Working Group', International Seminar on Training for Nonviolent Action (ISTNA), Pax Christi Netherlands, and Fernando Claudin, director of the Pablo Iglesias Foundation, *Bulletin of the European Network for East-West Dialogue*, Trial Number (September 1987), 16–24.
20. *Giving Real Life to the Helsinki Accords: A Memorandum to the European Peoples and Government* (second draft), 2.
21. *Giving Real Life to the Helsinki Accords: A Memorandum, Drawn Up in Common by Independent Groups and Individuals in Eastern and Western Europe* (Berlin: European Network for East-West Dialogue, April 1987), 4.
22. *Giving Real Life to the Helsinki Accords: A Memorandum to the European Peoples*.
23. Ibid.
24. *Giving Real Life to the Helsinki Accords: A Memorandum, Drawn Up in Common*.
25. Christie Miedema writes that Western peace activists 'could not accept all proposals from their Eastern European allies. Especially the Polish and Czechoslovak appeals for a German unification that emerged in the discussion process about the Memorandum of 1986 were a bridge too far'. Miedema, 'A Transnational Movement', 17–18.
26. *Giving Real Life to the Helsinki Accords: A Memorandum, Drawn Up in Common*.
27. P.D.M. Burke, *European Nuclear Disarmament: A Study of Transnational Social Movement Strategy*, thesis submitted in partial fulfilment of the requirements of the University of Westminster for the degree of Doctor of Philosophy, June 2004.
28. Spokesman Janusz Onyszkiewicz claimed: 'Solidarity doesn't want to play a role on the international political scene. We want to play a role as a factor on the Polish political scene. That's why this group Freedom and Peace is breaking new ground'. P. Duncan, 'Uniting for Independence', an interview with Janusz Onyszkiewicz, *Sojourners* (October 1987), 24–25.
29. G. Wylie, *Creating Alternative Visions: The Role of National and Transnational Social Movements in the Demise of Polish State Socialism*, PhD thesis, Aberdeen, 1996, 176.
30. 'Joint Declaration of the members of Die Grünen and the "Freedom and Peace" Movement from Cracow, Breslau and Warsaw', April 1986, in *'WiP' a Zieloni* ['Freedom and Peace' and The Greens] (Warsaw: Wydawnictwo Dezerter, 1987), 3.
31. 'Letter of the Freedom and Peace Movement to Michail Gorbachev', in *Wolność i Pokój (WiP), Documents of Poland's 'Freedom and Peace' Movement*

(Seattle: A World Without War Council Publication, 1989), 36–37. See also 'Two Freedom and Peace Activists Visit Soviet Consulate in Cracow', CN103 A-Wire, Warsaw, 29 May, 87.
32. *Bulletin of the European Network for East-West Dialogue*, Trial Number (September 1987), 7; Ch. Peterson, 'Seeing the Value of the Helsinki Accords: Human Rights, Peace and Transnational Debates about Détente, 1981–1988', in this volume.
33. For example, the Dutch peace activist Herbert Reitenbach had to return from Warsaw's airport on the very same plane on which he arrived. 'Warsaw Fails to Halt Talks on Helsinki Pact', *The New York Times*, 7 May 1987. The authorities denied visas or otherwise made it impossible to come to Warsaw for Petr Uhl and a number of other Charter 77 activists from Czechoslovakia, Wolfgang Templin from East Germany, Janos Kis from Hungary, Irina and Andrei Krivov from the Moscow Trust Group, Pelle Voight and Keldow Elbrechtsem, Danish MPs, Erkki Pulliainen, a Finnish MP, Mient Jan Faber, Janeke Houdijk and Wolfgang Müller from the Dutch IKV, Mary Kaldor, John Fletcher, Mark Thompson from END, Stephen Brown from Campaign for Nuclear Disarmament, Michael Randle from War Resistance International, Franco Corleone, Ivan Novelli, Paulo Pietro Santi from the Italian Radical Party, Alberto Tridente, a member of the European Parliament, as well as Luciano Negri from Proletarian Democracy. *Seminarium pokojowe w Warszawie, 7–9 V 87. Dokumenty* [Documents from the Peace Seminar in Warsaw], 'Freedom and Peace' Movement (Warsaw: Wydawnictwo Dezerter, 1987), 12.
34. J. Fleischman, 'Beyond the Blocs? Peace and Freedom Hosts International Seminar in Warsaw', *Across Frontiers* (Summer/Fall 1987), 27.
35. P. Duncan, 'A New Generation of Opposition', *Sojourners* (October 1987), 18; cf. J. Landy, 'Worth Every Disrupted Minute: Interview', *East European Reporter* 3(3) (1988), 22–24.
36. B. Geremek, 'Pokój i prawa człowieka' [Peace and Human Rights], *Czas Przyszły* 1(1) (September/December 1987), 4–8. See also H.M. Ferderowicz, 'East-West Dialogue: Detente from Below', *Peace Research Reviews* XI(6) (Dundas, Canada: Peace Research Institute, June 1991), 33–34. Geremek held an address at a panel session, 'Peace Has a Name – Introducing Real Life into the Helsinki Accords', next to Stefan Bratkowski, Standfah Forswell, Aaron Epstain, Jacek Szymanderski, Dieter Esche and Zbigniew Romaszewski. Lech Wałesa 'didn't come to Warsaw because he thought that his presence was not necessary and in order to give this happening an identity of its own'. P. Duncan, 'An Intent on Democracy', *Sojourners* (October 1987), 21.
37. 'Declaration on Conscientious Objection', in *Seminarium pokojowe w Warszawie*, 18. See also M. Litwińska, *WiP kontra PRL, Ruch Wolność i Pokój 1985–1989* ['Freedom and Peace' against the Polish People's Republic 1985–1989] (Krakow: Wydawnictwo Wysoki Zamek, 2015), 329–37.
38. J. Kis, 'Can We Have a Joint Programme? Message to Warsaw', *Bulletin of the European Network for East-West Dialogue*, Trial Number (September 1987), 44.

39. The liaison from the SPD was Gert Weisskirchen, and the liaison from the Green Party was Elisabeth Weber, members of the Bundestag. Letters were also sent by Petra Kelly from the German Green Party, Mary Kaldor from END, Senator Jo Vallentine from Australia, Bruno Coppieters on behalf of VAKA, as well as Andrei and Irina Krivov and thirty-one people from the Moscow Trust Group. *Seminarium pokojowe w Warszawie*, 27–29.
40. J. Diehl, 'Poles Host East-West Peace Rally', *The Washington Post*, 11 May 1987. See also M.T. Kaufman, 'Rights Conference Stirs Warsaw Ire', *The New York Times*, 14 May 1987; R. Brier, 'Entangled Protest: Dissent and the Transnational History of the 1970s and 1980s', in Brier, *Entangled Protest*, 39.
41. 'Speech of the Chairman of the Council of State of the Polish People's Republic Wojciech Jaruzelski at the second congress of the Patriotic Movement for National Rebirth (PRON)', *Rzeczypospolita*, 9–10 May 1987. See also 'Memorandum of the Government of the Polish People's Republic of Poland on Decreasing Armaments and Increasing Confidence in Central Europe', 19870909 DPA(87)609.
42. 'Press Conference for Foreign Press (Stenographic Record)', *Rzeczpospolita* 114(1640) (18 May 1987), 5. One of the participants of the seminar, Richard Bloom, wrote: 'The Polish state remained unenthusiastic about the seminar's contribution to détente. Recommending that the peace movement turn its attention instead toward the new "Jaruzelski Plan" for disarmament, Jerzy Urban accused WiP of advocating "unilateral disarmament in the name of weakening the socialist states"; consequently, he claimed, it is "no peace movement, but one which objectively acts in support of forces boycotting the peace initiatives forwarded by the socialist states". All of which, if you change a word or two, sounds quite familiar, don't you think?' R. Bloom, 'Provoking Peace in Poland', *END Journal* 28/29 (Summer 1987), 5.
43. J. Czaputowicz, 'Freedom and Peace Are Inseparable', in *Wolność i Pokój (WiP), Documents*, 55–62.
44. Ibid.; 'The Wave of the Future?' *Newsweek* 33 (15 August 1988), 48. As observed by the spokesperson of Solidarity, Janusz Onyszkiewicz: 'For us peace cannot be the peace of a cemetery, in which our aspirations and hopes are buried'. Duncan, 'Uniting for Independence', 25.
45. V. Orban, 'Recapturing Life', *Across Frontiers* (Spring–Summer 1988), 34–35.
46. D. Lewis, 'East, West Peace Blocs Hold Budapest Meeting', *The Washington Post*, 22 November 1986; 'Seminarium Pokojowe w Budapeszcie, 21–22 listopada 1987' [Peace Seminar in Budapest, 21–22 November 1987], *Czas Przyszły* 2 (1988), 51–53.
47. M. Henderson, 'Report on the Independent Human Rights Seminar in Moscow in December 1987', *Bulletin of the European Network for East-West Dialogue* 1–2 (1988), 21–27. The authorities blocked entry to the country for some Western and Polish activists. S.B. Snyder, *Human Rights Activism and the End of the Cold War: A Transnational History of the Helsinki Network* (Cambridge: Cambridge University Press, 2011), 195.
48. J. Laber, *The Courage of Strangers: Coming of Age with the Human Rights Movement* (New York: Public Affairs, 2012), 292–93; Snyder, *Human Rights Activism*, 199–202.

49. Mary Kaldor, Lynne Jones, Joan Landy, Jan Minkiewicz, Thomas Mastnak and Ferenc Miszlivetz were forced to leave the country.
50. J. Hempfling, 'Prague: The Tale of Two Seminars, June 1988', *Peace & Democracy News* 3(2) (Winter 1988/89), 11.
51. J. Landy, 'Prague: The Tale of Two Seminars, November 1988', *Peace & Democracy News* 3(2) (Winter 1988/89), 11. See also Laber, *The Courage of Strangers*.
52. J. Tagliabue, '7 More Dissidents Convicted in Prague', *The New York Times*, 23 February 1989; J. Fleischman, 'Political Trials in Czechoslovakia', *Across Frontiers* 5(2) (Summer 1989), 27–28; P. Hunt, 'Cracks in the Ice', *END Journal of European Nuclear Disarmament* 37 (1989), 23.
53. *Międzynarodowa Konferencja Praw Człowieka, Kraków–Mistrzejowice, 25–28 sierpnia 1998 r.* [International Conference for Human Rights, Krakow–Mistrzejowice, 25–28 August 1998] (Krakow, 1989), 437.
54. J.M. Rokita, 'The Sickness of Law: Speech to the International Human Rights Conference in Cracow', in *Wolność i Pokój (WiP), Documents*, 80–83.
55. H. Ruffin, *Report on Trip to Poland and Czechoslovakia, August–September 1988* (Seattle: A World Without War Council, 1988).
56. 'Resolution no. 6 on the Integration Processes in Europe', in *Międzynarodowa Konferencja Praw Człowieka*, 405–6.
57. See Peterson's chapter in this volume.
58. K. Szulecki, 'Hijacked Ideas: Human Rights, Peace and Environmentalism in Czechoslovak and Polish Dissident Discourses', *East European Politics and Societies* 25(2) (2011), 272–95.

Bibliography

Bloom, R. 'Provoking Peace in Poland'. *END Journal* 28/29 (Summer 1987), 5.

Brier, R. 'Entangled Protest: Dissent and the Transnational History of the 1970s and 1980s', in R. Brier (ed.), *Entangled Protest: Transnational Approaches to the History of Dissent in Eastern Europe and the Soviet Union* (Osnabrück: Fibre Verlag, 2013), 11–42.

Bukovsky, V. 'The Peace Movements and the Soviet Union'. *Commentary* (May 1982), 25–41. https://www.commentarymagazine.com/articles/the-peace-movement-the-soviet-union/.

Burke, P.D.M. *European Nuclear Disarmament: A Study of Transnational Social Movement Strategy*. Thesis submitted in partial fulfilment of the requirements of the University of Westminster for the degree of Doctor of Philosophy, June 2004.

'Charter 77 Document 12/86'. *East European Reporter* 2(1) (1986), 24–27.

Chilton, P. 'Mechanics of Change: Social Movements, Transnational Coalitions, and the Transformation Processes in Eastern Europe', in Th. Risse-Kappen (ed.), *Bringing Transnational Relations Back In* (Cambridge: Cambridge University Press, 1995), 189–226.

'Commentaries on the Memorandum from the END German-German Working Group', International Seminar on Training for Nonviolent Action (ISTNA),

Pax Christi Netherlands, and Fernando Claudin, director of the Pablo Iglesias Foundation. *Bulletin of the European Network for East-West Dialogue,* Trial Number (September 1987), 16–24.

Czaputowicz, J. 'Freedom and Peace Are Inseparable', in *Wolność i Pokój (WiP), Documents of Poland's 'Freedom and Peace' Movement* (Seattle, WA: A World Without War Council Publication, 1989), 55–62.

Diehl, J. 'Poles Host East-West Peace Rally'. *The Washington Post,* 11 May 1987.

Duncan, P. 'An Intent on Democracy'. *Sojourners* (October 1987), 20–22.

Duncan, P. 'A New Generation of Opposition'. *Sojourners* (October 1987), 14–19.

Duncan, P. 'Uniting for Independence', an interview with Janusz Onyszkiewicz. *Sojourners* (October 1987), 23–25.

Ferderowicz, H.M. 'East-West Dialogue: Detente from Below'. *Peace Research Reviews* XI(6). Dundas, Canada: Peace Research Institute, June 1991.

Fleischman, J. 'Beyond the Blocs? Peace and Freedom Hosts International Seminar in Warsaw'. *Across Frontiers* (Summer/Fall 1987), 27.

Fleischman, J. 'Political Trials in Czechoslovakia'. *Across Frontiers* 5(2) (Summer 1989), 27–28.

Fry, J. *The Helsinki Process: Negotiating Security and Cooperation in Europe.* Washington, DC: National Defense University Press, 1993.

Geremek, B. 'Pokój i prawa człowieka' [Peace and human rights]. *Czas Przyszły* 1(1) (September/December 1987), 4–8.

Giving Real Life to the Helsinki Accords: A Memorandum to the European Peoples and Governments. Typescript.

Giving Real Life to the Helsinki Accords: A Memorandum to the European Peoples and Governments (second draft). Typescript.

Giving Real Life to the Helsinki Accords: A Memorandum, Drawn Up in Common by Independent Groups and Individuals in Eastern and Western Europe. Berlin: European Network for East-West Dialogue, April 1987.

Hauner, M. 'Anti-militarism and the Independent Peace Movement in Czechoslovakia', in V. Tismaneanu (ed.), *In Search of Civil Society: Independent Peace Movement in the Soviet Bloc* (New York and London: Routledge, 1990), 88–117.

Hempfling, J. 'Prague: The Tale of Two Seminars, June 1988'. *Peace & Democracy News* 3(2) (Winter 1988/89), 11.

Henderson, M. 'Report on the Independent Human Rights Seminar in Moscow in December 1987'. *Bulletin of the European Network for East-West Dialogue* 1–2 (1988), 21–27.

Hunt, P. 'Cracks in the Ice'. *END Journal of European Nuclear Disarmament* 37 (1989), 23.

Jarząbek, W. 'Hope and Reality: Poland and the Conference on Security and Cooperation in Europe, 1964–1989'. Working Paper of the Woodrow Wilson International Center for Scholars 56 (May 2008).

Jones, L. *The Process of Engagement in Non-Violent Collective Action.* PhD dissertation, University of Bath, 1995.

Kaufman, M.T. 'Rights Conference Stirs Warsaw Ire'. *The New York Times,* 14 May 1987.

Kis, J. 'Can We Have a Joint Programme? Message to Warsaw'. *Bulletin of the European Network for East-West Dialogue*, Trial Number (September 1987), 44.
Kowalczuk, I.-S., and A. Polzin (eds). *Fasse Dich kurz! Der grenzüberschreitende Telefonverkehr der Opposition in den 1980er Jahren und das Ministerium für Staatssicherheit*. Analysen und Dokumente 41. Göttingen: Vandenhoeck & Ruprecht 2014.
Laber, J. *The Courage of Strangers: Coming of Age with the Human Rights Movement*. New York: Public Affairs, 2012.
Landy, J. 'Prague: The Tale of Two Seminars, November 1988'. *Peace & Democracy News* 3(2) (Winter 1988/89), 11.
Landy, J. 'Worth Every Disrupted Minute: Interview'. *East European Reporter* 3(3) (1988), 22–24.
Lazarski, Ch. 'The Polish Independent Peace Movement', in V. Tismaneanu (ed.), *In Search of Civil Society: Independent Peace Movement in the Soviet Bloc* (New York and London: Routledge, 1990), 118–34.
'Letter of the Freedom and Peace Movement to Michail Gorbachev', in *Wolność i Pokój (WiP), Documents of Poland's 'Freedom and Peace' Movement* (Seattle: A World Without War Council Publication, 1989), 36–37.
Lewis, D. 'East, West Peace Blocs Hold Budapest Meeting'. *The Washington Post*, 22 November 1986.
Litwińska, M. *WiP kontra PRL, Ruch Wolność i Pokój 1985–1989* ['Freedom and Peace' against the Polish People's Republic 1985–1989]. Krakow: Wydawnictwo Wysoki Zamek, 2015.
Miedema, Ch. 'Struggling Against the Bomb or Against the Bloc Divide? The Dutch Peace Movement and Eastern Europe'. *Dutch Crossing* 39(3) (2015), 261–74.
Miedema, Ch. 'A Transnational Movement Breaking Down the Blocs? The "Alliance" between the Western Peace Movement and the Polish Opposition in the 1980s'. Paper prepared for the conference *New Perspectives in the Transnational History of Communism in East-Central Europe*, Institute of National Remembrance, Poznań, October 2014.
Miedema, Ch. 'The Transnationality of Dutch Solidarity with the Polish Opposition 1980–1989'. *Revue Belge de Philologie et d'Histoire* 89 (2011), 1307–30.
Międzynarodowa Konferencja Praw Człowieka, Kraków–Mistrzejowice, 25–28 sierpnia 1998 r. [International Conference for Human Rights, Krakow–Mistrzejowice, 25–28 August 1998]. Krakow, 1989.
Nowak, J. 'An East European Perspective', in N. Andren and K.E. Birnbaum (eds), *Belgrade and Beyond: The CSCE in Perspectives* (Alphen aan den Rijn: Sijthoff & Noordhoff, 1980), 39–50.
Orban, V. 'Recapturing Life'. *Across Frontiers* (Spring–Summer 1988), 34–35.
'Polish Underground and European Nuclear Disarmament: An Exchange on Peace, Human Rights and the Cold War'. *Peace and Democracy News* (Spring 1984), 8–9.
'The Prague Appeal'. *East European Reporter* 1(1) (1985), 27–28.
'Press Conference for Foreign Press (Stenographic Record)'. *Rzeczpospolita* 114(1640) (18 May 1987), 5.

Rokita, J.M. 'The Sickness of Law: Speech to the International Human Rights Conference in Cracow', in *Wolność i Pokój (WiP), Documents of Poland's 'Freedom and Peace' Movement* (Seattle, WA: A World Without War Council Publication, 1989), 80–83.

Ruffin, H. *Report on Trip to Poland and Czechoslovakia, August–September 1988*. Seattle: A World Without War Council, 1988.

'Seminarium Pokojowe w Budapeszcie, 21–22 listopada 1987' [Peace Seminar in Budapest, 21–22 November 1987]. *Czas Przyszły* 2 (1988), 51–53.

Seminarium pokojowe w Warszawie, 7–9 V 87. Dokumenty [Documents from the Peace Seminar in Warsaw], 'Freedom and Peace' Movement. Warsaw: Wydawnictwo Dezerter, 1987.

Smółka-Gnauck, A. *Między Wolnością a Pokojem: Zarys historii Ruchu 'Wolność i Pokój'* [Between Freedom and Peace: An Outline of the History of the 'Freedom and Peace' Movement]. Warsaw: IPN, 2012.

Snyder, S.B. *Human Rights Activism and the End of the Cold War: A Transnational History of the Helsinki Network*. Cambridge: Cambridge University Press, 2011.

'Speech of the Chairman of the Council of State of the Polish People's Republic Wojciech Jaruzelski at the second congress of the Patriotic Movement for National Rebirth (PRON)'. *Rzeczypospolita*, 9–10 May 1987.

Szulecki, K. 'Freedom and Peace Are Indivisible', in R. Brier (ed.), *Entangled Protest: Transnational Approaches to the History of Dissent in Eastern Europe and the Soviet Union* (Osnabrück: Fibre Verlag, 2013), 208–16.

Szulecki, K. 'Heretical Geopolitics of Central Europe: Dissidents, Intellectuals and an Alternative European Order'. *Geoforum* 65 (2015), 25–36.

Szulecki, K. 'Hijacked Ideas: Human Rights, Peace and Environmentalism in Czechoslovak and Polish Dissident Discourses'. *East European Politics and Societies* 25(2) (2011), 272–95.

Tagliabue, J. '7 More Dissidents Convicted in Prague'. *The New York Times*, 23 February 1989.

Thompson, E.P., and D. Smith (eds). *Protest and Survive*. Harmondsworth: Penguin Books, 1980.

'Warsaw Fails to Halt Talks on Helsinki Pact'. *The New York Times*, 7 May 1987.

'The Wave of the Future?' *Newsweek* 33 (15 August 1988), 48.

'WiP' a Zieloni ['Freedom and Peace' and The Greens]. Warsaw: Wydawnictwo Dezerter, 1987.

Wylie, G. *Creating Alternative Visions: The Role of National and Transnational Social Movements in the Demise of Polish State Socialism*. PhD thesis, Aberdeen, 1996.

 8

THE LIMITS OF REPRESSION
Soviet Bloc Security Services vs. Transnational Helsinki Networks, 1976–1986

Douglas Selvage

Introduction

In his landmark work, *The Helsinki Effect* (2001), Daniel Thomas argued that the Soviet bloc's acceptance of human rights provisions in the CSCE Final Act sparked the establishment of dissident groups in Eastern Europe that pressured their respective governments to fulfil these provisions. Groups and movements such as the Moscow Helsinki Group, Charter 77 and the Workers' Defense Committee (KOR) in Poland made use not only of the mandated CSCE follow-up meetings, but also growing contacts with governments, non-government organizations (NGOs), journalists and other individuals in the West to put external pressure on their governments to observe human rights. Transnational networks began to form that put pressure on the East, but also on Western governments, to further the cause of human rights in Eastern Europe. Thomas concludes that 'the Helsinki Final Act's formal commitment to respect human rights contributed significantly to the demise of Communism and the end of the Cold War'.[1]

This chapter will analyse and evaluate to what extent the communist regimes of the Warsaw Pact, but especially the Soviet Union and its East German ally, the German Democratic Republic (GDR), perceived such a 'Helsinki Effect'; how they sought to repress the ensuing transnational activism that arose regarding human rights; and to what extent they were successful. The chapter concludes with an evaluation of Thomas's argumentation based on these findings.

The Soviet Bloc Security Services and Transnational Relations

The Soviet bloc secret police with the Soviet KGB (Komitet gosudarstvennoy bezopasnosti or Committee for State Security) at the fore were clearly aware of a 'Helsinki Effect' in the form of growing cross-border activism regarding human rights. Based on what the KGB, the Stasi and their 'fraternal organs' had supposedly learned, East German Minister of State Security Erich Mielke sounded the alarm in a missive to all units of the Stasi in March 1977. 'Imperialism' intended to 'inspire and organize a broad "internal" opposition, a "dissident and human rights movement" a "political underground"' in the communist states.[2] One of the goals of the 'enemy' was to accuse the East of violating the Helsinki Accords with the goal of pressuring the Warsaw Pact states to accept new proposals in the 'so-called humanitarian realm' at the upcoming CSCE follow-up meeting in Belgrade.[3] Mielke stressed in particular the threat of the 'internationalization' of the opposition – what we today would call transnational relations – and noted the danger of the growing contacts between groups and individuals in East and West.[4] Mielke sketched the danger of transnational contacts as noted in Figure 8.1. Groups and individuals inside the Soviet bloc were

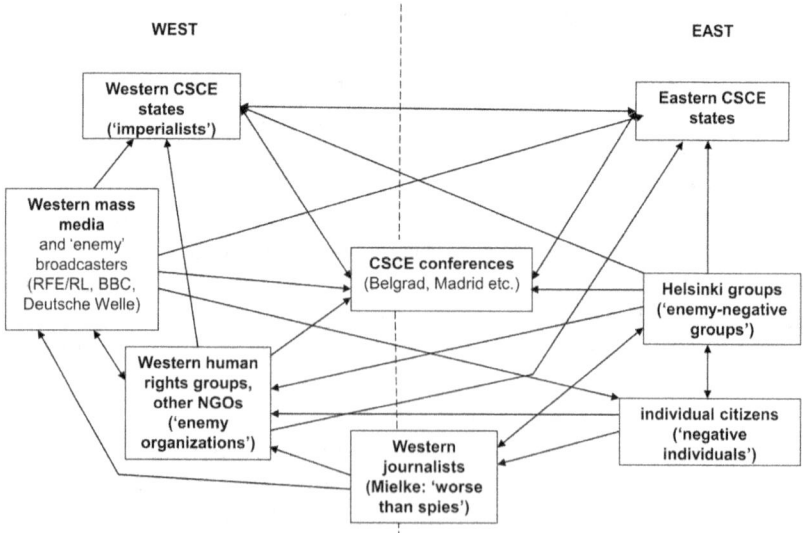

Figure 8.1 Transnational relations in the CSCE process (as viewed by the East German Stasi). Figure created by Douglas Selvage.

establishing contacts with Western journalists, NGOs and even Western governments to put pressure on the communist regimes of the East to respect human rights at home and to resolve individual human rights cases. Through the international mass media and 'enemy' broadcasters to the Soviet bloc, such as Radio Free Europe and Radio Liberty (RFE/RL), the West and especially the United States sought to popularize such human rights activism in the East and to put increased domestic and international pressure on the communist governments.[5] The model sketched by Mielke of the 'internationalization' of the opposition within the Soviet bloc after the signing of the CSCE Final Act in Helsinki, including the most important actors in East and West, conforms closely to what most scholars have subsequently written regarding transnational human rights networks that arose on the basis of the Helsinki Final Act.[6] Not pictured in the diagram, but central to the worldview of the Stasi, the KGB and the other 'fraternal' security organs of the Soviet bloc were Western intelligence agencies, which allegedly orchestrated all the new activism after the signing of the Helsinki Final Act with regard to human rights and gave orders directly or indirectly to Western journalists, NGOs, the mass media and Eastern activists.[7]

Despite Mielke's forebodings, no 'Helsinki group' arose in the communist GDR before 1985 – that is, a group publicly lobbying for human rights on the basis of the Helsinki Final Act. This stood in open contrast to the Soviet Union, where Helsinki groups originated; Czechoslovakia, where the Charter 77 movement remained active from its establishment in 1977 until the collapse of communism in 1989; and Poland, where the Workers' Defense Committee (Komitet Obrony Robotników, KOR) and the Movement to Defend Human and Civil Rights (Ruch Obrony Praw Człowiek i Obywatela, ROPCiO) made various appeals for reforms based on the Helsinki Final Act. How can this difference be explained?

The Stasi, of course, took credit for the lack of a 'Helsinki group' in the GDR. In the summer of 1977, there was a false alarm. According to the Stasi, initial contacts between opposition circles in Jena and Naumburg in the GDR, Charter 77 in neighbouring Czechoslovakia, and the West Berlin organization 'Schutzkomitee Freiheit und Sozialismus' (Committee for the Protection of Freedom and Socialism) were threatening to lead to the development of a 'so-called civil-rights movement'[8] in the GDR, 'similar to the ... infamous Charter 77'.[9] A group of theology students in Naumburg were also privately distributing their own human rights charter from a Christian perspective under the title 'Peace and Justice Today'.[10] Through various 'demoralization measures', individual arrests and disciplinary measures undertaken within the Lutheran and Catholic churches – under pressure from the

East German government – the Stasi successfully silenced and dispersed these various opposition circles and thus its own manufactured threat of an East German 'Helsinki group'.[11] The Stasi, contrasting its work with the other 'fraternal' security organs in Eastern Europe, then bragged about its successes in talks with the KGB.[12]

Despite the Stasi's assertions, the CSCE had little direct influence upon dissidents in the GDR before 1985. Although an active dialogue took place in some church circles regarding the CSCE and human rights,[13] the East German opposition had no intention of establishing a Helsinki group. East German dissident Ulrike Poppe writes: 'The members of the opposition in the GDR did not devote as much attention to the CSCE process as in the other Eastern bloc states'.[14] Those opposed to the policies of the East German regime assembled mainly in the independent peace movement in response to the growing militarization of East German society that began at the end of the 1970s.[15]

Nevertheless, the Helsinki process did have a large, indirect influence upon the opposition in East Germany. Dissidents in the GDR who would later play a key role in the 'Peaceful Revolution' of 1989 – including Gerd Poppe, Wolfgang Templin and Ludwig Mehlhorn – had already made contact with Charter 77, KOR and ROPCiO at the end of the 1970s. Through these contacts they learned new strategies for opposition, including 'living in the truth' and 'living as if' (i.e. as if the guarantees of human and civil rights in the various communist constitutions and in the CSCE Final Act were binding and true).[16] Based on an appeal by Charter 77 to join the struggle for peace with that of human rights, contacts between the Czechoslovak and East German opposition grew in the mid 1980s and culminated in the formation within the East German peace movement of the first Helsinki group in the GDR in 1985, the Initiative for Peace and Human Rights (Initiative Frieden und Menschenrechte).[17]

Ironically, from the viewpoint of the East German opposition, the Helsinki Final Act arguably served, indirectly, to limit the potential for opposition inside the GDR, especially in the quantitative sense. The individuals in the GDR who made most active and successful use of the Helsinki Final Act were petitioners seeking to emigrate to West Berlin and West Germany. Their relatively successful appeals, citing the Helsinki Final Act, meant that tens of thousands of people disenchanted with the East German regime simply left for the West, rather than engage in demonstrations and active opposition inside the GDR. Because of this exodus, the opposition movements inside the GDR had fewer recruits and were thus much smaller than in Czechoslovakia or Poland.[18] Thus, some opposition activists in East Germany came to disdain the applicants for emigration, whom they urged to remain in the GDR and to fight for reforms. However, given that such petitions to leave the GDR were illegal, one can also interpret this ongoing movement to emigrate, which sometimes took the form of group demonstrations and actions, as a form of opposition unique to East Germany, at least on such a large scale.[19]

East Germans seeking to emigrate were among the first to cite the Helsinki Final Act to demand their rights. After the formation of the Moscow Helsinki Group, but before the establishment of KOR or the promulgation of Charter 77, a group of applicants to emigrate in the city of Riesa submitted a petition to the East German government in August 1976, with copies to the West German press and NGOs, demanding that they be permitted to emigrate on the basis of the Helsinki Final Act.[20] East German leader Erich Honecker reacted quickly by forbidding the emigration of anyone to West Germany who cited the Helsinki Final Act, and the ministries of the East German government, with the Stasi at the fore, pushed through changes in East German law to further criminalize public demonstrations and contacts with the West, whether for emigration or otherwise protesting against the human rights situation in the GDR.[21]

From Belgrade to Madrid: The Successes of Repression, 1977–1980/82

As the Soviet Union, the GDR and the other communist countries had feared, the West – and especially the United States – made human rights a central issue at the CSCE follow-up conference in Belgrade in 1977–78. As Sarah Snyder has demonstrated, a growing network of transnational actors in East and West, often in coordination with the US Congress's Commission for Security and Cooperation in Europe, pushed for concrete gains for human rights at the Belgrade meeting. In the end, they failed, because all concrete proposals at the meeting regarding human rights (Principle VII) were blocked by the East, and the United States' West European allies were more concerned about human contacts (Basket Three). The one major achievement of the transnational Helsinki network centred in the United States was to successfully exploit the Belgrade meeting to publicize the human rights violations of the communist countries – a precedent for future CSCE follow-up meetings.[22]

It is important to note, however, that the Soviet Union and its allies, for their part, also failed in their efforts at the Belgrade meeting to push through their own, one-sided programme for 'military détente' – Moscow's top priority after the achievement of the 'political détente' embodied in the 1975 Helsinki Final Act. The Soviet Union thus obtained relatively little or nothing at Belgrade to push forward its international 'peace offensive' aimed at attaining beneficial arms control and disarmament agreements with the West.[23] The East also obtained no substantive concessions in the realm of trade or economic cooperation from the West – yet another priority for Moscow and its allies in the Helsinki process.[24] The Belgrade meeting thus ended in a stalemate between East and West. Its concluding document did little more than simply confirm that the meeting had taken place and set the time and place for the next follow-up meeting: 1980 in Madrid.[25]

As Thomas himself notes, by the time of the Madrid CSCE follow-up meeting in 1980, three of the communist countries that had been most impacted by the 'Helsinki Effect' had secured the political status quo through a sustained campaign of political repression.[26] In Czechoslovakia, many leading activists of Charter 77 were imprisoned and put on trial during the Belgrade meeting, and in 1979, several Charter activists in the Committee for the Defense of the Unjustly Prosecuted (Výbor na obranu nespravedlivě stíhaných, VONS) were sentenced to longer prison terms.[27] In the GDR, the number of applications for emigration fell in 1977 and 1978.[28] The government began to deny such applications on a regular basis and passed a number of laws criminalizing the activities of 'intractable' applicants for discrimination. Such applicants faced serious sanctions, including loss of employment and the denial of opportunities to their children. The Stasi also began to persecute them just like any other enemy of the state – opening their mail, tapping their phones and mobilizing its collaborators for demoralization or 'disintegration' measures.[29] The GDR's criminal code was further hardened against political crimes associated with would-be emigres, for example the paragraphs relating to 'impairment of state or social activity', 'conspiracy to criminal ends', 'illegal contact' and a new creation, 'public vilification'. A number of applicants for emigration who contacted NGOs or journalists in the West regarding their plight or engaged in public demonstrations were imprisoned.[30] East German leader Erich Honecker later bragged to his Polish counterparts that there had been no second 'Riesa' in the GDR – that is, no further signs of an organized movement to emigrate from East to West Germany – and that in the GDR, unlike Poland, there were no groups like KOR, publicly lobbying for human rights.[31] The Stasi, despite its self-proclaimed success against potential human rights groups, was more muted about the emigration issue in its talks with the KGB.[32] The number of applications to emigrate began to grow anew in 1979,[33] and the Stasi knew that public demonstrations could occur at any time, despite its best efforts and standing orders to pre-empt and suppress them.[34]

In the Soviet Union, leading dissidents from Soviet Helsinki groups, most of whom had been arrested before the Belgrade meeting, were put on trial, condemned and sentenced to prison and work camps after its conclusion. After US–Soviet détente collapsed in December 1979 in the wake of NATO's dual-track decision and the Soviet invasion of Afghanistan, Andrei Sakharov was exiled with his wife, Yelena Bonner, from Moscow to the Russian city of Gorky, where both were kept under heightened surveillance by the KGB.[35] In November 1980, Colonel V.N. Schadrin, the director of the KGB division responsible for the suppression of dissidents (Div. 9, 5th Chief Directorate), told his Stasi counterparts: 'The organized political underground in the USSR was crushed in 1979–80 in preparation for the Olympic Games through a variety of political and operational measures. This is especially the case with the so-called "Helsinki groups"; its branches in Moscow, Ukraine, Lithuania and Georgia were fully exposed and liquidated. A total of 150 persons were arrested'.[36] Schadrin also cited the fate of the dissidents' Working Commission for the Disclosure of the Abuse of Psychiatry. By 1980, all leading members of the group had been arrested, thanks in part to information gathered by the East German Stasi. One leader of the group, Irena Kaplun, had been persuaded by an unofficial collaborator of the Stasi to apply – successfully – to emigrate to Israel. Somewhat eerily, Schadrin noted that Kaplun had died, however, in an auto accident before she could leave the USSR.[37] In September 1982, during the CSCE follow-up meeting in Madrid, Yelena Bonner announced the dissolution of the Moscow Helsinki Group, which had been decimated through arrests, repression and exile.[38]

Even in Poland, where the domestic opposition had succeeded in compelling the communist government to recognize the Solidarity trade union and to make temporary concessions, also with regard to human rights, the government's successful introduction and implementation of martial law in December 1981 demonstrated the limitations of any 'Helsinki Effect'.[39] The example of Poland also served as a warning to the other communist regimes, and especially their state security services, regarding the dangers of making concessions on human rights for the sake of otherwise much-needed economic assistance from the West.[40]

Other Factors in the Collapse of Communism: Economic Weakness and the Need for Arms Control

Given the successes of the Soviet bloc in repressing dissidents and human rights groups in the East at the beginning of the 1980s, why can Daniel Thomas – and we – still speak of a 'Helsinki Effect' after 1980/82?

Thomas gives two reasons. First, by the time of the repressions, a transnational Helsinki network had already come into existence. Although many of the Eastern activists had been repressed and largely silenced, the NGOs and other state and non-state actors in the West lobbied all the harder on behalf of the implementation of human rights in accordance with the Helsinki Final Act.[41] Sarah Snyder demonstrates this convincingly, especially in the case of the US and specifically with regard to Helsinki Watch and the Congressional CSCE Commission.[42] As will be shown in a forthcoming book, the communist security services, with the KGB and Stasi at the fore, did their best to hinder, demoralize and eliminate the Western actors in the transnational Helsinki network, but despite occasional tactical successes, their effectiveness was limited.[43] The communist authorities also unwittingly created martyrs out of the human rights activists, who now received all the more publicity in the West and in Western broadcasting to the East.

Of course, just because Western actors took up the slack in lobbying for human rights did not mean that the communist governments would listen to them. This was especially the case for the Soviet Union, which considered the case closed, especially after the collapse of US–Soviet détente. Thomas cites a second factor, at least for the years until 1982, that helps explain the ongoing openness of at least some communist governments to Western arguments on human rights: the growing crisis of their planned economies, which necessitated loans and trade with the West. He cites Poland and Hungary – correctly – as prime examples.[44]

Still, in the end, in arguing for a 'learning process' in the East with regard to human rights norms, in which Mikhail Gorbachev is the prime example, Thomas suddenly downplays the role of the same economic factors after 1982. Indeed, the period from 1982 until Gorbachev's assumption of power in 1985 basically drops out of Thomas's analysis.[45] He ignores the fact that the Soviet Union and its allies – in contrast to Belgrade – made concessions to the West in order to obtain a concluding document at the Madrid follow-up meeting of the CSCE in 1983. In the case of the US, Moscow made concessions in the form of permission to emigrate for a group of Pentecostalists in the US embassy in Moscow, along with their families, and agreed to a CSCE experts' conference on human rights – another platform for the US and the transnational Helsinki network to attack the East for its human rights abuses.⁴⁶ In the case of Western Europe, Moscow had already proposed a series of concessions in Basket Three in 1980 based on earlier Western proposals at the Belgrade meeting. Among other things, Moscow was prepared to agree to 'handle favourably' applications for family meetings, family unification and cross-border marriages, but also 'to decide upon them in the same spirit'; to process applications for family meetings in 'emergency cases … as expeditiously as possible'; to make determinations regarding family reunification and cross-border marriages 'in normal practice within six months and for other family meetings within gradually decreasing time limits'; to 'provide the necessary information on the procedures to be followed by the applicants in these cases and on the regulations to be observed, as well as, upon the applicant's request, provide the relevant forms'; and a commitment not to discriminate against individuals who resubmitted such applications or their families in terms of 'employment, housing, access to social, economic or educational benefits, as well as any other rights and obligations flowing from the laws and regulations of the respective participating State'.⁴⁷ Eventually, the Eastern bloc would also agree not to discriminate against re-applicants for emigration in terms of 'residence status' and 'family support'.⁴⁸ The country, of course, that would be hardest hit by these concessions was the GDR, which would have to change its laws to conform to the new concessions and had just begun to get the emigration movement under control. The East Germans had protested the proposed concessions,⁴⁹ and Mielke confronted KGB Chief Yuri Andropov about them in the summer of 1981.⁵⁰ He posed, in effect, the question that scholars would pose today: why did the Soviet Union, after its allies had largely succeeded in repressing the activism in their countries based upon the Helsinki Final Act (i.e. the 'Helsinki Effect'), suddenly demonstrate a willingness to make new concessions to the West with regard to human rights and human contacts at Madrid, which would only serve to revive such activism?

In defending the planned concessions to Mielke, Andropov cited Moscow's need to preserve its ongoing détente with Western Europe.⁵¹ Two grounds were decisive. After the collapse of US–Soviet détente, Moscow needed to maintain good economic relations with Western Europe due to its own economic difficulties – i.e. due to the very factor that Thomas downplays. A second factor that Andropov cited – and Thomas completely dismisses in his book – was the geopolitical balance between East and West, especially the nuclear-strategic balance, which threatened to turn against the East. Moscow sought a successful concluding document at Madrid with a planned conference on confidence-building and disarmament measures in Europe in order to strengthen its 'peace offensive' in the West, aimed at derailing the stationing of US long-range theatre nuclear forces (LRTNF) in Western Europe – the so-called 'Euromissiles'.[52] The concerns that Andropov cited – the Reagan administration's unprecedented nuclear and conventional arms build-up, its worldwide counter-offensive against Soviet- and Cuban-supported insurgencies, its economic warfare against the Soviet Union, and its anti-détente rhetoric – made détente with Western Europe and a future conference on security and confidence-building measures in the CSCE process all the more valuable to the Soviet Union. There was a note of pessimism in Andropov's assessment of the world situation. 'Perhaps it is my subjective opinion', he said. 'The USA is preparing for war, but it is not prepared to start it. They are not building the enterprises and palaces in order to destroy them. They want military superiority in order to put us in "check" and to declare "mate" without beginning a war.' He then added, 'Perhaps I am deceiving myself'.[53] The US arms build-up, Andropov noted, was putting Moscow under increasing economic pressure:

> The most complicated problem is that we cannot avoid the burden of military expenditures for us and the other socialist countries. Reagan obtained approval for 220 billion dollars in military expenditures. Therefore, we must do everything possible in order to provide the corresponding funds for the defence industry. ... The Americans know that parity exists. We cannot permit them to overtake us. If we did not have to make these expenditures, we could solve all the other problems in two or three years. Over and beyond this, there is the assistance for Vietnam, Laos, Kampuchea, Angola, Cuba, Afghanistan, etc. The People's Republic of Poland recently received four billion dollars in order to remain creditworthy.[54]

Reagan's economic warfare against Moscow was also having an impact. Andropov said: 'The banks have suddenly stopped giving us loans (USA, FRG). We are currently conducting negotiations with the FRG and France over the natural-gas pipeline. This is useful for us and also for them. But the USA is putting pressure on other countries, saying that they are allegedly making themselves dependent upon us'. Nevertheless, Andropov was 'optimistic' that the 'business people' would prevail over the 'rulers' with regard to the pipeline.[55]

In January 1983, now as General Secretary of the CPSU, Andropov explained to the assembled leaders of the Warsaw Pact why the Soviet bloc needed to make concessions for a concluding document at Madrid, which would include a Conference on Disarmament in Europe. Front and centre in his argumentation stood Moscow's deteriorating geostrategic position vis-à-vis the US and the need to derail the planned stationing of US Euromissiles. He stressed the need to 'give détente a second wind' by 'engaging in a broad, meaningful dialogue with the West European countries and strengthening cooperation with them'.[56] The need for reviving détente, especially in Europe, was clear to Andropov, given the growing threat from the US. He told the Warsaw Pact's leaders:

> Whereas before, the Americans, in speaking about their nuclear weapons, preferred to emphasize that they were above all else a means of 'intimidation' and 'deterrence', now, as they create advanced missile systems, they do not hide the fact that they are actually intended for future wars. Hence, the doctrines of 'rational' and 'limited' nuclear war; hence, the assertions about the possibility of surviving and winning a protracted nuclear conflict. It is difficult to distinguish between what constitutes blackmail and what constitutes a genuine readiness to take the fatal step.[57]

The Warsaw Pact leaders' final declaration reflected Andropov's bleak assessment of US policy. 'The dangers to peace', it read, 'are growing, and it is necessary to counter the heating up of the international situation. ... Détente, which brought positive results for the peoples, has suffered heavy damages. ... The danger of a war, especially a nuclear war, is growing'.[58] Thus, in the end, the deteriorating economic situation in the Soviet Union and the Eastern bloc in general and Soviet concerns about limiting Western military potential, especially in the nuclear arena, explain why the East was still compelled to make concessions in the Helsinki process.

Not surprisingly, the same factors that had led Moscow to compromise on human contacts and later on human rights at Madrid led the Soviet Politburo to reject the request of Poland's communist leader, General Wojciech Jaruzelski, to use Soviet forces to assist in the imposition of martial law in Poland in December 1981. In explaining Moscow's decision not to engage directly in the military suppression of human rights in Poland, Thomas cites Andropov's statement at the climactic Soviet Politburo meeting on 10 December 1981. For Andropov, Moscow's dire economic situation and thus, indirectly, the need to preserve economic relations with Western Europe were decisive in his rejection of Soviet military intervention.[59] Practically everyone – including Thomas – has ignored, however, the statement of hardline ideological secretary Mikhail Suslov in opposition to Soviet military intervention. He cited the need to maintain the peace movement in the West and to bolster ongoing Soviet diplomacy in the same direction – most importantly, to prevent the planned stationing of US 'Euromissiles' in keeping with NATO's dual-track decision.[60]

Ironically, the factors that led Moscow to make concessions to the West in Basket Three at the Madrid meeting and to reject military intervention in Poland were the very same factors that had led Moscow to seek détente and a Conference on Security and Cooperation in Europe over ten years before: not only to obtain Western recognition of the territorial and political status quo in Europe, but also to obtain access to Western loans, trade and technology and, in the end, to 'complete' political détente with 'military détente' in the form of favourable disarmament and arms control agreements with the West.[61] After the communist victory in Vietnam and the conclusion of the CSCE Final Act, the Soviets seemed to have forgotten the weaknesses that had brought them to a policy of détente with the West in the first place. After the collapse of US–Soviet détente, the imposition of US economic sanctions and an accelerating US conventional and nuclear arms build-up, the Soviets came to remember the factors that had originally brought them to détente. Thus, they were willing to make concessions to save the Helsinki process and Soviet–West European détente in general.

Nevertheless, the Soviet concessions at Madrid did not prove enough to prevent the stationing of US Euromissiles as part of NATO's dual-track decision, and Moscow found itself in economic and political *Zugzwang* at the end of the Andropov era, as Vladislav Zubok has pointed out. Under Konstantin Chernenko's short rule, it continued a policy of muddling through.[62] His successor might have continued such a policy, but Moscow's East European allies, due to their growing economic dependence on Western Europe, were more and more susceptible to demands for reforms in the realm of human rights. This was even the case for the GDR, which permitted a mass exodus of around forty thousand émigrés to West Germany in 1984, only to try to close the floodgates again, with lessening success.[63] To Mielke's dismay, not only had Moscow forced the GDR to make the aforementioned concessions in Basket Three at Madrid, which led to an increase in applications for emigration and public demonstrations for the same inside the GDR, but East German leader Erich Honecker had decided to permit the emigration wave after a number of East Germans occupied the West German mission and other Western missions in Berlin, along with the West German embassy in Prague.[64] Honecker's goal in permitting the emigration – instead of embarking on a new wave of repression – was to maintain good relations with the FRG after obtaining a guarantee for a billion Deutschmark (DM) loan from the West German government.

Soon after Honecker's approval of the mass exodus from East Germany, the GDR obtained a guarantee for yet another billion DM loan from Bonn.[65] If Moscow had continued a policy of muddling through after Chernenko's death, the case of East Germany suggested that Moscow's allies would have continued to slip further into the West's economic orbit and to make further concessions in the realm of human contacts and human rights. Crises, such as in Poland in 1980–81, would have likely arisen more often, and Moscow would have been compelled to decide between military intervention or a loss of political influence in East Central Europe.[66]

Another option for Andropov's successor would have been to 'free' its allies and the Soviet Union itself from the shackles of economic relations with the West through a policy of economic self-sufficiency and re-Stalinization. This would have proved difficult, given the Soviet elite's own taste for the privileges that they had gained from increased contacts with the West since the 1970s.[67] Moscow's East European allies, for their part, would have likely balked, although the Soviet bloc's maverick, Romania, stood as a counter-example: a country with a national Stalinist regime that had repaid its Western loans. None of the other Eastern bloc regimes, it seems, wanted to follow Romania's example.[68]

The policy of the United States in the CSCE process, bolstered and shaped by the transnational Helsinki network, suggested another possibility for Moscow. A Soviet leader willing to make certain concessions on human rights might find a partner in Washington that was willing to discuss arms control and disarmament. As chance would have it, Mikhail Gorbachev turned out to be such a leader.[69] The Soviet concessions in Basket Three at the Vienna CSCE follow-up meeting (1986–89) undermined the East German dictatorship – for example, the legal review of administrative decisions, freedom to travel and mobility, the legalization of Helsinki groups, and review of implementation of decisions related to the CSCE. This meant that most of the provisions in East German criminal law against applicants for emigration had to be dropped or revised. Once again, this did not mean an end to legal discrimination, especially since the GDR refused to be bound by the decisions of the Vienna meeting, but the GDR's difficulties in suppressing the emigration movement only grew.[70] This was even more the case when Hungary's communist government announced on 10 September 1989 its decision to open its border. It thus legalized the mass flight of East Germans that had already begun across its border. The Hungarians justified their decision by citing not only United Nations (UN) conventions, but also the decisions of the Vienna meeting.[71]

Conclusion

Summing up, the 'Helsinki Effect', even though it contributed to the collapse of communism, was not decisive. Long-term factors, exacerbated by the backlash in the US after the collapse of US–Soviet détente, proved more important: the growing economic crisis of the East, which made it increasingly dependent on loans and trade from the West, and the perceived need of Soviet leaders to maintain the strategic and conventional military balance with the West. This meant, given the economic weakness of the Soviet Union, a need for arms control and disarmament agreements with the West and especially the US.

This does not mean that the CSCE process was unimportant with regard to the collapse of communism in Eastern Europe. In particular, it helps explain why communism collapsed the way it did: largely peacefully in a process of ongoing rapprochement between East and West. It helped show Gorbachev a peaceful path towards ending the Cold War. It also provided Gorbachev with an excuse vis-à-vis Soviet hardliners for implementing political reforms; such reforms were necessary, he could argue, in order to promote Western peace movements, to stabilize the Soviet economy (in part through trade with the West) and to obtain beneficial arms control and disarmament agreements with the West, which would not only lessen the danger of war, but also further relieve the Soviet economy from excessive expenditures for arms.[72]

Douglas Selvage (Ph.D., Yale University, History, 1998) is a project director in the Education and Research Division of the Office of the Federal Commissioner for Stasi Records (BStU) in Berlin. He recently completed a book with Walter Süß entitled *Staatssicherheit und KSZE-Prozess: MfS zwischen SED und KGB* [State Security and the CSCE Process: The Ministry of State Security between SED and KGB], Göttingen: Vandenhoeck & Ruprecht, forthcoming 2019. In his previous position as a historian at the US Department of State, his publications included *Foreign Relations of the United States, 1969–1976: European Security, 1969–76* (Washington: U.S. Government Printing Office, 2007).

Notes

1. D.C. Thomas, *The Helsinki Effect: International Norms, Human Rights, and the Demise of Communism* (Princeton, NJ: Princeton University Press, 2001), 4.

2. Mielke an die Leiter aller Diensteinheiten des MfS, Zusammenfassung von Hinweisen über Aktivitäten antisozialistischer, feindlich-negativer Kräfte in einigen Staaten der sozialistischen Gemeinschaft und über in diesem Zusammenhang erfolgte Reaktionen und Aktivitäten führender westlicher Kreise und einiger kommunistischer Parteien kapitalistischer Staaten, 14 March 1977, in Bundesbeauftragte für die Unterlagen des Staatsicherheitsdienstes der ehemaligen DDR (BStU), Ministerium für Staatssicherheit (MfS), Büro der Leitung (BdL), Dok. Nr. 6040, 4.
3. Ibid., 7–8.
4. Referat des Genossen Minister auf dem zentralen Führungsseminar über die weitere Vervollkommnung und Gewährleistung der Sicherheit der DDR durch vorbeugende Verhinderung und Bekämpfung des subversiven Missbrauchs des Einreiseverkehrs aus nichtsozialistischen Staaten und Westberlin, GVS, MfS 008-4/77, 6 July 1977, in BStU, MfS, BdL, Dok. Nr. 06332, 12–13.
5. Mielke an die Leiter aller Diensteinheiten, 14 March 1977, 4–10, 23–25.
6. See, for example, S. Rohde-Liebenau, *Menschenrechte und internationaler Wandel: Der Einfluß des KSZE-Menschenrechtsregimes auf den Wandel des internationalen Systems in Europa* (Baden-Baden: Nomos Verlag, 1996), 67–70.
7. Mielke an die Leiter aller Diensteinheiten, 14 March 1977, 5–6.
8. Oberstltn. Horn, Kreisdienststelle Jena, MfS, Bericht IMV 'Heinz Muller' vom 24.06.1977, 27 June 1977, BStU, Außenstelle (Ast) Gera, AOP 452/79, Bd. II, 191.
9. Zusammenfassender Bericht über die Feindorganisation 'Schutzkomitee für [sic] Freiheit und Sozialismus', n.d., BStU, MfS, Zentrale Koordinierungsgruppe (ZKG), Bd. 358, 3. See also H. Schwenger, 'Das Schutzkomitee Freiheit und Sozialismus in Selbstzeugnissen, Dokumenten, Briefen und im Zerrspiegel des MfS-Akten', *Europäische Ideen* (1995, Sonderheft), 61–67. On the actual contacts between the *Schutzkomitee*, East German dissidents and Charter 77, see also R. Ellmenreich, 'Begegnungen in Prag', in D. Liebermann, J. Fuchs and V. Wallat (eds), *Dissidenten, Präsidenten und Gemüsehändler: Tschechische und ostdeutsche Dissidenten 1968–1998* (Essen: Klartext Verlag, 1998), 39–40; and U. Scheer, *Vision und Wirklichkeit: Die Opposition in Jena in den siebziger und achtziger Jahren*, 2nd ed. (Berlin: Ch. Links Verlag, 1999), 181.
10. L. Tautz (ed.), *Friede und Gerechtigkeit Heute: das 'Querfurter Papier' – ein politisches Manifest für die Einhaltung der Menschenrechte in der DDR*, Sachbeiträge (22) (Magdeburg: Landesbeauftragte für die Unterlagen des Staatsicherheitsdienstes der ehemaligen DDR in Sachsen-Anhalt, 2002), passim.
11. W. Janssen, 'Das "Querfurter Papier" im Spiegel der Akten des Ministeriums für Staatssicherheit – Der Zentrale Operative Vorgang (ZOV) "Korinther"', in Tautz, *Friede und Gerechtigkeit*, 70; HA XX/5, 4. Maßnahmeplan zur Bearbeitung des Operativ-Vorganges 'Kontakt', 16 November 1977, BStU, MfS, AOP 12003/83, Bd. IV, Bl. 4–12; Scheer, *Vision und Wirklichkeit*, 195–97.
12. Ausführungen des Hauptabteilungsleiters im Ministerium für Staatssicherheit der DDR, Generalmajor Kienberg, auf der Beratung mit der

V. Verwaltung des KGB (Auszug), Moskau, 23–24. Mai 1978, in D. Hofmann, H.-H. Jansen and A. Löbnitz (eds), *Dokumente zur Deutschlandpolitik. VI. Reihe. Band 5: 1. Januar 1977 bis 31. Dezember 1978* (Munich: Oldenbourg, 2011), 658.
13. E. Neubert, *Geschichte der Opposition in der DDR 1949–1989*, 2nd ed. (Bonn: Bundeszentrale für politische Bildung, 1997), 257–62.
14. U. Poppe, '"Der Weg ist das Ziel": Zum Selbstverständnis und der politischen Rolle oppositioneller Gruppe der achtziger Jahren', in U. Poppe, R. Eckert and I.-S. Kowalczuk (eds), *Zwischen Selbstbehauptung und Anpassung: Formen des Widerstandes und der Opposition in der DDR* (Berlin: Ch. Links, 1995), 248.
15. Ibid., 245–46.
16. G. Poppe, 'Begründung und Entwicklung internationaler Verbindungen', in E. Kuhrt (ed.), *Opposition in der DDR von den 70er Jahren bis zum Zusammenbruch der SED-Herrschaft* (Opladen: Heske und Budrich, 1999), 359–60; Neubert, *Geschichte der Opposition*, 322–23; T. Vilímek, *Solidarita napříč hranicemi: Opozice v ČSSR a NDR po roce 1968* (Vyšehrad: Ústav pro soudobé dějiny AV ČR, v. v. i., 2010), 155–73.
17. G. Poppe, 'Begründung und Entwicklung', 353–57; Neubert, *Geschichte der Opposition*, 559–61, 597–604.
18. U. Poppe, 'Der Weg ist das Ziel', 263–66.
19. B. Eisenfeld, 'Die Ausreisebewegung – eine Erscheinungsform widerständigen Verhaltens', in Poppe, Eckert and Kowalczuk, *Zwischen Selbstbehauptung und Anpassung*, 192–224, passim.
20. A. Hanisch, *Die DDR im KSZE-Prozess 1972–1985* (Munich: Oldenbourg Verlag, 2012), 169–74.
21. Ibid., 157–66.
22. S.B. Snyder, *Human Rights Activism and the End of the Cold War: A Transnational History of the Helsinki Network* (Cambridge and New York: Cambridge University Press, 2011), 81–114. Regarding the greater concern of Washington's allies for 'Basket Three', see D. Selvage, 'The Superpowers and the Conference on Security and Cooperation in Europe, 1977–1983: Human Rights, Nuclear Weapons, and Western Europe', in M. Peter and H. Wentker (eds), *Die KSZE im Ost-West-Konflikt: Internationale Politik und gesellschaftliche Transformation 1975–1990* (Munich: Oldenbourg Verlag, 2012), 22–26.
23. See, for example, Soviet leader Leonid Brezhnev's speech at the meeting of the Political Consultative Committee (PCC) of the Warsaw Pact, 26 November 1976, in V. Mastny, C. Nuenlist, A. Locher and D. Selvage (eds), *Records of the Warsaw Pact Political Consultative Committee, 1955–1990*, Parallel History Project (PHP) on Collective Security, retrieved 15 June 2017 from http://www.php.isn.ethz.ch/lory1.ethz.ch/collections/colltopic439e.html?lng=en&id=19359&navinfo=14465. In October 1973, the World Congress of Peace Forces in Moscow had proclaimed the following two goals for communist-influenced peace organizations around the globe: conclusion of the CSCE negotiations ('political détente'), which would then be 'completed' with arms control and disarmament agreements between

East and West ('military détente'). See Kommuniqué des Weltkongresses der Friedenskräfte, Moskau, 25-31. Oktober 1973, in Friedensrat der DDR (ed.), *Dokumente der Weltfriedensbewegung, Oktober 1962 bis Dezember 1974* (Berlin: Friedensrat der DDR, 1976), 226.

24. In a speech to the foreign ministers of the other Warsaw Pact states in December 1975, Soviet Foreign Minister Andrei Gromyko had called the 'multilateral entrenchment of the [territorial] status quo' in the Helsinki Final Act the 'central point' for the communist states. It also offered a starting point, however, for 'very much that was useful' in the realm of 'economic and scientific-technical cooperation'. Stiftung Archiv der Parteien und Massenorganisationen der ehemaligen Deutschen Demokratischen Republik im Bundesarchiv (SAPMO BA), DY 30, J IV 2/2A-1940, 102–3.

25. At the Belgrade meeting, Moscow submitted proposals for an agreement to prohibit the expansion of the existing military alliances in Europe and a treaty among all CSCE member states on the non-first-use of nuclear weapons. The two proposals had a highly propagandistic character. The first, directed against Spain's planned accession to NATO, stood no chance of acceptance by the West, especially since there was no corresponding danger of the Warsaw Pact's expansion. The second proposal, which had a long history in Soviet peace campaigns, had been rejected by NATO even before the Belgrade meeting opened. As Moscow knew, NATO's defence strategy was based on the willingness of the US to use nuclear weapons first in the event of a Soviet invasion of Western Europe – a necessity, given the Warsaw Pact's superiority in conventional forces. Selvage, 'Superpowers', 25–26; W. Korey, *The Promises We Keep: Human Rights, the Helsinki Process, and American Foreign Policy* (New York: St. Martin's Press, 1993), 95 ff.

26. Thomas, *Helsinki Effect*, 22.

27. H.G. Skilling, *Charter 77 and Human Rights in Czechoslovakia* (London: George Allen & Unwin, 1981), 140–42, 145–46.

28. Hanisch, *DDR im KSZE-Prozess*, 233.

29. Ibid., 233–34. Regarding the psycho-terror of the Stasi against individuals, so-called *Zersetzungsmaßnahmen* or 'disintegration measures', see J. Gieseke, *The History of the Stasi: East Germany's Secret Police, 1945–1990* (New York and Oxford: Berghahn Books, 2014), 146–48.

30. J. Raschka, *Justizpolitik im SED-Staat: Anpassung und Wandel des Strafrechts während der Amtszeit Honeckers* (Cologne: Böhlau Verlag, 2000), 89–124; H.-H. Lochen and C. Meyer-Seitz (eds), *Die geheimen Anweisungen zur Diskriminierung Ausreisewilliger: Dokumente der Stasi und des Ministeriums des Innern* (Cologne: Bundesanzeiger, 1992), passim.

31. Ausführungen des Genossen Erich Honecker im Gespräch mit Genossen Andrzej Zabinski, Mitglied des Politbüros und Sekretär des ZK der Polnischen Vereinigten Arbeiterpartei am 13. September 1980, SAPMO BA, DY 30/2477, 61.

32. See, for example, the comments of Mielke on the topic to a visiting delegation from the KGB, in Niederschrift zum Empfang der sowjetischen Delegation durch den Genossen Minister (Erstfassung), 26 May 1978, BStU, MfS, HA IX, Bd. 10251, 144.

33. Hanisch, *DDR im KSZE-Prozess*, 234.
34. By the end of the 1970s, both the Stasi and Honecker – who had the final say – had begun to approve on a growing basis the emigration applications of individuals who were likely to demonstrate publicly during major events such as the East German Party Congress, which could lead to negative publicity for the GDR in the West German media, which practically all East Germans could receive in their homes. Already in 1975–76, fears that an individual might engage in a public demonstration could lead to accelerated approval of their emigration – or, alternatively, especially after 1976, to imprisonment for various political crimes. See ibid., 144–77, 239–54.
35. S. Savranskaya, 'Human Rights Movement in the USSR after the Signing of the Helsinki Final Act, and the Reaction of Soviet Authorities', in L. Nuti (ed.), *The Crisis of Détente in Europe: From Helsinki to Gorbachev, 1975–1985* (Abingdon: Routledge, 2009), 35.
36. Teilbericht von Oberstleutnant Jaekel vom 2.12.1980 über die Ereignisse seiner Dienstreise nach Moskau 24.-28.11.1980, BStU, MfS, HA XX, Bd. 1386, Bl. 215–20, hier 216.
37. Ibid. Kaplun's husband, the trade unionist Vladimir Borisov, blamed the KGB for her death. He saw it as revenge for her call to boycott the 1980 Olympics in Moscow. See 'Soviets Killed My Wife: Exile', *Montreal Gazette*, 26 July 1980, 95.
38. Savranskaya, 'Human Rights Movement in the USSR', 35.
39. Thomas, *Helsinki Effect*, 206–8.
40. W. Süß, 'Wandlungen der MfS-Repressionstaktik seit Mitte der siebziger Jahre im Kontext der Beratungen der Ostblock-Geheimdienste zur Bekämpfung der "ideologischen Diversion"', in L. Ansorg, B. Gehrke, T. Klein and D. Kneipp (eds), *'Das Land ist still – noch!': Herrschaftswandel und politische Gegnerschaft in der DDR (1971–1989)* (Cologne, Weimar and Vienna: Böhlau Verlag, 2009), 130–31.
41. Thomas, *Helsinki Effect*, 197.
42. Snyder, *Human Rights Activism*, 131–34.
43. See D. Selvage and W. Süß. *Staatssicherheit und KSZE-Prozess: MfS zwischen SED und KGB* (Göttingen: Vandenhoeck & Ruprecht, forthcoming 2019).
44. Thomas, *Helsinki Effect*, 167–74, 183–86.
45. Ibid., 195–219.
46. Selvage, 'Superpowers', 53–56.
47. Bemerkungen zu den inoffiziell vereinbarten Texten eines Schlußdokumentes des Madrider Treffens, 19 June 1981, BStU, MfS, Rechtsstelle (RS), Bd. 605, 273–80.
48. OSCE Archives, Prague, Proposal Submitted by the Delegations of Austria, Cyprus, Finland, Liechtenstein, San Marino, Sweden, Switzerland and Yugoslavia: Draft Concluding Document (CSCE/RM.39), 16 December 1981, 24.
49. Hanisch, *DDR im KSZE-Prozess*, 271–79.
50. Hinweise für Gespräche in Moskau (Juli 1981), o.D., BStU, MfS, ZAIG, Bd. 5169, 25.

51. Thomas implies that the Soviet bloc's détente with Western Europe collapsed along with US–Soviet détente. Thomas, *Helsinki Effect*, 198, 211. However, this was not the case. The end of US–Soviet détente and the desire of the West Europeans to preserve it had already become a source of tensions and debates between Washington and its European allies, particularly France and West Germany. See Selvage, 'Superpowers', 22–26; K. Wiegrefe, *Das Zerwürfnis: Helmut Schmidt, Jimmy Carter und die Krise der deutsche-amerikanischen Beziehungen* (Berlin: Propyläen-Verlag, 2005), 145 ff.
52. Selvage, 'Superpowers', 29 ff. Regarding the importance of the security and military aspects of the CSCE and the ensuing 'Conference on Confidence and Security Building Measures and Disarmament in Europe' (CDE) in Stockholm, see Oliver Bange's contribution to this volume (Chapter 12).
53. Notiz über die Gespräche des Genossen Minister mit dem Vorsitzenden des KfS, Genossen ANDROPOW, am 11.7.1981 in Moskau, n.d., 8, in Selvage and Süß, 'Das MfS und die Zusammenarbeit', retrieved 8 June 2017 from http://www.bstu.bund.de/DE/Wissen/MfS-Dokumente/Downloads/KGB-Projekt/81_07_11_Gespraech_Mielke_Andropow.pdf;jsessionid=85C21847 5C48FEB7F78BFE89B4DA2E65.2_cid354?__blob=publicationFile.
54. Ibid., 5–6.
55. Ibid., 4.
56. Speech by the General Secretary of the CC of the CPSU (Yuri V. Andropov), 3 January 1983, English transl., 9, in Mastny et al., *Records of the Warsaw Pact*, retrieved 15 March 2017 from http://www.php.isn.ethz.ch/kms2.isn.ethz.ch/serviceengine/Files/PHP/18854/ipublicationdocument_singledocument/1bd8b661-d3cf-4ea4-97a4-b50cb8184ea8/en/Speech_Andropov_1983_en.pdf.
57. Ibid., 3.
58. Politische Deklaration der Teilnehmerstaaten des Warschauer Vertrages, 5.1.1983, in Ministerium für Auswärtige Angelegenheiten (MfAA) der DDR, *Die Organisation des Warschauer Vertrages. Dokumente und Materialien 1955–1985* (Berlin: MfAA, 1986), 272.
59. Thomas, *Helsinki Effect*, 207. Andropov declared: 'We do not intend to introduce troops into Poland. That is the correct position, and we must observe it to the end. I do not know how matters will develop in Poland, but even if Poland comes under the authority of Solidarity that will be one thing. But if the capitalist countries fall upon the Soviet Union, and they already have a suitable agreement, with various kinds of economic and political sanctions, then that will be very difficult for us. We must show concern for our country, for the strengthening of the Soviet Union. That is our main line'. Transcript of CPSU CC Politburo Meeting, 10 December 1981, in A. Paczkowski and M. Byrne (eds), *From Solidarity to Martial Law: The Polish Crisis of 1980–1981* (Budapest and New York: Central European University Press, 2007), 450.
60. Ibid., 452 ff.
61. See endnotes 23 and 24 (above).
62. V.M. Zubok, *A Failed Empire: The Soviet Union in the Cold War from Stalin to Gorbachev* (Chapel Hill: University of North Carolina Press, 2007), 305–7.

63. Hanisch, *DDR im KSZE-Prozess*, 349–59.
64. Notiz über die Gespräche des Genossen Minister mit dem Stellvertreter des Vorsitzenden des KfS, Genossen W.A. Krjutschkow, am 19.9.1983 in Berlin, 18, in Selvage and Süß, 'Das MfS und die Zusammenarbeit', retrieved 8 June 2017 from http://www.bstu.bund.de/DE/Wissen/MfS-Dokumente/Downloads/KGB-Projekt/83_09_19_Gespr_Mielke_Krjutschkow.pdf;jsessionid=85C218475C48FEB7F78BFE89B4DA2E65.2_cid354?__blob=publicationFile.
65. With regard to the loan, see H.-H. Hertle, 'Die DDR an die Sowjetunion verkaufen? Stasi-Analysen zum ökonomische Niedergang der DDR', *Deutschland Archiv* 42(3) (2009), 476–77. Mielke belonged to the informal 'Moscow wing' of the East German Politburo. This wing opposed the growing economic relations between East and West Germany, which it associated with Honecker and especially his Central Committee Secretary for Economics Günter Mittag. For the sake of such economic relations, Honecker had been making concessions with regard to humanitarian matters to West Germany, including with regard to emigration. In this case, the GDR received 5,000 West German marks for every émigré. Ibid., 477. With regard to the 'Moscow wing', see also W. Süß, *Die Staatssicherheit im letzten Jahrzehnt der DDR: Geschichte der Staatssicherheit, Teil III* (Berlin: BStU, 2009), 24, https://www.bstu.bund.de/DE/Wissen/Publikationen/Publikationen/handbuch_stasi-im-letzten-jahrzehnt_suess.pdf?__blob=publicationFile.
66. I.T. Berend, *Central and Eastern Europe 1944–1993: Detour from the Periphery to the Periphery* (Cambridge: Cambridge University Press, 1996), 230–32.
67. Zubok, *A Failed Empire*, 277.
68. Berend, *Central and Eastern Europe*, 231–32. The term 'national Stalinism' for Romania comes from Vladimir Tismaneanu. See V. Tismaneanu, *Stalinism for All Seasons: A Political History of Romanian Communism* (Berkeley: University of California Press, 2003).
69. See Y. von Saal, *KSZE-Prozess und Perestroika in der Sowjetunion: Demokratisierung, Werteumbruch und Auflösung* (Munich: Oldenbourg Verlag, 2014), especially 357–60. See also Thomas, *Helsinki Effect*, 233, 236–38, 241–44; Snyder, *Human Rights Activism*, 215–16.
70. W. Süß, 'Die Wiener KSZE-Folgekonferenz und Handlungsspielraum des DDR-Sicherheitsapparates 1989', in Peter and Wentker, *Die KSZE im Ost-West-Konflikt*, 220–25, 228–30.
71. See the chapter by Graf in this volume (Chapter 10) and also Thomas, *Helsinki Effect*, 249.
72. Von Saal, *KSZE-Prozess und Perestroika*, 305–72; A. Adamishin and R. Schifter, *Human Rights, Perestroika, and the End of the Cold War* (Washington, DC: United States Institute of Peace Press, 2009), 111–81, 236–38.

Bibliography

Adamishin, A., and R. Schifter. *Human Rights, Perestroika, and the End of the Cold War*. Washington, DC: United States Institute of Peace Press, 2009.

Berend, I.T. *Central and Eastern Europe 1944–1993: Detour from the Periphery to the Periphery*. Cambridge: Cambridge University Press, 1996.
Eisenfeld, B. 'Die Ausreisebewegung – eine Erscheinungsform widerständigen Verhaltens', in U. Poppe, R. Eckert and I.-S. Kowalczuk (eds), *Zwischen Selbstbehauptung und Anpassung: Formen des Widerstandes und der Opposition in der DDR* (Berlin: Ch. Links, 1995), 192–224.
Ellmenreich, R. 'Begegnungen in Prag', in D. Liebermann, J. Fuchs and V. Wallat (eds), *Dissidenten, Präsidenten und Gemüsehändler: Tschechische und ostdeutsche Dissidenten 1968–1998* (Essen: Klartext Verlag, 1998), 37–40.
Friedensrat der DDR (ed.). *Dokumente der Weltfriedensbewegung, Oktober 1962 bis Dezember 1974*. Berlin: Friedensrat der DDR, 1976.
Gieseke, J. *The History of the Stasi: East Germany's Secret Police, 1945–1990*. New York and Oxford: Berghahn Books, 2014.
Hanisch, A. *Die DDR im KSZE-Prozess 1972–1985*. Munich: Oldenbourg Verlag, 2012.
Hertle, H.-H. 'Die DDR an die Sowjetunion verkaufen? Stasi-Analysen zum ökonomische Niedergang der DDR'. *Deutschland Archiv* 42(3) (2009), 476–95.
Hofmann, D., H.-H. Jansen and A. Löbnitz (eds). *Dokumente zur Deutschlandpolitik. VI. Reihe. Band 5: 1. Januar 1977 bis 31. Dezember 1978*. Munich: Oldenbourg, 2011.
Janssen, W. 'Das "Querfurter Papier" im Spiegel der Akten des Ministeriums für Staatssicherheit – Der Zentrale Operative Vorgang (ZOV) "Korinther"', in L. Tautz (ed.), *Friede und Gerechtigkeit Heute: das 'Querfurter Papier' – ein politisches Manifest für die Einhaltung der Menschenrechte in der DDR* (Magdeburg: Landesbeauftragte für die Unterlagen des Staatssicherheitsdienstes der ehemaligen DDR in Sachsen-Anhalt, 2002), 63–70.
Korey, W. *The Promises We Keep: Human Rights, the Helsinki Process, and American Foreign Policy*. New York: St. Martin's Press, 1993.
Lochen, H.-H., and C. Meyer-Seitz (eds). *Die geheimen Anweisungen zur Diskriminierung Ausreisewilliger: Dokumente der Stasi und des Ministeriums des Innern*. Cologne: Bundesanzeiger, 1992.
Mastny, V., C. Nuenlist, A. Locher, and D. Selvage (eds). *Records of the Warsaw Pact Political Consultative Committee, 1955–1990*. Parallel History Project (PHP) on Collective Security, n.d. Retrieved 15 February 2018 from http://www.php.isn.ethz.ch/lory1.ethz.ch/collections/colltopic3bcf.html?lng=en&id=14465.
Ministerium für Auswärtige Angelegenheiten (MfAA) der DDR. *Die Organisation des Warschauer Vertrages. Dokumente und Materialien 1955–1985*. Berlin: MfAA, 1986.
Neubert, E. *Geschichte der Opposition in der DDR 1949–1989*. 2nd ed. Bonn: Bundeszentrale für politische Bildung, 1997.
Paczkowski, A., and M. Byrne (eds). *From Solidarity to Martial Law: The Polish Crisis of 1980–1981*. Budapest and New York: Central European University Press, 2007.
Poppe, G. 'Begründung und Entwicklung internationaler Verbindungen', in E. Kuhrt (ed.), *Opposition in der DDR von den 70er Jahren bis zum Zusammenbruch der SED-Herrschaft* (Opladen: Heske und Budrich, 1999), 349–77.

Poppe, U. '"Der Weg ist das Ziel": Zum Selbstverständnis und der politischen Rolle oppositioneller Gruppe der achtziger Jahren', in U. Poppe, R. Eckert and I.-S. Kowalczuk (eds), *Zwischen Selbstbehauptung und Anpassung: Formen des Widerstandes und der Opposition in der DDR* (Berlin: Ch. Links, 1995), 244–72.

Raschka, J. *Justizpolitik im SED-Staat: Anpassung und Wandel des Strafrechts während der Amtszeit Honeckers*. Cologne: Böhlau Verlag, 2000.

Rohde-Liebenau, S. *Menschenrechte und internationaler Wandel: Der Einfluß des KSZE-Menschenrechtsregimes auf den Wandel des internationalen Systems in Europa*. Baden-Baden: Nomos Verlag, 1996.

Savranskaya, S. 'Human Rights Movement in the USSR after the Signing of the Helsinki Final Act, and the Reaction of Soviet Authorities', in L. Nuti (ed.), *The Crisis of Détente in Europe: From Helsinki to Gorbachev, 1975–1985* (Abingdon: Routledge, 2009), 26–40.

Scheer, U. *Vision und Wirklichkeit: Die Opposition in Jena in den siebziger und achtziger Jahren*. 2nd ed. Berlin: Ch. Links Verlag, 1999.

Schwenger, H. 'Das Schutzkomitee Freiheit und Sozialismus in Selbstzeugnissen, Dokumenten, Briefen und im Zerrspiegel des MfS-Akten'. *Europäische Ideen* (1995, Sonderheft), 61–67.

Selvage, D. 'The Superpowers and the Conference on Security and Cooperation in Europe, 1977–1983: Human Rights, Nuclear Weapons, and Western Europe', in M. Peter and H. Wentker (eds), *Die KSZE im Ost-West-Konflikt: Internationale Politik und gesellschaftliche Transformation 1975–1990* (Munich: Oldenbourg Verlag, 2012), 15–58.

Selvage, D., and W. Süß (eds). 'Das MfS und die Zusammenarbeit mit anderen kommunistischen Geheimdiensten: Staatssicherheit und sowjetischer KGB'. Retrieved 15 February 2018 from https://www.bstu.bund.de/DE/Wissen/MfS-Dokumente/MfS-KGB/_inhalt.html.

Selvage, D., and W. Süß. *Staatssicherheit und KSZE-Prozess: MfS zwischen SED und KGB* (Göttingen: Vandenhoeck & Ruprecht, forthcoming 2019).

Skilling, H.G. *Charter 77 and Human Rights in Czechoslovakia*. London: George Allen & Unwin, 1981.

Snyder, S.B. *Human Rights Activism and the End of the Cold War: A Transnational History of the Helsinki Network*. Cambridge and New York: Cambridge University Press, 2011.

'Soviets Killed My Wife: Exile'. *Montreal Gazette*, 26 July 1980, 95.

Süß, W. *Die Staatssicherheit im letzten Jahrzehnt der DDR: Geschichte der Staatssicherheit, Teil III*. Berlin: BStU, 2009. https://www.bstu.bund.de/DE/Wissen/Publikationen/Publikationen/handbuch_stasi-im-letzten-jahrzehnt_suess.pdf?__blob=publicationFile.

Süß, W. 'Wandlungen der MfS-Repressionstaktik seit Mitte der siebziger Jahre im Kontext der Beratungen der Ostblock-Geheimdienste zur Bekämpfung der "ideologischen Diversion"', in L. Ansorg, B. Gehrke, T. Klein and D. Kneipp (eds), *'Das Land ist still – noch!': Herrschaftswandel und politische Gegnerschaft in der DDR (1971–1989)* (Cologne, Weimar and Vienna: Böhlau Verlag, 2009), 111–34.

Süß, W. 'Die Wiener KSZE-Folgekonferenz und Handlungsspielraum des DDR-Sicherheitsapparates 1989', in M. Peter and H. Wentker (eds), *Die KSZE*

im Ost-West-Konflikt: Internationale Politik und gesellschaftliche Transformation 1975–1990 (Munich: Oldenbourg Verlag, 2012), 219–32.
Tautz, L. (ed.). *Friede und Gerechtigkeit Heute: das 'Querfurter Papier' – ein politisches Manifest für die Einhaltung der Menschenrechte in der DDR*, Sachbeiträge (22). Magdeburg: Landesbeauftragte für die Unterlagen des Staatssicherheitsdienstes der ehemaligen DDR in Sachsen-Anhalt, 2002.
Thomas, D.C. *The Helsinki Effect: International Norms, Human Rights, and the Demise of Communism*. Princeton, NJ: Princeton University Press, 2001.
Tismaneanu, V. *Stalinism for All Seasons: A Political History of Romanian Communism*. Berkeley: University of California Press, 2003.
Vilímek, T. *Solidarita napříč hranicemi: Opozice v ČSSR a NDR po roce 1968*. Vyšehrad: Ústav pro soudobé dějiny AV ČR, v. v. i., 2010.
von Saal, Y. *KSZE-Prozess und Perestroika in der Sowjetunion: Demokratisierung, Werteumbruch und Auflösung*. Munich: Oldenbourg Verlag, 2014.
Wiegrefe, K. *Das Zerwürfnis: Helmut Schmidt, Jimmy Carter und die Krise der deutsche-amerikanischen Beziehungen*. Berlin: Propyläen-Verlag, 2005.
Zubok, V.M. *A Failed Empire: The Soviet Union in the Cold War from Stalin to Gorbachev*. Chapel Hill: University of North Carolina Press, 2007.

 9

HELSINKI AT HOME
NGOs, the Helsinki Final Act and Politics in the United States, 1975–1985

Carl J. Bon Tempo

Introduction

In 2001, Daniel Thomas, one of the first scholars of the CSCE, posited a 'Helsinki Effect' in Cold War geopolitics.[1] In the intervening years, other scholars have followed in Thomas's footsteps, producing an explosion of scholarship on the CSCE that has deepened our understanding of the CSCE and documented the multiple effects it had in a variety of arenas. Scholars of international affairs demonstrate persuasively that the Helsinki Final Act helped bring about the Cold War's end and hastened the collapse of the Soviet Union's Eastern European empire.[2] Historians of human rights assert that the Final Act played a key role in the 'breakthrough' of human rights in global affairs in the 1970s.[3] Finally, scholars of American politics argue that the Helsinki Final Act quickly reframed the domestic politics of national security, especially among Republicans, conservatives and neo-conservatives.[4] The pace of the growth of our knowledge has been breathtaking.

However, as this volume demonstrates, questions remain. In that spirit, this chapter asks whether a 'Helsinki Effect' occurred in American domestic politics, beyond the established narrative of the CSCE final document upending the status quo among conservatives on the political centre and right. Or, more pointedly, did the Helsinki Final Act shape the agendas, strategies and politics of organizations and interest groups working in the United States – and if so, how, why and on which issues? The chapter utilizes two case studies to explore these questions: the National Association for the Advancement of Colored People (NAACP), a key African American civil rights organization in this period, and a variety of immigration advocates and organizations who sought to liberalize American immigration law. These groups, for the most part, existed outside of the Helsinki 'process'. They did not write the Final Act or enact it, and they played small roles in enforcing it. Instead, these groups came to the Helsinki Final Act with little investment in its failure or success, which makes their utilization of it all the more revealing.

Both sets of political actors used the Helsinki Final Act – and the human rights ideas inherent in it – in their appeals. For the NAACP and immigration advocates, the United States' participation in the CSCE presented an opportunity to push for policy changes they strongly desired. In this sense, the Final Act was a form of leverage. These political actors tried to use the Helsinki Final Act to draw a logical, and ineluctable, path to domestic political and policy reform: if the United States signed the CSCE, and held to the principles embodied in it, then political and policy change at home had to follow. At the same time, some of these actors, especially those involved in immigration issues, rather stretched the meaning of the Helsinki Final Act far from its original purposes to fit their agendas. This dynamic was not, of course, new. Human rights advocates, as Carol Anderson showed in her landmark study of the NAACP's efforts in the United Nations during the early post-World War II years, shaped notions of human rights to their ends as they fought American racial segregation.[5] In the 1970s, then, the NAACP and immigration advocates followed a worn path when they redefined the Helsinki Final Act as they employed it to achieve particular policy goals.

Indeed, the ability of advocates to give the Helsinki Final Act new meaning indicates its flexibility as a political concept, but also its inherent weakness and failure to resonate beyond the Cold War and the politics of national security. Unsurprisingly, these groups employed the Final Act in select and targeted ways, its principles often emerging as secondary to other concerns or framings. The Helsinki Final Act, then, holds a complicated place in American domestic politics. It had an influence on political life in the United States, to be sure. But that impact had its limits and it paled in comparison to the policy and political ramifications the CSCE unleashed in Eastern Europe and the Soviet Union.

The NAACP and the Helsinki Final Act

By the Helsinki Final Act of 1975, the NAACP's power and prestige had waned. Beset by leadership problems, a shrinking membership and disputes over its direction, the Association had fallen from its singular perch at the forefront of the fight for African American civil rights in the United States, where it had proven an especially powerful force in the political and legal arenas. Moreover, by the 1970s, the NAACP's leadership understood that the American political environment was rapidly becoming less hospitable to claims of equal rights, economic equality and a federal government deeply committed to improving race relations. In the late 1970s, the NAACP saw the conservative turn in American politics, which would define the last decades of the twentieth century, on the near horizon.[6]

This diminished stature did not leave the NAACP powerless. It still maintained decent resources, a sizeable membership and access to politicians, especially Democrats. Moreover, it still had its name, history and reputation, which garnered it media attention and a prominent voice in public affairs. As a result, the NAACP remained through the 1980s one of the key African American voices – but not *the* key African American voice – in American life. Its agenda stretched from a litany of domestic legal, political and economic issues to American foreign policy and global affairs.

During the 1970s, the NAACP wrestled with that era's human rights revolution.[7] The group never became full converts to a human rights agenda, or saw themselves as a human rights group rather than a civil rights group. Rather, the NAACP selectively engaged with human rights principles and integrated them into some of its policy agenda. At times, the group seemed more enamoured with human rights as a political tool, using human rights to prove a political point or to build common cause with other liberal groups. Finally, it must be said that the NAACP's engagement with human rights peaked in the late 1970s and early 1980s. The NAACP's foreign policy agenda addressed many of the same issues as it had in the early 1980s – the end of apartheid in South Africa and a call for the empowerment of Third World nations – but those issues had been framed in terms of human rights early in the decade, a frame that disappeared as the decade wore on.[8]

If the NAACP was going to engage with the Helsinki Final Act and the human rights principles inherent in it, one might reasonably have expected that to occur in foreign policy. Yet this did not happen. The NAACP had little interest in traditional Cold War foreign policy questions or with East–West relations. Instead, the Association viewed the Cold War as only one of many issues facing people of colour around the world. The NAACP did highlight the importance of human rights in US foreign policy in the late 1970s and early 1980s. In its January 1981 brief to the incoming Reagan administration, the group called the Universal Declaration of Human Rights 'integral' to American foreign policy. The group went further, describing what it thought should be at the centre of America's 'global human rights goals': 'support for the rights of indigenous people to self-governance wherever external governments control or administer their lands and to full political status and participation where nations are controlled by settlers'.[9] A few years later, human rights emerged as one of the NAACP's key talking points on South Africa, especially after the Reagan administration's chief Africa diplomat, Chester Crocker, implemented his 'constructive engagement' policy. Constructive engagement held that the United States should not isolate or shun South Africa's apartheid government, but instead should maintain cordial relations with it in order to bring about changes in South Africa's racial system. Unsurprisingly, anti-apartheid activists like the NAACP saw the policy both as morally reprehensible and as much more likely to ensure apartheid's survival than its demise. Broadus Butler, the NAACP's foreign policy expert, used human rights ideas to attack constructive engagement, arguing that it made the US a party to the white South African government's human rights violations.[10]

The NAACP's framing of human rights in these instances cut against some of the ways that the Helsinki Final Act framed human rights concerns. The NAACP explicitly tied human rights to a broad notion of anti-colonialism and self-determination, each of which was grounded in the status of individual nation-states, ethno-national groups or racial minorities. On the other hand, the Helsinki Final Act seemed more concerned with the place of human rights vis-à-vis individuals. When the NAACP did invoke the importance of protecting individual rights in the international arena, it did so by referencing the Universal Declaration of Human Rights, not the CSCE.[11] And even when the NAACP made a case for the rights of refugees to migrate – a situation most closely analogous to some of the CSCE's provisions about freedom of movement and the right to migrate – the Association referenced the human rights of refugees but without invoking the Helsinki Final Act.[12]

Surprisingly, the Helsinki Final Act found its way more noticeably into the NAACP's domestic vision. First, it is clear that one strategy of the Association in the second half of the 1970s was to leverage American interest in human rights abroad into concern for human rights at home.

The NAACP laid down an explicit challenge to those who advocated for human rights' centrality to US foreign policy – especially the Carter administration – to also show equal concern for human rights issues at home. No one put this better than NAACP head Benjamin Hooks in 1980:

> While it makes good print to talk about human rights in South Africa, Iran, Yugoslavia, Afghanistan, or France, I am told that charity begins at home. We cannot tell the leaders of South Africa about the shooting down of innocent blacks by vicious police officers until we end the slaughter of blacks by white policemen in South Carolina. We cannot admonish Ayatollah Khomeini's government to safeguard human rights until we get the officials in Indiana to protect the rights of blacks in that state. We cannot talk about the importance of maintaining stability in Yugoslavia until we establish stability in our urban centers of York, Pennsylvania and Yuma, Arizona. We cannot lift up our voices with conviction in human rights in Afghanistan until we correct the problems we face in Alabama.[13]

Hooks' point, delivered with devastating comparative clarity, stung only because the United States had recently committed itself to fostering and protecting human rights around the globe. The Helsinki Final Act was a very public statement of that commitment and thus it opened up the possibility for Hooks and others in the NAACP to make these claims in the late 1970s and early 1980s. The Final Act, of course, was just one of many pledges made by American leaders to honour human rights and the NAACP often tried to leverage those promises into greater emphasis on human rights at home. In fact, on multiple occasions, Hooks or another NAACP official demanded that Carter forthrightly make human rights real in the United States.[14] In this case, then, the Final Act was just one arrow in the NAACP's quiver as it pressed for domestic change.

Second, the Helsinki Final Act, especially Principle VII, committed all of its signatories to protect and promote human rights at home. This obligation gave Hooks' statement added punch, but it also led to efforts to monitor human rights in each signatory. The monitoring system – especially the organizations that worked to monitor human rights in the USSR and its Eastern European empire – is well known. Less well known are the efforts of the US Helsinki Watch Committee (and others) to report on human rights in the United States.[15] That group produced a number of papers on human rights conditions in the United States in the 1970s and early 1980s, before largely abandoning the effort.

Two examples indicate that the NAACP engaged at least somewhat enthusiastically in this monitoring process. In 1979, the NAACP's policy director Michael Meyers indicated that he was scrambling to contribute to Helsinki Watch's forthcoming report on human rights in the United States, which he described as a 'priority'.[16] Much more striking, the NAACP – specifically Assistant Counsel to the NAACP's Legal Defense and Educational Fund, Bill Lee – wrote the 1980 Helsinki Watch report on racial discrimination in the United States.[17] Lee ended this report by arguing that if the recommendations of the US Commission on Civil Rights were observed – which the Association and other civil rights groups generally supported – then the US would be in compliance with the CSCE. Here, Lee argued that in order for the US to live up to its commitments made at Helsinki, it had to take concrete steps to address the black condition and attack racial inequality. In short, it was a leverage play to muster support for civil rights claims at home and give the issue of minority rights more lustre and attention.

Of course, the NAACP was not the only politically disempowered group employing this strategy. Across Eastern Europe and the Soviet Union, dissident groups like Charter 77, the Polish Workers' Defense Committee and the Moscow Helsinki Group demanded that communist governments change their policies to live up to the CSCE.[18] But for those dissident groups behind the Iron Curtain, appeals to the Final Act drove their strategy and tactics. The NAACP, which had elections, lobbying and a free and functioning press, among many venues, to press for their policy changes, never relied on the Final Act so deeply. Thus, the Helsinki Final Act emerged as just another weapon in the NAACP's arsenal, and one that was not of the first order.

Immigration Advocates and the Helsinki Final Act

By the late 1970s and early 1980s, the foundations of post-1965 immigration affairs in the United States finally became apparent. Liberals had destroyed the hated national origins quota immigration system in 1965,[19] but reform did not wipe the slate clean. Rather, the end of national origins, accomplished via amendments to existing law, effectively left in place some restrictionist codicils that impeded the flow of migrants to the US. Two additional challenges further stressed the immigration system. First, a series of refugee crises in the late 1970s and 1980s saw hundreds of thousands of refugees arriving, ultimately leading to the regularization of refugee entry in 1980 via the Refugee Act. Second, tens of thousands of migrants, mostly from Mexico and Central America, began to arrive each year in the United States, but outside of legal mechanisms used to admit newcomers. This was the beginning of what contemporary Americans understand as the 'illegal immigration problem', though it had its roots earlier in the twentieth century.[20] Taken together, a clear picture emerges: a powerful surge of (sometimes) desperate newcomers arriving (or hoping to arrive) in the United States but not always with a legal claim to entering or staying.[21] In this environment, immigration and refugee advocates fought fiercely to make sure that refugees and immigrants, regardless of their legal status, might come and stay in the country. They confronted in the political and legal arena equally determined opponents, who began in the early 1980s to search for legislative solutions to what they saw as overwhelming migration to the US.

The domestic policy issue of immigration, then, was fertile ground for the principles of the Helsinki Final Act to take root. The CSCE contained explicit provisions about the free movements of people between the East and the West. And, from 1975 to the end of the Cold War, the Final Act played a key role in easing the movement of individuals from behind the Iron Curtain to the West. As the famed Romanian gymnastics coach Gheza Pozsar (who tutored the star gymnast Nadia Comaneci) put it in 1981 as he tried to arrange for his family to join him in the United States, 'They have to release my family, they signed the Helsinki accords'.[22]

However, the CSCE's effects on immigration and refugee affairs expanded beyond Cold War migration from behind the Iron Curtain. Indeed, the Final Act became a weapon in the arsenal of immigration advocates looking to liberalize American immigration law generally, and to solve some of the aforementioned problems. As the Indochinese boat people refugee crisis crested, the labour union leader Albert Shanker in May 1979 argued that if the CSCE allowed the United States to demand the movement of dissidents from Russia, they should also commit the United States to an aggressive campaign to aid – and admit – refugees from Southeast Asia.[23] In 1980, as the Carter administration pondered a larger revision to immigration law, the White House addressed a long-standing (since 1952) ban on the rights of homosexual (and suspected homosexual) aliens to immigrate to the US. The Carter administration publicly supported repeal of this ban, arguing that it conflicted with the US pledge to uphold the Helsinki Final Act's sections on freedom of migration.[24] Finally, in 1983, the American Bar Association (ABA)'s Section on Individual Rights and Responsibilities weighed in on proposed immigration legislation (mainly the restrictionist Simpson-Mazzoli bill) that would have given the Executive Branch more discretion in immigration and refugee affairs, especially more powers to restrict entry. The ABA criticized these proposals, citing the 'fundamental aspects of human liberty' that they violated – and that if passed they would put the United States in violation of the Helsinki Final Act.²⁵

By far the most expansive use of the Helsinki Final Act by immigration advocates came in the lingering controversy over one aspect of the 1952 McCarran-Walter Immigration Act, a key piece of twentieth-century immigration law. That law had two subsections that outlined specific grounds for excluding immigrants on the basis of ideology. Subsection 27 banned the entry of those whom the Attorney General or consular officials believed endangered the public interest of the US and its citizens. Subsection 28 banned the entry of aliens who were – or had been – anarchists or communists. Subsection 27 was absolute; no appeal or waiver mechanisms existed. But Subsection 28 – the anticommunist and anarchist ban – had a waiver process, and it was used quite frequently in the 1960s and 1970s, but with much confusion, effort and generation of ill-will and suspicion.²⁶

The debate about reforming these provisions stretched over the course of a decade, and the Helsinki Final Act was at the centre of discussions. First, in 1977, Senator George McGovern (D-South Dakota) pushed through an amendment to immigration law that weakened Subsection 28 and made it easier for communists (and anarchists) to receive visas to visit the United States. Supporters of the so-called McGovern Amendment noted that the Helsinki Final Act required signatories to support the free movement of ideas and people, and thus the McGovern reform brought the US into compliance with the Final Act.²⁷ But the battle was only beginning over the government's ability to control who could visit the United States. The McGovern Amendment left in place Subsection 28's cumbersome and inefficient waiver process on the one hand, and did nothing to Subsection 27 on the other hand. The National Lawyers Guild in 1980 urged that Congress erase Subsection 28 from the statute books, on the grounds that 'not only does it violate America's long-standing commitment to intellectual freedom but also it violates the spirit of the Helsinki accords, which at this time of increased tension with the Soviet Union must be reemphasized as affirming the basic freedoms we cherish'.²⁸

The Reagan administration retreated from its enforcement of Subsection 28, but, as the liberal group Campaign for Political Rights noted in late 1983, began to rely on the more amorphous Subsection 27 to ban controversial visitors of all political persuasions (from Tomas Broge and Roberto d'Aubuisson, both of El Salvador's rightist party, to Nino Pasti, an Italian politician critical of US foreign policy and the North Atlantic Treaty Organization, to Hortensia de Allende, widow of Chile's murdered leftist political leader).²⁹ The Campaign for Political

Rights and the American Civil Liberties Union objected to the administration's reliance on, and even the existence of, Subsection 27 on the grounds that it violated the Helsinki Final Act's sections on easing the entry and exit processes visitors faced.[30] Others made the same point but without legalisms. The *New York Times* editorialized that the Helsinki Final Act's codicils on freedom of movement were 'Good words, those, for lubricating our gates'.[31]

A year later, the Helsinki Watch Executive Director Jeri Laber joined this chorus. Laber emerged in the late 1970s as a tireless advocate of human rights groups in the Soviet Union and Eastern Europe, offering vital support to dissidents living behind the Iron Curtain. In her memoirs, Laber makes clear that she and Helsinki Watch were not principally concerned with migration issues. Laber recalls telling State Department official Rozanne Ridgeway in the mid 1980s that 'Helsinki Watch isn't working for Jewish emigration. We support the right to emigrate, of course, but our main goal is to make the Soviet Union a better place for *everyone*, so that people will want to *stay*'.[32] Yet, during these same years – and not detailed in the memoirs – Laber turned her fire on the American government's immigration policies. She castigated the United States for its 'shameful and embarrassing' visa regulations that 'give the world the impression that the Government is so fearful and defensive that it will not give foreigners who are critical of its policies an opportunity to express their views'. Laber noted, of course, that American restrictions violated the Helsinki Final Act, but also made the US into a hypocrite for its criticism of other nations' violations of those very same principles.[33] This episode, while short-lived, showed Laber taking up a new issue – US immigration policies – and attacking them with a tool, the Helsinki Final Act, that she employed regularly in her work as a human rights advocate.

In these examples, the Helsinki Final Act obviously affected immigration affairs and policy in the United States. Of course, Helsinki was just one of many arguments offered by immigration advocates as they pressed their policy agendas. Sometimes – as in the case of refugee admissions – it played a minor role, but in other instances – like the McGovern Amendment and the fight over Subsections 27 and 28 – it emerged more forcefully. But in all of these episodes, immigration advocates clearly stretched the meaning of the Helsinki Final Act. The Final Act's commentary on migration stressed the right of an individual to leave a country. Vitally, however, the Final Act did not make a commensurate demand upon receiving countries to admit individuals. In the instances detailed here, immigration advocates were rarely, if ever, concerned about barriers of exit (whether migrants could leave their country of origin) but instead focused on lowering barriers of entry (whether migrants could enter the United States). And to make this case, they used the Helsinki Final Act's freedom of movement principles, stretching – or perhaps perverting – their original meaning and focus. If the historian Elizabeth Borgwardt in her work on the Atlantic Charter and the human rights moment of the 1940s reminds us that principles matter in international affairs because nations and governments can be asked to live up to them,[34] the story of the Final Act and immigration illuminates a subsidiary: activists can twist and utilize principles – in this case relating to freedom of migration and basic human rights – in ways that travel fairly far from their origins.

Conclusion

The Helsinki Final Act found its way into the thinking of some of the key activists and organizations working on the domestic political issues of civil rights and immigration. Perhaps unsurprisingly, the Final Act made its strongest appearance in immigration policy. But here, the CSCE's influence extended beyond Cold War immigration concerns and into the general issues of movement of peoples, American immigration law and the right to enter a country, not just the right to leave one. The Final Act may have been borne of the Cold War (and migration), but it moved beyond this genesis. When it came to race, the Helsinki Final Act emerged most powerfully in the eyes of advocates like the NAACP as a reminder of the relationship of human rights to American ideals, and thus as a tool to try to force more policy and political changes that made those ideals a reality on racial issues.

But, and it is vital to be clear on this point, the Helsinki Final Act and its principles never emerged for immigration advocates or the NAACP as the centrepiece of their efforts. In most ways, Helsinki's principles were an additional argument, another tool, a secondary concern – with the exception of the history of the McGovern Amendment – in the arsenal of these groups and organizations. Moreover, the Helsinki Final Act, as the immigration advocates learned, was most useful when stretched beyond its original meanings, which points again to the Final Act's relative weakness in American politics and political culture: it had to be changed for it to be truly useful.

Why did the power of the Helsinki Final Act find itself limited in this way? Of course, expanding the case studies beyond these two groups might very well lead to a different set of conclusions. But the CSCE never gained traction in American domestic politics in any powerful way for a few reasons.

First, and most important, the rise of human rights in the 1970s United States – and its place in the political culture of the 1980s – was accompanied (and perhaps aided) by a powerful 'othering' of human rights. Put another way, human rights came to be seen by many Americans as something that happened elsewhere: Vietnam, South Africa, Greece and the Soviet Union, to name a few examples. Barbara Keys makes this powerful point in *Reclaiming American Virtue*, and while Keys overstates the degree to which human rights disappeared from domestic politics and culture, this 'othering' did occur.[35] As a result, domestic political actors had to question the utility of applying human rights ideas – like those embodied in the Final Act – in their appeals. Not even the efforts of Helsinki Watch groups writing on human rights issues in the United States – which they did with frequency in the 1970s and early 1980s – could overcome this challenge.

Second, the thin corpus of human rights law in the United States likely hindered the Final Act's influence in domestic politics. Human rights principles simply were not deeply embedded in American legal culture in the way that civil rights or political rights were. The most notable enunciations of rights in American political and legal discourse – such as the 1964 Civil Rights Act, the 1965 Voting Rights Act, the Bill of Rights, the 1935 Wagner Act and a variety of constitutional amendments and laws in the Civil War's wake – trafficked in civil and political rights. By the 1970s, the United States was party to some of the major post-1945 human rights treaties,[36] but rather than arousing a focus on human rights at home, Americans saw these agreements as committing the nation to protecting human rights abroad, intensifying the 'othering' dynamic. On the domestic front, human rights found its way into the legal arena most prominently through a variety of state and municipal Human Rights Commissions. These bodies, charged largely with adjudicating racial and gender discrimination, as well as labour law complaints, reinforced the centrality of political and civil rights at the expense of a human rights agenda.

As a result, the human rights ideas at the centre of the Helsinki Final Act, and so celebrated by activists in the East and West in the 1970s and 1980s, found less purchase in American domestic political and legal culture and history than they perhaps needed in order to be effective. And there was one final complicating factor: the Helsinki Final Act was not a treaty but a non-binding agreement between its signatories, its provisions existing under a gentlemen's agreement rather than obligatory under force of international law. Moreover, most treaties, after signing and approval by two-thirds of the Senate, are part of American law. The Final Act, in other words, did not bind any of the signatories in international law, and it was not part of the corpus of law in the United States. It is fair to wonder whether, if the Final Act had been a binding treaty, giving it more power and weight, American political actors would have utilized it differently. Of course, many of the actors in this chapter cited the Final Act as if it were a treaty and as if its principles were ones the United States was legally bound to under international law.

Finally, it is also clear that at this moment – the late 1970s and early 1980s – many in American politics, and especially the groups covered in this chapter, were still unsure of the power of the human rights revolution and human rights moment. The NAACP, for instance, understood that human rights had new power in the late 1970s, but they debated how to engage with human rights ideas. They asked whether they wanted to be a human rights group or a civil rights group. At most turns – and this solidified in the 1980s – they chose the latter. Additionally, the political right and the Republican Party at this moment offered their own definition of human rights – and even of the Helsinki Final Act – that found a good number of adherents in American political life.[37] The conservative definition of human rights, stressing anticommunism, often diverged fairly significantly from the definition emerging on the liberal left, among groups like the NAACP and immigration advocates. As a result, human rights, and the Helsinki Final Act, were novel and contested ideas and terms in American politics, a dynamic that likely made embracing the Final Act and its principles a less urgent, and perhaps too fraught, matter.

Carl J. Bon Tempo is Associate Professor of History at the University at Albany, State University of New York. He is the author of *Americans at the Gate: The United States and Refugees during the Cold War* (Princeton University Press, 2008) and is currently co-authoring, with Hasia Diner, *Immigration: An American History* for Yale University Press. He is also writing a monograph, *Human Rights at Home: The United States and Human Rights in the 1980s* for the University of Pennsylvania Press.

Notes

The author would like to thank Kristin Celello and Paul Kramer, as well as the editors of this volume, for their comments on this chapter.

1. D. Thomas, *The Helsinki Effect: International Norms, Human Rights, and the Demise of Communism* (Princeton, NJ: Princeton University Press, 2001).
2. S. Snyder, *Human Rights Activism and the End of the Cold War: A Transnational History of the Helsinki Network* (Cambridge, UK: Cambridge University Press, 2013); G. Domber, *Empowering Revolution: America, Poland, and the End of the Cold War* (Chapel Hill: University of North Carolina Press, 2014). Soon to join this group is an important book by Robert Brier, *A Contested Icon: Poland's Solidarity and the Global Politics of Human Rights* (forthcoming).
3. B. Keys, *Reclaiming American Virtue: The Human Rights Revolution of the 1970s* (Cambridge, MA: Harvard University Press, 2014); S. Moyn, *The Last Utopia: Human Rights in History* (Cambridge, MA: Belknap Press, 2010); S. Moyn and J. Eckel (eds), *The Breakthrough: Human Rights in the 1970s* (Philadelphia: University of Pennsylvania Press, 2014).
4. J. Vaisse, *Neoconservatism: The Biography of a Movement* (Cambridge, MA: Belknap Press, 2011); J. Zelizer, 'Conservatives, Carter, and the Politics of National Security', in B. Schulman and J. Zelizer (eds), *Rightward Bound: Making America Conservative in the 1970s* (Cambridge, MA: Harvard University Press, 2008), 265–88; J. Suri, 'Détente and its Discontents', in Schulman and Zelizer, *Rightward Bound*, 227–45; C. Bon Tempo, 'From the Center-Right: Freedom House and Human Rights in the 1970s and 1980s', in A. Iriye, P. Goedde and W. Hitchcock (eds), *The Human Rights Revolution: An International History* (New York: Oxford University Press, 2012), 223–44.
5. C. Anderson, *Eyes Off the Prize: The United Nations and the African American Struggle for Human Rights, 1944–1955* (New York: Cambridge University Press, 2003).
6. No scholar has written a post-1970 history of the NAACP, although Timothy Minchin has done excellent work on the NAACP's legal strategies in the 1970s American south. On the troubles of the NAACP, see S. Rule, 'Leadership Conflict Just One Problem Facing NAACP at Meeting Today', *The New York Times*, 11 July 1983, 7; R. Norrell, *The House I Live In: Race in the American Century* (New York: Oxford University Press, 2005), 301; G. de Jong, *Invisible Enemy: The African American Struggle after 1965* (New York: Wiley-Blackwell, 2010), 76, 78, 85, 141–42, 166. On the NAACP and conservatism, see Benjamin Hooks, 4 July 1984, Papers of the NAACP, VIII, Box 33, File 17, Library of Congress, Washington, DC. See also Michael Meyers, The Office of Research, Policy, and Plans, '1982 Annual Report', Papers of the NAACP, VIII, Box 54, Folder 1, Library of Congress, Washington, DC; 'Long Range Planning CA 1979', Papers of the NAACP, VIII, Box 335, Folder 10, Library of Congress, Washington, DC.
7. The 1970s was not the first time the NAACP engaged with human rights. The most significant episode occurred in the late 1940s, when the organization took its fight against segregation to the United Nations with a strategy of using the recently birthed corpus of international human rights laws to build international pressure for domestic change in the US. Here, the NAACP made clear that it saw human rights as the partner of civil rights at home. As Carol Anderson documents in her study of this vital episode, the strategy failed in large part because the US government, especially the

Eisenhower administration, worked very hard to delegitimize the NAACP and to shift the meaning of human rights. See Anderson, *Eyes Off the Prize*.
8. This abbreviated history of the NAACP and human rights is drawn from the research for my forthcoming book, *Human Rights at Home: The United States and Human Rights in the 1980s*. For the NAACP and human rights in the late 1980s, see 'NAACP Long Range Plan, the Year 2000 and Beyond', July 1987, Papers of the NAACP, VIII, Box 335, Folder 7, Library of Congress, Washington, DC.
9. 'NAACP Speaks to the Reagan Administration', January 1981, Papers of the NAACP, VIII, Box 310, Folder 5, Library of Congress, Washington, DC.
10. Broadus Butler, Testimony at the Hearing 'US Corporate Activities in South Africa', 22 October 1981, Committee on Foreign Affairs, House of Representatives (Washington, DC: U.S. Government Printing Office, 1982.)
11. See, for instance, S. Pearl Schilling, 'Two Anniversaries, NAACP Dinner', 11 December 1977, Papers of the NAACP, VIII, Box 49, File 7, Library of Congress, Washington, DC.
12. 'Resolutions Adopted by the 71st Annual Convention of the NAACP at Miami Beach, Florida, June 30–July 4, 1980', Papers of the NAACP, VIII, Box 30, File 2, Library of Congress, Washington, DC.
13. Benjamin Hooks, 'Speech to the Opening Plenary Session on Monday, June 30, 1980, 71st Annual Convention', Papers of the NAACP, VIII, Box 30, File 5, Library of Congress, Washington, DC.
14. For example, Margaret Bush Wilson, Chairman of the NAACP National Board of Directors, cited President Carter's famous 1977 University of Notre Dame speech that outlined the president's human rights vision as she pushed for domestic reform. See 'Keynote Address by Margaret Bush Wilson', 27 June 1977, Papers of the NAACP, VIII, Box 20, File 6, Library of Congress, Washington, DC. See also Michael Meyers, 'Remarks at Rally for Wilmington Ten', 11 May 1978, Papers of the NAACP, VIII, Box 441, File 7, Library of Congress, Washington, DC; Benjamin Hooks, 'Speech of Dr. Benjamin L. Hooks, NAACP Executive Director, Plenary Session, 69th Annual Convention, Portland, Oregon', 4 July 1978, Papers of the NAACP, VIII, Box 24, File 11, Library of Congress, Washington, DC.
15. A great starting point for this activity in the US context is P. Slezkine, 'From Helsinki to Human Rights Watch', *Humanity* 5(3) (2014), 345–70, http://humanityjournal.org/issue-5-3/from-helsinki-to-human-rights-watch-how-an-american-cold-war-monitoring-group-became-an-international-human-rights-institution/.
16. Michael Meyers to Benjamin Hooks, 'Weekly Activity Report', 29 March 1979, Papers of the NAACP, VIII, Box 442, File 2, Library of Congress, Washington, DC.
17. US Helsinki Watch Committee, 'A Helsinki Record: Racial Discrimination in the United States' (New York, NY: US Helsinki Watch Committee, 1980).
18. See, for instance, Snyder, *Human Rights Activism and the End of the Cold War*.
19. Designed in the 1920s, the national origins quota immigration system capped total migration to the US from the eastern hemisphere at around 150,000 persons annually and it established national quotas that granted

the largest admissions to immigrants from northwestern Europe. Both of these measures reversed migration trends of the previous decades, as the new immigration system's supporters desired. Opponents of the national origins quota system decried it as racially discriminatory and unworthy of American ideals. With reform in 1965, immigration supporters accomplished two of their main goals: they eliminated the national origins quotas and they won a new immigrant admissions system that gave preference to newcomers with family in the US and with employable skills.

20. On the longer history of 'illegal immigration', see M. Ngai, *Impossible Subjects: Illegal Aliens and the Making of Modern America* (Princeton, NJ: Princeton University Press, 2004).
21. On refugee affairs, see C. Bon Tempo, *Americans at the Gate: The United States and Refugees during the Cold War* (Princeton, NJ: Princeton University Press, 2008). On immigration affairs, see A. Zolberg, *A Nation by Design: Immigration Policy in the Fashioning of America* (Cambridge, MA: Harvard University Press, 2008).
22. Penny Spar, 'Nadia Comaneci's Coach, in US, Seeks Another Star', *Los Angeles Times*, 13 December 1981.
23. Albert Shanker, 'US Funds Running Out for Refugee Aid', *The New York Times*, 13 May 1979.
24. 'Resolving Policy on Homosexual Aliens', *The New York Times*, 29 June 1980.
25. 'Justice Detained: The Immigration Crisis', American Bar Association, Human Rights, Section of Individual Rights and Responsibility, Summer 1983, Volume 11, No. 2, 40.
26. F. Fink, 'Abourezk v. Reagan: Curbing Recent Abuses of the Executive Immigration Power', *Cornell International Law Journal* 21(1), Article 4, retrieved 21 April 2017 from http://scholarship.law.cornell.edu/cilj/vol21/iss1/4.
27. Ibid., 151–52; Graham Hovey, 'French Labor Leader Is Granted US Visa', *The New York Times*, 27 August 1977, 2. For the Carter administration's thinking on the McGovern Amendment vis-à-vis larger human rights policies, see 'Briefing Memorandum from the Assistant Secretary of State for Congressional Relations (Benett) to the Deputy Secretary of State (Christopher)', 18 June 1977, *Foreign Relations of the United States, 1977–1980, Volume II, Human Rights and Humanitarian Affairs*, retrieved 20 April 2017 from https://history.state.gov/historicaldocuments/frus1977-80v02/d62.
28. 'Immigration Newsletter', National Lawyers Guild Foundation, 9(3), (May–June 1980), 19.
29. 'Why Is Everyone Talking about the Immigration Act?', Campaign for Political Rights, *Organizing Notes* 7(6) (Winter 1983–84), 4.
30. Ibid. See also the efforts of the New York Civil Liberties Union to protest the Reagan policies in David Margolick, 'Reprise on McCarran Act', *The New York Times*, 4 June 1982, B1.
31. 'Nervous Nellies at the Gates', *The New York Times*, 14 March 1983.
32. J. Laber, *The Courage of Strangers: Coming of Age with the Human Rights Movement* (New York: Public Affairs, 2002), 253.

33. Jeri Laber, 'Why Some Writers Aren't Welcome Here', *The New York Times*, 29 April 1984, BR28.
34. E. Borgwardt, *A New Deal for the World: America's Vision for Human Rights* (Cambridge, MA: Belknap Press, 2007), 8–9.
35. Keys, *Reclaiming American Virtue*, 7.
36. For instance, in 1968 the United States acceded to the United Nations' 1967 Protocol to the 1951 Convention Related to the Status of Refugees. In 1977, President Carter signed – but did not win Senate ratification of – the International Covenant on Political and Civil Rights and the International Covenant on Economic, Social, and Cultural Rights. In 1980, Carter signed the Convention on the Elimination of All Forms of Discrimination Against Women, but that agreement did not receive Senate ratification either. For a fantastic overview of international human rights agreements and treaties and the United States' relationship to them, see 'Ratification of International Human Rights Treaties – United States' by the University of Minnesota's Human Rights Library, retrieved 20 April 2017 from http://hrlibrary.umn.edu/research/ratification-USA.html.
37. On the political right's definition of human rights in the late 1970s, see C. Bon Tempo, 'Human Rights and the US Republican Party in the Late 1970s', in Moyn and Eckel, *The Breakthrough* (Philadelphia: University of Pennsylvania Press, 2014), 146–165.

Bibliography

Archival and Primary Sources

Committee on Foreign Affairs, United States House of Representatives
The New York Times
Records of the NAACP, Library of Congress, Washington, DC.

Secondary Sources

Anderson, C. *Eyes Off the Prize: The United Nations and the African American Struggle for Human Rights, 1944–1955*. New York: Cambridge University Press, 2003.
Bon Tempo, C.J. *Americans at the Gate: The United States and Refugees during the Cold War*. Princeton, NJ: Princeton University Press, 2008.
Bon Tempo, C.J. 'From the Center-Right: Freedom House and Human Rights in the 1970s and 1980s', in A. Iriye, P. Goedde and W. Hitchcock (eds), *The Human Rights Revolution: An International History* (New York: Oxford University Press, 2012), 223–44.
Borgwardt, E. *A New Deal for the World: America's Vision for Human Rights*. Cambridge, MA: Belknap Press, 2007.
De Jong, G. *Invisible Enemy: The African American Struggle after 1965*. New York: Wiley-Blackwell, 2010.

Domber, G. *Empowering Revolution: America, Poland, and the End of the Cold War*. Chapel Hill: University of North Carolina Press, 2014.
Keys, B. *Reclaiming American Virtue: The Human Rights Revolution of the 1970s*. Cambridge, MA: Harvard University Press, 2014.
Laber, J. *The Courage of Strangers: Coming of Age with the Human Rights Movement*. New York: Public Affairs, 2002.
Moyn, S. *The Last Utopia: Human Rights in History*. Cambridge, MA: Belknap Press, 2010.
Moyn, S., and J. Eckel (eds). *The Breakthrough: Human Rights in the 1970s*. Philadelphia: University of Pennsylvania Press, 2014.
Ngai, M. *Impossible Subjects: Illegal Aliens and the Making of Modern America*. Princeton, NJ: Princeton University Press, 2004.
Norrell, R. *The House I Live In: Race in the American Century*. New York: Oxford University Press, 2005.
Slezkine, P. 'From Helsinki to Human Rights Watch'. *Humanity* 5(3) (2014), 345–70. http://humanityjournal.org/issue-5-3/from-helsinki-to-human-rights-watch-how-an-american-cold-war-monitoring-group-became-an-international-human-rights-institution/.
Snyder, S. *Human Rights Activism and the End of the Cold War: A Transnational History of the Helsinki Network*. Cambridge, UK: Cambridge University Press, 2013.
Suri, J. 'Détente and Its Discontents', in B. Schulman and J. Zelizer (eds), *Rightward Bound: Making America Conservative in the 1970s* (Cambridge, MA: Harvard University Press, 2008), 227–45.
Thomas, D. *The Helsinki Effect: International Norms, Human Rights, and the Demise of Communism*. Princeton, NJ: Princeton University Press, 2001.
Vaisse, J. *Neoconservatism: The Biography of a Movement*. Cambridge, MA: Belknap Press, 2011.
Zelizer, J. 'Conservatives, Carter, and the Politics of National Security', in B. Schulman and J. Zelizer (eds), *Rightward Bound: Making America Conservative in the 1970s* (Cambridge, MA: Harvard University Press, 2008), 265–88.
Zolberg, A. *A Nation by Design: Immigration Policy in the Fashioning of America*. Cambridge, MA: Harvard University Press, 2008.

PART III

THE POLITICS OF THE CSCE IN EUROPE

 10

EUROPEAN DÉTENTE AND THE CSCE
Austria and the East-Central European Theatre in the 1970s and 1980s

Maximilian Graf

Introduction

Détente in Europe was a precondition for the realization of a Conference on Security and Cooperation in Europe (CSCE), but some aspects of the Helsinki Final Act had already been implemented in bilateral East–West-relations and therefore constituted elements of a genuine European détente. European détente was fostered by the Helsinki process. It even came through the final peak of the Cold War at the turn of the 1970s to the 1980s and the rather burdened CSCE process of those years unscathed. This chapter addresses the interactions of European détente and the CSCE by examining Austria's relations with Hungary, Czechoslovakia, East Germany and Poland from the 1970s to the end of the Cold War. Focusing on the implementation of the provisions of Basket Three of the Helsinki Final Act, it addresses the limits and possibilities of both the CSCE and European détente in overcoming the 'Iron Curtain'. The end of the Cold War and the revolutions of 1989 cannot be explained without the 'Gorbachev factor',[1] the international context of superpower détente re-emerging in the second half of the 1980s and the more general socio-economic changes from the 1970s onwards leading to the economic decline of the socialist states and increasing unrest among their populations.[2] Yet, without European détente and the repercussions of the CSCE process on socialist countries of Eastern Europe, it is highly unlikely that history would have gone the way it finally did in 1989. Against the background of the developments in the second half of the 1980s, the long-term effects of détente unfolded and significantly contributed to the speed-up of events prior to and during 1989. Hence, it was no coincidence that the close of the Third Follow-up Meeting to the CSCE in Vienna (1986–89) and the fall of the Iron Curtain both took place in 1989.[3]

The last decade brought a number of studies on the CSCE process within the international context, the CSCE policies of almost all European countries as well as the repercussions on socialist regimes (dissidents, Helsinki groups, societal changes).[4] However, there is a lack of contextualized studies bringing together the narratives of implementation, non-implementation or even overachievement of the humanitarian (but also other cooperative) provisions of the CSCE in the domestic Eastern, bilateral East–West and international context. By bringing together the rather 'national' narratives on Austria, Czechoslovakia, the German Democratic Republic (GDR), Poland and Hungary and analysing them within the international context, this chapter provides an analysis of interactions between the CSCE and European détente in the East-Central European theatre on the road from Helsinki 1975 to the revolutions of 1989. Moreover, it will also show the limits of the CSCE in times of eroding détente.

Austria and the CSCE: Origins, Actors and Contribution

Until recently, studies on Austrian CSCE politics had to rely on older works by political scientists and the memoirs of Austrian diplomats and politicians. Recent research has revealed that the resulting interpretations have to be revisited by multi-archival research. Thomas Fischer was one of the pioneers of the recent boom of CSCE research. His works on the role of the Neutral and Non-Aligned states (NNA) were the first to address the role of this crucial factor of the CSCE process.[5] Fischer was also the first to provide an overview on Austria's CSCE politics and diplomacy.[6] Concerning the humanitarian dimension of the Helsinki process, Benjamin Gilde provided us with a distinct analysis of Austria's policy in this regard until 1983. His study is based on in-depth archival research and changed our interpretation of the differing roles played by politicians and diplomats and deconstructed the hitherto mythologized picture. Nevertheless, his general conclusion on the role of the Austrian CSCE delegation remained unambiguous: 'It was always a party, a Western actor in neutral clothes'.[7]

In large parts, this also holds true for Austria's Ostpolitik after 1955. Relations of neutral Austria with socialist Eastern Europe developed constantly after the conclusion of the Austrian State Treaty and the adoption of the neutrality law in 1955 that among other things has to be regarded as the 'price' for the country's regaining of its sovereignty.[8] The reasons for that were twofold. First, the Soviet Union aimed at shaping Austrian neutrality within its foreign policy concept of 'peaceful coexistence' and encouraged Vienna to develop relations with the socialist countries. Second, Austria aimed at enhancing détente and profiting from improved relations with the 'people's democracies', not least in the economic field. Austrian–Soviet relations led the way, not least because Moscow aimed at shaping Austrian neutrality alongside its own needs. Austria became a diplomatic 'ice breaker' first for the Soviet Union after 1956 and later for the entire socialist camp. Nevertheless, after 1956, Western doubts about Austrian neutrality being oriented towards the East had decreased to a minimum.[9]

Austria actively contributed to the policy of détente in Europe by continuously improving its relations with the socialist camp. Even the crushing of the 'Prague Spring' in 1968 marked only a short setback. In contrast to its (relatively) sharp reaction to the 1956 crackdown on the Hungarian revolution, Austria abstained from an official condemnation. This marked a certain shift in the Austrian interpretation of its neutrality. Austrian historian Wolfgang Mueller identified a 'mental neutralization' of leading Austrian politicians.[10] The tendency of equalling 'coexistence' with détente grew, but this was not only an Austrian phenomenon. Despite Soviet violations of Austrian airspace and accusations against Austria for violating its neutrality, in the end there was 'no damage done to Austrian–Soviet relations'.[11] However, the same holds true for many other Western countries engaging in détente. Austria's neutrality remained only a military one. Hence, within the CSCE process and especially with regard to the economic, political, societal, humanitarian and ideological dimensions of East–West détente, the Alpine republic was a neutral, but in fact determined Western actor, like many other non-communist NNA states.[12]

Unsurprisingly, the Soviets tried to win over Austria to promote their goal of a Conference on Security in Europe. The Austrian government refused to fulfil Moscow's desire in the 1960s, and in the end it was Finland that officially launched the idea with its memorandum of 1969. Austria welcomed the initiative and finally constructively participated in the CSCE.[13] The Austrian CSCE memorandum of 24 July 1970 was primarily dominated by questions of security and paid almost no attention to the topic of freedom of movement, which the NATO countries had brought up when reacting to the Finnish initiative. New evidence shows that Austrian politicians were reserved about a number of issues in the CSCE negotiations, especially the inclusion of human rights questions.¹⁴ The main reason for this was the Austrian expectation that negotiations on that matter would lead to nothing. Leading politicians had learnt that in humanitarian hardship cases, *stille Diplomatie* ('silent diplomacy', an approach of negotiating and solving these problems on the sidelines of political encounters without any publicity) was usually more successful.

At the beginning of the CSCE process, hardly any humanitarian questions between Austria and Poland or Hungary existed. The situation in relation to Czechoslovakia and its post-1968 'normalization' regime was more difficult. Austria had recognized the GDR only in 1972 and the problems in the humanitarian sector were unsolved. When East German Foreign Minister Otto Winzer and his Austrian counterpart Rudolf Kirchschläger, a practising Catholic, met in spring 1973, the latter declared on the prospects of the CSCE: 'More difficult is the question of the third item on the agenda. On this point distrust is the strongest. ... Austria does not want humanitarian contacts as a Trojan horse'. Kirchschläger added that he did not have 'the intention to proselytize'.¹⁵ However, the Austrian foreign minister stressed that solutions for humanitarian questions on the bilateral level were very much needed. They even constituted a precondition for the improvement of bilateral relations that East Berlin was seeking. The Austrian stance was a result of its strictly bilateral approach of Ostpolitik.

Bruno Kreisky had an ambiguous attitude towards the CSCE.¹⁶ The Austrian Chancellor (1970–83) did not believe in changes within the socialist countries through conferences. Instead, Kreisky hoped for an inclusion of the conflict in the Middle East on the agenda of the CSCE. Throughout his political career, Kreisky pursued several peace initiatives with regard to the Middle East and contributed to making Yasser Arafat an international recognized negotiating partner, not least by Austrian recognition of the Palestine Liberation Organization in 1980. However, his abortive CSCE proposal was not taken seriously by Austrian diplomats and finally sanded up. It seems obvious that the intention to solve this (still today unsolved) conflict within the framework of the CSCE would probably have led to a premature failure of the negotiations on security and cooperation in Europe. Another aim of the Austrian Chancellor that was gaining importance by the mid 1970s was closer cooperation in the fields of economics and energy supplies between East and West within the framework of the CSCE. This was paramount to a similar shift in his bilateral Ostpolitik, which had primarily domestic political reasons: against the background of global economic changes since the beginning of the 1970s, Austria's nationalized industries were facing a severe crisis.¹⁷ Since his personal ambitions all came to naught, Kreisky never warmed to the seemingly endless conference of diplomats, which the CSCE represented to him. However, on the occasion of the signing of the Helsinki Final Act, he made the most distinct statements by a Western politician regarding the third basket, stressing readiness for a continued ideological argument with communism. This very statement led to an overrating of Kreisky's role in Austria's CSCE politics – a misinterpretation Benjamin Gilde has revised thoroughly.[18]

In contrast to Austrian politicians, the country's diplomats quickly realized the importance of the third basket, and within the NNA group contributed to making the Helsinki Final Act possible. Not least, the potential repercussions of an engagement in humanitarian questions on Austria's international reputation finally led the Foreign Ministry to back the respective actions by its diplomats in the multilateral preparatory talks and the early CSCE negotiations. Austrian diplomacy played a decisive role in this early phase of the CSCE. It formulated the preamble of the third basket and became a driving force in negotiating the contents of this basket. Led by Helmut Liedermann, the Austrian delegation supported Western positions, and as a pretended 'mediator' fought for their inclusion in the Final Act. Austrian diplomats worked out compromise papers, formulations acceptable to East and West, and especially sounded out potential Eastern concessions. Nevertheless, the considerable mediatory efforts of Austria should not be overestimated, as the most crucial obstacles were overcome in superpower negotiations and compromises.[19] In the end, the Soviet struggle for a quick conclusion of the Final Act was most decisive. For what it perceived as the final acceptance of the postwar status quo in Europe, Moscow had to make concessions with regard to the third basket and underestimated the dynamics of the Final Act. From that very moment on, the citizens of socialist countries had a document signed by 'their' leaderships they could refer to when demanding their rights. The same holds true for the Western countries when bi- and multilaterally dealing with those regimes on humanitarian issues.

Austria and the Implementation of the Helsinki Final Act in East-Central Europe

With regard to the implementation of the Final Act, it was Austria's main task to observe how far the principles agreed upon were adhered to and – if necessary – to use them as a foreign policy instrument when dealing with the socialist states. The initial position differed from country to country. Poland had led the way in Austria's Ostpolitik in the early 1960s. After a period of stagnation and despite the severe inner-Polish crises at the turn of the 1960s, bilateral relations had once again intensified. In 1972, even a treaty on the abolition of mutual visa requirements was agreed upon, and Kreisky set high hopes on the future developments of economic relations. Interestingly enough, the abolition of visa requirements was the result of a surprising Polish initiative. Austrian diplomacy seized the opportunity and concluded the treaty within an extremely short period of time. Since no other such treaty between Poland and Western countries was agreed upon in the aftermath, Vienna was convinced that this was due to the 'concerns' of the other socialist countries.[20] Despite this, and being unaware how the treaty had become possible at all, the hitherto rather unrealistic idea of general visa-free travel across the Iron Curtain became an Austrian goal. From the state of the quality of bilateral relations, Hungary was the country most likely to be open to the Austrian desire. Thus, by 1972, and hence before the start of the CSCE negotiation process, there was already an example of freer movement between East and West.

Hungary

Austrian–Hungarian relations had hit rock bottom after the bloody Soviet crackdown on the revolution in 1956. Thereafter, it took until 1964 to solve the most severe bilateral problems between Austria and Hungary. However, the common border remained a minefield. Seeking an improvement of relations with the West, the Hungarian regime gradually softened its border regime. Even though the border remained 'iron', the area was demined by 1971. By the beginning of the 1970s, mutual visiting diplomacy had increased by leaps and bounds.[21]

The almost complete absence of bilateral and especially humanitarian problems resulted in a focus on the development of economic relations. By the early 1970s, Hungary had become Austria's second most important Eastern European commercial partner, after the Soviet Union. Economic cooperation went beyond the principles agreed upon in the second basket of the Final Act.[22] In some fields, the results of the CSCE were already part of Austrian–Hungarian relations; in other fields, they were expected to reveal new possibilities for further improvement. By the mid 1970s, bilateral relations were consequently called a 'masterpiece of a friendly good neighbourly relationship between states of different societal systems'.[23] Kreisky paid a private visit to Hungary and met with János Kádár in the summer of 1976, stating on bilateral relations: 'Because of us, there was no need for the Helsinki conference'.[24]

Austria acted as a diplomatic 'ice breaker' for Hungary, most strikingly in December 1976 when Austria became the first Western country to receive the Hungarian party leader Kádár officially.[25]

Subsequently, Hungary rewarded the Austrian attitude with several concessions. Austrian loans for the modernization of Hungarian tourism infrastructure made something possible that Vienna had sought for years: in 1978, a treaty on the abolition of mutual visa requirements was agreed upon, an unusual step by neighbours with an immediate border on either side of the Iron Curtain. Economic relations, regional cooperation and mutual tourism grew significantly in the 1980s. The Hungarian political system was subsequently perceived, or, more accurately, misperceived as 'Goulash communism',[26] due to the economic reforms and the moderate border regime. Nevertheless, despite visa-free travel, the party and state security still regulated the travel regime,[27] a situation that changed only in the late 1980s. As reforms in Hungary further proceeded, by the end of the 1980s relations became even closer and significantly contributed to overcoming the Iron Curtain – an aspect to be dealt with at the end of this chapter.

In the case of Austrian–Hungarian relations, there was no Helsinki effect at all, since there was no need for it. Bilateral relations already went beyond the principles of the Final Act and their quality was preserved throughout the last peak of the Cold War. The post-1975 permanent mentioning of the 'spirit of Helsinki' in bilateral conversations and statements showed the importance both countries dedicated to the CSCE process; on the bilateral level, this 'spirit' was more than simply lip service, as it had been established before the conclusion of the Final Act.

Poland

Chancellor Kreisky had high hopes for the development of Austrian–Polish relations at the beginning of the 1970s. He hoped especially to foster and grow economic relations and grant energy supplies – something that had also shaped his interpretation of the aims of the CSCE. In bilateral meetings throughout the second half of the 1970s, the economic cooperation between Austria and Poland was described as being in 'the spirit of the CSCE'.[28] In the end, despite many Austrian large-scale loans, the effect was a complete default, as Poland usually needed the fresh foreign currency to pay its national debts. In 1980, it became obvious that Poland would soon be insolvent. To Kreisky, this constituted a shock. He had completely misjudged the risks of Austria's expansive credit policy and believed that in the case of a default the

Soviet Union would step in.[29] Despite the Polish and bilateral economic fiascos, in mid 1980 overall relations were still valued by Austria as 'being of privileged character'.[30] Humanitarian hardship cases hardly existed, and Austria had abstained from openly criticizing the Polish domestic political turbulences. In early 1971, only six weeks after the massacre of Gdansk,[31] Austrian Foreign Minister Kirchschläger paid an official visit to Poland.[32] Increasing societal and intellectual unrest, as evidenced through workers' turmoil in June 1976 and the foundation of the Workers' Defense Committee later the same year, did not burden bilateral relations. When the regime took a growingly repressive stance, doubts among Austrian diplomats about the future economic and societal stability arose.[33] The appearance of Solidarność complicated this – in economic terms highly irrational – East–West 'love affair'.

Public protest started in August 1980 and soon the independent trade union Solidarność turned into a political factor. Austria reacted with sympathy and caution. With the increasing escalation, Kreisky became more and more reserved and the inner-Austrian debate turned more controversial. The reasons for this were twofold. First was the economic dimension and the crisis-related absence of Polish coal deliveries. Within this context, Kreisky made inconsiderate statements (calling the Polish workers back to the mines or criticizing the role of the Catholic Church in Poland) that caused domestic political conflict with the opposition as well as the Church. Second, before the imposition of martial law in December 1981, more than thirty thousand Poles had already travelled to Austria as tourists and subsequently claimed asylum. Supposedly, large parts of the Austrian population showed hardly any understanding for Polish refugees and the yellow press put pressure on the Kreisky government to do something. Only a few days before the imposition of martial law, Austria unilaterally suspended the treaty on visa-free travel. However, after the first bloodshed, Austria granted asylum to all potentially persecuted persons. Austria, however, aimed at being a transit country only; it intensively sought third countries to accommodate refugees and requested financial aid from the international community.[34] Within a few years, Poland, once regarded as a role model in the socialist camp, had become the most severe case of violations against human rights.

To Kreisky, the CSCE had made the appearance of Solidarność possible and at the same time the regime's treatment of the independent trade union was a violation of the principles agreed upon in Helsinki. Considering Kreisky (and many other Western politicians), sustaining détente and not risking a Soviet intervention dominated over supporting Solidarność. Despite his permanent advocacy for an end to martial law and the release of all political detainees, Warsaw was grateful for his rejection of a boycott of the Polish regime.[35] After the suspension of martial law in 1983, Austrian–Polish relations recovered, but this time no illusions arose about the Polish regime and future stable political and economic development in Poland.[36] Relations re-intensified in the second half of the 1980s. Visiting diplomacy increased once again. Starting from January 1988, the suspended treaty on visa-free travel was put back into effect.[37] Not least because of the renewed growth in domestic political unrest, this increased the number of Poles claiming asylum in Austria.[38] In 1989, the Polish reform process was regarded as a 'historic chance for real change'. Hence, Austria assisted with food supplies and the foundation of joint ventures.[39] In 1988, Austria and Poland even became the first East–West tandem jointly sponsoring a proposal for a symposium on 'cultural heritage' during the Third Follow-up Meeting to the CSCE in Vienna.[40]

East Germany

After 1945, some twenty thousand Austrians were living in the GDR. In the period of non-recognition until 1972, Austrian diplomacy had only limited means to represent their interests, whether it was their wish to permanently leave East Germany or other consular matters. The situation was worsened by the fact that the GDR had issued identity cards to those Austrians and claimed them to be East German or at least dual citizens. Austria did not accept this practice but was unable to take action against it and 'silent diplomacy' through unofficial channels offered only limited success. Furthermore, with international recognition approaching, the GDR increasingly refused any concessions in this field.[41] Unsurprisingly, the East German regime's attitude did not change following diplomatic recognition in 1972. However, the GDR sought recognition of its citizenship, something West Germany had consequently rejected during the negotiations of the basic treaty. In 1975 (months before the signing of the Helsinki Final Act), a consular treaty was concluded. This treaty – much to the displeasure of Bonn – explicitly recognized East German citizenship. Thanks to an intervention by Austria's first ambassador to the GDR, Friedrich Bauer, the Austrian Foreign Ministry had linked the conclusion of the treaty with the solution of humanitarian hardship cases. Because of the German-German dimension of this treaty, the GDR reluctantly accepted this deal and other repercussions of the treaty, such as granting Austrian diplomats the right to visit imprisoned Austrian citizens. More than one thousand humanitarian hardship cases were solved in connection with the consular treaty.⁴² With the signing of the treaty, despite heavy West German interventions, Austria had become a diplomatic 'ice breaker' for the GDR.

In August 1976, Austrian Foreign Minister Erich Bielka visited the GDR, and in a conversation with his East German counterpart Oskar Fischer he highlighted Austria's interest in an intensification of bilateral relations under the terms of the Helsinki Final Act. Bielka emphasized human contacts and called for a next round of solving humanitarian hardship cases. As an incentive, he mentioned that due to the abolition of visa requirements and economic cooperation, relations with Poland and Hungary already went 'beyond Helsinki'.⁴³ However, the GDR was the wrong addressee for such remarks.

The GDR was the Eastern regime most reluctant to implement the Final Act, not least because it had to deal with a steadily growing number of citizens demanding their right to leave their country.⁴⁴ Hence, any reference to the CSCE in the East German Foreign Ministry was more likely to hinder humanitarian solutions than make them possible. There is good reason to exemplify both the Austrian position and the GDR's reluctance to accept any reference to the provisions of the Helsinki Final Act. Interestingly enough, the expatriation of famous dissident Wolf Biermann in 1976 did not cause a setback in bilateral relations, although Kreisky had publicly offered Biermann the chance to continue his work in Austria. The principle of humanitarian concessions prevailed as Austria continued to act as a diplomatic 'ice breaker'. This was the case when Bruno Kreisky officially visited East Berlin as the first Western head of government in 1978.⁴⁵ Thereafter, economic relations became the determining factor in bilateral relations.

According to international diplomatic conventions, after mutual visits by the foreign ministers and the respective heads of government of one country, a return visit by their counterparts would take place, before moving on to mutual visits by the heads of state. After Kreisky had visited East Berlin in 1978, a return visit by East German Prime Minister Willi Stoph was scheduled.⁴⁶ At that time, the East German writer Rolf Schneider, who had been invited to Austria for a lecture, was denied permission to travel abroad. Kreisky and Schneider had known each other for some years, and in the course of his visit to the GDR the Austrian Chancellor had met the author in the Austrian embassy. East German authorities disliked this encounter, but since Kreisky was the first Western head of government to visit East Berlin they decided to reluctantly let it happen and not to cause any arguments.⁴⁷ Perhaps due to Schneider's prominence and Kreisky's sympathy for him, the Austrian Foreign Ministry publicly protested against the regime denying Schneider the right to travel, with direct reference to the CSCE. East German diplomats spoke of Austrian interference in the GDR's domestic policies likely to threaten bilateral relations and called Schneider a 'very disloyal' person. Neither side changed its position, and finally the Politburo of the Sozialistische Einheitspartei Deutschlands (Socialist Unity Party of Germany, SED) cancelled Stoph's visit to Austria.[48] However, not least for economic reasons, Austria was not interested in deteriorating bilateral relations. Only shortly after the 'Schneider affair', Kreisky sent his foreign minister Willibald Pahr on an unofficial visit to East Berlin that aimed to soundlessly restore a positive climate.[49] Such visits are part of the forgotten history of Austria's humanitarian engagement in the Cold War. In the end, due to economic interests, Austria allowed East Germany to 'absorb' the Stoph visit by a visit of head of state Erich Honecker.[50] The East German state and party leader garnished his Western premiere with a large-scale order for Austria's nationalized industries amounting to almost two billion Deutschmark. This resulted in another Austrian construction site in the GDR, and the presence of thousands of Austrian workers once again resulted in humanitarian questions, namely the demand for marriages of Austrians with East German women. Without any mention of the CSCE, most of these cases were accepted by the GDR in the course of the next top-level visits by Austrian politicians. A dialogue between Austrian President Kirchschläger and Honecker in November 1983 best illustrates this fact; when Kirchschläger handed over a list of the requested marriages, he said: 'It is unavoidable. There is no country in the world from which the VÖEST workers have not brought home women. This even holds true for America and Africa and in a German-speaking country this tendency is even stronger'. Austrian Foreign Minister Erwin Lanc interjected: 'That seems to be a potent enterprise'. Honecker answered: 'We got to know it in the economic field, there it has dynamic forces'. The SED leader continued in an ambiguous way: 'It is natural that such things happen, due to the frequent dealings between Austria and the GDR. No one is going to make a problem out of it. The questions will be solved, since they constitute real and not fake problems. In this regard, we are relatively liberal and open. I would like to say that in this field we are better than our reputation'.[51]

The main reason for this was the all-time peak of bilateral relations that occurred in the early 1980s, when German-German relations were also strained. Additionally, one has to mention that within those crucial years Austria and the GDR had become economic partners, not least because Austrian loans significantly helped to keep the GDR solvent during the debt crisis of the early 1980s, before Bavarian Prime Minister Franz Josef Strauß provided loans in 1983/84.⁵²

Not only in German-German relations but also in the case of neutral Austria, the CSCE was a taboo subject when aiming to solve humanitarian questions on a bilateral level. For the GDR, the Soviet humanitarian concessions in Madrid were problematic. The number of people demanding their right to leave their country grew once more. The regime tried to appear accommodating, but in fact repression was enforced in stages – ultimately with limited success. The domestic political situation did not stabilize and societal disappointment grew constantly. In the end, the cyclically permitted right to emigrate for groups who persistently demanded it also contributed to increasing the numbers of those who wanted to leave the country. However, it was only in the mid 1980s that the first relevant East German Helsinki groups appeared. The impulse came from Czechoslovakia.⁵³

Czechoslovakia

Austrian–Czechoslovakian relations, despite some occasional gleams of hope, were constantly heavily burdened from 1945 until the early 1970s. The expulsion of the German-speaking minority, the communist takeover in 1948 and the implementation of the Iron Curtain drew a dividing line between the somehow ever since 'begrudging neighbours'.⁵⁴ Natural cross-border contacts intensified again with the beginning of liberalization in Czechoslovakia in the 1960s. East–West tourism increased and even boomed during the 'Prague Spring'.⁵⁵ In contrast, political relations remained highly strained throughout the 1950s and 1960s. No top-level visits took place and diplomatic relations were not normalized until the 1970s. After the conclusion of the treaty on proprietary rights in 1974, relations improved, diplomatic representations were raised to the level of embassies in 1975 and mutual state visits by foreign ministers and heads of government became possible. After Kreisky had visited Czechoslovakia in February 1976, it seemed that relations had finally normalized. Yet this 'honeymoon' phase of Austrian–Czechoslovakian relations lasted less than a year. In fact, relations remained at least cyclically burdened and became a minefield when it came to humanitarian questions and dissent.⁵⁶

The first scandal resulted from denying Václav Havel (who was awarded the Austrian State Prize for European Literature in 1968) the right to travel to Austria in autumn 1976. In that very year, Kreisky had spoken out in favour of dissidents several times. Inspired by this and the SED's expatriation of the East German dissident singer-songwriter

Wolf Biermann in November 1976, Kreisky offered all East European dissidents asylum in Austria by the end of 1976. After the publication of Charter 77, which criticized the government for failing to implement human rights provisions it had signed for example in the Helsinki Final Act, many of the responsible Czechoslovakian dissidents were traced. The Czechoslovakian regime's reinforced repression was decried in the West. Kreisky unconditionally stood up for the dissidents and renewed his offer for asylum in Austria. Not all dissidents were happy about Kreisky's offer, as it was suitable for abetting their expatriation. However, some, like Zdeněk Mlynář, accepted the offer and claimed asylum in Austria in 1977. Thereafter relations between Prague and Vienna once again hit rock bottom.[57] Normalization started again only at the end of summer 1977.[58] This pattern of ups and downs continued in the following years.

Already in early 1978, Austrian ambassador to Prague Johann Pasch warned his ministry that the award of the Austrian State Prize for European Literature to the 'dissident author' Pavel Kohout could harm the 'spring in Austrian–Czechoslovakian relations'.[59] Shortly after the visit by Austrian President Rudolf Kirchschläger in 1979, rounding out the formal normalization process of diplomatic relations, Czechoslovakian authorities expatriated Kohout, who at the time worked in Austria, refusing him re-entry to his home country. Kreisky publicly spoke out in the case of Kohout and claimed it to be a violation of the Helsinki principles.[60] Yet once again, Foreign Minister Pahr was sent on an unofficial visit to Prague to calm things down.[61] Border incidents and espionage affairs contributed to this infinite loop. The 'Josef Hodic affair', the revealing of a supposed dissident as an agent of the Czechoslovakian intelligence service, resulted in the postponement of the return visit by party leader and head of state Gustav Husák to the year 1982.[62] Both sides had agreed on the new date as they aimed to provide an unbiased atmosphere for the visit.

Even though both neighbouring states aimed at normalizing bilateral relations, these remained cyclically burdened until 1989 (and in fact even beyond). In 1984, Czechoslovakian border guards killed a refugee on Austrian soil. This constituted another setback that both sides wanted to avoid in the future. By the second half of the 1980s, Austrian diplomacy drew a dismal picture of Czechoslovakia. However, despite the declining standard of living, a weak opposition and the ongoing conflict between state and Church, the situation was regarded as stable. Without any fundamental domestic reforms, there were no prerequisites for an intensification of bilateral relations. Only small steps seemed possible.[63] Even though relations had improved to some extent and had become less polemic, one can hardly find any 'CSCE effect'. The CSCE had constituted a challenge for the regime in Prague and yet another severe burden for Austrian–Czechoslovakian relations. Mutual visiting diplomacy intensified towards 1989, several treaties aiming at closer cooperation were signed and travel restrictions somehow liberalized. The conservative Austrian People's Party increasingly criticized socialist Chancellor Franz Vranitzky for not paying enough attention to the dissidents of neighbouring Czechoslovakia. In the course of his visit to Czechoslovakia in June 1988, he had avoided meeting them. After the end of the Vienna CSCE follow-up, Václav Havel was once again imprisoned, and Austria protested. Just how ambivalent Austria's dealings with the Czechoslovakian regime were became obvious only weeks before the 'velvet revolution', when Prime Minister Ladislav Adamec was received in Vienna in October 1989. Only after the ousting of the communist regime did Czechoslovakia follow the Hungarian example and tear down the Iron Curtain at its border with Austria.[64]

Conclusions and Outlook: The Vienna CSCE Follow-up, European Détente and the End of Communism in East-Central Europe

Turning back to the rather stagnating post-1975 CSCE process, Austria contributed to keeping the process alive. Despite his engagement with East European dissidents, Kreisky warned against reducing the Belgrade CSCE follow-up meeting (1977–78) to the question of dissidents, and Austrian diplomacy did its best to secure another follow-up.[65] Since the international climate was further aggravated at the turn of the 1970s, Kreisky was in favour of a postponement of the next follow-up meeting, which started in Madrid in 1980.[66] There, the Austrian delegation, an integral part of the NNA group, was decisive in finding a way to a conclusion of the meeting, despite the fact that it took place during the last peak of the Cold War. After the implementation of martial law in Poland on 13 December 1981, the solution was an adjournment for several months, proposed and negotiated by the Austrian and French delegations. Hence, the fact that the Madrid meeting lasted until 1983 can be regarded as a success for Austrian diplomacy, not only because Austria additionally managed to get the Third Follow-up Meeting to the CSCE to Vienna, but also because in the end a substantial document was signed. Benjamin Gilde even characterized it as a 'moment of glory' for Austrian diplomacy. Yet the role of the NNA states, despite their merits, should not be overestimated. The main reason a substantial document was signed resulted from the Soviet aim to receive a mandate for a Conference on Confidence and Security Building Measures and Disarmament in Europe. Therefore, Moscow made substantial concessions in the third basket. In the final phases of Madrid, the West and Austria had stood as one, an attitude that was to be continued at the next follow-up meeting starting in late 1986.[67] At the same time, Austria had made economic and sometimes even political concessions towards the socialist states on a bilateral level. Hence, Vienna's relations with the East survived the last peak of the Cold War without severe setbacks. Relations with the GDR had even reached their heyday. Bilateral détente was always oriented around the status quo, and by the mid 1980s none of the actors expected a change or aimed to overcome it.

After Madrid, several special meetings took place, which forecast that the need for NNA mediatory efforts was in decline.[68] Furthermore, before the onset of the Vienna CSCE follow-up meeting, the international climate had significantly changed. The Stockholm Conference on Confidence and Security Building Measures and Disarmament in Europe ended with a substantial document in September 1986. Meanwhile, Mikhail Gorbachev had come to power in the Soviet Union and the first signs of a renaissance of superpower détente loomed on the horizon. The most remarkable international sign was the Intermediate Range Nuclear Forces Treaty signed in 1987. These developments were fostered during the Third Follow-up Meeting to the CSCE. At the beginning, the NNA states acted in their customary manner. Austria did so not least because it was still one of the most affected countries. While the border with Hungary had become more permeable, the border to Czechoslovakia was still 'iron'. What complicated the initial negotiations in Vienna was – according to the Austrian view – the West's attempt to test Gorbachev's readiness to make concessions in the humanitarian field. In its initial stages, the debate about the implementation of humanitarian issues did not differ much from what had happened in Belgrade and Madrid, but this time no one doubted the legitimacy of such a controversial debate. The West and the Western neutrals, like Austria, Sweden and Switzerland, heavily criticized the situation in the Soviet Union, Czechoslovakia, the GDR, Romania and Bulgaria. With the progression of Gorbachev's reforms, the Western critique focused on Czechoslovakia, the GDR and Romania, who refused domestic reforms. Against the background of proceeding reforms in Eastern Europe, the main reason for slow work on the final document resulted from the growing expectations in the West. The insufficient implementation of certain humanitarian provisions should be overcome by the new document and the agreements should be more binding. As the negotiations continued, divergences within the socialist bloc became more and more obvious. Finally, in January 1989, all countries involved accepted a concluding document that once again originated from an NNA proposal. Romania had openly announced that it would not implement the humanitarian provisions and in those very days, the regimes in Prague and East Berlin brutally suppressed demonstrations. Now pariahs even in the socialist bloc, those weeks forecast their fate in the months to come. One of the principles agreed upon in Vienna was the right to travel abroad and permanently leave the home country.[69]

The GDR had resisted this principle and other formulations on humanitarian issues. Finally, Moscow *de facto* forced the East Germans to sign the concluding document. The leadership in East Berlin planned not to implement the results of the Vienna follow-up meeting, especially the expiration of minimum exchange for foreigners travelling to the GDR. With regard to the freedom of movement, the Vienna document was published only selectively. Like all other CSCE conferences, the Vienna meeting once again increased the number of people demanding their right to leave the GDR permanently. Despite the new procedures implemented in the GDR, the domestic situation worsened in the months to come.[70]

Turning to the Austrian–Hungarian border, Vienna had pushed for an agreement on local border traffic for more than a decade. The Austrian pressure in combination with inner-Hungarian dynamics initiated a process that led to an entirely different and more far-reaching result. In 1987, after an intense discussion, the Hungarian Politburo abandoned local border traffic from its agenda, and decided that in the future the frequency of journeys to the West should not be regulated by the Hungarian state.[71]

From 1 January 1988, every Hungarian citizen was entitled to claim a so-called 'world passport'. The passport enabled one to leave the country at any time without restrictions, a very unusual permission in the Eastern bloc. A travel boom soon started, and Austria served as Hungary's gate to the West. By 1988, millions of Hungarians crossed the border to Austria.[72] 'Technical barriers' and the alarm system at the border had become faulty over the years. After the introduction of the 'world passport', they had ultimately become redundant too. In the second half of the 1980s, internal discussions on the future border regime had started. However, it took until the change in Hungarian leadership in 1988 for true reforms to be possible.[73]

For his first official visit to a foreign country, the new Hungarian Prime Minister Miklós Németh visited Austria in February 1989, where he announced that the border security would be removed. In May of the same year, the dismantling of the Iron Curtain began. However, this brave step did not imply that the border was open for citizens of other socialist countries still maintaining a restrictive visa policy. For example, tourist visas for GDR citizens were only valid for a stay in Hungary and did not allow travel further abroad. Nonetheless, the pictures of the dismantling of the Iron Curtain became known across the globe, including in East German living rooms. The more efficacious, but at this moment still inappropriate picture of an entirely open border between Austria and Hungary resulted from the staged cutting of the fence by Austrian Foreign Minister Alois Mock and his Hungarian counterpart Gyula Horn in June 1989. Interestingly enough, this was an Austrian idea and took place in the course of a bilateral meeting.[74]

The rest of the story is well known. In the summer of 1989, the exodus of East Germans gathered pace. Throughout the summer months, West German embassies were filled with East Germans unwilling to return to the GDR.[75] Since the number of GDR citizens trying to escape via Hungary increased constantly, the Hungarian government decided to open the borders for all East German citizens on 11 September 1989. Within the following few weeks, some fifty thousand East German citizens used Austria as their transit country on the way to West Germany. The developments of summer 1989 clearly sped up because of the dynamics of the time and had severe repercussions for the 'peaceful revolution' and the 'fall' of the Berlin Wall, and further consequences for the end of the communist regimes in Czechoslovakia and Romania. Even though these developments can hardly be explained without the 'Gorbachev factor' and the renaissance of superpower détente or the socio-economic changes since the 1970s, it would be equally wrong to explain them without the politics of a 'long European détente'[76] and the effects of the CSCE. Their interaction on the long way to 1989 is one of the underestimated factors – often borne by neutrals or small states – that contributed to ending the Cold War.

Maximilian Graf (European University Institute, Florence) is a historian who specializes in Cold War studies and the history of communism. His most recent publications include a prize-winning book on Austrian–East German relations during the Cold War, entitled *Österreich und die DDR 1949–1990: Politik und Wirtschaft im Schatten der deutschen Teilung* (ÖAW, 2016) and the co-edited volume *Europa und die deutsche Einheit: Beobachtungen, Entscheidungen und Folgen* (Vandenhoeck &Ruprecht,

2017). In 2014 he was awarded the Karl von Vogelsang Prize – Austrian State Prize for the History of Social Sciences.

Notes

1. A. Brown, *The Gorbachev Factor* (Oxford: Oxford University Press, 1996).
2. For a well-balanced interpretation, see W. Mueller, 'The Revolutions of 1989: An Introduction', in W. Mueller, M. Gehler and A. Suppan (eds), *The Revolutions of 1989: A Handbook* (Vienna: ÖAW, 2015), 3–30.
3. However, given the importance of the factors mentioned above, I doubt that this was a result of intentional 'change through rapprochement'. Despite its primordial intentions, in my view, throughout the 1970s this policy concept evolved into a status quo realpolitik that aimed at making divided Europe more livable and no longer anticipated fundamental political change. For controversial positions on this debate, see the articles by Gottfried Niedhart and Oliver Bange as well as the editorial remarks by Mark Kramer who qualified their interpretations as 'teleological nonsense' in *Journal of Cold War Studies* 18 (2016), 3.
4. To name but a selection of the most recent ones going beyond a solely 'national' approach: S. Kieninger, *Dynamic Détente: The United States and Europe 1964–1975* (Lanham, MD: Lexington Books, 2016); M. Peter and H. Wentker (eds), *Die KSZE im Ost-West-Konflikt: Internationale Politik und gesellschaftliche Transformation 1975–1990* (Munich: Oldenbourg, 2012); H. Altrichter and H. Wentker (eds), *Der KSZE-Prozess: Vom Kalten Krieg zu einem neuen Europa 1975 bis 1990* (Munich: Oldenbourg, 2011); O. Bange and G. Niedhart (eds), *Helsinki 1975 and the Transformation of Europe* (New York: Berghahn Books, 2008); S. Snyder, *Human Rights Activism and the End of the Cold War: A Transnational History of the Helsinki Network* (New York: Cambridge University, 2011); A. Romano, *From Détente in Europe to European Détente: How the West Shaped the Helsinki CSCE* (Brussels: Peter Lang, 2009); D.C. Thomas, *The Helsinki Effect: International Norms, Human Rights, and the Demise of Communism* (Princeton, NJ: Princeton University Press, 2001).
5. T. Fischer, *Neutral Power in the CSCE: The N+N States and the Making of the Helsinki Accords 1975* (Baden–Baden: Nomos, 2009).
6. T. Fischer, 'Austria and the Helsinki Process', in A. Suppan and W. Mueller (eds), *Peaceful Coexistence or Iron Curtain? Austria, Neutrality, and Eastern Europe in the Cold War and Détente, 1955–1989* (Vienna: Lit, 2009), 168–202.
7. B. Gilde, *Österreich im KSZE-Prozess 1969–1983: Neutraler Vermittler in humanitärer Mission* (Munich: Oldenbourg, 2013), 439.
8. On the Austrian State Treaty, see G. Stourzh, *Um Einheit und Freiheit: Staatsvertrag, Neutralität und das Ende der Ost-West-Besetzung Österreichs 1945–1955* (Vienna: Böhlau, 2005); A. Suppan, G. Stourzh and W. Mueller (eds), *Der Österreichische Staatsvertrag: Internationale Strategie, rechtliche Relevanz, nationale Identität* (Vienna: ÖAW, 2005); R. Steininger, *Der*

Staatvertrag: Österreich im Schatten von deutscher Frage und Kaltem Krieg 1938–1955 (Innsbruck: Studienverlag, 2005).
9. W. Mueller, *A Good Example of Peaceful Coexistence? The Soviet Union, Austria, and Neutrality, 1955–1991* (Vienna: ÖAW, 2011), 39–132. On Austrian 'Ostpolitik' in general, see Suppan and Mueller, *Peaceful Coexistence or Iron Curtain?*
10. Mueller, *A Good Example*, 179.
11. S. Karner and P. Ruggenthaler, 'Austria and the End of the Prague Spring: Neutrality in the Crucible?', in G. Bischof, S. Karner and P. Ruggenthaler (eds), *The Prague Spring and the Warsaw Pact Invasion of Czechoslovakia in 1968* (Lanham, MD: Lexington Books, 2010), 419–39.
12. See Fischer, *Neutral Power in the CSCE*.
13. T. Fischer, 'A Mustard Seed Grew into a Bushy Tree: The Finnish CSCE-Initiative of 5 May 1969', *Cold War History* 9 (2009), 177–201; Fischer, 'Österreich und die finnische KSZE-Initiative vom 5. Mai 1969', in W. Mueller and M. Portmann (eds), *Osteuropa vom Weltkrieg bis zur Wende* (Vienna: ÖAW, 2007), 313–39.
14. B. Gilde, '"Kein Vorreiter": Österreich und die humanitäre Dimension der KSZE 1969–1973', in Altrichter and Wentker, *Der KSZE-Prozess*, 41–50.
15. Memcon Winzer–Kirchschläger, 12 April 1973, Politisches Archiv des Auswärtigen Amts (PA/AA), Ministerium für auswärtige Angelegenheiten der DDR (MfAA), C 795/75, Bl. 75–82.
16. On Kreisky's foreign policy with almost no attention to Ostpolitik and the CSCE, see E. Röhrlich, *Kreiskys Außenpolitik: Zwischen österreichischer Identität und internationalem Programm* (Zeitgeschichte im Kontext 2) (Göttingen: V&R unipress, 2009).
17. I have shown this in detailed case studies on economic relations between Austria and the GDR as well as on Austria and Poland. M. Graf, *Österreich und die DDR 1949–1990: Politik und Wirtschaft im Schatten der deutschen Teilung* (Vienna: ÖAW, 2016), 381–404, 425–33, 459–70, 497–528, 535–47; Graf, 'Kreisky und Polen: Schlaglichter auf einen vernachlässigten Aspekt der österreichischen "Ostpolitik"', in L. Dreidemy et al. (eds), *Bananen, Cola, Zeitgeschichte: Oliver Rathkolb und das lange 20. Jahrhundert*, 2 vols (Vienna: Böhlau, 2015), 692–706, here 700–4. On Austria's economic relations to Eastern Europe in general, see A. Resch, 'Der österreichische Osthandel im Spannungsfeld der Blöcke', in M. Rauchensteiner (ed.), *Zwischen den Blöcken: NATO, Warschauer Pakt und Österreich* (Vienna: Böhlau, 2010), 497–556; G. Enderle-Burcel et al. (eds), *Gaps in the Iron Curtain: Economic Relations between Neutral and Socialist Countries in Cold War Europe* (Cracow: Jagiellonian University Press, 2009).
18. Gilde, *Österreich im KSZE-Prozess*, 445–46.
19. Ibid., 255–57.
20. Graf, 'Kreisky und Polen', 700–1.
21. See T. Bárányi, M. Graf, M. Krajczár and I. Lehner, 'A Masterpiece of European Détente? Austrian–Hungarian Relations from 1964 until the Peaceful End of the Cold War', *Zeitgeschichte* 41(5) (2014), 311–38, here 313–23.

22. On Austrian–Hungarian trade, see A. Pogány, 'Co-operation through the Iron Curtain: Economic Relations between Austria and Hungary after the Second World War', in Enderle-Burcel et al., *Gaps in the Iron Curtain*, 142–62.
23. Official visit by Prime Minister György Lazar to Austria, 16–19 May 1976, Kreisky-Archive, Vienna, Box Ungarn 2.
24. Memorandum on the unofficial visit by Kreisky, 13 September 1976. Highly confidential! Magyar Nemzeti Levéltár – Országos Levéltár, Budapest (MNL–OL), XIX–J–1–j Österreich, 27. d. 1. t. 003795/10/1976.
25. See M. Graf, 'Ein Musterbeispiel der europäischen Entspannung? Die österreichisch–ungarischen Beziehungen von 1964 bis 1989', in C. Szabó (ed.), *Österreich und Ungarn im 20. Jahrhundert* (Vienna: Collegium Hungaricum, 2014), 261–80, here 268–74.
26. 'Goulash communism' or the 'happiest barrack of the socialist camp' are popular but inadequate descriptions of the – in comparison with other socialist countries – more liberal Hungarian regime, which nonetheless was a single party dictatorship. For a critique on these terms highlighting the human consequences of the Hungarian system (such as the high suicide rate), see G. Dalos, *Der Vorhang geht auf: Das Ende der Diktaturen in Osteuropa* (Munich: C.H. Beck, 2009), 63–68.
27. Z. Mlynar, 'Die österreichisch-ungarischen Beziehungen als Sonderfall der Ost-West-Beziehungen', in Z. Mlynar et al. (eds), *Die Beziehungen zwischen Österreich und Ungarn: Sonderfall oder Modell?* (Vienna: Wilhelm Braumüller, 1985), 145–62.
28. Memcon, Kreisky–Jaroszewicz, Innsbruck, 16 September 1977, Kreisky-Archive, Box Polen 3.
29. Staribacher-diaries, 8 November 1977, Kreisky-Archive. Kreisky confirmed his judgement regularly. See also O. Klambauer, *Der Kalte Krieg in Österreich: Vom Dritten Mann zum Fall des Eisernen Vorhangs* (Vienna: Ueberreuter, 2000), 149.
30. Official visit by the Polish Prime Minister to Austria, Kreisky-Archive, Box Polen 2.
31. After an increase in prices for consumer goods decreed by the regime, several enterprises in Gdansk went on strike. When the police intervened, local riots broke out. Without any negotiation attempt, the Polish party leader Władysław Gomułka gave a firing order. This led to countrywide unrest and at least forty-five people died. Thereafter, on 19 December 1970, Gomułka had to resign as First Secretary and was replaced by Edward Gierek who immediately took back the decisions of his predecessor and thereby managed to end the strikes. See W. Borodziej, *Geschichte Polens im 20. Jahrhundert* (Munich: C.H. Beck, 2010), 316–18.
32. Language Regime on the visit by the Foreign Minister to Poland, Austrian Foreign Ministry (AFM) to all diplomatic representations, Vienna, 25 January 1971, Österreichisches Staatsarchiv (ÖStA), Archiv der Republik (AdR), Bundesministerium für Auswärtige Angelegenheiten (BMfAA), II-Pol 1971, Polen 2, Gr.Zl. 105.030-6/71, GZ. 106.039-6(Pol)/71, Karton 1801.

33. Briefing papers for the visit by the Polish Foreign Minister Wojtaszek to Austria, 21–23 March 1978, Kreisky-Archive, Länderbox Polen 3.
34. See O. Rathkolb, 'Austria: An Ambivalent Attitude of Trade Unions and Political Parties', in I. Goddeeris (ed.), *Solidarity with Solidarity: Western European Trade Unions and the Polish Crisis, 1980–1982* (Lanham, MD: Lexington Books, 2010), 269–88. My interpretations slightly differ from Rathkolb's. See Graf, 'Kreisky und Polen', 703–6.
35. Ambassador Wotava to AFM, Warsaw, 16 March 1982, Zl. 133-Res/82, Kreisky-Archive, Box Polen 1; AFM to all diplomatic representations, Vienna, 25 January 1982, GZ. 166.03.00/109-II.3/82, Kreisky-Archive, Box Polen 1; AFM to all diplomatic representations, Vienna, 19 March 1982, GZ. 166.03.00/246-II.3/82, Kreisky-Archive, Box Polen 1.
36. See M. Graf and P. Ruggenthaler, 'Polnisch-österreichische Beziehungen im Kalten Krieg', in A. Kisztelińska-Węgrzyńska (ed.), *Austria w polskim dyskursie publicznym po 1945 roku: Österreich im polnischen Diskurs nach 1945* (Cracow: Universitas, 2016), 25–60.
37. Memorandum, Bilateral relations, 18 October 1988, in folder 'Besuch Premierminister Rakowski; 24.–26.11.1988', Kreisky-Archive, Depositum Franz Vranitzky, AP, Box 'MP Grosz Ungarn Nov. 88; MP Rakowski (Polen) Nov. 88; AM Johannes CSSR'.
38. Memorandum, Refugees situation, 16 November 1988, ibid.
39. Poland, Domestic political situation, October 1989, in folder 'Off. Besuch des poln. AM Prof. Krzystof Skubiszewski in Österreich, 5.–8.11.1989', Kreisky-Archive, Depositum Franz Vranitzky, AP, Box 'AM Skubiszewski Polen 1989; MP Adamec CSSR 24.10.1989; MP Nemeth Ungarn 1989; MP Komarek CSSR 1990; MP Modrow DDR 1990'.
40. Poland – Vienna CSCE follow up, November 1988, Kreisky-Archive, Depositum Franz Vranitzky, AP, Box 'MP Grosz Ungarn Nov. 88; MP Rakowski (Polen) Nov. 88; AM Johannes CSSR'.
41. See Graf, *Österreich und die DDR*, 174–98.
42. E. Seewald, 'Die Aufnahme der diplomatischen Beziehungen zwischen der DDR und Österreich', in J. Staadt (ed.), *Schwierige Dreierbeziehung: Österreich und die beiden deutschen Staaten* (Studien des Forschungsverbundes SED-Staat an der Freien Universität Berlin) (Frankfurt: Peter Lang, 2013), 81–135, here 102–18.
43. Report on the visit by Bielka to the GDR, 23–26 August 1976, PA/AA, MfAA, C 3751, Bl. 4–9.
44. A. Hanisch, *Die DDR im KSZE-Prozess 1972–1985: Zwischen Ostabhängigkeit, Westabgrenzung und Ausreisebewegung* (Munich: Oldenbourg, 2012), 124–78. Also see the chapter by Douglas Selvage in this volume.
45. F. Bauer and E. Seewald, *Bruno Kreisky in Ost-Berlin: Ein Besuch der besonderen Art* (Innsbruck: Studienverlag, 2011).
46. Fischer to Stoph, Berlin, 4 October 1978, Bundesarchiv, Berlin (BArch), Abteilung DDR, DC/20/4750, Bl. 53.
47. R. Schneider, *Leben in Wien* (Munich: Hanser, 1994), 113–23; Bauer and Seewald, *Bruno Kreisky in Ost-Berlin*, 35–36.

48. Meeting of the SED-Politburo, 5 June 1979, Stiftung Archiv der Parteien und Massenorganisationen der ehemaligen DDR, Berlin (SAPMO-BArch), DY 30/J IV 2/2/1780, Bl. 4, 57 and SAPMO-BArch, DY 30/J IV 2/2A/2232, Bl. 140–42.
49. Information on the visit by Foreign Minister Pahr to the GDR, 13–14 October 1979, BArch, Abteilung DDR, DC 20/5288, Bl. 231–34.
50. Walser to Kreisky, Berlin, 18 October 1979, Kreisky-Archive, Länderbox DDR 2, Mappe Diverses 1976–1982.
51. Stenographic record on the conversation Honecker–Kirchschläger, Berlin, 11 October 1983, SAPMO-BArch, DY 30/2474, Bl. 210–61.
52. See Graf, *Österreich und die DDR*, 497–528.
53. Hanisch, *Die DDR im KSZE-Prozess*, 317–65. Also see the chapter by Douglas Selvage in this volume.
54. A. Suppan, *Missgünstige Nachbarn: Geschichte und Perspektiven der nachbarschaftlichen Beziehungen zwischen Tschechien und Österreich* (Vienna: Club Niederösterreich, 2005).
55. See D. Schriffl, 'Der "Prager Frühling" 1968 und die österreichisch-slowakischen Beziehungen', in Mueller and Portmann, *Osteuropa vom Weltkrieg bis zur Wende*, 299–311, here 306–8.
56. Hitherto research on Austrian–Czechoslovakian relations has hardly touched the 1970s and 1980s. See P. Ullmann, *Eine schwierige Nachbarschaft: Die Geschichte der diplomatischen Beziehungen zwischen Österreich und der Tschechoslowakei 1945–1968* (Vienna: Lit, 2006), 223–34.
57. Gilde, *Österreich im KSZE-Prozess*, 289–97.
58. Ambassador Pasch to Pahr, Prague, 2 September 1977, Zl. 11-Pol/77, Kreisky-Archive, Box ČSSR 2.
59. Ambassador Pasch to AFM, 24 January 1978, Zl. 2-Pol/78, ÖStA, AdR, BMfAA, II-Pol 1978, ČSSR, GZ. 35.02.02/1-II.3/78.
60. Gilde, *Österreich im KSZE-Prozess*, 297–304.
61. Again, this emergency visit also had vital economic reasons. See König to Fischer, Prague, 28 December 1979, PA/AA, MfAA, C 3750, Bl. 33–35.
62. Preparatory papers for the visit by Husák to Austria, 16–18 November 1982, Kreisky-Archive, Box ČSSR 4.
63. Final report by Ambassador Ullmann, Prague, 7 January 1987, in Ullmann, *Eine schwierige Nachbarschaft*, 275–82.
64. M. Kunštát, 'Die Tschechoslowakei und Österreich vor dem Umbruch 1989/90', in A. Brait and M. Gehler (eds), *Grenzöffnung 1989: Innen- und Außenperspektiven und die Folgen für Österreich* (Vienna: Böhlau, 2014), 367–84; Folder 'MP Adamec CSSR', in Kreisky-Archive, Depositum Franz Vranitzky, AP, Box 'AM Skubiszewski Polen 1989; MP Adamec CSSR 24. 10. 1989; MP Nemeth Ungarn 1989; MP Komarek CSSR 1990; MP Modrow DDR 1990'.
65. V. Bilandžić, D. Dahlmann and M. Kosanović (eds), *From Helsinki to Belgrade: The First CSCE Follow-up Meeting and the Crisis of Détente* (Göttingen: V&R unipress, 2012).
66. Record on the conversation Honecker–Kreisky, Vienna, 10 November 1980, SAPMO-BArch, DY 30/J IV 2/2/1866, Bl. 36–47.

67. Gilde, *Österreich im KSZE-Prozess*, 397–431; T. Fischer, 'Bridging the Gap between East and West: The N+N as Catalysts of the CSCE Process, 1972–1983', in P. Villaume and O. Westad (eds), *Perforating the Iron Curtain: European Détente, Transatlantic Relations and the Cold War, 1965–1985* (Copenhagen: Museum Tusculanum Press, 2010), 143–78, here 159–66.
68. T. Fischer, *Keeping the Process Alive: The N+N and the CSCE Follow-up from Helsinki to Vienna (1975–1986)* (Züricher Beiträge zur Sicherheitspolitik Nr. 84) (Zurich: Center for Security Studies (CSS), ETH Zürich, 2012).
69. Final internal report by the Austrian Foreign Ministry on the Vienna CSCE Follow-up Meeting, January 1989, Archives of the Bundesministerium für Europa, Integration und Äußeres. For a contemporaneous analysis, see S. Lehne, *The Vienna Meeting of the Conference on Security and Cooperation in Europe, 1986–1989: A Turning Point in East-West Relations* (Boulder, CO: Westview Press, 1991).
70. Hanisch, *Die DDR im KSZE-Prozess*, 373–74; W. Süß, 'Die Wiener KSZE-Folgekonferenz und der Handlungsspielraum des DDR-Sicherheitsapparates 1989', in Peter and Wentker, *Die KSZE im Ost-West-Konflikt*, 219–31.
71. Meeting of the Hungarian Politburo, 19 May 1987, MNL-OL M-KS 288. f. 5. cs. 997. ő.e.
72. M. Graf, 'Die Welt blickt auf das Burgenland. 1989 – die Grenze wird zum Abbild der Veränderung', in M. Graf, A. Lass and K. Ruzicic-Kessler (eds), *Das Burgenland als internationale Grenzregion im 20. und 21. Jahrhundert* (Vienna: Neue Welt Verlag, 2012), 135–79, here 145–53.
73. A. Oplatka, *Der erste Riß in der Mauer: September 1989 – Ungarn öffnet die Grenze* (Vienna: Zsolnay, 2009), 30–37.
74. Graf, 'Die Welt blickt auf das Burgenland', 153–62.
75. K. Stokłosa, 'Die letzte Fluchtwelle aus der DDR im Jahr 1989: Aus den Berichten der westdeutschen Botschaften in Budapest, Prag und Warschau', *Zeitschrift für Ostmitteleuropa-Forschung* 64(1) (2015), 40–80.
76. P. Villaume and O. Bange (eds), *The Long Détente: Changing Concepts of Security and Cooperation in Europe from the 1940s to the 1980s* (Budapest: Central European University Press, 2016).

Bibliography

Altrichter, H., and H. Wentker (eds). *Der KSZE-Prozess: Vom Kalten Krieg zu einem neuen Europa 1975 bis 1990*. Munich: Oldenbourg, 2011.

Bange, O., and G. Niedhart (eds). *Helsinki 1975 and the Transformation of Europe*. New York: Berghahn Books, 2008.

Bárányi, T., M. Graf, M. Krajczár and I. Lehner. 'A Masterpiece of European Détente? Austrian–Hungarian Relations from 1964 until the Peaceful End of the Cold War'. *Zeitgeschichte* 41(5) (2014), 311–38.

Bauer, F., and E. Seewald. *Bruno Kreisky in Ost-Berlin: Ein Besuch der besonderen Art*. Innsbruck: Studienverlag, 2011.

Bilandžić, V., D. Dahlmann and M. Kosanović (eds). *From Helsinki to Belgrade: The First CSCE Follow-up Meeting and the Crisis of Détente*. Göttingen: V&R unipress, 2012.

Borodziej, W. *Geschichte Polens im 20. Jahrhundert*. Munich: C.H. Beck, 2010.

Brown, A. *The Gorbachev Factor*. Oxford: Oxford University Press, 1996.

Dalos, G. *Der Vorhang geht auf: Das Ende der Diktaturen in Osteuropa*. Munich: C.H. Beck, 2009.

Enderle-Burcel, G., et al. (eds). *Gaps in the Iron Curtain: Economic Relations between Neutral and Socialist Countries in Cold War Europe*. Cracow: Jagiellonian University Press, 2009.

Fischer, T. 'Austria and the Helsinki Process', in A. Suppan and W. Mueller (eds), *Peaceful Coexistence or Iron Curtain? Austria, Neutrality, and Eastern Europe in the Cold War and Détente, 1955–1989* (Vienna: Lit, 2009), 168–202.

Fischer, T. 'Bridging the Gap between East and West: The N+N as Catalysts of the CSCE Process, 1972–1983', in P. Villaume and O. Westad (eds), *Perforating the Iron Curtain: European Détente, Transatlantic Relations and the Cold War, 1965–1985* (Copenhagen: Museum Tusculanum Press, 2010), 143–78.

Fischer, T. *Keeping the Process Alive: The N+N and the CSCE Follow-up from Helsinki to Vienna (1975–1986)* (Züricher Beiträge zur Sicherheitspolitik Nr. 84). Zurich: Center for Security Studies (CSS), ETH Zürich, 2012.

Fischer, T. 'A Mustard Seed Grew into a Bushy Tree: The Finnish CSCE-Initiative of 5 May 1969'. *Cold War History* 9 (2009), 177–201.

Fischer, T. *Neutral Power in the CSCE: The N+N States and the Making of the Helsinki Accords 1975*. Baden-Baden: Nomos, 2009.

Fischer, T. 'Österreich und die finnische KSZE-Initiative vom 5. Mai 1969', in W. Mueller and M. Portmann (eds), *Osteuropa vom Weltkrieg bis zur Wende* (Vienna: ÖAW, 2007), 313–39.

Gilde, B. '"Kein Vorreiter": Österreich und die humanitäre Dimension der KSZE 1969–1973', in H. Altrichter and H. Wentker (eds), *Der KSZE-Prozess: Vom Kalten Krieg zu einem neuen Europa 1975 bis 1990* (Munich: Oldenbourg, 2011), 41–50.

Gilde, B. *Österreich im KSZE-Prozess 1969–1983: Neutraler Vermittler in humanitärer Mission*. Munich: Oldenbourg, 2013.

Graf, M. 'Kreisky und Polen: Schlaglichter auf einen vernachlässigten Aspekt der österreichischen "Ostpolitik"', in L. Dreidemy et al. (eds), *Bananen, Cola, Zeitgeschichte: Oliver Rathkolb und das lange 20. Jahrhundert*, 2 vols (Vienna: Böhlau, 2015), 692–706.

Graf, M. 'Ein Musterbeispiel der europäischen Entspannung? Die österreichisch–ungarischen Beziehungen von 1964 bis 1989', in C. Szabó (ed.), *Österreich und Ungarn im 20. Jahrhundert* (Vienna: Collegium Hungaricum, 2014), 261–80.

Graf, M. *Österreich und die DDR 1949–1990: Politik und Wirtschaft im Schatten der deutschen Teilung*. Vienna: ÖAW, 2016.

Graf, M. 'Die Welt blickt auf das Burgenland. 1989 – die Grenze wird zum Abbild der Veränderung', in M. Graf, A. Lass and K. Ruzicic-Kessler (eds), *Das Burgenland als internationale Grenzregion im 20. und 21. Jahrhundert* (Vienna: Neue Welt Verlag, 2012), 135–79.

Graf, M., and P. Ruggenthaler. 'Polnisch-österreichische Beziehungen im Kalten Krieg', in A. Kisztelińska-Węgrzyńska (ed.), *Austria w polskim dyskursie publicznym po 1945 roku: Österreich im polnischen Diskurs nach 1945* (Cracow: Universitas, 2016), 25–60.

Hanisch, A. *Die DDR im KSZE-Prozess 1972–1985: Zwischen Ostabhängigkeit, Westabgrenzung und Ausreisebewegung.* Munich: Oldenbourg, 2012.

Karner, S., and P. Ruggenthaler. 'Austria and the End of the Prague Spring: Neutrality in the Crucible?', in G. Bischof, S. Karner and P. Ruggenthaler (eds), *The Prague Spring and the Warsaw Pact Invasion of Czechoslovakia in 1968* (Lanham, MD: Lexington Books, 2010), 419–39.

Kieninger, S. *Dynamic Détente: The United States and Europe 1964–1975.* Lanham, MD: Lexington Books, 2016.

Klambauer, O. *Der Kalte Krieg in Österreich: Vom Dritten Mann zum Fall des Eisernen Vorhangs.* Vienna: Ueberreuter, 2000.

Kunštát, M. 'Die Tschechoslowakei und Österreich vor dem Umbruch 1989/90', in A. Brait and M. Gehler (eds), *Grenzöffnung 1989: Innen- und Außenperspektiven und die Folgen für Österreich* (Vienna: Böhlau, 2014), 367–84.

Lehne, S. *The Vienna Meeting of the Conference on Security and Cooperation in Europe, 1986–1989: A Turning Point in East-West Relations.* Boulder, CO: Westview Press, 1991.

Mlynar, Z. 'Die österreichisch-ungarischen Beziehungen als Sonderfall der Ost-West-Beziehungen', in Z. Mlynar et al. (eds), *Die Beziehungen zwischen Österreich und Ungarn: Sonderfall oder Modell?* (Vienna: Wilhelm Braumüller, 1985), 145–62.

Mueller, W. *A Good Example of Peaceful Coexistence? The Soviet Union, Austria, and Neutrality, 1955–1991.* Vienna: ÖAW, 2011.

Mueller, W. 'The Revolutions of 1989: An Introduction', in W. Mueller, M. Gehler and A. Suppan (eds), *The Revolutions of 1989: A Handbook* (Vienna: ÖAW, 2015), 3–30.

Oplatka, A. *Der erste Riß in der Mauer: September 1989 – Ungarn öffnet die Grenze.* Vienna: Zsolnay, 2009.

Peter, M., and H. Wentker (eds). *Die KSZE im Ost-West-Konflikt: Internationale Politik und gesellschaftliche Transformation 1975–1990.* Munich: Oldenbourg, 2012.

Pogány, A. 'Co-operation through the Iron Curtain: Economic Relations between Austria and Hungary after the Second World War', in G. Enderle-Burcel et al. (eds), *Gaps in the Iron Curtain: Economic Relations between Neutral and Socialist Countries in Cold War Europe* (Cracow: Jagiellonian University Press, 2009), 142–62.

Rathkolb, O. 'Austria: An Ambivalent Attitude of Trade Unions and Political Parties', in I. Goddeeris (ed.), *Solidarity with Solidarity: Western European Trade Unions and the Polish Crisis, 1980–1982* (Lanham, MD: Lexington Books, 2010), 269–88.

Resch, A. 'Der österreichische Osthandel im Spannungsfeld der Blöcke', in M. Rauchensteiner (ed.), *Zwischen den Blöcken: NATO, Warschauer Pakt und Österreich* (Vienna: Böhlau, 2010), 497–556.

Röhrlich, E. *Kreiskys Außenpolitik: Zwischen österreichischer Identität und internationalem Programm* (Zeitgeschichte im Kontext 2). Göttingen: V&R unipress, 2009.

Romano, A. *From Détente in Europe to European Détente: How the West Shaped the Helsinki CSCE*. Brussels: Peter Lang, 2009.

Schneider, R. *Leben in Wien*. Munich: Hanser, 1994.

Schriffl, D. 'Der "Prager Frühling" 1968 und die österreichisch-slowakischen Beziehungen', in W. Mueller and M. Portmann (eds), *Osteuropa vom Weltkrieg bis zur Wende* (Vienna: ÖAW, 2007), 299–311.

Seewald, E. 'Die Aufnahme der diplomatischen Beziehungen zwischen der DDR und Österreich', in J. Staadt (ed.), *Schwierige Dreierbeziehung: Österreich und die beiden deutschen Staaten* (Studien des Forschungsverbundes SED-Staat an der Freien Universität Berlin) (Frankfurt: Peter Lang, 2013), 81–135.

Snyder, S. *Human Rights Activism and the End of the Cold War: A Transnational History of the Helsinki Network*. New York: Cambridge University Press, 2011.

Steininger, R. *Der Staatsvertrag: Österreich im Schatten von deutscher Frage und Kaltem Krieg 1938–1955*. Innsbruck: Studienverlag, 2005.

Stokłosa, K. 'Die letzte Fluchtwelle aus der DDR im Jahr 1989: Aus den Berichten der westdeutschen Botschaften in Budapest, Prag und Warschau'. *Zeitschrift für Ostmitteleuropa-Forschung* 64(1) (2015), 40–80.

Stourzh, G. *Um Einheit und Freiheit: Staatsvertrag, Neutralität und das Ende der Ost-West-Besetzung Österreichs 1945–1955*. Vienna: Böhlau, 2005.

Suppan, A. *Missgünstige Nachbarn: Geschichte und Perspektiven der nachbarschaftlichen Beziehungen zwischen Tschechien und Österreich*. Vienna: Club Niederösterreich, 2005.

Suppan, A., G. Stourzh and W. Mueller (eds). *Der österreichische Staatsvertrag: Internationale Strategie, rechtliche Relevanz, nationale Identität*. Vienna: ÖAW, 2005.

Suppan, A., and W. Mueller (eds). *Peaceful Coexistence or Iron Curtain? Austria, Neutrality, and Eastern Europe in the Cold War and Détente, 1955–1989*. Vienna: Lit, 2009.

Süß, W. 'Die Wiener KSZE-Folgekonferenz und der Handlungsspielraum des DDR-Sicherheitsapparates 1989', in M. Peter and H. Wentker (eds), *Die KSZE im Ost-West-Konflikt: Internationale Politik und gesellschaftliche Transformation 1975–1990* (Munich: Oldenbourg, 2012), 219–31.

Thomas, D.C. *The Helsinki Effect: International Norms, Human Rights, and the Demise of Communism*. Princeton, NJ: Princeton University Press, 2001.

Ullmann, P. *Eine schwierige Nachbarschaft: Die Geschichte der diplomatischen Beziehungen zwischen Österreich und der Tschechoslowakei 1945–1968*. Vienna: Lit, 2006.

Villaume, P., and O. Bange (eds). *The Long Détente: Changing Concepts of Security and Cooperation in Europe from the 1940s to the 1980s*. Budapest: Central European University Press, 2016.

# 11

Saving Détente
The Federal Republic of Germany and the CSCE in the 1980s

Matthias Peter

Despite the signing of the Helsinki Final Act on 1 August 1975, the 1980s saw a sharp increase in East–West tensions. The North Atlantic Treaty Organization's dual-track decision (12 December 1979), Soviet military intervention in Afghanistan (24 December 1979) and martial law in Poland (13 December 1981) deteriorated superpower relations and threatened Western unity. This situation challenged West German foreign policy, which was firmly rooted in the Harmel Doctrine's twin strategy of military defence and dialogue with the East. Bonn's policy of détente was based firstly on the bilateral treaties with Moscow (1970), Warsaw (1970), East Berlin (1972) and Czechoslovakia (1973) (*Ostverträge*) and secondly on the implementation of the final document of the Conference on Security and Cooperation (CSCE). As a divided nation at the front line of the Cold War, the Federal Republic's *Ostpolitik* – its policy of easing the consequences of and ultimately overcoming the division of Europe – depended on keeping the lines of communication between East and West open. Subsequently, Bonn made every effort to keep détente alive using the CSCE process as the most important forum to stabilize East–West relations.

As recent research has shown, détente significantly increased the Western alliance's flexibility in dealing with the Warsaw Pact and from the late 1960s onwards strengthened the political clout of the European Community, laying the ground for a 'European détente'.[1] Scholars are still divided, however, as to how exactly détente and *Ostpolitik* contributed to the end of the Cold War.[2] This chapter will demonstrate that the CSCE in particular was a complex process of multilateral conference diplomacy, only gradually unfolding its dynamics on the state as well as the societal level.³ It will explore the various CSCE follow-up conferences and expert meetings in the 1980s as an indispensable multilateral stage for West Germany's policy of détente. In the preparatory phase of the CSCE the coalition government, which the Social Democratic Party (SPD) and the Free Democratic Party (FDP) had formed in 1969, had used Moscow's interest in a conference on European security to pursue a policy of 'linkage' to push through the *Ostverträge* and the Four Power Agreement on Berlin, making sure to keep the German question open.⁴ Immediately after the Helsinki summit in 1975, Bonn began to use the final document as a point of reference to settle issues of national interest in consultations with the Warsaw Pact countries, for example family reunification, immigration and human contacts. Starting with the Madrid follow-up meeting (1980–83), however, the CSCE became an ever more important tool for the Federal government to rebalance the lopsided discussion on arms control by stressing the significance of the CSCE process with a view towards countering Soviet propaganda, restoring the credibility of the West's commitment to mutual disarmament and fighting domestic opposition against the deployment of US nuclear missiles in the Federal Republic. The chapter will also demonstrate that the experience of the Madrid conference and the subsequent expert meetings, especially the Stockholm Conference on Confidence- and Security-Building Measures and Disarmament in Europe (1984–86), convinced West Germany's minister of foreign affairs, Hans-Dietrich Genscher, that the CSCE had the potential for societal change in Eastern Europe and could provide a blueprint for a new European peace order.

The Federal Republic and the CSCE after Helsinki (1975–80)

The Helsinki summit in 1975, rather than being the climax of East–West détente, marked the beginning of the CSCE process proper as the Final Act's much underrated Basket Four provided for a conference reviewing the implementation of the obligations signed by the thirty-five heads of state. Expectations as to their implementation were low and many contemporaries expected that diplomatic routine would now set in again. In the Federal Foreign Office (Auswärtiges Amt), too, there was widespread insecurity as to how the many recommendations could be implemented. It quickly emerged that the Warsaw Pact countries in particular were in no rush to adopt the Helsinki norms. The Kremlin was busy trying to keep the potential consequences of the Accords under control and resumed the persecution of dissidents with renewed force as numerous monitoring groups were set up in the USSR as well as in the West.[5] Similarly, Moscow ignored the confidence-building measures (CBM) agreed on in Helsinki, refraining in 1975 and 1976 from announcing Warsaw Pact manoeuvres and from inviting military observers as it should have.[6]

The rather bumpy beginning was a foretaste of what was to come at the first follow-up meeting, which began in October 1977 in Belgrade. The conference saw a shift of emphasis in the CSCE process. While the US had hitherto been only a reticent CSCE supporter, President Jimmy Carter took a special interest in the Final Act's human rights principle. This not only led to a clash with the Soviet delegation but also led to tensions with Washington's European allies.[7] Bonn was concerned that narrowing the CSCE to the human rights principle would be to the detriment of measures from Basket Three as the Federal government felt responsible for the millions of Germans in the GDR and ethnic Germans living under communist rule. West German diplomats, therefore, maintained that human rights could not be reduced to prominent victims but should aim at the 'greatest happiness of the greatest number'.[8]

Moscow, on the other hand, had no intention either of being rushed into implementing the Helsinki obligations or of being put in the dock by the West for its human rights abuses. Soviet leader Leonid Brezhnev had signed the Final Act believing that he had at long last secured Soviet hegemony over Eastern Europe.[9] His interest in an agreement at Belgrade, therefore, was muted at best. With the Soviet attitude hardening and Washington being content having criticized Moscow's human rights record, the West German delegation worked to prevent a breakdown of the conference. In the end, with the help of the Neutral and Non-Aligned Countries (NNA), delegations approved a meagre text in which the participating states concurred that a number of expert meetings should take place to be followed by a second review meeting to be convened at Madrid in 1980. Although disappointed, the FRG did not consider Belgrade a failure but proof that the CSCE process would only reap benefits for the West in the long term. After all, despite heavy criticism, the East did not break off negotiations, thus proving that it was principally interested in continuing the CSCE. This was something the West could take advantage of in the future if the CSCE process could be enriched with something in which Moscow had a particular interest.[10]

Between 1978 and 1980, East–West relations rapidly deteriorated. Superpower negotiations on SALT II stalled. Moscow, meanwhile, started modernizing its arsenal of nuclear missiles. Chancellor Helmut Schmidt pointed out that Soviet long-range theatre nuclear forces (SS-20) opened up a gap in the West's nuclear defences. France, although not part of NATO's integrated defences, became more active in the field of disarmament, too. In spring 1978, the French government suggested a Conference on Disarmament in Europe (CDE) covering the area 'from the Atlantic to the Urals'.[11] At this point Hans-Dietrich Genscher was increasingly concerned that the domination of disarmament issues in East–West relations would 'dry up' the substance of and marginalize the CSCE process. The Federal Foreign Office, therefore, which now was the key player formulating Bonn's CSCE policy, worked towards upgrading the next review meeting in Madrid by, firstly, lifting its political status to the level of foreign ministers. Secondly, the Federal government put special emphasis on the three expert meetings on the peaceful settlement of disputes, on security in the Mediterranean and on scientific cooperation taking place between 1978 and 1980.[12] Often neglected by contemporaries and historians alike, these meetings were of particular importance for West Germany at a time in which East–West communication appeared to be dominated by military issues, working as bridges between the Review Conferences. Thirdly, Bonn viewed the French CDE proposal as an important lever to advance the CSCE process. The Federal government supported Paris unreservedly yet insisted that a CDE should not be independent of the CSCE but rather should be convened under the roof of the CSCE. The CDE should in its first stage be restricted to military confidence-building and officially be introduced to the Madrid meeting. This strategy would substantially enrich the CSCE process and provide NATO with a welcome 'carrot' for a future trade-off with Moscow, which had been interested in a disarmament conference for some time. When, in December 1979, NATO took its dual-track decision, it also approved a new MBFR (Mutual and Balanced Force Reductions) initiative and declared its support for a CSCE conference dedicated to CBMs and, at a later stage, conventional disarmament. With decisive help from Bonn, the alliance, for the first time, had approved a balanced strategy, which combined nuclear and conventional disarmament with the CSCE process.[13]

The Madrid Experience (1980–83)

This concept of striking a balance between issues of military security and progress in the humanitarian field also determined Bonn's strategy at the second CSCE review meeting, which opened on 11 November 1980. The meeting was different in nearly every respect from its predecessor in Belgrade. For the first time a large number of human rights groups, although not allowed to take part in the proceedings, lobbied delegations in front of and in the conference building, underlining that five years after Helsinki, non-governmental organizations (NGOs) had become an important player in the CSCE process. But most importantly, tensions between East and West had come to a head and cast a dangerous shadow over the meeting. NATO's dual-track decision in December 1979 and Soviet intervention in Afghanistan a few days later ushered in a new phase of the Cold War. Furthermore, Ronald Reagan, who took office in January 1981, had always been critical of US involvement in the CSCE process and remained sceptical concerning the Madrid meeting.[14] This development forced the FRG to embark on a risky diplomatic course, constantly shifting between loyalty to its allies and saving détente, the prerequisite of which was keeping the lines of communication with the Warsaw Pact open.[15] The renewed crisis, the Auswärtiges Amt concluded, made it all the more imperative to keep the CSCE process alive. The communist states, Bonn's diplomats kept reminding the allies, must not be relieved of the commitments they had agreed to in Helsinki.

But Bonn's strategy, indeed the whole CSCE process, was suddenly called into question when on 13 December 1981, following months of unrest in Poland, General Wojciech Jaruzelski put Poland under martial law. This decision constituted a flagrant violation of the Helsinki Final Act and increased the likelihood of a military intervention by Moscow and its allies, threatening the sovereignty of a CSCE participating state. But while the Reagan administration pressed for sanctions against Poland and the USSR, West Germany, France and Great Britain hesitated to support Washington's course.[16] The CSCE process had now reached its most dangerous moment yet. Bonn, therefore, was of the opinion that Warsaw and Moscow had to be openly criticized in Madrid but that the review meeting had to be continued. West German diplomats pointed out that the CSCE process worked as an 'umbrella' protecting, on a state-to-state level, the Polish opposition movement.[17] The Soviets, Genscher told the allies, would not dare to intervene militarily as long as they were tied to the CSCE conference table. At the same time, he repeatedly reminded Warsaw Pact governments of what they had signed in Helsinki: to refrain from the use of force and to respect the sovereignty of the CSCE countries. To many of Bonn's partners, however, this attitude appeared too optimistic if not outright naive, and Genscher subsequently faced heavy criticism domestically and internationally as well as from the independent labour union Solidarność (Solidarity).[18]

To be sure, there were also domestic reasons for Bonn to insist that the Madrid meeting be continued by any means. In the FRG the deployment of US theatre nuclear forces (TNF) met with stiff resistance from the West German peace movement, which doubted the will of NATO to engage in serious disarmament talks. Appearing reticent in Madrid, Bonn maintained, would play into the Kremlin's hands. Moscow could take advantage of the situation and style itself as an advocate of peace. Chancellor Helmut Kohl, who succeeded Schmidt in November 1982, assured Washington that his country, as a loyal member of the alliance, would make every effort to enforce the dual-track decision. But he also expected a 'peace dividend' in return, in Madrid and elsewhere. The Federal government, he wrote to Reagan, had promised in parliament to work hard for results in all ongoing disarmament talks.[19] The Chancellor and Genscher insisted that they viewed agreement on a CDE as a key element of their efforts to cushion the deployment of American TNF missiles for an increasingly hostile public, counter Soviet propaganda and keep the credibility of détente intact. In Madrid, therefore, the FRG delegation strived for a substantive concluding document.

Four weeks before delegates resumed negotiations in Madrid in November 1982, the Polish government had prohibited Solidarność, casting an even darker shadow over the review meeting. Subsequently, Washington pressed for more Soviet concessions, even at the cost of a concluding document. In spring 1983, to everybody's surprise, the Soviet delegation appeared to negotiate more constructively. From Moscow's point of view, time was running out as the deployment of Pershing II and cruise missiles was set to begin by the end of the year. Moscow, therefore, felt under pressure to reach an agreement in Madrid on a CDE, which could be used to influence the West German peace movement. Moscow was also prepared to accept the draft concluding document the Neutrals had tabled on 15 March 1983 in return for Western consent for a CDE. Bonn, too, thought that the text was a considerable improvement on previous drafts. In particular it included a date for the beginning of the CDE (15 November), just in time for the scheduled start of the deployment of US missiles in West Germany.[20]

When Kohl and Genscher travelled to Washington in mid April 1983, they used their trip to campaign for a successful conclusion of the review meeting. The Chancellor assured Reagan yet again that, despite heavy domestic pressure, he stood by the decision to deploy Pershing II and cruise missiles but in return expected the US's consent for a CSCE concluding document.[21] Back in Bonn, the Federal Foreign Office instructed the embassy in Washington to lobby state officials and Congress alike. Genscher, meanwhile, in bilateral talks as well as letters, tried to convince Warsaw Pact governments not to reject Western demands for text revisions out of hand. The US government, however, remained adamant and demanded that Moscow be more forthcoming concerning the release of dissidents before it would agree to a concluding document.

At the beginning of July, Genscher invited US head of delegation Max Kampelman, who was on his way to Washington to receive further instructions, to his private house in Bonn. He told the American diplomat that, at this stage of the conference, the West should not appear to block an agreement. He also promised that he would try to convince Soviet Foreign Minister Andrei Gromyko on his forthcoming visit to Moscow to be more flexible concerning Washington's list of human rights cases.[22] A few days later, Genscher flew to Washington to inform Reagan and Secretary of State George Shultz of his talks with the Soviet government. Washington, he warned, should not act as the 'conference killer'.[23] He also warned them not to underestimate the effect the CSCE had begun to show on communist societies.[24] In the Spanish capital, meanwhile, Kampelman received Soviet diplomat Sergei Kondrashev's promise that Moscow would favourably consider further human rights cases. With the last obstacle removed, delegates (with the exception of Malta) on 15 July approved the concluding document.[25]

The successful conclusion of the follow-up meeting was also due to the USSR's overriding interest in a CDE. In return, Moscow agreed to include its European territory in the area of control. Furthermore, in the humanitarian field the Kremlin conceded further obligations and consented to expert meetings on human rights and on human contacts as well as on cultural cooperation. In order to reach an agreement about the disarmament conference, Moscow was even prepared to ignore the misgivings of its allies, most prominently voiced by Erich Honecker who had to deal with a growing movement of people wanting to leave the GDR.[26] Lastly, a third review meeting was scheduled to begin in Vienna in November 1986. Thus, the CSCE's system of diplomatic conferences was substantially enlarged and its scope enriched.

For Foreign Minister Hans-Dietrich Genscher, too, Madrid proved to be a turning point. The meeting, he told Reagan and Vice-President George W. Bush in 1982, had opened a 'window', through which 'fresh air' would blow towards Eastern Europe. Madrid had 'stimulated the will of the people in favour of self-determination and against oppression' and was proof that the CSCE 'had developed into a dynamic and powerful process'.[27] He explained his strategy even more directly in a personal letter of 20 December 1983 to his former State Secretary Berndt von Staden:

> The Soviets know exactly, and have officially taken note, that our political goal is directed towards changing conditions in Europe. Given their mistrust, they will insinuate methods we don't even think of. I believe

that it serves confidence-building if we say openly how we imagine this change: no secret Trojan horses, no crusaders assaulting the castle walls, no other unfriendly means, but the CSCE process, which makes them aware that advancement and change is necessary and which gives them the opportunity to participate.[28]

To Genscher, Madrid was also proof that the CSCE could be the nucleus of a European peace order. Two months after the review meeting, on 2 November 1983, in a speech at Helsinki, he sketched five elements of a peace order based on the Helsinki Final Act: first, an extended declaration on the non-use of force, which should apply not only between states but in domestic policies as well; second, a continuous dialogue between the CSCE countries, especially between East and West, 'even at times of rising tensions'; third, the full implementation of the Basket Two provisions on economic cooperation; fourth, the recognition of the 'rule of law', in particular human rights and the principle of self-determination; fifth, the 'common ground of European culture'.[29] In his opinion, the CSCE's system of conference diplomacy could provide both the framework and the driving force for the 'desirable and necessary changes in Eastern Europe'.[30]

Stockholm and the Expert Meetings at Ottawa, Budapest and Bern

By the mid 1980s and with the CSCE process unfolding, Genscher's policy of 'realistic détente' had become more assertive and more independent of the concept of détente as practised by the rival SPD. This was made clear by Wolfgang Schollwer, a long-time member of Genscher's FDP and the Policy Planning Staff of the Federal Foreign Office, who at the end of 1985 aptly wrote that the *Ostverträge* and the Helsinki Final Act did not mark the end of the East–West conflict but instead put it on a basis that ruled out military conflict. Unlike the Social Democrats, who in 1985 had started talks with the GDR's Socialist Unity Party (SED) on security policy,[31] he maintained that Bonn's policy did not aim at 'change through rapprochement', as Egon Bahr had put it in the 1960s, since the Federal Republic had no reason to 'converge' with the East in the first place. Rather, its policy should strive towards 'change through influence (CSCE)'.[32] The ideological conflict, he thought, ought not to be blurred and the CSCE process be used to induce change in Eastern Europe without compromising the West's security interests.

Against that backdrop it is clear that Bonn viewed the densely scheduled set of forthcoming CSCE conferences as important steps on the way to the third follow-up meeting in Vienna. At the top of the list of priorities was the conference on Confidence- and Security Building Measures and Disarmament (CSBM) which began in January 1984. Stockholm was considered indispensable for West Germany's strategy to balance military security and disarmament negotiations in the context of NATO's dual-track decision. As ambassador Friedrich Ruth, the head of the armaments control and disarmament department of the Auswärtiges Amt, wrote, the CSBM conference marked the beginning of a new phase of the CSCE and should be used to test the Warsaw Pact's 'future policy towards the West'. However, a Soviet-style pan-European security conference had to be avoided, and every care had to be taken to keep the balance of all baskets.[33]

Accordingly, Bonn worked closely with the allies to prepare a set of substantive, obligatory and verifiable confidence-building measures. NATO's proposal filed in January 1984 contained six measures ranging from the exchange of military information and the prior notification of military activities to measures of verification such as on-site inspections and observations on the ground and from the air.[34] But it soon emerged that the West's and the East's goals at Stockholm were far from compatible. While NATO aimed towards more military transparency, the Kremlin stuck to its strategy of 'military détente' and advocated an agreement on the non-use of force. The West, in turn, refused to notify sea and air activities independent of mainland activities demanded by Moscow in return for the inclusion of Soviet territory in a CBM regime. Bonn was not averse to considering some text or other on the non-use of force as this could be a useful 'carrot' in a trade-off with Moscow. The draft text the Soviets filed on 29 January 1985, however, was considered a propaganda instrument.[35]

By the end of 1985, neither side seemed willing to make concessions.[36] With the Stockholm meeting slowly grinding to a halt, all eyes were set on the three expert meetings scheduled for 1985/86. The West German government considered the meetings on human rights in Ottawa (7 May to 17 June 1985), on cultural cooperation in Budapest (15 October to 25 November 1985) and on human contacts in Bern (15 April to 26 May 1986) as far from being of only minor interest. Hopes in Bonn were high that the two human rights meetings would come up with further obligations concerning freedom of movement as the numbers of ethnic Germans who were allowed to leave the Soviet Union had been declining for some years. Furthermore, the meetings came at a time when, in January 1985, Secretary of State George P. Shultz and Soviet Foreign Minister Gromyko agreed to resume the disarmament talks at Geneva, which Moscow had ended in November 1983 when the first US nuclear missiles had arrived in West Germany. The FRG also hoped that a successful outcome of the expert meetings would boost the CSBM conference in Stockholm.

Ambassador Ekkehard Eickhoff, the head of the West German delegation, arrived in Canada with three proposals which his government wanted to table. Firstly, all participating states should reaffirm the right of the individual to know and act upon his or her rights as embodied in the Helsinki Final Act. They should, therefore, agree to re-publish the Final Act and the concluding document from Madrid and make them permanently available. Secondly, all CSCE states should reaffirm their determination to give full effect to their human rights obligations. Thirdly, they should recognize the right of the individual to travel, including the right to leave or re-enter their home country.[37]

As was customary, in the first half of the meeting, delegates took stock of the implementation of the human rights obligations. Richard Schifter, the US head of delegation, repeatedly addressed human rights violations in the USSR, including high-profile cases ranging from Andrei Sakharov and Anatoly Shcharanksy to Yuri Orlov. He demanded the right to religious freedom and criticized Moscow's practice of psychological confinement. The Soviets, on the other hand, accused Washington of racism, high unemployment rates and the suppression of women but surprisingly also took up the subject of Jewish emigration.[38] Eickhoff in his statements called for the GDR and the USSR to abide by the set of Helsinki norms but did not mention particular cases. He addressed the problem that many families were still separated by the Iron Curtain and cultural ties of ethnic minorities severed. On 16 May, again without naming particular countries, he intervened on behalf of the Helsinki monitors still being persecuted for invoking the Helsinki human rights norms.[39]

The second stage of the meeting began on 29 May and within a few days the delegations in quick succession filed forty-six new proposals. However, it soon became clear that the Soviet Union had no interest in drafting a conference report containing numerous recommendations on human rights. Instead, Moscow's diplomats insisted that a set of economic and social rights be included.[40] The US was not keen either on a consensus document that did not fully reflect Washington's human rights goals and was content that the meeting had been used to put pressure on the Soviets to comply with the human rights norms agreed upon in Helsinki.[41] As a result, on 12 June the Warsaw Pact countries tabled a draft report of their own, which was followed by a NATO draft the following day. A last-minute compromise by the Neutral and

Non-Aligned Countries calling simply for another expert meeting was finally rejected by the Warsaw Pact.[42]

To be sure, the FRG would have preferred an agreement enlarging the human rights obligations. Far from being disappointed, however, Bonn came to a positive conclusion and warned that the Ottawa meeting should not publicly be judged a failure.[43] Diplomats pointed out that at least the West had continued its human rights dialogue with the East. Most importantly, a number of proposals had been tabled which, although not formalized in a concluding document, could be taken up again at the next review meeting. Ottawa also showed that a rift had begun to open up within the Warsaw Pact when Hungary spoke up in favour of protecting the rights of minorities, thereby implicitly criticizing Romania's and Bulgaria's handling of ethnic Hungarian and Turkish minorities. Similarly, discussion on religious freedom showed very different approaches by communist governments, ranging from relative tolerance (Poland) to outright persecution (Czechoslovakia).[44] Lastly, Ottawa marked the first occasion on which the USSR was prepared to discuss the subject of human rights openly. In future, the East would no longer be in a position to brush off any critique as interference in domestic affairs.[45] Given this balance sheet, Bonn pointed out to its allies that the inconclusive expert meeting should not influence NATO's strategy for the CSBM conference and should not raise barriers for an agreement in Stockholm.[46]

The Culture Forum in Budapest (15 October to 25 November 1985) had the task of improving the conditions of creating and disseminating works of art in CSCE-participating states and promoting cultural cooperation in general. At first glance, the meeting's subject did not carry the same weight as the human rights meeting in Ottawa. The FRG, however, had always maintained that each CSCE basket was indispensable to the CSCE's fabric. Therefore, it recognized the meeting's importance as a forum dedicated to an integral part of the Helsinki Final Act. In the run-up to the meeting, Hans-Dietrich Genscher told other foreign ministers from allied countries as well as from the Warsaw Pact that the forum played an important part in boosting the CSCE process as a whole. He also hoped that success at Budapest could foster the cultural identity of Europe to stabilize a future European peace order, a point that had already featured prominently in his speech in Helsinki in 1983.[47] Germany as a divided nation also harboured a special interest in cultural relations since it shared a common cultural ground with its neighbours in East and South Eastern Europe. After all, as Karl-Günther von Hase, the retired former ambassador in London who headed the West German delegation, pointed out in his opening speech, the German language was the only language spoken by millions in countries on both sides of the Iron Curtain.[48] In order to underline the importance of the forum, the FRG integrated a large number of prominent cultural figures in its delegation. Non-diplomatic representatives from cultural organizations as well as eminent writers like Günter Grass dominated the conference scene just as much as diplomats. Bonn's diplomats supported their projects and had three proposals of their own: the right to open cultural institutes, the annual proclamation of a 'cultural capital of Europe' and the idea of opening three 'European Cultural Institutes' in Amsterdam, Budapest and Vienna.[49]

It quickly became clear that the Soviet Union was promoting its very own understanding of 'culture', emphasizing the artist's prime responsibility to advocate 'peace' and 'disarmament'. From early on, therefore, the irreconcilable notions in East and West of what constituted 'culture' proved a crucial stumbling block for the working groups editing the recommendations. On the other hand, German diplomats did not fail to notice that some smaller Warsaw Pact countries displayed signs of cultural independence from Moscow. Delegates from Czechoslovakia and Hungary occasionally delivered their statements in German as if to prove von Hase's remarks in the opening session.[50] This contrasted sharply with the reticence displayed by some Western delegations, which, as von Hase reported back to Bonn, for political as well as financial reasons had no specific interest in deepening their cultural relations with the communist countries. For the US, Great Britain and the Netherlands, von Hase complained, the forum was more important as an opportunity to criticize the lack of artistic freedom in the Warsaw Pact countries.[51] In the NATO caucus on 30 October, he reminded his colleagues that a concluding document was in the West's interest since the Culture Forum had been their idea in the first place and ought to signal to the public that the CSCE process was progressing.[52]

By mid November, almost seventy official proposals had been submitted, two-thirds by the Warsaw Pact countries. In addition, more than 250 proposals by artists had been filed informally by the Secretariat. As for a final text, NATO countries again were of different opinions as to its general importance. While some pointed out that the forum had served its purpose by bringing together people from the art world across the East–West divide, the FRG still favoured a concluding document and insisted that at any rate the proposals should be saved for Vienna. West German diplomats were under pressure from the artists in their delegation to save as many of their projects as possible. They were also under the impression that Moscow was inclined to adopt a final text and that therefore a greater effort should be made by the West to press for more concessions during the meeting's 'end game'.[53]

On 16 November, the European Political Cooperation (EPC) and NATO caucuses approved a non-paper to be handed to the NNA group containing their main demands. It was strongly influenced by the US delegation, which had insisted that the paper emphasized human and cultural rights. As von Hase noted, Washington preferred a text that was presentable to the American public rather than a 'watered down' consensus with the East. Bonn, on the other hand, remained interested in a document that described the forum's proceedings and the principles of cultural cooperation, followed by a set of recommendations approved by all thirty-five participating states; more projects could be listed in an annex. The situation was further complicated by the fact that the NNA countries were far from unanimous themselves and could not play their usual role as intermediaries. The Swiss delegation especially pressed for an NNA draft which would come out strongly in favour of a text calling for more cultural freedom and cooperation.[54] After further discussion, however, the NNA on 20 November tabled an informal draft, which contained passages on human as well as cultural rights but said nothing about the state of cultural freedoms in Eastern Europe. As von Hase noted, it also lacked a call for common actions and did not mention West Germany's proposals for cultural centres and for the annual proclamation of cultural capitals of Europe.[55] The Warsaw Pact countries quickly submitted a number of amendments to redress what they perceived as a bias towards NATO's position. The NATO countries, too, asked for amendments. In particular, they wanted the role in cultural life played by individuals and NGOs to be addressed more prominently. When the NNA draft was discussed on 24 November, the Warsaw Pact delegations insisted that their amendments be included in the final draft and reference be made to the societal role of artists. This, of course, was unacceptable to the West as well as the NNA countries. With the latter's informal draft effectively buried and time running out, Luxemburg for the NATO countries and Bulgaria for the Warsaw Pact countries officially submitted draft documents 'for the record'. On 25 November at 4:00 a.m., the latter broke off the negotiations. A subsequent effort by Hungary to adopt a text merely recommending that the Vienna meeting be informed of the proposals was rejected by Romania.[56]

Again, the West German Foreign Office did not publicly consider the forum a failure.[57] Diplomats pointed out that Budapest had provided a forum for direct contacts of the art world across the East–West divide. They also agreed that the communist understanding of 'culture' had been effectively challenged and that the proposals tabled by the West could be saved for the Vienna follow-up meeting. However, unlike with Ottawa, the Federal Foreign Office was disappointed at the outcome. At an EPC meeting in Brussels in December 1985, Bonn's diplomats pointed out that the FRG would have welcomed even a small amount of progress to smooth the path for the Bern meeting the following year. Moreover, although responsibility for the meeting's failure rested firmly with the Soviets, from Bonn's point of view some partners lacked the will to negotiate with a view towards adopting a concluding document. From West Germany's point of view, this had led to a series of missed opportunities in the CSCE process and reduced Bonn's room to manoeuvre to successfully negotiate in the field of family unification and the migration of ethnic Germans.[58]

In the Federal Foreign Office, diplomats were acutely aware that after two inconclusive expert meetings an effort had to be made to boost the CSCE process. This applied to the CSBM negotiations in Stockholm, which by the end of 1985 had stalled over the questions of mandatory on-site inspections and the threshold for the notification of military activities. Agreement on these questions had not been possible as Moscow considered this an invitation to NATO to spy on Soviet military secrets. Bonn, therefore, pinned all hopes on the next expert meeting as an incentive for Stockholm to finish successfully in time for the Vienna follow-up meeting in November.

The CSCE Meeting of Experts in Bern began on 15 April 1986. Diplomats had the task of discussing the development of 'contacts between people, institutions and organizations' among the CSCE participants. Unlike Ottawa, the meeting would not discuss the principle of human rights but review practical obligations laid down in Basket Three of the Helsinki Final Act. To underline the high priority West Germany attributed to the subject of human contacts, Bonn was prepared to address particular Warsaw Pact countries openly and present exemplary cases but without naming names. Most importantly, the Federal Foreign Office hoped for progress, however small, in the field of family reunifications but also, for example, the improvement of travel conditions for relatives.[59] Ambassador Eickhoff, who again led the FRG delegation, intensively lobbied NATO allies and EPC partners in Brussels to work towards substantive recommendations and pointed to Bonn's responsibility for millions of Germans behind the Iron Curtain. However, as Eickhoff's consultations in Washington and with Warsaw Pact countries showed, a concluding document was far from certain.[60] Against that backdrop, the FRG intended to file a small number of proposals all aimed at increasing freer movement across the East–West divide. In particular, the Federal government wanted an obligation to permit visits for relatives and to simplify the application procedure for family reunifications. Other proposals included the development of youth exchange programmes and guarantees that applicants for travel or emigration permits would not be persecuted.[61]

After the usual acrimonious review of implementation, deliberations gradually improved. The West German delegation was also pleased that upon entering the discussion of new proposals, the subjects of family reunification and the improvement of travel conditions had the broad support of EPC partners. It subsequently presented the FRG's proposals as planned and co-sponsored a number of other NATO proposals. The delegation also conducted separate talks outside the conference rooms with representatives from the USSR, Romania, Poland and Czechoslovakia on the migration of ethnic Germans.[62] Finally, forty-six proposals were filed with the Secretariat, almost all of which were sponsored either by the Warsaw Pact or the EPC countries.

On 22 May, the Neutrals tabled a non-paper which, although some of the Western proposals had been deleted, included central Western demands, foremost of which was the right of minorities to be reunited with their families, to visit relatives and to marry across borders. However, this proved to be too much for Moscow and its allies, who feared the consequences for their own large minorities. The draft was referred to a Contact Group, which in the night of 25/26 May hammered out a new version of the NNA paper and obtained the support of all thirty-five delegations. To the surprise of the delegations, however, on the afternoon of 26 May the US head of delegation Michael Novak told delegates that Washington would not give its consent to the text. Given the East's still unsatisfactory human rights performance, Novak explained, his government could only have accepted a document of the 'highest standard'. The draft, however, contained nothing to ensure that the Soviets would implement already existing CSCE obligations.[63] Even a last-minute effort by Genscher, who phoned Shultz to get his assent, was to no avail.[64] There was widespread consternation among the delegations, since Novak as a member of the Contact Group had given his consent *ad personam* the previous night. Also, Washington's veto alienated the host country, which had been supporting the US human rights course since Madrid.[65] Washington's decision not to sign a document at Bern was generally supported by the American public.[66] US diplomats pointed to the great interest in human rights issues among members of Congress, some of whom had attended the NATO caucus meetings in Bern. It was also indicated that the veto might have been triggered by the lack of support from European allies after US fighter planes on 15 April had attacked targets in Libya in retaliation for the bombing of the 'La Belle' nightclub in West Berlin a fortnight earlier, which had killed two American soldiers. On the other hand, the US stance at Bern caused considerable acrimony among the allies. West German diplomats in particular sharply criticized Washington's U-turn at the very last minute and without prior consultation with European allies. With some bitterness they asked why Washington, for purely domestic reasons, had withdrawn its consent for a text that might have helped millions of Germans.[67]

No doubt, from the FRG point of view, Bern was a disappointment. Diplomats feared that the meeting was yet another example of the tendency of the Reagan administration to act unilaterally. On the day before Novak's about-face, Washington had announced that without a more significant Soviet disarmament effort it would no longer feel bound by the SALT II treaty and would refit its B-52 bombers with cruise missiles by the end of the year.[68] In particular, Bonn was worried about the effect the American veto could have on public opinion in Europe. What if the public concluded that the doves were sitting in the Kremlin while the hawks dominated politics in Washington?[69] But again, the Auswärtiges Amt publicly maintained that Bern was not a failure, sticking to its mantra that the East–West dialogue had been kept alive.

The trio of inconclusive expert meetings had not seriously damaged the CSCE process. However, their outcome put pressure on Bonn to conclude the Stockholm conference successfully in time for the Vienna follow-up meeting. Therefore, its delegation worked towards a compromise solution on the two remaining contentious subjects, namely notification (to ensure that enough military activities on the USSR's European territory would have to be notified) and verification (i.e. on-site inspections). FRG diplomats warned of a cut-off date for negotiations and pointed out that, like in Madrid, the West must not leave the conference table. Instead, they pressed the allies for a package deal with the East. Genscher in particular favoured a new initiative by the West in the run-up to his visit to Moscow scheduled for July 1986. With all three expert meetings having ended without results and the Stockholm conference stalled, Genscher's forthcoming talks with the Soviet government were of the utmost importance. Bonn's foreign secretary was under pressure to explain the FRG's disarmament policy to the Soviets, press for more concessions in Stockholm and generally smooth the way for the Vienna follow-up meeting.

New Horizons: Gorbachev, the CSCE and Arms Control

When Mikhail Gorbachev became General Secretary of the Communist Party of the Soviet Union (CPSU) on 11 March 1985, Soviet foreign policy became more flexible and dynamic, which was first visible in the field of arms control. On the following day, Washington and Moscow resumed negotiations on strategic as well as intermediate-range missiles, followed by talks on strategic defence weapons, which foreign secretaries Shultz and Gromyko had agreed on in January.[70] In mid November, the General Secretary met President Ronald Reagan for the first time in Geneva. As a result, both sides agreed in principle to reduce their strategic systems by 50 per cent and to conclude an interim agreement on intermediate-range nuclear weapons. It also ushered in what Shultz called a 'slow, incremental' process of improving the 'rollercoaster' relationship of the two superpowers.[71] Conscious that he had to ease the burden of military expenditure, Gorbachev launched a comprehensive disarmament drive a few weeks later. On 15 January 1986, he suggested the abolishment of all nuclear weapons by the year 2000. In mid April, there followed proposals on the reduction of conventional forces 'from the Atlantic to the Urals'. Gorbachev also declared that Moscow was prepared for concessions concerning the verification of CSBMs and in particular to allow on-site inspections.[72]

Gorbachev's more forthcoming attitude towards the Stockholm conference marked the starting point for a new Soviet approach towards the CSCE. Unlike his predecessors, he and his reformist advisers gradually embraced the CSCE as a major point of reference for shaping cooperative relations with the West and gaining economic and political leeway for domestic reforms. While in the course of 1986 the Kremlin still adhered to the Soviet primacy of arms control, the General Secretary soon concluded that a cautious reorientation of Soviet human rights policy might win the West's support for his reforms and broaden acceptance of *perestroika*, Gorbachev's ambitious reform plans to modernize Soviet society.[73]

The question of arms control also became an issue of increasing importance to the Federal government. First, with a superpower agreement on strategic and intermediate-range nuclear weapons on the horizon, Bonn was anxious to solve the problem of short-range nuclear weapons (SRINF), which were not covered by the Geneva talks. Second, the conclusion of the CSBM conference would open the prospect of negotiations on conventional arms reductions within the CSCE framework. Thus, the CSCE process became all the more important for Bonn to redress the balance between military security and détente. Moreover, as Bonn pointed out, boosting the CSCE by including the issue of conventional arms control would preserve Europe's voice and in particular give Moscow's smaller allies more leverage.[74]

West German–Soviet relations, meanwhile, did not develop as the Federal government had wished. Ever since the United States had begun deploying Pershings and cruise missiles in 1983, Moscow had frozen its bilateral relations with Bonn. Things worsened when on 18 December 1985 the West German cabinet decided to support Washington's Strategic Defense Initiative (SDI) programme and enter into negotiations about an agreement allowing German companies to take part in US research on SDI. The West German government was subsequently the target of Soviet accusations and was ostentatiously shunned by Gorbachev on his visits to Western capitals.

It was at this point that Genscher travelled to Moscow for talks with the Soviet leadership. The previous summer, he had met the newly appointed foreign secretary, Eduard Shevardnadze, at the tenth anniversary meeting of the CSCE summit in Helsinki. The meeting had gone well as Shevardnadze, despite criticizing Bonn's stance on disarmament, had struck a new tone. But there had not been any substantive talks.[75] To the surprise of the West German delegation, immediately after Genscher's plane touched Soviet ground he was informed that the Kremlin had changed the arranged timetable. Instead of the Soviet foreign secretary, he first met with Gorbachev on 21 July 1986 for a frank talk that lasted more than three hours.

At the beginning, Gorbachev accused Bonn of closely following America's military course and of dismissing the Soviet drive for disarmament. Germany, Gorbachev maintained, pretended to pursue a policy of détente while in fact unreservedly supporting what Moscow perceived as Washington's policy of military brinkmanship. In the end, however, the Soviet party chief warmed to his guest and spoke of the need to 'turn the page' in Soviet–German relations. He talked frankly about the poor state of the Soviet economy, leaving Genscher in no doubt that he wanted to intensify economic relations, especially alleviating Western rules of trade with communist countries as set by the Coordinating Committee on Multilateral Export Controls (COCOM), in order to support his domestic reforms. He also pointed to the importance of building a 'Common European Home' and assured Genscher that he did not wish to drive a wedge between Bonn and Washington.

Genscher, on the other hand, explained in detail Germany's attitude towards arms control and the future of détente. Picking up Gorbachev's notion of a 'Common European Home', Genscher told the General

Secretary that the Eastern treaties and the Helsinki Final Act, namely the principle of the non-violation of borders, were West Germany's contribution towards building a peaceful Europe. They were 'not things of the past' but formed the basis on which to mould 'perspectives for the future'. At the same time, Genscher made clear that a 'Common European Home' would have to accommodate 'different and conflictive societies', providing freedom and equal security for all states. He called on Gorbachev to deliver on his calls for disarmament at the conference table in Geneva, Stockholm and Vienna. Moreover, while for Moscow the subject of German reunification was not on the agenda, Genscher reminded Gorbachev that a 'Common European Home' was not conceivable as divided.[76] At the end of Genscher's visit, a number of bilateral agreements were concluded, among them the agreement on scientific and technical cooperation, which had been in the making since 1973.[77] The Federal Foreign Office's Political Director, Gerold von Braunmühl, summed up the visit: 'A good deal of normalcy has been regained'.[78]

Genscher returned to Bonn with the impression that the Soviet Union was prepared to make concessions to overcome the deadlock at the CSBM conference. This impression proved to be true as the main obstacles for an agreement were removed during the summer of 1986. The Warsaw Pact at long last conceded to on-site inspections and withdrew its veto on the inclusion of independent sea and air activities in the CSBM regime. Subsequently, on 22 September, a concluding document was signed which established a set of confidence-building measures and for the first time included European territory of the USSR in the area of control. Military activities with more than thirteen thousand troops or three hundred tanks would have to be notified forty-two days in advance. Observers would have to be invited for military exercises with more than seventeen thousand troops; in the case of noncompliance, mandatory on-site inspections on the ground and by air could be carried out.[79]

Bonn was pleased with the outcome of the conference. As has been seen, the inclusion of Soviet territory in any CSBM regime had been one of the FRG's main goals since the Madrid follow-up meeting. Furthermore, the agreement had brought NATO's and the Warsaw Pact's points of view closer to military confidence-building and substantively enlarged the area of CSBMs.[80] With a view to conventional disarmament, it laid the ground for the solution of one of the most contested arms control problems in the Cold War even before the beginning of the new thaw in superpower relations. Subsequently, the Vienna follow-up meeting (1986–89) passed the mandate for a conference on the limitation of conventional troops in Europe. This finally meant the end of the MBFR talks in Vienna and their inclusion in the CSCE conference system.

Conclusion

The CSCE, this chapter has shown, was a slow and incremental learning process. Its consequences could not be foreseen by any of the participating states. It was not teleological as many forces contributed to the end of the Cold War, including the improvement of superpower relations after 1985, the economic decline of the Warsaw Pact countries, the 'Gorbachev factor' and the rise of opposition movements in Eastern Europe, forces which, in turn, strongly influenced the course of the CSCE. It is also important to bear in mind that the CSCE progressed in steps, each one dependent on the unanimous decision of all participating states to continue, and was saddled with different, often opposing sets of national interests. However, the CSCE gradually unfolded its potential as a force of transformation with the Madrid follow-up meeting marking a breakthrough for the West's policy of 'antagonistic cooperation'.[81] In Madrid, the Kremlin, despite objections from East Berlin, made concessions in the humanitarian field in order to ensure a European disarmament conference. Madrid, therefore, was a decisive step in the Kremlin's long journey in the CSCE process, which led from Brezhnev's policy of saving the postwar status quo in Europe to Gorbachev's interest in the CSCE as a means to safeguard *perestroika* at home and support his vision of a 'Common European Home' on the international level.[82]

Likewise, Bonn's *Ostpolitik* and CSCE policy must be seen in different contexts, varying from Brandt/Scheel to Schmidt/Genscher and Kohl/Genscher. The Federal Republic of Germany, with a view to its national agenda and exposed position at the front line of the East–West divide, had by far the greatest interest in successful negotiations. Saving détente, therefore, was a pillar of Bonn's foreign and security policy in addition to a strategy of sufficient military preparedness as a member of NATO. Communication was central to West Germany's strategy. With a view to the plight of millions of Germans in the GDR and Eastern Europe, Bonn's main goal in the CSCE process was to keep the dialogue between East and West alive in order to ease tensions in Europe and open up opportunities for more transnational contacts across the Iron Curtain. Starting as a lever to push through the *Ostverträge* in the early 1970s, the CSCE, after the hapless first review meeting in Belgrade, slowly became an important element of soft power, complementing NATO decisions in the fields of military security and disarmament. With tensions rising again at the end of the decade, Bonn used the CSCE process as an instrument to de-escalate East–West relations. Even at the height of the crisis in Poland, with the fate of the conference hanging by a thread, the Auswärtiges Amt staunchly defended the CSCE and pressed allies and Warsaw Pact countries to continue negotiations, believing that this would have a soothing effect on Moscow's and Warsaw's behaviour.

It was the second follow-up conference from 1980 to 1983 in Madrid that made Hans-Dietrich Genscher aware of the CSCE's full potential. It not only underlined the importance of the CSCE as a diplomatic tool for weathering the stormy East–West relations. The deliberations led him to conclude that the CSCE could lay the foundation of a new European peace order. Subsequently, its concluding document became, alongside the Helsinki Final Act of 1975, a further reference document for the Federal government in conducting relations with the East.

Despite several setbacks following the expert meetings from 1984 to 1986, Bonn saw its view confirmed by the successful conclusion of the CSBM negotiations. It is important to note that as the 1980s progressed, questions of arms control and the CSCE process slowly began to merge. The Stockholm accords opened the prospect to overcome the deadlock of the MBFR talks in Vienna and negotiate the issue of conventional arms control between the two military alliances, including France, as part of the CSCE. They also redressed the balance of military security, humanitarian issues and economic cooperation, thus upgrading the CSCE and paving the way for the third review meeting to begin shortly in Vienna. More and more people, Genscher told Yugoslav Foreign Secretary Raif Dizdarević in November 1986, were now beginning to understand the CSCE's philosophy. If there were a school for foreign secretaries, he quipped, the CSCE would have to be compulsory reading.[83]

Matthias Peter is Research Associate at the Institut für Zeitgeschichte München–Berlin and a member of the editorial staff of the Akten zur Auswärtigen Politik der Bundesrepublik Deutschland. He received his Ph.D. from the Justus-Liebig-Universität Gießen. As well as numerous volumes in the series of West German diplomatic documents, he has published widely on the CSCE process. His most recent book is *Die Bundesrepublik Deutschland im KSZE-Prozess 1975–1983: Die Umkehrung der Diplomatie* (Oldenbourg De Gruyter, 2015).

Notes

 1. On European Political Cooperation, détente and the CSCE, see A. Romano, *From Détente in Europe to European Détente: How the West Shaped the Helsinki CSCE* (Brussels: P.I.E. Peter Lang, 2009); D. Möckli, *European Foreign Policy during the Cold War: Heath, Brandt, Pompidou and the Dream of Political Unity* (London and New York: I.B. Tauris, 2009). On détente as an inherent strategy of Cold War diplomacy, see G. Niedhart, *Entspannung in Europa: Die Bundesrepublik Deutschland und der Warschauer Pakt* (Munich: De Gruyter Oldenbourg Verlag, 2014); W. Loth, *Die Rettung der Welt: Entspannungspolitik im Kalten Krieg 1950–1991* (Frankfurt am Main: Campus Verlag, 2016). See also G. Niedhart, 'Der Ost-West-Konflikt: Konfrontation im Kalten Krieg und Stufen der Deeskalation', *Archiv für Sozialgeschichte* 50 (2010), 589f. On 'European détente', see J.M. Hanhimäki, 'Détente in Europe, 1962–1975', in M.P. Leffler and O.A. Westad (eds), *The Cambridge History of the Cold War*, 3 vols (Cambridge: Cambridge University Press, 2010), vol. II: *Crises and Détente*, 198–218.
 2. On the debate about Ostpolitik and the CSCE as driving factors of the transformation process in communist Eastern Europe, see the special issue 'CSCE, the German Question, and the Warsaw Pact' of the *Journal of Cold War Studies*, especially M. Kramer, 'Editor's Note'; G. Niedhart, 'Introduction'; G. Niedhart, 'Ostpolitik: Transformation through Communication and the Quest for Peaceful Change'; O. Bange, 'Onto the Slippery Slope: East Germany and East-West Détente under Ulbricht and Honecker, 1965–1975', all in *Journal of Cold War Studies* 18(3) (2016). For analyses of Western pre-1975 détente as an important tool in Western Cold War strategy, see also O. Bange and G. Niedhart (eds), *Helsinki 1975 and the Transformation of Europe* (New York and Oxford: Berghahn Books, 2008); S. Kieninger, *Dynamic Détente: The United States and Europe 1964–1975* (Lanham, MD: Lexington Books, 2016).
 3. See the results of the research project 'The CSCE Process: Multilateral Conference Diplomacy and Its Consequences' undertaken by the Institute for Contemporary History Munich-Berlin, which looked at the CSCE process on the societal as well as the state level: M. Peter and H. Wentker (eds), *Die KSZE im Ost-West-Konflikt: Internationale Politik und gesellschaftliche Transformation 1975–1990* (Munich: Oldenbourg Verlag, 2012); A. Hanisch, *Die DDR im KSZE-Prozess 1972–1985: Zwischen Ostabhängigkeit, Westabgrenzung und Ausreisebewegung* (Munich: Oldenbourg Verlag, 2012); B. Gilde, *Österreich im KSZE-Prozess 1969–1983: Neutraler Vermittler in humanitärer Mission* (Munich: Oldenbourg Verlag, 2013); Ph. Rosin, *Die Schweiz im KSZE-Prozess 1972–1983: Einfluß durch Neutralität* (Munich: Oldenbourg Verlag, 2014); Y. von Saal, *KSZE-Prozess und Perestroika in der Sowjetunion: Demokratisierung, Werteumbruch und Auflösung 1985–1991* (Munich: Oldenbourg, 2014); M. Peter, *Die Bundesrepublik im KSZE-Prozess 1975–1983: Die Umkehrung der Diplomatie* (Berlin, Munich and Boston: De Gruyter Oldenbourg Verlag, 2015); V. Heyde, *Frankreich im KSZE-Prozess:*

Diplomatie im Namen der europäischen Sicherheit 1969–1983 (Berlin and Boston: De Gruyter Oldenbourg Verlag, 2017).
4. P. Hakkarainen, *A State of Peace in Europe: West Germany and the CSCE, 1966–1975* (New York and Oxford: Berghahn Books, 2011).
5. On Helsinki Watch and the rising movement of monitoring groups in the USSR, see S.B. Snyder, *Human Rights Activism and the End of the Cold War: A Transnational History of the Helsinki Network* (Cambridge: Cambridge University Press, 2011), chapter 5.
6. See S. Savranskaya, 'Human Rights Movement in the USSR after the Signing of the Helsinki Final Act, and the Reaction of Soviet Authorities', in L. Nuti (ed.), *The Crisis of Détente in Europe: From Helsinki to Gorbachev, 1975–1985* (London and New York: Routledge, 2009), 26–40. On Soviet CBM compliance, see Peter, *Die Bundesrepublik im KSZE-Prozess*, 138–51.
7. D. Selvage, 'The Superpowers and the Conference on Security and Cooperation in Europe, 1977–1983', in Peter and Wentker, *Die KSZE im Ost-West-Konflikt*, 15–58, here 18–26; Peter, *Die Bundesrepublik im KSZE-Prozess*, 225–38.
8. Meyer-Landrut to mission NATO Brussels, 29 June 1977, in *Akten zur Auswärtigen Politik der Bundesrepublik Deutschland 1977*, ed. on behalf of the Auswärtiges Amt by the Institut für Zeitgeschichte (Munich: Oldenbourg Verlag, 2008), vol. I, Doc. 170, fn. 2 (hereafter AAPD 1977). All translations from German documents are by the author.
9. See A. Dobrynin, *In Confidence: Moscow's Ambassador to America's Six Cold War Presidents (1962–1986)* (New York: Random House, 1995), 346, on the Politburo debates about the Helsinki Final Act. See also T. Judt, *Postwar: A History of Europe since 1945* (London: Heinemann, 2005), 501f.; J.L. Gaddis, *The Cold War: A New History* (New York: The Penguin Press, 2005), 187f.; M.P. Leffler, *For the Soul of Mankind: The United States, the Soviet Union and the Cold War* (New York: Hill and Wang, 2007), 234f., 248–51.
10. See Peter, *Die Bundesrepublik im KSZE-Prozess*, chapter IV.
11. See Heyde, *Frankreich im KSZE-Prozess*, 254–83.
12. The expert meeting on the peaceful settlement of disputes took place from 31 October to 11 December 1978 in Montreux, the meeting on security in the Mediterranean from 13 February to 26 March 1979 in Valletta (Malta) and the two-part Scientific Forum from 20 June to 28 September 1976 in Bonn and from 18 February to 3 March 1980 in Hamburg. See Peter, *Die Bundesrepublik im KSZE-Prozess*, 355–86.
13. See Peter, *Die Bundesrepublik im KSZE-Prozess*, 330–55.
14. See Snyder, *Human Rights Activism*, 135f.
15. On Genscher's strategy of communicative foreign policy, see A. Bresselau von Bressensdorf, *Frieden durch Kommunikation: Das System Genscher und die Entspannungspolitik im Zweiten Kalten Krieg 1979–1982/83* (Berlin and Boston: De Gruyter Oldenbourg Verlag, 2015).
16. See Peter, *Die Bundesrepublik im KSZE-Prozess*, 482–85.
17. See for example Wieck (NATO Brussels) to Auswärtiges Amt, 25 April 1981, in AAPD 1981 (Munich: Oldenbourg Verlag, 2012), vol. I, Doc. 115, 641; Politisches Archiv des Auswärtigen Amts (hereafter PA-AA), B 14

(ZA), 125582, Pfeffer to German embassy Washington, 24 April 1981 (No. 2255), transmitting a letter by Genscher to Secretary of State Haig.
18. On criticism of Bonn's attitude, see Selvage, 'The Superpowers and the Conference of Security and Cooperation in Europe'; G. Dehnert, 'Entspannung gegen das Volk – Sanktionen für das Volk? Die Solidarność nach Ausrufung des Kriegsrechts und die Nachfolgekonferenz von Madrid', in Peter and Wentker, *Die KSZE im Ost-West-Konflikt*, 249–66.
19. See Chancellor Kohl to President Reagan, 1 December 1983, in AAPD 1983 (Munich: Oldenbourg Verlag, 2014), vol. II, Doc. 365.
20. See Peter, *Die Bundesrepublik im KSZE-Prozess*, 501f.
21. On Kohl's and Genscher's talks in Washington on 14/15 July 1985, see AAPD 1983, vol. I, Doc. 101 and Doc. 102.
22. See meeting Genscher and Kampelman, 2 July 1983, in AAPD 1983, vol. II, Doc. 196.
23. 'KSZE: "Der Präsident ist sehr zufrieden"', *Der Spiegel*, No. 29 (1986), 18 July 1986, 89.
24. On Genscher's meetings with Shultz and Reagan on 10/11 July 1983, see AAPD 1983, vol. II, Doc. 210, Doc. 211 and Doc. 212.
25. See Peter, *Die Bundesrepublik im KSZE-Prozess*, 518–21.
26. On the clash between the USSR and the GDR over Moscow's human rights policy at Madrid, see Hanisch, *Die DDR im KSZE-Prozess*, 261–64.
27. Meetings Genscher with Reagan and Bush, 9 March 1982, in AAPD 1982 (Munich: Oldenbourg Verlag, 2013), vol. I, Doc. 77 and Doc. 78, 388, 392.
28. Letter Genscher to von Staden, 30 December 1983, in AAPD 1983, vol. II, Doc. 388.
29. H.-D. Genscher, *Deutsche Aussenpolitik: Ausgewählte Reden und Aufsätze 1974–1985* (Bonn: Bonn Aktuell, 1985), 386–91.
30. Hans-Dietrich Genscher, 'Konsequente Fortsetzung der Friedens- und Entspannungspolitik', *Bulletin der Bundesregierung* 1983 (Bonn, 1983), 1209.
31. See T. Garton Ash, *In Europe's Name: Germany and the Divided Continent* (London: Jonathan Cape, 1993), 319–30; H. Potthoff, *Die 'Koalition der Vernunft': Deutschlandpolitik in den 80er Jahren* (Munich: Deutscher Taschenbuch Verlag, 1995), 47–52.
32. 'Nicht "Wandel durch Annäherung" (Bahr), eine Politik, die heute offenbar von der SPD-Mehrheit praktiziert wird, sondern Wandlung durch Einwirkung (KSZE) ist die der Bundesrepublik Deutschland gestellte deutschlandpolitische und gesamteuropäische Aufgabe.' Memorandum Schollwer, 27 December 1985, in AAPD 1985 (Berlin and Boston: De Gruyter Oldenbourg Verlag, 2016), vol. II, Doc. 356, 1890.
33. Memo Ruth, 18 January 1984, AAPD 1984 (Munich: Oldenbourg Verlag, 2015), vol. I, Doc. 11.
34. See memo Holik, 9 January 1984, AAPD 1984, vol. I, Doc. 4.
35. See Citron (CSBM Stockholm) to Auswärtiges Amt, 15 February 1985 (No. 43), and memo Hartmann, 19 February 1985, in AAPD 1985, vol. I, Doc. 42 and Doc. 43.
36. See Citron (CSBM Stockholm) to Auswärtiges Amt, 9 December 1985 (No. 229), in AAPD 1985, vol. II, Doc. 336.

37. See PA-AA, B 28 (ZA), 133513, memo Referat 212, 25 April 1985.
38. Sergei Kondrashev, the Soviet deputy head of delegation in Ottawa, in the plenary meeting of 16 May 1985, denied any persecution of Jews in the USSR, maintaining that despite Soviet support of Jewish emigration to Israel, 90 per cent of those who had been allowed to leave had stayed in Europe and the US. Moscow, he went on, was now approaching this question more cautiously and wanted to solve each case of family reunion on an individual basis. PA-AA, B28 (ZA), 133515, Eickhoff (Ottawa) to Auswärtiges Amt, 16 May 1985 (No. 372). For Schifter's account of the Ottawa meeting, see A. Adamishin and R. Schifter, *Human Rights, Perestroika, and the End of the Cold War* (Washington, DC: United States Institute of Peace Press, 2009), 102.
39. PA-AA, B 28 (ZA), 133515, Eickhoff (Ottawa) to Auswärtiges Amt, 9 May 1985 (No. 347), 15 May 1985 (No. 363 and No. 369), 16 May 1985 (No. 373), 22 May 1985 (No. 404).
40. PA-AA, B 28 (ZA), 133515, Eickhoff (Ottawa) to Auswärtiges Amt, 4 June 1985 (No. 446).
41. See S.B. Snyder, 'The Foundation for Vienna: A Reassessment of the CSCE in the Mid-1980s', *Cold War History* 10(4) (2010), 498.
42. PA-AA, B 28 (ZA), 133515, Eickhoff (Ottawa) to Auswärtiges Amt, 12 June 1985 (No. 476), 13 June 1985 (No. 479), 17 June 1985 (No. 491).
43. PA-AA, B 28 (ZA), 133514, Vollmar-Libal to CSCE delegation Ottawa, 12 June 1985 (No. 141).
44. PA-AA, B 28 (ZA), 133514, Eickhoff (Ottawa) to Auswärtiges Amt, 31 May 1985.
45. See Hans-Dietrich Genscher's statement in the West German Bundestag on 27 June 1985, at http://dip21.bundestag.de/dip21/btp/10/10149.pdf, 11152. See also Y. von Saal, 'Die Folgen des KSZE-Prozesses in der Sowjetunion der Perestroika: Der KSZE-Faktor in der Eigendynamik des Wertewandels', in Peter and Wentker, *Die KSZE im Ost-West-Konflikt*, 288; Snyder, 'The Foundation for Vienna'. This view was shared by the US State Department. See PA-AA, B 28 (ZA), 133514, van Well (Washington) to Auswärtiges Amt, 3 July 1985.
46. PA-AA, B 28 (ZA), 133514, Wieck (NATO Brussels) to Auswärtiges Amt, 4 July 1985. On the US position of a link between security and human rights, see Snyder, 'The Foundation for Vienna', 497. For Eickhoff's own appraisal of the Ottawa meeting, see E. Eickhoff, 'Das KSZE-Expertentreffen über Menschenrechte in Ottawa – eine Bewertung', *Europa-Archiv* 40(19) (1985), 573–80.
47. See for example meeting Genscher and Dizdarević (Yugoslavia), 30/31 January 1985; EPC foreign ministers' meeting in Rome, 12 February 1985; meeting Genscher and Gromyko (USSR) in Moscow, 3/4 March 1985; meeting Genscher and Jaruzelski/Olszowski (Poland), 6 March 1985 in Warsaw; meeting Genscher and Chňoupek (Czechoslovakia), 22 August 1985; EPC foreign ministers' meeting in Luxemburg, 10 September 1985; meeting Genscher with Fischer (GDR) in New York, 25 September 1985; in AAPD 1985, vol. I, Doc. 27, Doc. 38, Doc. 54 and Doc. 56; vol. II, Doc. 230, Doc. 245 and Doc. 261.

48. See the opening remarks by Karl-Günther von Hase in Budapest, 16 October 1985, *Bulletin der Bundesregierung 1985*, 1016–18, here 1016f.
49. PA-AA, B 28 (ZA), 133516, Memo Altenburg, 28 October 1985.
50. PA-AA, B 28 (ZA), 133517, von Hase (Budapest) to Auswärtiges Amt, 21 October 1985 (No. 1093).
51. PA-AA, B 28 (ZA), 133517, von Hase (Budapest) to Auswärtiges Amt, 28 October 1985 (No. 1138).
52. PA-AA, B 28 (ZA), 133517, von Hase (Budapest) to Auswärtiges Amt, 30 October 1985 (No. 1160).
53. PA-AA, B 28 (ZA), 133517, von Hase (Budapest) to Auswärtiges Amt, 13 November 1985 (No. 1248); PA-AA, B 150, memo von Studnitz, 26 November 1985 ('Cultural Forum in Budapest').
54. PA-AA, B 28 (ZA), 133517, von Hase (Budapest) to Auswärtiges Amt, 18 November, 20 November and 21 November 1985 (No. 1271, No. 1280 and No. 1286).
55. PA-AA, B 28 (ZA), 133517, von Hase (Budapest) to Auswärtiges Amt, 21 November 1985 (No. 1283).
56. PA-AA, B 28 (ZA), 133517, von Hase (Budapest) to Auswärtiges Amt, 23 November, 25 November 1985 (No. 1309, No. 1312 and No. 1318).
57. For an evaluation by the West German deputy head of delegation, see W. Pabsch, 'Das Kulturforum der KSZE in Budapest: Bericht und Bewertung', *Europa-Archiv* 20(7) (1986), 211–16.
58. PA-AA, B 28 (ZA), 133516, von Hase (Budapest) to Auswärtiges Amt, 28 October 1985 (No. 1138); Graf zu Rantzau (NATO Brussels) to Auswärtiges Amt, 17 December 1985 (No. 2028); memorandum Referat 212, 9 December 1985.
59. See the instructions for the FRG delegation to the Expert Meeting in Bern: Memo von Braunmühl, 19 March 1986, in AAPD 1986 (Berlin and Boston: De Gruyter Oldenbourg Verlag, 2017), vol. I, Doc. 77.
60. Assistant Secretary of State Rozanne Ridgway told Eickhoff in January 1986 that the US did not necessarily need a concluding document, while the USSR 'categorically rejected' the idea of a final text. See PA-AA, B 28 (ZA), 133556, Eickhoff (Washington) to Auswärtiges Amt, 24 January 1986 (No. 369); Memo von Braunmühl, 19 March 1986, in AAPD 1986, vol. I, Doc. 77, 438.
61. PA-AA, B 28 (ZA), 133524, memo Eickhoff, 6 March 1986 ('German proposals'); memo Eickhoff, 19 March 1986 ('Negotiation goals and tactics for Bern').
62. Several delegations tried, often in vain, to use the Bern meeting to solve individual human rights cases, but not as part of substantive negotiations like West Germany. See A. Doepfner, 'Das KSZE-Expertentreffen über menschliche Kontakte in Bern: Einordnung, Beschreibung, Bewertung', *Europa-Archiv* 20(17) (1986), 521.
63. PA-AA, B 28 (ZA), 133525, Eickhoff (Bern) to Auswärtiges Amt, 24 May, 26 May and 27 May 1986 (No. 298, No. 300 and No. 301).
64. See 'Memmen und Cowboys', *Der Spiegel*, No. 23 (1986), 2 June 1986, 25f.

65. PA-AA, B 28 (ZA), 133525, Eickhoff (Bern) to Auswärtiges Amt, 27 May 1986 (No. 301). On Swiss CSCE policy and the support for Washington's human rights policy, see Rosin, *Die Schweiz im KSZE-Prozess*.
66. See Snyder, 'The Foundation for Vienna', 501f.
67. See memo von Ploetz, 4 June 1986, about his conversation with James F. Dobbins, in AAPD 1986, vol. I, Doc. 162, 835f.
68. See W. Loth, *Helsinki, 1. August 1975: Entspannung und Abrüstung* (Munich: Deutscher Taschenbuch Verlag, 1998), 239; van Well (Washington) to Auswärtiges Amt, 28 May 1986, in AAPD 1986, vol. I, Doc. 157.
69. See memo von Braunmühl, 3 July 1986, in AAPD 1986, vol. II, Doc. 183, 968.
70. See Graf zu Rantzau (NATO Brussels) to Auswärtiges Amt, 24 April 1985, in AAPD 1985, vol. I, Doc. 101.
71. See memos von Braunmühl, 21 November and 22 November 1985; Hansen (NATO Brussels) to Auswärtiges Amt, 13 December 1985 (No. 2015), in AAPD 1985, vol. II, Doc. 317, Doc. 319 and Doc. 345.
72. See Loth, *Helsinki*, 237–40.
73. For a detailed analysis of the influence of the CSCE process on perestroika, see von Saal, *KSZE-Prozess und Perestroika*, 49–78, 357–66. See also S. Savranskaya, 'The Logic of 1989: The Soviet Peaceful Withdrawal from Eastern Europe', in S. Savranskaya, T. Blanton and V. Zubok (eds), *Masterpieces of History: The Peaceful End of the Cold War in Europe, 1989* (Budapest and New York: Central European University Press, 2010), 1–48, here 19f.
74. See Chancellor Kohl to President Reagan, 16 October 1985, in AAPD 1985, vol. II, Doc. 284.
75. See meeting Genscher with Shevardnadse in Helsinki (1 August 1985), in AAPD 1985, vol. II, Doc. 215.
76. See Braunmühl (Moscow) to Auswärtiges Amt, 22 July 1986, in AAPD 1986, vol. II, Doc. 209; Politburo meeting, 24 July 1986, in A. Galkin and A. Tschernjajew (eds), *Michail Gorbatschow und die deutsche Frage: Sowjetische Dokumente 1986–1991* (Munich: Oldenbourg Verlag, 2011), Doc. 6. See also G.A. Ritter, *Hans-Dietrich Genscher, das Auswärtige Amt und die deutsche Vereinigung* (Munich: C.H. Beck, 2013), 17–19; H.-D. Genscher, *Erinnerungen* (Berlin: Siedler Verlag, 1995), 493–505. On Gorbachev's 'Common European Home', see M.-P. Rey, "Europe is Our Common Home": A Study of Gorbachev's Diplomatic Concept', *Cold War History* 4(2) (2004), 33–65; Savranskaya, 'The Logic of 1989', 22. As early as 30 January 1986, Chancellor Kohl, in a letter to Gorbachev, picked up the idea and told the General Secretary that a 'Common European Home' could only be free of tensions 'if the relationship of the two German states were boosted as a stabilizing factor in the overall development of East-West relations'. See Kohl to Gorbachev, 30 January 1986, in AAPD 1986, vol. I, Doc. 27, 166.
77. Pleuger to German embassies, 22 July 1986, in AAPD 1986, vol. II, Doc. 212.
78. Memo von Braunmühl, 25 July 1986, in AAPD 1986, vol. II, Doc. 218. The arrangements, however, were temporarily put on hold by the Kremlin when Chancellor Kohl, in an interview with *Newsweek* later that year, drew a comparison between Gorbachev's public relations skills and those of

Hitler's minister for propaganda Joseph Goebbels. See Memo Kastrup, 25 November 1986, in AAPD 1986, vol. II, Doc. 339; H. Wentker, 'Vom Gegner zum Partner: Gorbatschow und seine Politik im Urteil Helmut Kohls', *Historisch-Politische Mitteilungen* 22(1) (2015), 1–34, here 10.
79. See Loth, *Helsinki*, 240.
80. For an evaluation of the Stockholm CSBM conference, see Citron to Auswärtiges Amt, 22 September 1986; memo Hartmann, 30 September 1986, in AAPD 1986, vol. II, Doc 253 and Doc. 267.
81. Niedhart, 'Ostpolitik', 59. Niedhart and Bange are, therefore, right in pointing out the long-term effects of the West's policy of 'antagonistic cooperation'. This, of course, does not mean that West German *Ostpolitik* from its beginning provided a 'blueprint' for overcoming the East–West conflict. See Niedhart, 'Ostpolitik', and Bange, 'Onto the Slippery Slope'. On the other hand, the assertion that the CSCE in the 1980s 'was largely irrelevant' understates the role played by the CSCE on the state level. See Kramer, 'Editor's Note', 2.
82. For more detail, see von Saal, *KSZE-Prozess und Perestroika in der Sowjetunion*; Savranskaya, 'The Logic of 1989', 20–22; S. Savranskaya, 'In the Name of Europe: Soviet Withdrawal from Eastern Europe', in F. Bozo, M.-P. Rey, N.P. Ludlow and L. Nuti (eds), *Europe and the End of the Cold War: A Reappraisal* (London and New York: Routledge, 2008), 36–48.
83. Conversation Genscher and Dizdarević, 7 November 1986, in AAPD 1986, vol. II, Doc. 319, 1642f.

Bibliography

Adamishin, A., and R. Schifter. *Human Rights, Perestroika, and the End of the Cold War*. Washington, DC: United States Institute of Peace Press, 2009.

Akten zur Auswärtigen Politik der Bundesrepublik Deutschland 1977–1986, ed. on behalf of the Auswärtiges Amt by the Institut für Zeitgeschichte. Munich: Oldenbourg Verlag, 2008–2015; Berlin and Boston, MA: De Gruyter Oldenbourg Verlag, 2016–2017.

Bange, O. 'Onto the Slippery Slope: East Germany and East-West Détente under Ulbricht and Honecker, 1965–1975'. *Journal of Cold War Studies* 18(3) (2016), 60–94.

Bange, O., and G. Niedhart (eds). *Helsinki 1975 and the Transformation of Europe*. New York and Oxford: Berghahn Books, 2008.

Bresselau von Bressensdorf, A. *Frieden durch Kommunikation: Das System Genscher und die Entspannungspolitik im Zweiten Kalten Krieg 1979–1982/83*. Berlin and Boston: De Gruyter Oldenbourg Verlag, 2015.

Dehnert, G. 'Entspannung gegen das Volk – Sanktionen für das Volk? Die Solidarność nach Ausrufung des Kriegsrechts und die Nachfolgekonferenz von Madrid', in M. Peter and H. Wentker (eds), *Die KSZE im Ost-West-Konflikt: Internationale Politik und gesellschaftliche Transformation 1975–1990* (Munich: Oldenbourg Verlag, 2012), 249–66.

Dobrynin, A. *In Confidence: Moscow's Ambassador to America's Six Cold War Presidents (1962–1986)*. New York: Random House, 1995.
Doepfner, A. 'Das KSZE-Expertentreffen über menschliche Kontakte in Bern: Einordnung, Beschreibung, Bewertung'. *Europa-Archiv* 20(17) (1986), 513–22.
Eickhoff, E. 'Das KSZE-Expertentreffen über Menschenrechte in Ottawa – eine Bewertung'. *Europa-Archiv* 40(19) (1985), 573–80.
Gaddis, J.L. *The Cold War: A New History*. New York: The Penguin Press, 2005.
Galkin, A., and A. Tschernjajew (eds). *Michail Gorbatschow und die deutsche Frage: Sowjetische Dokumente 1986–1991*. Munich: Oldenbourg Verlag, 2011.
Garton Ash, T. *In Europe's Name: Germany and the Divided Continent*. London: Jonathan Cape, 1993.
Genscher, H.-D. *Deutsche Aussenpolitik: Ausgewählte Reden und Aufsätze 1974– 1985*. Bonn: Bonn Aktuell, 1985.
Genscher, H.-D. *Erinnerungen*. Berlin: Siedler Verlag, 1995.
Gilde, B. *Österreich im KSZE-Prozess 1969–1983: Neutraler Vermittler in humanitärer Mission*. Munich: Oldenbourg Verlag, 2013.
Hakkarainen, P. *A State of Peace in Europe: West Germany and the CSCE, 1966– 1975*. New York and Oxford: Berghahn Books, 2011.
Hanhimäki, J.M. 'Détente in Europe, 1962–1975', in M.P. Leffler and O.A. Westad (eds), *The Cambridge History of the Cold War*, 3 vols (Cambridge: Cambridge University Press, 2010), vol. II: *Crises and Détente*, 198–218.
Hanisch, A. *Die DDR im KSZE-Prozess 1972–1985: Zwischen Ostabhängigkeit, Westabgrenzung und Ausreisebewegung*. Munich: Oldenbourg Verlag, 2012.
Heyde, V. *Frankreich im KSZE-Prozess: Diplomatie im Namen der europäischen Sicherheit 1969–1983*. Berlin and Boston, MA: De Gruyter Oldenbourg Verlag, 2017.
Judt, T. *Postwar: A History of Europe since 1945*. London: Heinemann, 2005.
Kieninger, S. *Dynamic Détente: The United States and Europe 1964–1975*. Lanham, MD: Lexington Books, 2016.
Kramer, M. 'Editor's Note'. *Journal of Cold War Studies* 18(3) (2016), 1–2.
Leffler, M.P. *For the Soul of Mankind: The United States, the Soviet Union and the Cold War*. New York: Hill and Wang, 2007.
Loth, W. *Helsinki, 1. August 1975: Entspannung und Abrüstung*. Munich: Deutscher Taschenbuch Verlag, 1998.
Loth, W. *Die Rettung der Welt: Entspannungspolitik im Kalten Krieg 1950–1991*. Frankfurt am Main: Campus Verlag, 2016.
Möckli, D. *European Foreign Policy during the Cold War: Heath, Brandt, Pompidou and the Dream of Political Unity*. London and New York: I.B. Tauris, 2009.
Niedhart, G. *Entspannung in Europa: Die Bundesrepublik Deutschland und der Warschauer Pakt*. Munich: De Gruyter Oldenbourg Verlag, 2014.
Niedhart, G. 'Introduction'. *Journal of Cold War Studies* 18(3) (2016), 3–13.
Niedhart, G. 'Der Ost-West-Konflikt: Konfrontation im Kalten Krieg und Stufen der Deeskalation'. *Archiv für Sozialgeschichte* 50 (2010), 557–94.
Niedhart, G. 'Ostpolitik: Transformation through Communication and the Quest for Peaceful Change'. *Journal of Cold War Studies* 18(3) (2016), 14–59.
Pabsch, W. 'Das Kulturforum der KSZE in Budapest: Bericht und Bewertung'. *Europa-Archiv* 20(7) (1986), 211–16.

Peter, M. *Die Bundesrepublik im KSZE-Prozess 1975–1983: Die Umkehrung der Diplomatie*. Berlin, Munich and Boston, MA: De Gruyter Oldenbourg Verlag, 2015.
Peter, M., and H. Wentker (eds). *Die KSZE im Ost-West-Konflikt: Internationale Politik und gesellschaftliche Transformation 1975–1990*. Munich: Oldenbourg Verlag, 2012.
Potthoff, H. *Die 'Koalition der Vernunft': Deutschlandpolitik in den 80er Jahren*. Munich: Deutscher Taschenbuch Verlag, 1995.
Rey, M.-P. '"Europe Is Our Common Home": A Study of Gorbachev's Diplomatic Concept'. *Cold War History* 4(2) (2004), 33–65.
Ritter, G.A. *Hans-Dietrich Genscher, das Auswärtige Amt und die deutsche Vereinigung*. Munich: C.H. Beck, 2013.
Romano, A. *From Détente in Europe to European Détente: How the West Shaped the Helsinki CSCE*. Brussels: P.I.E. Peter Lang, 2009.
Rosin, Ph. *Die Schweiz im KSZE-Prozess 1972–1983: Einfluß durch Neutralität*. Munich: Oldenbourg Verlag, 2014.
Savranskaya, S. 'Human Rights Movement in the USSR after the Signing of the Helsinki Final Act, and the Reaction of Soviet Authorities', in L. Nuti (ed.), *The Crisis of Détente in Europe: From Helsinki to Gorbachev, 1975–1985* (London and New York: Routledge, 2009), 26–40.
Savranskaya, S. 'The Logic of 1989: The Soviet Peaceful Withdrawal from Eastern Europe', in S. Savranskaya, T. Blanton and V. Zubok (eds), *Masterpieces of History: The Peaceful End of the Cold War in Europe, 1989* (Budapest and New York: Central European University Press, 2010), 1–48.
Savranskaya, S. 'In the Name of Europe: Soviet Withdrawal from Eastern Europe', in F. Bozo, M.-P. Rey, N.P. Ludlow and L. Nuti (eds), *Europe and the End of the Cold War: A Reappraisal* (London and New York: Routledge, 2008), 36–48.
Selvage, D. 'The Superpowers and the Conference on Security and Cooperation in Europe, 1977–1983', in M. Peter and H. Wentker (eds), *Die KSZE im Ost-West-Konflikt: Internationale Politik und gesellschaftliche Transformation 1975–1990* (Munich: Oldenbourg Verlag, 2012), 15–58.
Snyder, S.B. 'The Foundation for Vienna: A Reassessment of the CSCE in the Mid-1980s'. *Cold War History* 10(4) (2010), 493–512.
Snyder, S.B. *Human Rights Activism and the End of the Cold War: A Transnational History of the Helsinki Network*. Cambridge: Cambridge University Press, 2011.
von Saal, Y. 'Die Folgen des KSZE-Prozesses in der Sowjetunion der Perestroika: Der KSZE-Faktor in der Eigendynamik des Wertewandels', in M. Peter and H. Wentker (eds), *Die KSZE im Ost-West-Konflikt: Internationale Politik und gesellschaftliche Transformation 1975–1990* (Munich: Oldenbourg Verlag, 2012), 285–304.
von Saal, Y. *KSZE-Prozess und Perestroika in der Sowjetunion: Demokratisierung, Werteumbruch und Auflösung 1985–1991*. Munich: Oldenbourg Verlag, 2014.
Wentker, H. 'Vom Gegner zum Partner: Gorbatschow und seine Politik im Urteil Helmut Kohls'. *Historisch-Politische Mitteilungen* 22(1) (2015), 1–34.

 12

Transformation by Linkage?
Arms Control, Human Rights and the Rift between Moscow and East Berlin in the Late 1980s

Oliver Bange

Introduction

Neither the so-called Stockholm process nor the military and security-political side of the CSCE conference series has so far been the focus of historiographical research. As a result, the sources introduced here – although compiled for the top echelon of the Socialist Unity Party (SED) and the German Democratic Republic (GDR) leadership – are still unknown and have not been the subject of historiographical analysis. They show that a close link existed between 'military détente' and dissent throughout the 1980s, coming to a head in East Germany in the autumn of 1989 and forging the way for a new post-Cold War order in Europe.

When people in the public and academia talk today about the 'CSCE process' or the 'Helsinki effect', they are almost without exception referring to the importance that Basket Three of the Helsinki Final Act had for the dissident movements in the member states of the Warsaw Pact.[1] According to this narrative, the Final Document of the Conference on Security and Cooperation in Europe of August 1975 served as (1) a point of public and political reference, (2) a legitimation before the courts, and (3) important moral support and a source of self-assurance for the democracy movements. Meanwhile, against the communist authorities of state and party it served as a kind of foot-shackle, increasingly hindering and preventing them from conducting a decisive crack-down against the emerging opposition movements in their states.

The following analysis diverts from this well-established historiographical narrative by focusing on the security and military-political dimensions of the CSCE process. Like the much better known and researched human dimension (Basket Three) of the CSCE, the military dimension of the 'Helsinki process' also greatly influenced the outcome of the East–West conflict. At least six different aspects can be distinguished to this effect.

First, the confidence-building and arms control side of the CSCE provided for ongoing conversations and thus for *continuity* even in periods of crisis, especially in the years between 1979 and 1984. Second, precisely because of the common interest in arms control as a way out of the political and military-strategic impasse in the early 1980s, the military aspect embedded in the Final Act constituted an important *incentive* to continue if not with détente, then at least with bridge-building or bridge maintenance. Third, it provided an important *linkage* by connecting the military aspects such as arms control, disarmament and confidence-building measures (CBMs) with the human dimension (Basket Three, catalogue of principles). Fourth, it helped to build *confidence* between the blocs, because even a partial transparency – resulting from the CBMs of the 1970s – provided assurances about the non-belligerent or even peaceful intentions of the other side. This kind of security, often and aptly described as a security of the mind, could then transform, step by step, into trust. And this transformation can indeed be observed in the period between 1984 and 1990 in the negotiations on CBMs, on Intermediate-Range Nuclear Forces (INF) and on Conventional Forces in Europe (CFE).

Fifth, the confidence and trust built by security and military policy measures allowed for further *change* – not only in security but also in societal and economic questions. It thereby played a significant role in facilitating Germany's reunification. The fear of a reunified Germany, overly strong and uncontrollable, had virtually evaporated by 1990. The West Germans remained institutionally 'anchored' within the CSCE/OSCE, within NATO and within the EC/EU integration process. They and their intentions became transparent, and they would remain so even after 1990. This latter aspect was also supported by the fact that contacts between the military of both sides already existed in 1989–90 due to the system of observers and inspectors already established by the Conference on Confidence and Security Building Measures and Disarmament in Europe (CDE) in Stockholm in 1986. The system itself and the experience of participating in the CSCE proved to be essential when the Western Group of Forces (WGF) of the USSR had to be withdrawn from German territory in the years between 1990 and 1994. And although it never materialized, the mere hopes and expectations for a pan-European security system constituted an important factor in the peaceful reordering of the continent during these later years.

But it is the sixth impact that this chapter will focus on: the CDE, INF and CFE negotiations all came with a price tag for Moscow. There would be no breather for the USSR's overstrung economy in the arms race if the communist leadership in Moscow would not allow for substantial improvement in human contacts and civil rights. This linkage and the predisposition of the new CPSU leadership to follow this route led to a *sustained rift* in security policies between East Berlin and Moscow. By late 1988 and early 1989, the external and internal security of the SED regime was thus compromised to such an extent that it seemed to make the public cessation of its state, the German Democratic Republic, only a matter of time.

The 'Madrid Effect': On the Interconnection between the Global Confrontation of the Superpowers, Security Interests in Central Europe and the Continuation of the CSCE Process, 1980–83

Despite the fact that in the early 1980s a so-called 'second Cold War' emerged between the two superpowers, the USA and the USSR, the antagonistic cooperation of the early détente never ceased in Europe and even intensified on a variety of levels.[2] A decisive factor in this was the CSCE follow-up conference in Madrid, which started in 1980.

The leadership of the ruling SED in East Berlin continued to monitor the negotiations in the Spanish capital under two guises: the external security of the GDR and the instruments for the party's projection of power within its own state. The reactions to the disarmament proposals, with which Leonid Brezhnev appealed to the NATO states in his speech during the twenty-sixth party conference of the CPSU, were a telling example of both the interests and the scepticism harboured in East Berlin. In the midst of public controversy in West European societies over NATO's dual-track decision, the General Secretary of the Communist Party in the Soviet Union proclaimed a 'programme for peace'. This entailed negotiations over substantial confidence-building measures covering the entire European part of the USSR, the renewal of bilateral negotiations about strategic (*ergo* global) nuclear weapons with the United States, and a moratorium against the deployment of new nuclear missiles of the intermediate-range class in Europe.[3] For Moscow, which had already begun to deploy substantial numbers of SS-20 missiles in Europe, this temporary freeze offered distinct advantages.

In the same year that Brezhnev put forward his 'programme for peace', economic recession led to a global shortage of money. At the end of 1981, East Berlin was even faced with a complete stop of credits for the East German economy. 'Hard' currency could now only be obtained through negotiations with Western governments and particularly with Bonn. The West Germans all too soon became aware of this instrument, linking credits to a variety of demands on East Berlin and other Eastern capitals. These included restraint in dealing with Poland, a mandate for a European conference on arms control and disarmament to be negotiated in Madrid, and a viable respect for the liberty rights of individuals as agreed upon in the CSCE process.[4] The compulsion for trade translated into a compulsion for détente – a détente that not only referred to security-political dealings with the West but which also contained a relaxation of rules within GDR society.[5]

When the Polish crisis heightened in early 1982, the common interest of the Europeans in meaningful CBMs – meaning more security from surprise attacks through more transparency about troops, dislocation and manoeuvres – proved to be an important glue holding the Madrid negotiations together. Enlarging political détente to encompass the military sphere was meant to be accomplished by a common decision in Madrid to convoke a special CSCE conference on disarmament in Europe. Western supporters of this idea – above all the French and the West Germans – knew about the personal interest that the ruler in the Kremlin had displayed in this project.[6] However, no reason for 'exaggerated expectations' was to be given to the public.[7] In his previously cited speech before the twenty-sixth CPSU party conference in March 1981, Brezhnev expanded on this idea, offering to place all European territories of the USSR under CBM regulations, putting the hitherto uncompromising position of the US administration into question. It was only now that the head of the US delegation Max Kampelman succeeded in obtaining consent from the White House to link the American focus on human rights to the interests of the Central Europeans in stabilizing the existing military antagonism.[8]

In the end, the conference in Madrid led to a surprisingly smooth perpetuation of the CSCE process, to an expansion of the CSCE process into military détente (including arms procurement, deployment and doctrines), to a new 're-engagement' under Ronald Reagan of both superpowers in security affairs and to significant improvements in the fields of human contacts and the freedom of information and opinion. The CSCE follow-up conference in Madrid ended on 9 September 1983 with a decision to establish a Conference on Confidence and Security Building Measures and Disarmament in Europe (CDE). It was only a few weeks later, on 25 October, that this first forum within the CSCE framework for arms negotiations began its work.

The 'Stockholm Process': From the Continuation of Multilateral Security Talks to a Policy of Superpower Deals, 1983–86

At the same time as the CDE negotiations started, NATO began the realization of the second part of its so-called 'dual-track decision'. The rapid deployment of the Pershing II and cruise missile systems had a profound impact on the military situation in Europe. The speed and reach especially of the Pershing II meant that, in an Eastern perspective, the forewarning time (the time to react) went down to a mere seven minutes.[9] The reach of both weapon systems enlarged the prospective battlefield right up to Moscow itself. Their precision and the East's inability to intercept practically discounted the 'second wave' of tank armies, hitherto thought to be the ultimate trump card in a conventional war between the two camps. Their capabilities introduced a so-called 'grey zone' between tactical and strategic tasks.[10]

During the first round of negotiations in Stockholm, the representatives of the Warsaw Treaty Organization (WTO) states did not hide their intention to use the CDE 'to limit the damage done by the USA missile stationing' by devising 'concrete measures for preventing nuclear war'.[11] These measures included a renunciation of military force, a non-first-use policy for nuclear weapons, the elimination of chemical weapons and the introduction of zones free of nuclear weapons. Reaching beyond the mere military level, the negotiations were thus meant to 'stabilize once again the relations between states of differing societal orders'.[12] It seems apt to say that fear was a driving motive behind the search for military détente and thus stood at the beginnings of the Stockholm process.

Warsaw Pact and NATO objectives within the second round of CDE negotiations differed accordingly. While the Warsaw Pact member states stressed 'the urgency' for measures to reduce the probability of a surprise attack and especially a nuclear 'confrontation', the NATO countries argued for Confidence and Security Building Measures (CSBMs). In their perspective, the exchange of annual manoeuvre plans, announcement of other military activities and the invitation of observers from the other bloc would create more transparency and thus allow for a better estimate of the opponent.[13]

The GDR's special dependency on the USSR in the field of military and security policies practically forced the party leadership in East Berlin and their negotiators in Stockholm to take on the role of Moscow's 'best pupil' and 'best ally'.[14] Similarly, the country's precarious geopolitical and ideological location at the frontline between the two blocs fed into East German interest in maintaining a common WTO front and peace rhetoric. Somewhat unsurprisingly, East German delegates were still told during the fourth round of negotiations in December 1984 to work hard for a 'coordinated approach [of the WTO delegations] on the basis of the Soviet conference document', a document that had been tabled at the very beginning almost a year earlier.[15]

Only three months later, however, Mikhail Gorbachev became the General Secretary of the CPSU. He almost immediately started to insert a new kind of dynamic into the CDE negotiations. In July 1985, the Warsaw Pact delegations tabled four proposals for the mutual announcement of military activities. This had been a long-standing Western demand (which remained unmentioned in East German documents) that signalled 'the will of the socialist states' to negotiate in earnest.[16] In the next round of negotiations, in autumn 1985, this signal was taken up by a number of NATO member states and the neutral and nonaligned countries present in Stockholm.[17] When the American delegates (in an attempt to link their agreement to a successful conclusion of the INF negotiations and human rights issues to be debated in the CSCE experts' forum in Bern) protracted the discussions, it was Gorbachev who once again pushed for a solution. In January and then again in April 1986, he offered partial and practical solutions to the key question of obligatory announcements of military activities.[18]

With this, Gorbachev had broken with the negotiating line agreed among WTO governments, but apparently he had also broken the deadlock in the negotiations. Only three months later, Soviet delegates confidentially informed their East German colleagues about the real state of the negotiations in Stockholm (meaning not the plenary sessions but the superpower talks behind the scenes). According to the head of the Soviet delegation, the problem of control and verification was and had to be 'solvable'.[19] It had to be solved in a pragmatic manner, because – as East German party leader Erich Honecker was informed only a fortnight later – 'without a formula for controlling the adherence to the agreements on the announcement of military activities acceptable to all [participants] there was no realistic chance' to conclude the conference in Stockholm successfully.[20] Honecker deemed this information to be so important that he immediately ordered it to be brought to the attention of all members and candidates of the SED politburo.

The outcome of the Stockholm negotiations in September 1986 mirrored the Soviet information from July and early August. It was a compromise with a direct impact on the GDR's security, but one with which East Berlin could still live. From now on, military activities had to be announced forty-two days in advance if they involved more than thirteen thousand soldiers or three hundred tanks.[21] The announcement had to describe the 'activity' in great detail, but East German authorities took consolation in the fact that under the agreed limits not every divisional exercise had to be announced and explained. It was obvious from the outset that most of the Eastern 'activities' falling under this provision were to take place within the GDR's territory. In an East German perspective, this would bring a flood of Western inspection teams, military observers and journalists in their wake. This of course had to be measured against the ideological background of East German security policies. After all, East Berlin's priority was still the fight against the so-called 'political-ideological diversion' (PID), an acronym describing the assumed subversion of the GDR's socialist society by visitors and ideas from the West. On the other hand, the Final Document from Stockholm worked both ways, and the GDR's authorities were determined to 'fully exploit the possibilities for [gathering] insights into the NATO and neutral states'.[22]

In retrospect, the number of manoeuvre observers and inspections under the Stockholm Document appears rather limited, but they apparently led to numerous sleepless nights in East Berlin. While the CDE negotiations lasted, the minister for state security had demanded an 'exposure' of Western 'peace rhetoric' at Stockholm. Subsequently he argued for an 'even better' ideological education of East German soldiers, particularly of those who might come into contact with military personnel from the West. In 1985/86 an internal analysis came to the conclusion that about one-third of the new recruits had no clear 'class position'.[23] This might have been pure coincidence – or already a kind of 'CDE effect'. As a reaction to this, East German Minister of State Security Erich Mielke demanded 'more influence of the party [meaning the Ministry for State Security (MfS)] within the army'.[24] This resulted in a wave of educational measures for a continuous 'communication of the enemy image'.[25] However, with the proclamation of the new defensive doctrine of the WTO in May 1987 and the publication of the INF treaty, the rhetorical split of those tasked with this indoctrination became ever more painful. All of this resulted in a gradual delegitimization of the SED system in the field of its official security ('peace') policies.

Arms Control and Civil Rights: Superpower Linkages with Fatal Implications for the GDR, 1986–88

In May 1986, only four months after the CSCE expert forum on the 'human dimension' had begun its work in Bern, MfS analysts drew their superiors' attention to the fact that the Soviet leadership appeared prepared to compromise on human rights in order to make headway with the West and especially the Americans in the military and economic field. American officials had indeed declared in internal consultations with other delegations from NATO states that they would only agree to progress in the field of military security in Europe if the Warsaw Pact states gave way on civil rights issues and human contacts.[26] Soviet delegates rather quickly gave into these demands and forced the entire Warsaw Pact to follow the line negotiated between them and the Americans. The initial compromise in Bern featured improved possibilities for communication and family contacts without an age limit, contacts between foreigners and citizens, and family reunions particularly if minors were involved. Furthermore, the 'human dimension' of the CSCE recommendations was to be turned into obligations, and the application within each state to be monitored by the CSCE conferences.

East Berlin's fears of having to pay the bill for a security deal between Moscow and Washington came to a head during the Warsaw Pact deputy foreign ministers' meeting in September 1986. Vadim Loginov, the head of the Soviet delegation, declared that a 'balanced progress' within the CSCE would 'practically mean a linkage between advances in military détente and compromises in human questions'.[27] The Soviets informed their surprised comrades from the Warsaw Pact that Moscow was 'working on a new approach' to civil rights questions: their foreign ministry had established a 'department for humanitarian and cultural relations' and a special group within the consular department was monitoring the transfer into practice of new legal directives on family reunions and family travel. All of this would be published at the start of the CSCE conference in Vienna.[28] Not only the leadership in East Berlin but also other 'brotherly states' took issue with this and in turn demanded that Moscow 'intensify the coordination on these questions and wage the tactic of this approach carefully and timely'.[29] Such a united opposition against policy directives from Moscow had rarely if ever been noted before in any of the Warsaw Pact committee meetings.

However, Gorbachev refused to change either direction or conduct. At the end of the same month, he and Egor Ligachev, the powerful secretary of the CPSU Central Committee, confirmed this link between security policies and human rights in internal speeches in Moscow.[30] When East German intelligence got scent of this and SED officials simultaneously drafted a memorandum on 'mutual security' between East and West together with West German social democrats, the GDR's minister for state security, Erich Mielke, must have felt surrounded by enemies within his own camp.[31]

Almost a year later, in October 1987, the East German Ministry for State Security (or Stasi) intelligence section once again warned the SED leadership that Gorbachev was intending to submit to Western human rights demands at the CSCE follow-up meeting in Vienna as a quid pro quo deal for American acquiescence to a 'double zero' solution on intermediate nuclear forces (the INF treaty) plus their participation in a disarmament conference on conventional forces in Europe.[32] Apparently, the Soviet delegation in Vienna had already been instructed accordingly.

For this, Gorbachev was prepared to allow a clause on 'free movement' (the entry and exit of persons to or from one country) to be inserted into the concluding document; to agree to bilateral mechanisms of control in civil rights questions (consultations between government officials, obligatory replies to questions posed by other states, discussions between members of the respective parliaments and the constitution of an international parliamentary commission); to grant written explanations in case of refused applications for travel; to acknowledge independent Helsinki watch groups; and to deal with 'unsolved cases' within six months.

As a consequence of the intended deal, the SED leadership would have to open East Germany's socialist society to a plethora of Western influences. All of this, of course, had to infringe on the livelihood of the SED regime and its state. East Germany's diplomats remonstrated accordingly. They told the Soviet delegation in Vienna and their Foreign Ministry in Moscow 'several times that the Soviet ideas went well beyond [the GDR's] national legislation'. They demanded that the Soviet leadership should 'respect the interests of the GDR'.[33]

At this point, the only other Warsaw Pact member state openly opposed to the Soviet-American deal was Nicolae Ceausescu's Romania. As a consequence, East Berlin's diplomats in Vienna saw themselves in a precarious state of isolation, and therefore requested that their mandate, to which Honecker had personally consented only in early October, ought to be changed as soon as possible.[34]

In order to maintain a common front of Warsaw Pact states in Vienna (on which Soviet guarantees for the GDR effectively hinged), the party and state leadership in East Berlin finally gave way and agreed to the draft of the concluding document in Vienna. The experts in the special working group, constituted in East Berlin for monitoring the drafting of the Vienna document, grudgingly conceded. For them it was all too obvious 'that the S[oviet] U[nion] is now prepared to grant far-reaching compromises in questions of key importance to the GDR – and that she is supported in this endeavour by Hungary, the CSSR and other socialist states'. From East Berlin's perspective, the new leadership in Moscow was thereby giving way to the economic and security-political 'blackmail' of the West.[35]

The only apparent exception to the SED politburo's general agreement to the Vienna draft concerned the admittance of 'Helsinki watch groups'. Appendix 2 of the briefing memorandum for the politburo maintained that these had 'to be rejected as before', even if this went against CSCE regulations. This concerned both 'the founding of and the toleration of activities of so-called national and international Helsinki watch groups', and particularly any 'right of individuals to monitor the state authorities' compliance with the CSCE documents'. Appendix 3 maintained that this control was 'strictly conducted' within the GDR 'by responsible state institutions, societal organizations and groups'.[36] This referred to the GDR's 'Committee for European Security and Cooperation', which was made up of representatives from all parties of the National Front, from other official mass organizations in the GDR and from churches. The members of this rather official 'Committee' were informed about CSCE-related issues by East German diplomats on a semi-annual basis. Control did certainly take place within the Committee, but this was not control by independent citizens over the application of the Helsinki Final Act. Rather, it was the party itself and its State Security who monitored the conformity of societal organizations with the party line.

The effects for the border regime of the GDR (the 'wall') and the mechanisms of domestic control were enormous. MfS analysts proclaimed a completely 'new situation' resulting from 'the dismantling of mines' along the German-German border, the 'non-application of guns – as is now required for political reasons', and the 'interruption of the modernization of the border installations'.[37]

From now on, reverting to 'armed intervention' – meaning the shooting of East Germans trying to escape to the West through, under or over the wall – was out of the question.[38] Instead, only 'preventive measures' could be applied.[39] Mielke's deputy, Lieutenant-General Neiber, aptly observed that the work of East German and Polish border troops in the 'hinterland' was however characterized by 'insufficient vigilance' and 'unfavourable conditions of distance and time', which seemed more to favour escape attempts than to hinder them.[40]

Just as with illegal emigrants, legal immigrants were becoming increasingly difficult to control: the documents accepted in Vienna practically granted free working conditions to foreign journalists within the GDR.[41] If fully applied, the Vienna document meant the 'end of the obligatory and centralized application and admission procedures for journalistic work'. It would also entail 'free access to public and private sources of information' (which included church and dissident groups in the GDR) and the 'uncontrolled' forwarding of information by journalists. And there would be no more personal 'advisers' for each journalist. From an MfS perspective, these 'changed conditions' seemed to necessitate even 'higher security precautions' than before – in both domestic and foreign affairs.[42]

Already in early 1988, when the sell-out of the security interests of the SED regime in return for benefits in the USSR's military security became apparent, the Stasi had tried to adapt to the new working conditions. In order to be able 'to limit the apparently improving opportunities of foreign journalists for intelligence and other subversive activities', the legal system of the GDR had to be adapted 'in time' and the State Security itself ought to be granted even more opportunities for control within 'all institutions and production sites within the GDR'.[43] MfS officials reminded their diplomatic colleagues in the summer of 1988 of a specific 'Enactment Regulation of the Directive about the activities of press organs of other states and their correspondents within the GDR'. According to this regulation from 1979, 'any law infringement' by foreign correspondents had to be documented in order to 'guarantee a differentiated application of sanctions'. It was obvious who had to document and to sanction, but what sanctions would be enacted 'always' depended on the 'political aims' and was therefore a 'political decision'.[44]

Once again, Honecker was confronted with a noticeable limitation of control and repression within his own sphere of power. And once again he withdrew to his imagination of the 'power of the factual', as he had already explained to Brezhnev at the very beginning of the CSCE process in the summer of 1975. He now explained this concept to a gathering of regional party secretaries: 'A state border, secured under all conditions, will remain a decisive factor for peace and security in the entire socialist community'.[45] With this he meant to describe the ongoing existence of the GDR and the continuation of the USSR's guarantee of military security for his country. On both accounts he was misleading himself and his audience.

When the CSCE conference in Vienna came to an end in January 1989, the unified position of the Warsaw Pact states on questions concerning civil rights and human contacts had evaporated; it had simply been 'lost' in the process, as Stasi analysts dryly remarked.[46] All that was left for the MfS to do was to advise the SED politburo to play a waiting game and to draw out any adaptations to the new international rules until September 1989 and thus prevent any legalization of Helsinki groups, at least temporarily.[47] This was possible because 'the citizen [obtained] a legal right' on the regulations codified in the Vienna document 'only after their transfer into domestic law'.[48] In early 1989 this still appeared to leave enough time to change East German legislation in order to outlaw Helsinki watch groups as 'acting outside the existing legal order and against the state'.[49]

The End Game: The Disintegration of the Warsaw Pact and the Disposal of the GDR, February 1988–April 1989

Predictably, these informal and successfully enacted deals between Washington and Moscow over arms control and civil rights resulted in an – albeit rather short-lived – period of superpower bilateralism. The consequences within the Warsaw Pact were severe, leading to an increasing de-coupling of the GDR and other member states from the USSR in the field of security policies. The increasing dissolution of the antagonism between East and West very soon translated into an existential threat for the already weakened GDR. The party and state leadership in East Berlin was practically excluded from the ensuing dialogue between the superpowers over security issues – a dialogue that had originally been reinitiated with the help of the two Germanies. Thus, during the 42nd United Nations General Assembly in February 1988, Soviet officials negotiated global peace-keeping missions with their American counterparts without even telling 'the group of socialist countries'. After finding out about this 'solo effort' of the Soviets, East Berlin's Foreign Minister Oskar Fischer angrily remarked to his own advisers that cooperation between Warsaw Pact delegations 'has never before been so bad'.[50] Fischer's defeatist remarks were immediately reported back to East Berlin by a Stasi informant within his own team.

When the departmental heads of the foreign ministries of the WTO countries met in the same month in Warsaw to discuss the further course after the Vienna CSCE conference, this did nothing but document the fast-moving disintegration of the Warsaw Pact. An apparently flabbergasted Honecker left numerous annotations on the report submitted to him. Like the delegates at the start of the meeting, Honecker too seems to have welcomed the negotiations on further CSBMs and large conventional troop cuts in Europe. He noted Gorbachev's priority to hold the next CSCE meeting in Moscow, but feared the centrifugal effects within the WTO with regard to human rights. While the GDR, the CSSR and Romania pointed to a number of problems connected with the Vienna agreements on human rights and human relations, 'the USSR, Hungary, Poland and even Bulgaria' claimed that the Final Document in Vienna 'does comply with the interests of the socialist states, mirroring the transformation processes within their own countries'.[51] The First Secretary of the SED marked this section of the paper with two black crosses.

Soon after the Vienna CSCE conference had closed, the SED politburo realized that the deal forced upon East Berlin would not bring the much-desired domestic stability. Instead, the Final Document from Vienna offered new possibilities particularly for West Germany in the field of human questions and human contacts. A briefing paper forwarded in April 1989 to all members and candidates of the politburo in East Berlin even judged that the 'mechanism for bi- and multilateral cooperation over human rights and human questions', agreed upon in Vienna, would constitute 'new options for blackmail and pressure against the GDR'.[52]

For the GDR, however, the situation could still worsen further. During the CSCE Information Forum in London in April 1989, the member states of the Warsaw Pact fought out their differences in front of a global public. East Berlin, Bucharest, Sofia and even Prague took a rather dogmatic position on the role of the media, claiming that they ought to support 'positive international processes'.[53] The representatives of the USSR, Hungary and Poland, however, argued for a 'maximum amount of transparency and information for the people' and for compliance with international standards. They were in favour of creating an all-European, trans-bloc information network. Representatives from Hungary and Poland even 'propagated bourgeois values about the freedom of information and opinion', such as the creation of a 'new "pluralistic" information system in Poland, the rejection of a monopoly on opinion, [and] the allowance of private media in Hungary'. In the plenum, Hungary even attacked Romania directly for hindering the work of Hungarian journalists. Thus, by April 1989 a deeply divided Warsaw Treaty Organization no longer merited the traditional description of a 'bloc'.[54]

Yet what the SED leadership accused its Soviet 'friends' of, namely the sell-out of societal security, East Berlin itself also practised. The only difference was the currency of these tit-for-tat deals with the West. Still in the final phase of the CSCE negotiations in Vienna, the socialist party leaders in East Berlin had sold off their agreement in the field of human questions and contacts in return for economic benefits from the West. As East Berlin's intelligence service aptly noticed, 'FRG government circles' and particularly West German commerce were cheering: 'Therefore, the conditions for turning CSCE obligations into real improvements ... with regard to East–West trade have never been so promising than after the conclusion of the meeting in Vienna'.[55]

The new Soviet leadership deserted the GDR hardliners not only ideologically but also in the military and security field – a quintessential condition for the continuation of SED rule in East Germany. During the conference series on conventional forces in Europe (CFE), which started in January 1989, the Soviet delegates negotiated large-scale troop withdrawals from central Europe, supported by some of their allies, while the attitude taken by East Berlin's diplomats remained for obvious reasons rather lacklustre.[56] In the wake of Gorbachev's arms control and disarmament initiatives, even the GDR announced in late January 1989 a unilateral reduction of its army by ten thousand. In the same month, acting in the spirit of the long-established loyalty with the 'friends' in Moscow, East German Minister of Defence Heinz Kessler even went out of his doctrinal way in explaining to his West German colleague the new data on soldiers and armaments in the Warsaw Pact armies.[57]

Despite or perhaps precisely because of these unilateral disarmament steps by the Soviet Union, experts in the GDR continued to fear NATO capabilities 'for a surprise attack or large-scale offensive operations'.[58] After all, the GDR remained a frontline state in the conflict between East and West, and Soviet troop withdrawals did nothing to ease the fears of NATO's growing military capabilities. This angst over the GDR's external security was nourished and perpetuated by intelligence information gathered just before the start of the CFE negotiations. Apparently, in December 1988 NATO's Ministerial Council had declared Soviet reductions to be irrelevant to the military balance in Europe. Furthermore, NATO ministers had agreed to further pursue their own programmes for arms procurement.[59]

Time and again during the CFE negotiations, East German officials were confronted with the necessity to define and pursue their own security interests rather than those of the Eastern bloc or the Soviet Union. These rifts and frictions between East Berlin and Moscow resulted from an informal linkage between the arms control and disarmament problems with the issue of an increasing liberalization of European societies within the CSCE framework. Soon enough, the West took due notice of this rather special effect within the Eastern bloc. Washington's analysts realized that the 'decreasing fear of the state authorities and swindling attitude to adapt' to the system not only changed the forms of protest but also led to a more moderate approach by state organs and to a significant drop in the 'motivation of soldiers'.[60]

In May 1989, SED leaders in East Berlin detected the first signs that the new US administration of George Bush was determined to capitalize on this situation by widening the gulf in East German–Soviet relations. According to East German information, the Americans intended to use the CFE framework in order to demonstrate to East German officials the necessity to define and pursue the GDR's own security interests. Washington's negotiators 'ought to explain' to the East Germans that the US administration would 'prefer a stable security system in Central Europe including two [!] German states'.[61]

Even if the West German government harboured any military intentions – meaning intentions to unify the two German states – this 'would meet with the decisive resistance of the other NATO member states'. But this American guarantee for the existence of the GDR, if necessary against West German desires, came with a price tag: the precondition was that 'offensive Soviet forces were no longer deployed on GDR territory'.[62] This was an obvious reference to the issues negotiated within the CFE framework. It did not necessarily mean that Soviet forces had to be withdrawn from the GDR in order to enable such a deal over the GDR's statehood. However, the units of the 'Group of Soviet Forces in Germany' (GSFG) had to lose their capabilities for large-scale offensive operations.[63] After all, this 'structural inability to attack' remained at the core of the CFE negotiations. The very concept was to constitute the essence of the CFE Treaty and the Vienna document in November 1990. It greatly facilitated Germany's reunification within a wider reordering of Europe, and it remains the central platform for security-building measures in Europe to this day.

With Gorbachev's proclamation in December 1988, just before the start of the CFE negotiations in Vienna, that the people of each nation had the right to choose their own societal system (the so-called 'Sinatra doctrine'), even the exit of individual states from their respective blocks and societal systems had become feasible.[64] In spring 1989, the Bush administration also judged that 'the end of the Cold War' had approached. US experts both at home and at the CFE negotiations assumed that Poland and Hungary would move out of the Warsaw Treaty Organization sooner rather than later. Geopolitically this would turn the GDR into a security and military-political island. To complicate things, this island would be inhabited by a larger number of Soviet troops with a rather precarious lifeline back home.

Of course, the Americans were interested in an end to communist rule in Central and Eastern Europe, but from Washington's perspective the new situation also demanded the prevention of a military crisis in Europe. Therefore, the destabilization of entire societies in Central and Eastern Europe had to be avoided.[65]

In an American – and in a wider sense also a Western – perspective, the months ahead promised 'great opportunities' but also contained 'severe risks'. The dialogue between the US and the USSR was therefore intended to be widened as soon as possible to cover all kinds of security-political questions relevant to both superpowers, comprising both military and societal security issues. Against this background, it was hardly surprising that Soviet and American delegates would soon sit down together in the back rooms of the CFE negotiations in Vienna to discuss cautiously – but never frankly – the options following a dissolution of communist rule in East Germany.[66]

In the end, it was the East German citizens themselves who prevented the kind of scenario envisaged in the 'immoral offer' by the US. At the time the offer was brought to the attention of the SED leadership via indirect channels, there was no dissident movement of considerable size detectable within the GDR. Unlike in Poland, a further duration of SED rule seemed highly likely, at least from an outside perspective. Things changed, however, when GDR citizens began to monitor the rigging of regional elections in their country in March 1989, an undertaking that involved detailed logistics over the entire country, which by its nature had to involve numerous people, and affected East German society well beyond the small circle of opposition groups. From then on, opposition against party rule widened continuously, from the embassy refugees in Budapest and Prague in the summer to the peace prayers and mass demonstrations in the autumn. Thus, from spring or early summer 1989 onwards there was simply no need to reiterate the kind of offer to the rulers in East Berlin that had been defeated earlier in the year.

Conclusion

The late 1970s and early 1980s saw a breakdown in the diplomatic relations between the superpowers. They also featured not only a continuation but a significant intensification of East–West contacts and cooperation on a wide variety of levels within Europe itself.[67] Much of this helped to put Soviet–American relations back on track in the second half of the 1980s. However, perhaps more importantly, the early

1980s saw the initiation of key developments in the military, economic, media and human rights fields that became momentous factors in the 'end game' of the Cold War between 1987 and 1989. Even the more indirect and less visible methods of repression developed and deployed by the Stasi in the 1970s and 1980s were found in breach of more and more international agreements signed by East German representatives in the wake of the CSCE process. East German experts had already warned of this development in the early 1970s, but increasing economic difficulties and the determination of the Gorbachev administration to pursue Soviet security interests within the CSCE in exchange for greater give in the 'human dimension' committed party and state leaders of the GDR to an irreversible multilateral process that eventually created the framing for the demise of their own state.

One might even argue that without the security framework that came out of the CSCE-CFE negotiations, Germany's reunification and Europe's reordering would not have taken place, or certainly not in the way and at the pace they did. The massive troop reductions and dislocations entailed in the CFE Treaty and the Vienna document practically guaranteed a 'structural inability to attack' just when it mattered in late 1990. The agreements also made for a seamless continuation of control-by-integration over Germany's now united armed forces. In November 1990, the CFE Treaty and the Vienna document became the main pillars of a system of military security in Europe (or what is left of it under the OSCE to this day). And it was no coincidence, but a central condition for the reordering of Europe, that the '2 plus 4' Treaty on Germany's unification was only enacted after the two documents on military security in Europe had been signed.[68]

Oliver Bange is a senior lecturer at the University of Mannheim and is currently working at the East Asia Desk at the German Ministry of Defence. He received his doctorate from the London School of Economics and his habilitation from the University of Mannheim. His research focuses include the diplomatic, military, social and nuclear history of the nineteenth and twentieth centuries. In 2017 he published *Sicherheit and Staat: Die Bündnis- und Militärpolitik der DDR im internationalen Kontext 1969 bis 1990* (ChLinks Verlag), and co-edited with Poul Villaume *The Long Détente: Changing Concepts of Security and Cooperation in Europe, 1950s–1980s* (Central European University Press, 2017).

Notes

 1. A selection of works in chronological order: D.C. Thomas, *The Helsinki Effect: International Norms, Human Rights and the Demise of Communism* (Princeton, NJ: Princeton University Press, 2001); A. Wenger, V. Mastny and C. Nuenlist (eds), *Origins of the European Security System: The Helsinki Process Revisited, 1969–1975* (London: Routledge, 2008); O. Bange and G. Niedhart (eds), *Helsinki 1975 and the Transformation of Europe* (New York and Oxford: Berghahn Books, 2008); T. Fischer, *Neutral Power in the CSCE: The N+N States and the Making of the Helsinki Accords 1975* (Baden-Baden: Nomos, 2009); S.B. Snyder, *Human Rights Activism and the End of the Cold War: A Transnational History of the Helsinki Network* (Cambridge: Cambridge University Press, 2011); C. Peterson, *Globalizing Human Rights: Private Citizens, the Soviet Union, and the West* (New York and London: Routledge, 2012); M. Peter and H. Wentker (eds), *Die KSZE im Ost-West-Konflikt: Internationale Politik und gesellschaftliche Transformation* (Munich: Oldenbourg, 2012). Most recently: G. Niedhart (ed.), 'CSCE, the German Question, and the Warsaw Pact', special issue of the *Journal of Cold War Studies* 18(3) (Summer 2016). The focus of most chapters in this volume also mirrors the preoccupation of the next generation of CSCE historians with Basket Three-related issues.
 2. Even before Ronald Reagan reintroduced the term 'Cold War' during his presidential campaign in 1979, it was Erich Honecker who praised the CSCE as an instrument against any 'second Cold War'. E. Honecker, 'Unsere Dokumente geben Antwort auf Fragen des Heute und Morgen', speech on 14 February 1976, edited, in E. Honecker, *Reden und Aufsätze*, vol. 4 (Berlin: Dietz Verlag, 1977), 200–15.
 3. The twenty-sixth party conference of the CPSU was held in Moscow from 23 February to 3 March 1981. Brezhnev made his speech on 23 February 1981; his proposals were officially presented to the US administration on 6 March 1981. See: XXVI. Parteitag der KPdSU—Dokumente (East Berlin, 1981); L.I. Brezhnev, *Rechenschaftsbericht des Zentralkomitees der KPdSU an den XXVI. Parteitag* (East Berlin: Dietz, 1981). For the importance of Brezhnev's 'programme for peace', see N. Inosemzew, 'Der XXVI. Parteitag der KPdSU und die Aussenpolitik der Sowjetunion', in Wissenschaftlicher Rat zur Erforschung der Friedens-und Abrüstungsprobleme (ed.), *Frieden und Abrüstung: Wissenschaftliche Forschungen* (Moscow: Progress, 1982), 22–34.
 4. This paragraph is based on information surveys on foreign policy from 1981 (Nos 1, 2, 14, 20, 23, 25, 29), between 5 January and 27 July 1981, Bundesbeauftragter für die Unterlagen des Staatssicherheitsdienstes der ehemaligen DDR (East German Stasi Archives – BstU): Hauptverwaltung A (Foreign Intelligence Section – HVA) 12.
 5. According to a detailed study of the legal history of the GDR, this interconnection between the foreign and domestic policies of the SED regime did indeed stop an already planned tightening of East German penal law

and even led to a partial relaxation of repression. J. Raschka, *Justizpolitik im SED-Staat: Anpassung und Wandel des Strafrechts während der Amtszeit Honeckers* (Cologne: Böhlau Verlag, 2000), 305.
6. Brezhnev's proposals for an extension of CBMs were included in the communiqué of the Committee of Foreign Ministers of the Warsaw Pact on 6 December 1979; edited in Europa Archiv Bd. 2 (1980), D49–D55. West German knowledge was confirmed in Information survey on foreign policy No. 2/81 from 12 January 1981, BStU: HVA 12.
7. 'Western opinions on the concluding document of the meeting in Madrid', Information survey on foreign policy No. 7/71 from 16 February 1981, BStU: HVA 12.
8. Albeit only under the condition that Moscow would accept the territorial framing of CBMs contained in the French draft. Information survey on foreign policy No. 15/81 from 20 April 1981, BStU: HVA 12. See also M. Kampelman, *Entering New Worlds: The Memoirs of a Private Man in Public Life* (New York: HarperCollins, 1991), 244; and Kampelman's memorandum from 9 January 1981 for the Reagan administration, Minnesota Historical Society, Kampelman Papers, Box 15. On Kampelman's important role, see Stephan Kieninger's chapter in this volume.
9. A public controversy ensued between NATO and Warsaw Pact countries over the question of whether the forewarning time was fifteen or only seven minutes. It would have taken about fifteen minutes for a Pershing II to reach Moscow. However, the missile would have appeared on Warsaw Pact radar systems only at its re-entry phase into the atmosphere, leaving at best seven minutes to react.
10. See O. Bange, 'SS-20 and Pershing II: Weapon Systems and the Dynamization of East-West Relations', in C. Becker-Schaum et al. (eds), *The Nuclear Crisis: The Arms Race, Cold War Anxiety, and the German Peace Movement of the 1980s* (New York and Oxford: Berghahn Books, 2016), 70–86.
11. In the following, both the official Eastern term (Warsaw Treaty Organization) and Western circumscriptions (Warsaw Pact, Eastern bloc etc.) are used in parallel. Neither term reflects an ideological or political position.
12. 'Report on the first round of negotiations at the Stockholm conference on confidence and security building measures in Europe', submitted to the SED politburo, 20 March 1984, Stiftung Archiv der Parteien und Massenorganisationen der DDR (Foundation archives of the parties and mass organisation of the GDDR – SAPMO): DY 30/11643. The code 'DY 30' refers to SED papers.
13. SED politburo information on the second round of CDE negotiations, 12 July 1984, SAPMO: DY 30/11643.
14. See, for example, the review of the mandate for East German negotiators in the third round of negotiations on 18 October 1984, SAPMO: DY 30/11643.
15. SED politburo information on the fourth round of negotiations, East Berlin, 19 December 1984, SAPMO: DY 30/11643.
16. SED politburo information on the sixth round of negotiations, East Berlin, 12 July 1985, SAPMO: DY 30/11643.

17. SED politburo information on the seventh round of negotiations, East Berlin, 24 October 1985, SAPMO: DY 30/11643.
18. Gorbachev announced his proposals on 15 January and 18 April 1986. The report to the SED politburo from 3 June 1986 on the tenth round of negotiations, while mentioning the proposals, did not however explain the deviation from the previous negotiating position which came with them. SAPMO: DY 30/11643.
19. SED politburo information from the eleventh round of CDE negotiations, 25 July 1986, SAPMO: DY 30/11643.
20. Secret note for Erich Honecker from 8 August 1986, SAPMO: DY 30/11643.
21. This was a compromise between NATO demands for an announcement level of six thousand troops involved and the WTO's initial offer of eighteen thousand troops.
22. Analysis 'On the Final Document of the Stockholm Conference', East Berlin, 22 September 1986, SAPMO: DY 30/11643.
23. For a detailed historiographical analysis of the military-sociological research conducted by the Political Main Department of the GDR's National People's Army (NVA) starting in 1971, see M. Metzler, *Nationale Volksarmee: Militärpolitik und politisches Militär in sozialistischer Verteidigungskoalition 1955/56 bis 1989/90* (Baden-Baden: Nomos, 2012), 678–705. Metzler observes a close connection between these results and the course of events in 1989/90. The NVA questionnaire looked at issues like the 'readiness to get involved in the realization of SED policies' or the belief in the 'victory of socialism on a global scale'.
24. Report of the NVA's Political Main Department 'on the political-ideological work necessary for realizing the class-order issued by the Politburo on 11.6.1985 following the X. SED-party conference', SAPMO: DY 30/J IV 2/2/2116.
25. Instructions for an intensified ideological education in order to establish a 'clear picture of the enemy' among troops, SAPMO: DY 30/J IV 2/2/2116.
26. 'Western analyses on the possible results of the experts' meeting on human contacts in Bern', Information survey on foreign policy No. 19/86 from 19 May 1986, BStU: HVA 57.
27. 'Report on the work meeting of the deputy foreign ministers of the Warsaw Treaty states on 2 September 1986 in Warsaw in preparation for the CSCE follow-up meeting in Vienna', Berlin, 3 September 1986, by Herbert Krolikowski, BStU: Zentrale Koordinierungsgruppe (ZKG) 12693.
28. For the Stasi's fight against family reunions (involving emigration from the GDR) and the problems resulting from the CSCE conference in Vienna, see B. Eisenfeld, *Die Zentrale Koordinierungsgruppe: Bekämpfung von Flucht und Übersiedlung* (Berlin: Bundesbeauftragter f. d. Unterlagen d. Staatssicherheitsdienstes d. ehem. DDR, 1995); and E. Crome and J. Franzke, 'Die SED-Führung und die Wiener KSZE-Konferenz 1986 bis 1989: Dokumente aus dem Parteiarchiv', *Deutschland Archiv* 26 (1993), 905–14.
29. 'Report on the work meeting of the deputy foreign ministers of the Warsaw Treaty states on 2 September 1986 in Warsaw in preparation for the CSCE follow-up meeting in Vienna'.

30. For the internal speeches by Gorbachev and Ligachev, see the MfS report from 1 October 1986, BStU: Hauptabteilung IX (HA IX) 2379. Ligachev addressed an assembly of university professors from the social sciences, explaining to them the new course to be followed.
31. Grundwertekommission der SPD und Akademie für Gesellschaftswissenschaften beim ZK der SED (eds), 'Der Streit der Ideologien und die gemeinsame Sicherheit', in *Politik: Informationsdienst der SPD* (3) (Bonn, 27 August 1987). East German perspectives are provided by R. Reißig, *Dialog durch die Mauer: Die umstrittene Annäherung von SPD und SED* (Frankfurt: Campus Verlag, 2002); and L. Mertens, *Rote Denkfabrik? Die Akademie für Gesellschaftswissenschaften beim ZK der SED* (Münster: Lit, 2004), chapter 6, 215ff.
32. 'Double zero' described the elimination of both classes of medium-range nuclear systems (subdivided into classes of longer and shorter reach) on both sides, excluding French and British as well as sea-launched systems; Information by the Ministry of State Security on the situation at the CSCE follow-up conference in Vienna, 10 October 1987, BStU: ZKG 16788; see also HVA 58.
33. Report for SED politburo members on the status of the CSCE follow-up conference in Vienna, 23 November 1987, SAPMO: DY 30/11644.
34. Draft memorandum for the politburo of the SED's Central Committee, Berlin, without date. This was apparently a draft prepared by the Ministry for Foreign Affairs for all ministries involved (the ministries for state security, domestic affairs, law and foreign affairs). The draft was titled 'Directive for the future approach of the GDR delegation during the drafting phase on civil rights and human questions at the CSCE', BStU: ZKG 16788.
35. 'Note on the consultation of the Main Department Press [Media] of the Ministry for Foreign Affairs regarding the issue of information in a working paper of the CSCE conference on 20.1.1988', Berlin, 20 January 1988, drafted by LtC Lachmund of the Central Analysis and Information Group of the MfS. The citation is taken from a previous paragraph and thus implicitly adds to the accusations against the Soviet Union. BStU: Central Analysis and Information Group (ZAIG) 26196.
36. See Appendix 2, 'Changes to the mandate of the GDR delegation …' and Appendix 3, 'Directive for the representation of the GDR delegation', BStU: ZKG 16788.
37. Presentation by Neiber in May 1988 on the 'Effectiveness of the contribution of the HA I/KGT to the reliable protection of the state borders of the GDR and to guaranteeing the territorial integrity and sovereignty as well as to new security demands resulting from changing circumstances'. LtG Gerhard Neiber was one of four deputies of the minister for state security. BStU: ZAIG 16338. Neiber did, however, point out some significant exceptions to the non-use of weapons: in case of 'terrorist intentions', in case of a forced break through the border installations and in case of a 'direct threat' to the lives of the border troops, exceptions 'might' [!] be feasible.
38. Speech by Neiber in May 1988 on the 'reliable protection of the state border', BStU: ZAIG 16338.

39. 'Information about attacks on the state border of the GDR', June 1988, BStU: ZKG 16338.
40. Speech by Neiber in May 1988, cited in note 37.
41. 'Support work' by the 'central group for analysis and information' (ZAIG) for the draft of an SED politburo decision on the legal consequences of the CSCE agreements in Vienna, coordinated by the Ministry for Foreign Affairs (Ministerium für Auswärtige Angelegenheiten – MfAA). The SED politburo had tasked the MfAA with this on 24 January 1989. The 'support work' of the ZAIG had to be submitted by mid March 1989 and was apparently meant to be discussed at the central service conference in April before being forwarded to the MfAA. BStU: ZAIG 15506.
42. BStU: ZAIG 15506.
43. 'Reaction to the proposal of the MfAA's Main Department Press regarding positions, which … could be accepted as a maximum option', appendix to the memorandum of the inter-ministerial working group of the MfAA in January 1988, BStU: ZAIG 26196.
44. Document dated 25 July 1988, no location, author or title given. The document was filed in the context of considerations about new legal directives for the work of foreign correspondents (comprising West German journalists) in the GDR. BStU: ZAIG 26196.
45. Cited in Neiber's presentation in May 1988; see note 37.
46. 'Note on consequences and contents-related questions regarding the course and results of the 3rd CSCE follow-up meeting in Vienna', no date (January 1989), BStU: HA IX-19667.
47. Letter from the head of the ZAIG, Lieutenant-General Werner Irmler, from 8 March 1989, to other departmental heads, BStU: HVA 975. The SED politburo had already decided on 10 January 1989 to prevent any legalization of 'Helsinki groups' within the GDR and had requested a draft for a CSCE-compatible solution. Dealing with Amnesty International and Greenpeace was treated in a similar fashion. With regard to both NGOs, Foreign Minister Fischer required from all ministries involved drafts for a 'special argumentation'. Fischer himself was tasked by the politburo to coordinate this approach within the Warsaw Treaty Organization.
48. Legal expertise included in the 'Note on consequences and contents-related questions …', cited in note 44.
49. Draft for a decision by the SED politburo in the annex to Irmler's letter from 8 March 1989, cited in note 45.
50. State Security report about internal utterances of the GDR's Minister for Foreign Affairs, 11 February 1988, BStU: HA II-43983.
51. 'Consultation between representatives of the foreign ministries of the states of the Warsaw Treaty on the further course in the CSCE-process', 13/14 February 1989, SAPMO: DY 30/11644.
52. 'Information for members and candidates of the politburo regarding measures resulting for the GDR from the punctuations in the Final Document of the Vienna CSCE-follow-up meeting', 14 April 1989, SAPMO: DY 30/11644.
53. 'Further information – At the start of the CSCE Information Forum in London', signed by Honecker on 21 April 1989, SAPMO: DY 30/11644.

54. Further information – At the start of the CSCE Information Forum in London', signed by Honecker on 21 April 1989, SAPMO: DY 30/11644.
55. Information for selected politburo members from the State Security, 9 February 1989, BStU: HVA 812/1.
56. R. Hartmann, W. Heydrich and N. Meyer-Landrut, *Der Vertrag über konventionelle Streitkräfte in Europa: Vertragswerk, Verhandlungsgeschichte, Kommentar, Dokumentation* (Baden-Baden: Nomos, 1994). The CFE Treaty was eventually signed on 19 November 1990 during the CSCE follow-up conference in Paris and is available online at http://www. https://www.auswaertiges-amt.de/blob/207276/b1196519ae7598a29c873570448a59e9/kse-vertrag-data.pdf (accessed 11 June 2018).
57. See for example telegram ct 25/89 of the GDR's Permanent Representation in Bonn, 2 February 1989, from Neubauer, on the conversations with the personal assistant of the Federal Minister of Defence Rupert Scholz. See also telegram ct 20/89 of the GDR's Representation at the United Nations in New York, 28 January 1989, from Zachmann, on the international reactions to the East German announcement on the demobilization of ten thousand of its troops; and telegram ct 16/89 of the Permanent Representation in Bonn, 26 January 1989, from Neubauer, on West German reactions to this announcement. All at BStU: ZAIG 6760.
58. Information No. 54/III of the Ministry for Foreign Affairs about 'Warsaw Pact and NATO positions at the start of the Vienna negotiations', 9 March 1989, BStU: ZAIG 6760. See also the memorandum 'Negotiations on conventional forces in Europe between 23 Warsaw Pact and NATO member states', 27 February 1989, BStU: ZAIG 6760.
59. Information from 12 December 1988, without author, location or title, BStU: ZAIG 6760. See also the memorandum 'On the further extension of NATO's ability to conduct war', without author and date, but according to the position within the file probably from May 1989, BStU: ZAIG 6760.
60. This paraphrase of US sources is contained in the 'Information on intelligence of the enemy about military policies and about force and arms developments within the Warsaw Treaty', Berlin, 12 June 1989, BStU: HVA 812/2.
61. 'Information on intelligence of the enemy about military policies and about force and arms developments within the Warsaw Treaty', Berlin, 12 June 1989, BStU: HVA 812/2.
62. Information No. 208/89, Berlin, 4 May 1989, 'on the anticipation of American divergence-activities with regard to the GDR', from Mielke to Honecker, read and signed by the latter on the same day, BStU: HVA 812/1.
63. The GSFG was renamed 'Western Group of Forces' (WGF) on 1 June 1989.
64. Information No. 219/89, Berlin, 6 May 1989, 'on the postulate of a "freedom of choice" within the new thinking in the USSR as perceived by government circles in the FRG', sent from Mielke to Honecker, BStU: HVA 812/1. For Gorbachev's speech before the UN General Assembly on 7 December 1988, see http://www.c-spanvideo.org/program/5292-1 (accessed 1 January 2015). The speech is edited in *Europa Archiv* 1989, Dokumente D23–D36.

65. 'Analysis of current aspects of the policy of the Bush administration towards the USSR', Berlin, 10 May 1989, BStU: HVA 812/1.
66. Author's conversation with an anonymous senior member of the US delegation to the CFE negotiations in 2009 and 2010.
67. For this, see the collected evidence in P. Villaume and O. Bange (eds), *The Long Détente: Changing Concepts of Security and Cooperation in Europe from the 1940s to the 1980s* (Budapest: Central European University Press, 2017).
68. The '2 plus 4' Treaty was signed on 12 September 1990 in Moscow. On 20 September 1990, both the East German Volkskammer and the West German Bundestag agreed to the Treaty on Germany's Unification. Accordingly, on 3 October 1990, the GDR acceded to the FRG. The CFE Treaty and the Vienna document were then signed at the CSCE summit conference in Paris on 19–21 November 1990. It was only then, on 15 March 1991, that the '2 plus 4' Treaty was enacted.

Bibliography

Bange, O. 'SS-20 and Pershing II: Weapon Systems and the Dynamization of East-West Relations', in C. Becker-Schaum et al. (eds), *The Nuclear Crisis: The Arms Race, Cold War Anxiety, and the German Peace Movement of the 1980s* (New York and Oxford: Berghahn Books, 2016), 70–86.

Bange, O., and G. Niedhart (eds). *Helsinki 1975 and the Transformation of Europe*. New York and Oxford: Berghahn Books, 2008.

Bange, O. and Villaume, P. (eds). *The Long Détente: Changing Concepts of Security and Cooperation in Europe from the 1940s to the 1980s*. Budapest: Central European University Press, 2017.

Brezhnev, L.I. *Rechenschaftsbericht des Zentralkomitees der KPdSU an den XXVI. Parteitag*. East Berlin: Dietz, 1981.

Crome, E., and J. Franzke. 'Die SED-Führung und die Wiener KSZE-Konferenz 1986 bis 1989: Dokumente aus dem Parteiarchiv'. *Deutschland Archiv* 26 (1993), 905–14.

Eisenfeld, B. *Die Zentrale Koordinierungsgruppe: Bekämpfung von Flucht und Übersiedlung*. Berlin: Bundesbeauftragter f. d. Unterlagen d. Staatssicherheitsdienstes d. ehem. DDR, 1995.

Fischer, T. *Neutral Power in the CSCE: The N+N States and the Making of the Helsinki Accords 1975*. Baden-Baden: Nomos, 2009.

Grundwertekommission der SPD und Akademie für Gesellschaftswissenschaften beim ZK der SED (eds). 'Der Streit der Ideologien und die gemeinsame Sicherheit', in *Politik: Informationsdienst der SPD* (3) (Bonn, 27 August 1987).

Hartmann, R., W. Heydrich and N. Meyer-Landrut. *Der Vertrag über konventionelle Streitkräfte in Europa: Vertragswerk, Verhandlungsgeschichte, Kommentar, Dokumentation*. Baden-Baden: Nomos, 1994.

Honecker, E. *Reden und Aufsätze*, vol. 4. Berlin: Dietz Verlag, 1977.

Inosemzew, N. 'Der XXVI. Parteitag der KPdSU und die Aussenpolitik der Sowjetunion', in Wissenschaftlicher Rat zur Erforschung der Friedens-und

Abrüstungsprobleme (ed.), *Frieden und Abrüstung: Wissenschaftliche Forschungen* (Moscow: Progress, 1982), 22–34.
Kampelman, M. *Entering New Worlds: The Memoirs of a Private Man in Public Life.* New York: HarperCollins, 1991.
Mertens, L. *Rote Denkfabrik? Die Akademie für Gesellschaftswissenschaften beim ZK der SED.* Münster: Lit, 2004.
Metzler, M. *Nationale Volksarmee: Militärpolitik und politisches Militär in sozialistischer Verteidigungskoalition 1955/56 bis 1989/90.* Baden-Baden: Nomos, 2012.
Niedhart, G. (ed.). 'CSCE, the German Question, and the Warsaw Pact'. Special Issue of the *Journal of Cold War Studies* 18(3) (Summer 2016).
Peter, M., and H. Wentker (eds). *Die KSZE im Ost-West-Konflikt: Internationale Politik und gesellschaftliche Transformation.* Munich: Oldenbourg, 2012.
Peterson, C. *Globalizing Human Rights: Private Citizens, the Soviet Union, and the West.* New York and London: Routledge, 2012.
Raschka, J. *Justizpolitik im SED-Staat: Anpassung und Wandel des Strafrechts während der Amtszeit Honeckers.* Cologne: Böhlau Verlag, 2000.
Reißig, R. *Dialog durch die Mauer: Die umstrittene Annäherung von SPD und SED.* Frankfurt: Campus Verlag, 2002.
Snyder, S.B. *Human Rights Activism and the End of the Cold War: A Transnational History of the Helsinki Network.* Cambridge: Cambridge University Press, 2011.
Thomas, D.C. *The Helsinki Effect: International Norms, Human Rights and the Demise of Communism.* Princeton, NJ: Princeton University Press, 2001.
Wenger A., V. Mastny and C. Nuenlist (eds). *Origins of the European Security System: The Helsinki Process Revisited, 1965–1975.* London: Routledge, 2008.

 13

CSCE

Albania, the Outsider in European Political Life

Hamit Kaba

Introduction

The refusal of the Albanian government to sign the Helsinki Final Act on 1 August 1975 should be considered a 'normal' step for Albanian foreign policy, given the Stalinist nature of the communist regime and its relations with both the Eastern and Western blocs during the Cold War period. After breaking off relations with the Soviet Union in 1961, a position maintained until the fall of the communist regime in 1991, Albania's history followed a different course from that of other European communist states. After the split with the Soviet Union, Albania was entirely oriented towards China for reasons of ideological affinity, security for the communist regime and pragmatism, to allow them to take advantage of its economic and military aid. The Albanian government maintained a hostile attitude towards the two superpowers – the United States and the Soviet Union – and to some extent also towards their allies.[1] Severing relations with China in 1978 would present Albania and its communist leadership with survival challenges. For the first time since 1945, Albania found itself without a great patron country, without international support and without adequate subsistence resources.[2] With no diplomatic relations with the two superpowers of the time, outside of the two major blocs of the Cold War – the North Atlantic Treaty Organization (NATO) and the Warsaw Treaty Organization (WTO) – and distanced from European and Balkan initiatives, Albania was the most isolated country in Europe. Owing to favourable international circumstances and its repressive character, the communist regime managed to survive until 1991, a year that would also mark its end. As one author succinctly put it, Albania's Labor Party (ALP) 'skillfully exploited conflicts within the global communist movement to preserve Albania's independence, [but] the policy of isolation and self-sufficiency aggravated the country's economic plight'.[3]

This chapter deals with the only European state that did not take part in the Conference on Security and Cooperation in Europe (CSCE). This study is the first attempt to deal with the topic; it explains and analyses the dynamics and real causes of Albania's rejection of the CSCE mainly in the period 1966–78. The last part of the chapter deals with the pressure applied by the West on Albania in the field of freedoms and human rights during the period 1985–90 (particularly emphasizing the role of the United Nations) and offers some partial reflections on the Albanian government after Ramiz Alia (First Secretary of the Central Committee of the ALP) came to power in 1985.[4]

The documentation available raises several questions and this chapter will attempt to provide answers to them. How did Albania's communist leadership conceive of European security and how did it view its solution? Why did it reject the idea of European security even though it had not yet been crystallized and clarified? What were the real causes of the Albanian government's long-lasting boycott of the CSCE? Did China really constitute a deterrent and binding factor in the Albanian policy of boycotting the CSCE? To answer these questions, it is necessary to carefully analyse the resources available, especially the ALP's funds and the archival documents of Albania's Ministry of Foreign Affairs, which were only recently declassified.[5]

Albania's Boycott of the CSCE, 1966–78

Albania's communist government did not take part in the Helsinki Conference in 1975, although it was well informed of the path followed by the CSCE. It had had knowledge of the idea and initiative of the Soviet Union for holding a Conference on European Security (CES) since 1966, and it was being informed of its evolution in the later stages through different sources.[6] The Albanian government was also well aware of the meetings between WTO countries and the reactions of the Western countries, inside as well as outside NATO, including the United States.[7]

For the first time, the Albanian government was informed of the meeting of the Political Consultative Committee of member countries of the Warsaw Pact in Bucharest, on 5 July 1966, and of the declaration it adopted, which, although not stated in so many words, left the door open for Albania's participation in the future Conference on European Security.[8] The fact that Albania had not taken part in the bloc's meetings since 1962 seems not to have prevented either Albania or the WTO member countries from considering themselves, at least from the legal perspective, part of the same bloc. Albania did not want to withdraw from the WTO in 1961, when it split from the Soviet Union, but withdrew in 1968, unwilling to suffer the same fate as Czechoslovakia.[9] The Albanian government protested against the declaration adopted at the Bucharest meeting, through a note sent to the participating countries: 'peace in Europe and worldwide was not brought about by Soviet–American cooperation', while it called the declaration itself 'a genuine crime against the peoples of the socialist camp, against the peoples of Europe and the world, against communism and peace'.[10]

The idea for holding a Conference on European Security was made known to the Albanian public for the first time on 13 April 1967, through an article in *Zëri i Popullit* [Voice of the People], the ALP's official newspaper. This happened only a few days before a meeting of European communist parties in Karlovy Vary, Czechoslovakia.[11] A few days after this meeting, on 5 May 1967, another article, entitled 'What the Meeting of Renegades at Karlovy Vary Showed', was published.[12] The strongest criticisms were directed at the French Communist Party, as an initiator of this meeting, and at the Soviet leadership who were behind it.

The Albanian government, like the others, was officially informed by the Finnish government about the CSCE in 1969, 1970, 1972 and 1973.[13] Another memorandum about the CSCE was sent to the Albanian government by the Austrian government in July 1970.[14]

ALP and state leadership made its attitude on European security clear through speeches and articles published in the daily newspaper *Zëri i Popullit* between 1967 and 1975,[15] through formal replies sent to the Finnish government, through notes kept by Enver Hoxha (First Secretary of the Central Committee of ALP) in his personal diaries, as well as through meetings with foreign diplomats in Albania and abroad.[16] Most of the articles published in *Zëri i Popullit* (although officially without authors) were written by Enver Hoxha himself, while a few of them were written by Ramiz Alia. Their content left no room for hesitation or assumptions. They unambiguously expressed the refusal of the Albanian leadership to be part of the CSCE or the Helsinki summit.

The CSCE became an object of criticism, especially after its conclusion. Enver Hoxha wrote two articles about this event in *Zëri i Popullit* in October 1974 and July 1975. He also wrote about it in his personal diary for international issues. These documents advanced no new arguments. However, in the articles studded with elaborate phraseology, one is struck by the complacency of the leader. In his general election speech of 3 October 1974, Enver Hoxha again returned to the European security problem. He said: 'Where is the security of the people of Europe? In the open and mysterious travels of a certain Kissinger, of a certain Gromyko, or in the scams of Brezhnev, who makes the Soviets and other people bleed...? Are these the people who will secure the future of the world? What a beautiful future that would be'.[17] In the same speech, Hoxha replied in the negative to offers from the US, the USSR, Great Britain and the FRG to establish diplomatic relations with Albania.

On 29 July 1975, Hoxha published another article in *Zëri i Popullit* entitled 'The Conference on the Insecurity of Europe'.[18] As on other occasions, the ideas in the article were well-known, but adapted to the daily press. The only 'enemies' of the people continued to be the two superpowers, which, according to Hoxha, imposed the Helsinki document on the people of Europe. By admitting the current status quo in Europe and the division of influence zones within it, the Helsinki Conference, according to this article, was detrimental to the peoples of Europe because it propagated the liberal and pacifistic idea that 'ostensibly, all the problems in the world, including the international class war, could be solved through "peaceful" negotiations and "personal contacts"'. It seems that Hoxha considered the CSCE a betrayal of the proletarian revolution and Marx's and Lenin's ideas according to which war was the best way towards revolution. On 31 July 1975, in his personal journal, Hoxha wrote again about the CSCE.[19] At the Helsinki Conference, he noted, they danced for more than two years only for 'the mountain to give birth to a mouse'. The Albanian phrase used by Hoxha could be interpreted as meaning that the Helsinki Conference ended as expected, without result.

The Albanian leader did not hold back when mocking European and American statesmen. According to Hoxha, the concessions made by the Soviet Union stemmed from their need for technology from the US and the West, while the latter wanted their ideas and their people to permeate Eastern European countries and the USSR in order to rot them from the core. Similarly, he continued, the West wanted to increase the anti-Soviet feelings within Eastern Europe, while the USSR satellites tried to get out of the Soviet sphere of influence.

Enver Hoxha's judgement on European security was unassailable both inside and outside the ALP's high-ranking leadership. It is rare to come across opposition voices in the Albania of the time, particularly on foreign policy issues, not only at high party and state levels, but also in the country's intellectual circles. Albania was an isolated country, where freedoms and human rights were non-existent and repression was among the harshest in the world. The Albanian leadership did not change its rejection of the CSCE either prior to signing the Helsinki Final Act or in the period after its adoption. The CSCE would remain 'forbidden fruit' for Albanians until Albania became an associate member in May 1990.

In 1970, the Albanian government continued to consider the proposals submitted by the Soviet government in 1954 and 1960, when Albania was part of the communist bloc, as the best models for solving the European security problem.[20] The declaration adopted by WTO member countries on 4 February 1960 was consistent with its vision of European security, which it did not separate 'from international security and the settlement of the German problem'. 'The conclusion of the peace treaty, repudiating any revanchism or border revisions as well as the policies of remilitarization and atomic armament – this is the best way of achieving the security of all European peoples'.[21] The Albanian government blamed Western countries for not adopting the above basis for European security. Following the split from the USSR, the Albanian leadership blamed not only the USA and its allies, but also the Soviet government and other socialist countries for how they were seeking to solve the European security problem. 'We oppose the conference of European security proposed by Soviet revisionists and their collaborators because it is a false security, demagogy and deception of peoples. One cannot expect security from revisionists because they have betrayed the interests of peoples and have been turned into enemies of their freedom and independence.'[22]

The critical attitude of the Albanian leadership towards the CSCE stemmed from pragmatism and ideology. Enver Hoxha failed to predict what would happen to the CSCE in the future and/or the consequences of the Helsinki Final Act. The factors that led Hoxha to reject the treaty with the CSCE were, *inter alia*, his long experience gained in governing Albania with an iron hand, the difficult relations with the USA in the aftermath of World War II, the conflict between Yugoslavia and the USSR, the détente and Soviet–American rapprochement, as well as his intuition as a paranoid communist.[23]

After the Soviet–Albanian split in 1961, the Albanian leadership began to oppose any USSR proposal on European security, because 'the Soviet leadership deviated from the path of Marxism-Leninism ... and introduced this issue in the context of Soviet–American cooperation'.[24] The two superpowers, according to the Albanian leadership, were not part of the solution to the problem on European security, but the major causes of insecurity and the instigators of tensions in Europe and around the world.[25] Attempts to exclude the USA and the USSR from the European security problems were actually an expression of fear, but also of the fact that the communist regime in Albania itself may be under threat from them. A clear indicator of this risk was the ongoing refusal of proposals made by US and Soviet governments to restore diplomatic relations with Albania, from the mid 1960s until the late 1980s. Memories of the Anglo-American covert operations in the period 1949–53 to overthrow the communist regime and the close relationships with Belgrade and Athens were still fresh in the memory of the Albanian communists.[26] Probably the most important factor affecting the rejection of Albania's rapprochement with the USA, however, was the communist leadership's suspicion of the impact on internal developments in the country. As one scholar duly noted, 'The success of Hoxha's hard-line policy and social experimentation, the most radical in Eastern Europe, depended to a great extent on Albania's isolation from outside influences'.[27]

The Albanian communist leadership continued to identify the two superpowers, the US and the USSR, and what it considered West German 'revanchism', as the biggest threats to the people. The Albanian leadership saw nothing positive in the diplomatic actions of the two superpowers to achieve an agreement between the two German states, the treaties Bonn-Moscow, Bonn-Warsaw and Bonn-Prague, as well as the quadripartite agreement on Berlin.[28] All these agreements, according to the Albanian leadership, had encouraged and strengthened revanchist tendencies in West Germany, which the superpowers were making an equal partner and the biggest power in Europe. The Albanian government did not like the fact that the plan and the procedures for calling the conference materialized and took their full form after the high-level talks between the Americans and the Soviets in Moscow. The Albanian leadership entertained serious doubts about the achievement of European security and the agreements already reached or under way in the early 1970s. The biggest suspicion related to the recognition of the existing borders of several countries of Eastern and Central Europe. 'Such obligations, as mentioned in a study undertaken in the Ministry of Foreign Affairs in December 1970, were declared long ago in the Charter of the United Nations. They did not halt the Cold War, campaigns of pressure and threats, or even the current invasion of a European country by armed forces of other countries allied to the same treaty', implying the invasion of Czechoslovakia by the USSR and its allies in August 1968.[29]

Tirana expressed its opinion that the CSCE would not provide equality for its participants or the chance for them to present their point of view. Assuming the role of a foreteller, the Albanian government believed that the participants would be disappointed quite quickly and that the great powers would not respect their commitments. This conference would spread a harmful illusion of peace and international security, it would weaken the European people's vigilance and it would serve the hegemonic goals of the two superpowers in Europe.

Albania's communist leadership opposed 'détente' for two main reasons. Firstly, it regarded it as a product of the two superpowers' policy, and secondly, easing of international tensions could cause undesirable consequences for Albania. In the new circumstances, Hoxha's regime could turn into a pariah and a subject of 'ideological, economic, cultural and psychological' pressure by the Western world.[30] On the contrary, a divided Europe meant more security for Albania's communist regime, allowing it to continue on its own path almost untroubled. Retention of the tense situation in East–West relations offered more space for Hoxha's regime, allowing him to follow the hardline policy. Such circumstances favoured some kind of 'comfort' for Albania's communist leadership. Albania became an object of concern to the West only in three cases: in 1961, when it broke away from the Soviet Union; in 1978, when it broke away from China; and in 1985, when Enver Hoxha died.[31] In all three cases, however, the Albanian leadership chose to maintain neutrality without approaching either of the two major groups. An especially delicate and worrying moment for the West emerged in the death of Hoxha. There was doubt as to what path his successor would follow. Albania's return into orbit around the USSR would disrupt the balance established in the region, and it would also be a loss to the West. This concern was more clearly expressed in the American policy.[32] But Ramiz Alia, who succeeded Enver Hoxha, continued to follow his path, and to stay on the same course vis-à-vis the USSR and the USA. He was not even tempted by invitations for rapprochement from the new USSR leader Mikhail Gorbachev.

In documentary sources, such as the press, and in Enver Hoxha's diaries, there is emphasis on the idea that it was the two superpowers and generally the Western countries that chiefly benefited from signing the Helsinki Final Act, while the losers would be the European socialist countries, and in particular the German Democratic Republic. In *Zëri i Popullit* and Enver Hoxha's personal diary, we find some writings and comments about the Bonn-Moscow treaty of August 1970 and the difficult position of Walter Ulbricht in relation to the Soviet leadership, as well as within his own party.[33]

According to Enver Hoxha, Willy Brandt's policy had put Ulbricht in trouble. He found himself under dual pressure from both the

Soviet-Poles and Bonn. On 4 December 1969, the highest leader of Albania wrote in his diary about the imminent end of Ulbricht's regime. He [Ulbricht] 'is likely to retire and be replaced by a real German Husak'.[34] In fact, the concern of Albania's communist leader was not the personal fate of Ulbricht, whom he considered 'a Prussian revisionist', but his Stalinist attitude and his intention to 'exercise a veto against Soviet-Poles and Germans'. Ulbricht's resistance to Willy Brandt's *Ostpolitik* and the Bonn-Moscow treaty was followed by tensions and disagreements between him and the Soviet leadership, but also within the Socialist Unity Party of Germany (GDR-SED). For these reasons, he tendered his 'resignation' as the SED leader and was replaced by Honecker.[35]

The CSCE became especially unacceptable to the Albanian government when a chapter on freedom and human rights was included. Accepting this could possibly undermine the 'stability' of the communist power and would encourage the phenomenon of dissidence and dissidents in Albania.[36] According to Hoxha, the West wanted the Eastern European countries to be linked to the Soviet Union, and the Soviet Union itself to become a 'two-gate inn' for people and ideas, so that it would be eaten away from inside.[37] Albania was facing major problems with the violation of freedoms and human rights. Criticism by the UN and several other organizations had become a common phenomenon for the Albanian government and this never changed, even after becoming a UN member in 1955. Albania refused to sign the Helsinki Final Act, as it had strong reservations regarding its implementation in general. However, had they signed it, this would have put the Albanian government in a difficult situation.

In 1967, religious belief and religious institutions were banned, proclaiming Albania as the only atheist country in the world, a stipulation laid down in the Constitution of the Socialist Republic of Albania of 1976, while 'a year earlier the Ministry of Justice had been done away with on the grounds that the establishment of "socialist legality" in Albania was complete'.[38] If the communist government had agreed to join the CSCE, it would have been obliged to meet at least some of the obligations with regard to freedoms and human rights. These changes could not happen in a country like Albania, where the most Stalinist and the most unreformed regime in Europe had constructed a totalitarian political structure that excluded all possible reform. Between 1973 and 1976 there were waves of purge campaigns within the country, while convictions were made inside the high leadership of the party, including those in the cultural, economic and defence sectors. Even after the Helsinki Conference, the Albanian government faced numerous criticisms and protests concerning the violation of freedoms and human rights, but the communist regime remained entrenched in its own 'bunker' until it collapsed in 1990.

Ideology had played an important role in the formation and dissolution of alliances with Albania in the aftermath of World War II. It can be said that the most positive periods of Albania's relations with Yugoslavia, the USSR and the People's Republic of China (PRC) coincided with the peak of Stalinism in these countries. However, in a small, poor country like Albania, surrounded by more powerful neighbours who, to some extent, even threatened its territorial integrity, economic and military needs prevailed over ideology. Marxist-Leninist ideology was also used as an 'argument' against European security and Albania's participation in the Helsinki Conference. The Albanian leadership did not renounce class struggle theory, the proletarian revolution and the danger posed by the two superpowers, the US and the Soviet Union. According to Tirana, European security was a falsity, as it involved the US and the Soviet Union, who were not viewed as guarantors of security in Europe and the world, but rather as instigators of insecurity, wars and tensions, and as the firefighters of proletarian revolutions. Hardly a single article in the Albanian press, an ALP official statement, a quote from Enver Hoxha's personal diaries, or minutes of meetings with foreign diplomats can be found without ideological character judgements.

We are inclined to believe that the communist leadership of Albania successfully used this ideological component, not only because it was loyal to communist dogma, but because it served as legitimate grounds to stay in power and to rule with Stalinist methods.[39] Obsessive dogma was not unsuccessfully employed within the country, to 'convince' the Albanian people that the ALP was the only true Marxist-Leninist party in the world. Maintaining unaltered 'Marxist-Leninist theory' allowed Albania's communist leadership to justify its long grip on power, to be protected from mistakes made and to oppose the changes that took place in the USSR in 1961 and in China in 1978. Tirana broke away from these two countries, just at the time of changes in their foreign policy and rapprochement with Yugoslavia. We are inclined to believe that the ideological factor both in the case of the split with the USSR and that with China had less of an impact than other causes on the break with these two countries.[40] Resorting to the ideological factor to reject the CSCE, as a consequence, had a chiefly domestic impact. Albanians had cherished the idea that their leadership was the best protector and implementer of 'Marxism-Leninism' and that they had consistently applied this theory.

How Influential Was the Chinese Factor in the Rejection of the CSCE?

In some foreign ministries and governments of Western countries there were hopes that US–Chinese rapprochement would be accompanied by Albania's rapprochement with the US.[41] The resulting situation could also have a positive impact on the attitude of the Albanian leadership towards the CSCE. Such illusions were expressed to the Maltese Prime Minister Dom Mintoff, who thought that China was not opposed to Albania's participation in the CSCE, but on the contrary wanted Albania to participate as its proxy.[42] At the end of October 1972, the Italian Embassy in Tirana reported indications that the Albanians were leaning towards participation. In fact, the Chinese up to that point had been ambiguous on the issue and had only just begun referring to the conference in public statements, which were lukewarm and sceptical. Publicly, the Albanian leadership did not give even the slightest indication that they were interested in participating and their attitude would subsequently remain unaltered. On 6 November 1972, Deputy Premier and Defense Minister Beqir Balluku, visiting Beijing, attacked the US and the USSR for raising a hue and cry about 'so-called European security' while their real intention was 'to bind the European people hand and foot to maintain the status quo over there, so as to free their own hands and direct their spearhead against Asia, and first of all against the PRC'.[43]

The Albanian leadership, starting from 1969, continued to repeatedly stress that one of the reasons for the CSCE refusal was the fact that it had another view of European security. Albania's government did not accept peace in Europe because, in its opinion, peace and security in Europe and peace and security in the world are indivisible. In order to give substance to this idea, it used examples of conflicts in the Middle East and the border dispute between China and the Soviet Union. In its opinion, security in Europe meant relaxing their rear lines and directing attention to other areas of the world.

A general view of Albania can give the idea that the official attitude of the Albanian leadership towards the CSCE was shaped mainly by the influence of the Chinese leadership's point of view.[44] But if we look carefully at Albanian and foreign documentary sources, we come to another conclusion. Without denying or underestimating the impact of the Chinese factor on this issue, we cannot consider it to be a key factor that 'forced' Albania to refuse to take part in the CSCE. The Chinese factor is not comparable, in terms of the impact, to the

Albanian communist leadership's paranoid suspicion and permanent fear of the US, the USSR and Great Britain.[45] In Albanian documents and even in the media, it is often mentioned that the PRC did not support the CSCE, because the latter, as soon as it achieved peace in Europe, would shift tensions outside it, to Asia, Africa and especially to China.[46] Enver Hoxha remained firmly attached to the idea that European security was in the interest of the Soviet Union, 'with the aim of securing its European flank in order to have its hands free against China'. 'Our Party [Albanian Labor Party]', he emphasized, 'follows a policy opposing political rapprochement between the Soviet Union and West Germany, against "European Security" and condemns the revisionist policy of Ceausescu as opportunistic...'.[47] On 11 December 1971, in a meeting with a Chinese commercial delegation, the highest leader of Albania once again criticized the Romanians, who 'shout, let's conclude the treaty on "European Security as soon as possible", which gives a free hand to imperialists and revisionists to attack China'.[48] Enver Hoxha strongly criticized Romanian policy on the CSCE, even though he had enough information about the good relations between Romania and China. He behaved in the same way with the Yugoslavian leader, Josip Broz Tito.

Changes that took place in the PRC's foreign policy led to doubts and presumptions that they would also be taking place in Albania, considering China's role in its relations with Albania. It should be mentioned that the suspicion that conflicts would shift to Asia, and especially to China, were embedded even in the minds of several European diplomats, namely the Dutch ambassador in Prague and the Australian ambassador in Vienna.[49] Some other European diplomats viewed the results that could be achieved by the CSCE with scepticism and suspicion. The Chinese ambassador in Helsinki claimed that China had been invited to attend the Helsinki meeting of August 1975 but had refused.[50] The congruence of opinions in this case was incidental and varying over time, while the attitudes of the Albanian government to the CSCE were stable and reflected the policy of Albania's communist leadership on European security.

In fact, China was against the CSCE. On 9 June 1971, at the end of the visit of Ceausescu to China, a joint communiqué on the CSCE was issued, which stated: 'the Chinese side expresses its support for these activities and believes that in order to preserve peace and security, the European people must fight with determination the imperialism and the politics of control and dictation'.[51] For the Chinese leadership, there could be no security in Europe as long as the Soviet and American troops were present. Withdrawing their troops from Europe was a necessary condition, according to them, for securing the independence of the European countries.

High-ranking Chinese leaders had expressed their own reservations regarding the thesis already repeated by the Albanian leadership on several occasions, according to which, following the CSCE, the war would shift to China. The records of Chinese–Albanian meetings note that the Chinese were more discreet and more careful than the Albanians in their attitudes, not only towards the CSCE, but also towards other international issues. The Chinese leadership was more realistic than that of Albania. China started to improve relations with the US after the visit of Richard Nixon in 1972 and established diplomatic relations with the Federal Republic of Germany (FRG) in the same year. In international relations, China started to act globally, while domestically it initiated a process of gradual change. The politics of the Albanian leadership, on the contrary, continued to follow its usual direction. Time would show that Albania could not follow the path of Chinese politics and divorce was a foregone conclusion.

The communist leadership of Albania expressed itself in harsh and anything but diplomatic tones against the Conference on European Security by highlighting especially the risk that it posed to China and its borders. But some diplomats and high-ranking PRC leaders felt that the main target of the USSR attacks was Europe rather than China. According to them, 75 per cent of the Soviet troops were deployed in the old continent, while in the area bordering China there were only one million Soviet soldiers, which was an inadequate number to engage in a general war with China. The inadequacy of the USSR's military forces and their deployment along a border of six to eight thousand kilometres might lead to a local conflict, but not a general one. China claimed that its military forces were able to face even an additional two million Soviet soldiers.[52] A member of the Political Bureau of the Communist Party of China, Jao Ven Juan, in a meeting with the Prime Minister of Albania, Mehmet Shehu, on 30 November 1974 expressed more or less the same opinion.[53] He informed the Albanian Prime Minister that the Soviets claimed they would attack in the East, but in fact they would attack Europe and then head towards the US, Japan and China: 'We have told the US', the Chinese leader stressed, 'that the white bear will bite you'.[54]

From 1971 to 1975, Albanian–Chinese relations were not at their best. Between the two, there were some disagreements that were not made public. The Albanian leadership had refused Chinese proposals to create an alliance with Yugoslavia and Romania in 1968, which would serve as a 'sanitary cordon' against the USSR in the Balkans.[55] It was not satisfied with the meeting between Zhou En Lai and Kosygin in 1969; it was against the visit of President Nixon to China in 1972 and American–Chinese rapprochement and it was against the theory of 'three worlds'.[56] The reservations of the Albanian leadership about Chinese foreign policy would be reflected in their bilateral relations and would gain momentum with the passing of time. In November 1971, the Chinese Communist Party did not take part in the Sixth Congress of the Albanian Labor Party.[57] Albanian–Chinese disputes could not avoid leaving their mark on bilateral relations, although the Albanian leadership endeavoured to mitigate them, labelling them 'tactical issues appropriate for Chinese rather than for Albanians'.[58]

The Albanian–Chinese disputes further intensified in the period 1975–78. The Albanian leadership expressed its disapproval of the cleansing of the 'Gang of Four' (Jiang Qing [Mao Ze Dong's wife], Zhang Chunqiao, Yao Wenyan and Wang Hongwen), who were arrested on 6 October 1976. It was against Tito's visit to China, as well as China's approach to the European Common Market and the visit of the French President to China.[59] The Albanian leadership took another step that further worsened its relations with China when it supported Vietnam in its conflict with China. But the prelude to the final split with China would come from the publication of the highly critical article on the 'theory of the three worlds' in *Zëri i Popullit* on 7 July 1977.[60] As a result, the joint path of Albania and China was finally interrupted in 1978.

After splitting with China, the Albanian government was 'free' to join the CSCE, but it did not do so until 16 September 1991 when it signed the Helsinki Final Act.[61] The Chinese factor was used by the Albanian communist leadership to cover up in a way the real causes of its refusal to take part in the CSCE. In the autumn of 1978, as a Mediterranean country, Albania was invited to participate in the Belgrade summit with observer status.[62] The Albanian government rejected any such participation, however, reiterating the previous 'arguments', except one – rejection due to the PCR.

Did the Helsinki Final Act Have Any Impact on Albania before 1990?

Taking into consideration the nature of the communist regime, the refusal to be part of the CSCE and also the non-binding character of its acts, it should be accepted that their impact on Albania was insignificant. The Albanian government continued its policy of repression even after the Helsinki Conference. What really changed, and could not help but have an influence in Albania, were international discussions on the matter. The principle of non-intervention in internal affairs and absolute sovereignty came to be given greater importance than human rights.[63] But it should be admitted that after breaking with the PRC, Albania did steadily become weaker and more isolated. In fact, the Albanian government did not lose its interest in the effects of the Helsinki Conference decisions in general, and of the chapter on freedoms and human rights in particular. The reaction of the European socialist countries to the 'third basket' captured the interest of the Albanian regime, due to the growing pressure from the West. Albania became the object of criticism from Amnesty International, the US Senate Committee on Foreign Relations and particularly from the UN. In addition, protests about the violation of human rights in Albania were also addressed by the Albanian political and economic emigré organizations in the USA, such as the Committee 'Free Albania', 'Legality' and the *Dielli* newspaper of the 'Vatra' organization.[64] But the Albanian government's reaction was insignificant. It viewed the Helsinki Final Act as 'a worthless piece of card' which had no legal power over Albania.[65]

The death of Enver Hoxha was one more reason for the West to increase its pressure on the Albanian government, particularly to improve its behaviour towards its citizens. Economic difficulties increased in Albania due to the new policy of Mikhail Gorbachev in the USSR, which in turn paved the way for changes. But Enver Hoxha's successor, Ramiz Alia, did not take steps to solve human rights problems in the period 1986–89. The Albanian government did not cooperate with the Commission on Human Rights, although it gave some faint signals with some cosmetic changes that did not affect the foundations of the regime. The Presidium of the People's Assembly of the Republic of Albania declared a partial amnesty for prisoners on 11 January 1986, but Amnesty International, the UN Commission on Human Rights as well as the European Parliament continued to exert pressure on the communist regime regarding the violence inflicted upon its own citizens.

On the eve of the visit of UN Secretary General Perez de Cuellar in May 1990, the People's Assembly adopted the draft on amendments to the Criminal Code and the Criminal Procedure Code. Article 55 of the Criminal Code for agitation and propaganda and twenty-four articles providing for the death penalty were cancelled. The Ministry of Justice advocacy system, among others, was re-established.[66] For the first time during the visit of Perez de Cuellar, Alia submitted a request for Albania to become part of the CSCE, but in 1990 this organization continued to have reservations about the degree to which the Albanian government, despite its reforms, respected the civil rights of its citizens.[67] The legalization of political pluralism and the first multiparty elections held in Albania as early as March 1991 would pave the way to Albania's accession to the CSCE.

Albania's path to the CSCE was too long. Its finalization in September 1991, when the communist regime collapsed, did not emerge through the raising of awareness and reflection of Albanians regarding their lack of rights during dictatorship, but through the changes that swept Europe in the late 1980s and the overall pressure that the communist regime was under. Let us recall a famous expression of French President François Mitterrand about Albania on 6 July 1990 at a NATO meeting in London, where thousands of Albanians rushed into foreign embassies in Tirana: 'The walls of the fortress that enslaves peoples must be torn down', Mitterrand stressed, so that 'the country and the people should be free, and Albania should participate more in the European concert'.[68] The French newspaper *Liberation* wrote: 'Albanian leaders should know that a Stalinist island cannot survive in the new Europe'.[69]

Hamit Kaba is Professor of Contemporary History at the Academy of Albanian Studies. His studies are focused mainly on Albanian international relations during World War II and the Cold War period. He received his doctorate from the University of Tirana in 1997. Professor Kaba is the author of *Albania and the Great Powers: From WWII to the Cold War* (KLEAN, 2015), *1981: Kosovo Demonstrations in the National Archives of London* (Institute of History 'Ali Hadri' Prishtinë, 2017), *Albania and Kosovo in Russian Archives, 1946–1962* (co-authored) (Brezi 81, 2011), *Albania in the Cold War Flow (Studies and Documents)* (Botimpex, 2007), and *UNRRA (United Nations Relief and Rehabilitation Administration) in Albania, 1944–1947* (Shkenca, 2000). He has also published in Albanian and international journals and edited volumes. Kaba has carried out archival research in the US, Great Britain, Russia and Italy. He is a former Woodrow Wilson Center scholar for the Cold War period. Lately he has been working on his new monograph *Albania and the USA: Between Alliance and Animosity, 1939–1991*.

Notes

1. H. Kaba, *Shqipëria në rrjedhën e Luftës së Ftohtë: studime dhe dokumente* (Tirana: Botimpex, 2007), 136–57. Relations between Albania and the United States were interrupted in 1939, after Albania's occupation by Italy. Efforts to

restore diplomatic relations between the US and Albania in 1945–46 proved unsuccessful.
2. H. Kaba, 'Përpjekje për afrim: Marrëdhëniet e Shqipërisë me SHBA dhe Anglinë në vite 1970–1980', *Studime Historike* 3–4 (2016), 225.
3. N.C. Pano, 'Albania', in J. Held (ed.), *The Columbia History of Eastern Europe* (Columbia: Oxford University Press, 1992), 53.
4. S. Boçi, 'The Beginning of the End: Western Pressure on Human Rights in Albania', in A. Pinari, E. Pandelejmoni and Th. Schrapel (eds), *The Call for Freedom: Studies on Totalitarianism and Transition in Albania* (Tirana: KAS Albania and Maluka, 2016), 125.
5. The fund i Arkivit te Ministrise se Puneve te Jashtme te Shqiperise (AMPJ) (Archive of Ministry of Foreign Affairs of Albania) contains some information and studies on European security, undertaken by the Second Department, which was part of the Albanian State Security structures.
6. AMPJ, Viti 1971, Dosja 673, 'Conference of Security in Europe', prepared by Frederik Nosi, Paris, 24 July 1971, 1–32; AMPJ, Viti 1970, Dosja 569, 'On the attitude of Western countries to the proposal for convening a conference of European Security', 257–71; AMPJ, Viti 1969, Dosja 472, 'Memorandum of the Finnish Government addressed to the Government of the People's Republic of Albania', 8–9.
7. AMPJ, Viti 1970, Dosja 569, 'On the attitude of Western countries to the proposal for convening a conference of European Security', 257–71.
8. The National Archives and Record Administration (NARA), RG 59, Department of State, 'The Warsaw Pact's Program for European Security – Seven Points and Seven Authors', Thomas L. Hughes to The Secretary, 20 July 1966, 8; AMPJ, Viti 1970, Dosja 569, 'On our attitude to European Security', September 1970, 220.
9. Arkivi Qendror Shteteror i Shqiperise (AQSH) (The Central and State Archive of Albania), Viti 1963, Fondi 14/AP, Dosja 7, 'Meeting of Beqir Balluku with Deng Xiaoping', Beijing, 24 September 1963, 81.
10. AMPJ, Viti 1970, Dosja 569, 'On our attitude to European Security', September 1970, 220.
11. 'Meeting at Karlovy Vary – a Meeting of Traitors', *Zëri i Popullit*, no. 88, Tirana, 13 April 1967.
12. 'What the Meeting of Renegades at Karlovy Vary Showed', *Zëri i Popullit*, 5 May 1967.
13. AMPJ, Viti 1969, Dosja 472, 8–9; AMPJ, Viti 1970, Dosja 569, 273–74; AMPJ, Viti 1972, Dosja 646, 71, 75–77; AMPJ, Viti 1973, Dosja 736, 2.
14. AMPJ, Viti 1970, Dosja 569, 199–201.
15. 'Soviet-American Collaboration Dominated the Budapest Meeting of the Warsaw Pact', *Zëri i Popullit*, 22 March 1969; 'European Security – Words and Reality', *Zëri i Popullit*, 7 December 1969; 'Sovereign Interests of the German Democratic Republic Must Be Resolutely Defended', *Zëri i Popullit*, 14 December 1969; 'Criminal Plots against the Sovereign Interests of the German DR Must Be Defeated', *Zëri i Popullit*, 5 August 1970; 'Soviet–German Treaty – a Dangerous Plot against Peoples of Europe and the Whole World', *Zëri i Popullit*, 22 August 1970; 'Our Policy is Open, Sincere,

Policy of Proletarian Principles', *Zëri i Popullit*, no. 238(8156), 4 October 1974; 'Conference of Insecurity', *Zëri i Popullit*, no. 179(8414), 29 July 1975.
16. E. Hoxha, *Ditar për Çështje Ndërkombëtare (1968–1969)* (Tirana: Instituti i Studimeve Marksiste-Leniniste pranë KQ të PPSH, 1982), 23, 352, 513, 537, 555; AMPJ, Viti 1970, Dosja 569, 266–69; AMPJ, Viti 1971, Dosja 29–33; AMPJ, Viti 1971, Dosja 325/1, Minutes of the Meeting between Mehmet Shehu-Prime Minister of Albania and Finnish ambassador Paul Jurkankallio, Tirana, 24 May 1971, 1–14; AMPJ, Viti 1971, Dosja 671, Information of Nesti Nase-Minister of Foreign Affairs of Albania relating Finnish ambassador Ralf Enckell, 27 May 1971, 29–33; NARA, RG 59, Telegram of American Embassy (Rome) to Department of State, 9 June 1971, 1–2
17. *Zëri i Popullit*, no. 238(8156), 4 October 1974.
18. The Conference on Insecurity of Europe, *Zëri i Popullit*, 29 July 1975.
19. E. Hoxha, *Ditar për Çështje Ndërkombëtare (1975–1976)* (Tirana: Instituti i Studimeve Marksiste-Leniniste pranë KQ të PPSH, 1984), 127–33.
20. AMPJ, Viti 1970, Dosja 569, 'On our attitude to European Security', prepared by the Second Directorate of the Ministry of Foreign Affairs, September 1970, 218–20. At the Berlin meeting of February 1954, the USSR government proposed to the Ministers of Foreign Affairs of the Communist Bloc Countries to reach an agreement on collective security in Europe, which would involve all countries of the region. The agreement proposed by the communist bloc, however, was rejected by Western countries. On 29 November–2 December 1954, Albania took part in another meeting of European socialist countries on European security, organized by the USSR government, which on 14 May 1955 signed the agreement for the establishment of the WTO.
21. AMPJ, Viti 1970, Dosja 569, 219.
22. Ibid., 230.
23. Enver Hoxha, like all dictators, had great and unlimited power. His name was synonymous with the ALP and his word was almost incontestable within the communist leadership. Numerous books written by him are a source of reference, of course by comparing them with archival sources declassified after the fall of the communist regime in Albania.
24. AMPJ, Viti 1970, Dosja 569, 220.
25. In 1986, one year after the death of Enver Hoxha, his book was published entitled *Superfuqitë, 1959–1984* (Tirana: Shtëpia Botuese '8 Nëntori', 1986).
26. N. Bethel, *The Great Betrayal: The Untold Story of Kim Philby's Biggest Coup* (London: Times Books, 1984).
27. E. Biberaj, *Albania and China: A Study of an Unequal Alliance* (Boulder, CO: Westview Press, 1986), 94.
28. The signing of the agreement and the treaties were successful steps for European and world politics because they served as cornerstones for post-war reconciliation, the right to the 'peaceful change of frontiers', détente as well as for creating the proper environment for finalizing the CSCE.
29. AMPJ, Viti 1970, Dosja 589, 'On the attitude of Western countries to the proposal for convening a conference of European Security', 25 November 1970, 262.

30. Biberaj, *Albania and China*, 105.
31. H. Kaba, *Shqipëria dhe të Mëdhenjtë: nga Lufta e Dytë Botërore në Luftën e Ftohtë* (Tirana: Botime KLEAN, 2015), 239–57; The National Archives (TNA), Foreign and Commonwealth Office (FCO) 28/3705, 'Recent Changes in Albania's Foreign Relations: Political Implications', R F Cooper to Foreign Office, 1 June 1979, 1–29.
32. Kaba, 'Përpjekje për afrim', 228–29.
33. 'Sovereign Interests of the German Democratic Republic Must Be Resolutely Defended', *Zëri i Popullit*, 14 December 1969; 'Criminal Plots against the Sovereign Interests of the GDR Must Be Defeated', *Zëri i Popullit*, 5 August 1970. 'Soviet/German Treaty – a Dangerous Plot against Peoples of Europe and the Whole World', *Zëri i Popullit*, 22 August 1970; 'Conference of Insecurity', *Zëri i Popullit*, no. 179(8414), 29 July 1975; E. Hoxha, 'Let's Defend the German Democratic Republic', 10 December 1969, 554, in Hoxha, *Ditar për çështje Ndërkombëtare (1969–1970)* (Tirana: Instituti i Studimeve Marksiste-Leniniste pranë KQ të PPSH, 1982); 'Rrëzimi i Valter Ulbrihtit', 4 May 1971, in Hoxha, *Ditar për Çështje Ndërkombëtare (1970–1971)* (Tirana: Instituti i Studimeve Marksiste-Leniniste pranë KQ të PPSH, 1983), 352–55.
34. E. Hoxha, 'Shqetësimet e Ulbrihtit', in *Ditar për Çështje Ndërkombëtare (1968–1969)*, 537.
35. O. Bange, 'Onto the Slippery Slope: East Germany and East-West Detente under Ulbricht and Honecker, 1965–1975', *Journal of Cold War Studies* 18(3) (2016), 75–78.
36. Due to the rigid policies of the Albanian communist regime, there were no dissident movements in the country. Nevertheless, dissidents were present. In fact, there were thousands of political prisoners who suffered long-term imprisonment because they did not agree with communist policies. Some of them were sentenced to death, while others died in prisons; most of them were released in 1990 when the communist regime was on its last breath.
37. Hoxha, *Superfuqitë*, 406.
38. Pano, 'Albania', 38.
39. Enver Hoxha, the main ALP leader, remained in power for forty-five years, longer than any other communist leader in Europe.
40. Biberaj, *Albania and China*, 141.
41. AMPJ, Viti 1973, Dosja 512, Information of Nako Naço, the Permanent Representative of Albania to UNO New York, 24 May 1973, 12–36; Kaba, *Shqipëria dhe të Mëdhenjtë*, 293; NARA, RG 59, 'Albania diversifies its Foreign Policy', prepared by Stephen Peters, 4 January 1972, 12.
42. NARA, RG 59, 'Albania: Attitudes toward CSCE', prepared by Bureau of Intelligence and Research, Department of State, 7 September 1973, ii.
43. AMPJ, Viti 1972, Dosja 330, 307.
44. NARA, RG 59, 'Albania: Attitudes toward CSCE', prepared by Bureau of Intelligence and Research, Department of State, 7 September 1973, ii.
45. NARA, RG 59, RESS-43, 7 September 1973, 1–3.
46. AMPJ, Viti 1970, Dosja 569, 222, 229, 231; Hoxha, *Ditar për Çështje Ndërkombëtare (1968–1969)*, 296–97; Hoxha, *Superfuqitë*, 420–21.

47. AQSH, Viti 1971, Fondi 14/AP, Dosja 5, Conversation of Enver Hoxha and Mehmet Shehu with Chinese Ambassador Liu Xhen Hua, Tirana, 30 September 1971, 13.
48. AQSH, Viti 1971, Fondi 14/AP, Dosja 7, Conversation of Enver Hoxha with Economic delegation of PRC, 11 December 1971, 7–8.
49. AMPJ, Viti 1974, Dosja 475, Radiogram of Albanian ambassador in Prague to the Ministry of Foreign Affairs of Albania, 20 August 1974, 220; AMPJ, Viti 1973, Dosja 737/2, Radiogram of Albanian ambassador in Vienna to the Ministry of Foreign Affairs of Albania, 14 July 1973.
50. AMPJ, Viti 1975, Dosja 669/3, Aerogram of Albanian ambassador in Helsinki to the Ministry of Foreign Affairs of Albania, 7 August 1975, 128–29.
51. Ibid., 26.
52. AMPJ, Viti 1974, Dosja 474, Radiogram of Albanian Embassy in Prague to Ministry of Foreign Affairs of Albania, 20 August 1974, 220–22.
53. AQSH, Viti 1974, Fondi 14/AP, Dosja 16, Lista 26, Relations with the Chinese Communist Party, 4.
54. Ibid.
55. E. Hoxha, *Shënime për Kinën II, 1973–1977* (Tirana: Shtëpia Botuese '8 Nëntori', 1979), 110, 125.
56. AMPJ, Viti 1978, Dosja 284, Letter of the Central Committee of Albanian Labor Party to Central Committee of Communist Party of China, 29 July 1978, 1–47.
57. Kaba, *Shqipëria dhe të Mëdhenjtë*, 293.
58. AQSH, Viti 1971, Fondi 14/AP, Dosja 7, Lista 23, The meeting of Enver Hoxha with the economic delegation of the PRC, on 11 December 1971.
59. AMPJ, Viti 1979, Dosja 730, 17–27.
60. 'The Theory and Practice of Revolution', *Zëri i Popullit*, 7 July 1977.
61. R. Alia, *Jeta ime, kujtime* (Tirana: Botimet Toena, 2010), 453.
62. The Belgrade meeting was held from 4 October 1977 to 9 March 1978.
63. Boçi, 'The Beginning of the End', 126.
64. AMPJ, Viti 1977, Dosja 1147, Radiogram of Muhamet Kapllani, Permanent Representative of Albania to UN to AMFA, 6 September 1977, 120; 'Vatra' and 'Legality' were two Albanian migration organizations in the USA.
65. AMPJ, Viti 1977, Radiogram of Albanian ambassador in Pekin (Sokrat Plaka) to Albanian Foreign Ministry, 20 June 1977, 93.
66. Boçi, 'The Beginning of the End', 125–34.
67. Pano, 'Albania', 61.
68. AMPJ, Viti 1990, Dosja 1334, 42.
69. Ibid., 105.

Bibliography

Archives

Arkivi i Ministrisë së Punëve të Jashtme te Shqiperise (AMPJ) (Archive of Ministry of Foreign Affairs of Albania)

Arkivi Qendror Shteteror i Shqiperise (AQSH) (The Central and State Archive of Albania)
The National Archives and Record Administration (NARA)
The National Archives (TNA)

Literature

Alia, R. *Jeta ime, kujtime.* Tirana: Botimet Toena, 2010.
Bange, O. 'Onto the Slippery Slope: East Germany and East-West Detente under Ulbricht and Honecker, 1965–1975'. *Journal of Cold War Studies* 18(3) (2016), 60–94.
Bethel, N. *The Great Betrayal: The Untold Story of Kim Philby's Biggest Coup.* London: Times Books, 1984.
Biberaj, E. *Albania and China: A Study of an Unequal Alliance.* Boulder, CO: Westview Press, 1986.
Boçi, S. 'The Beginning of the End: Western Pressure on Human Rights in Albania', in A. Pinari, E. Pandelejmoni and Th. Schrapel (eds), *The Call for Freedom: Studies on Totalitarianism and Transition in Albania* (Tirana: KAS Albania and Maluka, 2016), 125–34.
Hoxha, E. *Ditar për Çështje Ndërkombëtare (1968–1969).* Tirana: Instituti i Studimeve Marksiste-Leniniste pranë KQ të PPSH, 1982.
Hoxha, E. *Ditar për Çështje Ndërkombëtare (1969–1970).* Tirana: Instituti i Studimeve Marksiste-Leniniste pranë KQ të PPSH, 1982.
Hoxha, E. *Ditar për Çështje Ndërkombëtare (1970–1971).* Tirana: Instituti i Studimeve Marksiste-Leniniste pranë KQ të PPSH, 1983.
Hoxha, E. *Ditar për Çështje Ndërkombëtare (1975–1976).* Tirana: Instituti i Studimeve Marksiste-Leniniste pranë KQ të PPSH, 1984.
Hoxha, E. *Shënime për Kinën II, 1973–1977.* Tirana: Shtëpia Botuese '8 NËNTORI', 1979.
Hoxha, E. *Superfuqitë, 1959–1984.*Tirana: Shtëpia Botuese '8 NËNTORI', 1986.
Kaba, H. 'Përpjekje për afrim: Marrëdhëniet e Shqipërisë me SHBA dhe Anglinë në vite 1970–1980'. *Studime Historike* 3–4 (2016), 209–34.
Kaba, H. *Shqipëria dhe të Mëdhenjtë: nga Lufta e Dytë Botërore në Luftën e Ftohtë.* Tirana: Botime KLEAN, 2015.
Kaba, H. *Shqipëria në rrjedhën e Luftës së Ftohtë: studime dhe dokumente.* Tirana: Botimpex, 2007.
Pano, C.N. 'Albania', in J. Held (ed.), *The Columbia History of Eastern Europe* (Columbia: Oxford University Press, 1992), 16–64.
Zëri i Popullit, Tirana, April 1967–July 1975.

Conclusion

Nicolas Badalassi and Sarah B. Snyder

The chapters in *The CSCE and the End of the Cold War* depict the CSCE as a bridge both across the East–West divide and among European and North American countries. They also demonstrate that the Helsinki process served as a means of forging connections vertically, between high-level diplomats and lower-level actors. The volume reveals the significance of the human aspect in international relations and makes the case for how the CSCE contributed to the demise of communism and the end of the Cold War in Europe. In particular, the contributions here detail the CSCE's influence on the nature of that collapse, ensuring that it was peaceful.

Yet the significance of the CSCE to the end of the Cold War has not been accepted uniformly. One measurement of this phenomenon is that Odd Arne Westad only mentioned it on four pages in his recent 629-page history of the Cold War. More notably, Mark Kramer's editor's note in a special issue of the *Journal of Cold War Studies* demonstrates that claims regarding the significance of the CSCE remain strongly contested.

Kramer charges that Daniel C. Thomas, and presumably other scholars writing in this vein, 'wildly exaggerates the role of the CSCE in ending the Cold War'. In Kramer's view, the CSCE had been 'reduced to insignificance' by the early 1980s.[1] At the most, Kramer concedes that the CSCE 'may have played a very small role at the margin, but it was certainly not decisive'.[2] Kramer's view of the end of the Cold War, which is centred on the top leadership in the Soviet Union, is at odds with the thrust of this volume.

As much as the contributors here seek to expand the historiographical debate surrounding the CSCE, like Kramer, they nonetheless continue

Conclusion • 351

to engage with Daniel C. Thomas's *The Helsinki Effect*.[3] His book was one of the first scholarly accounts of the impact of the Helsinki Final Act, and it continues to inspire and provoke response. Selvage's chapter marks the clearest efforts to grapple with Thomas's arguments.[4] Selvage disagrees with Thomas to some extent, seeing his book as overplaying the causality of the CSCE. For Selvage, the CSCE explains the manner of the collapse of communism in Eastern Europe even if it was not the 'decisive' cause. Therefore, Selvage and Maximilian Graf agree to some extent with Kramer's assessment of the role of the CSCE, limiting the significance of the institution and the process to the pattern and nature of the end of the Cold War, rather than precipitating its collapse.

In contrast to Kramer's interpretation, Andrei Zagorski shows why and how the CSCE facilitated the infiltration of human rights and humanitarian commitments, or put another way, the human dimension, into the Soviet Union. In Zagorski's view, the CSCE played a significant role in the Soviet Union's slow move towards engagement with international human rights commitments. His chapter focuses on the role and contributions of non-governmental organizations to this effort, and it marshals evidence to support the claims of those who attribute great significance to the CSCE changing human rights practices in the Soviet Union. Selvage's chapter similarly offers documentation of the significance of activism inspired by the CSCE in that state security organs feared it and worked to combat it.

Matthias Peter's chapter, like Oliver Bange's, shows how the CSCE maintained a permanent dialogue between the two blocs despite the resurgence of tension in the late 1970s. Through the West German willingness to remain at the conference table in the 1980s, Peter demonstrates that the Helsinki process, thanks to its follow-up meetings and expert conferences, constituted a formidable East–West forum on most of the Cold War's constituent issues. Moreover, Peter shows that the CSCE in the 1980s was the starting point for the FRG's public officials – especially Foreign Minister Hans-Dietrich Genscher – to develop their vision of a European peace order based on the Helsinki Final Act.

Beyond engaging in broader debates about the intersection of the CSCE and the end of the Cold War, the volume also foregrounds issues that have been previously understudied, such as the security elements of the Helsinki process or the significance of scientists' activism; or neglected, such as the absence of Albania from the CSCE, and the contributions of individual diplomats, for example from France and the United Kingdom.

Christian Peterson's chapter fits well with Oliver Bange's as both contributors explore the intersection of the CSCE with peace and disarmament. Bange shows how the GDR particularly and other Eastern European states more generally reacted to Soviet leaders' decision in the mid 1980s to make human rights concessions to achieve security objectives. Peterson examines non-governmental actors involved in these issues, highlighting a myriad of engagement groups and demonstrating the capacity for citizens' engagement with the CSCE on issues beyond the human rights principle and human contacts provisions that have been the focus of much previous work.

Like Peterson, Jacek Czaputowicz is interested in the intersection of the CSCE, peace and human rights. In his telling, activists' priorities were determined by where they sat – in Eastern Europe or beyond. Czaputowicz also demonstrates how activists moved beyond focusing all of their attention on the official negotiations, turning to hold their own international conferences inspired by the CSCE.

Elisabetta Vezzosi's chapter focuses on scientific cooperation and scientific exchanges, aspects of the Helsinki Final Act that have received less attention in the scholarly literature.[5] Her work shows how these elements of the agreement spurred activism by scientists, principally based in the United States. The focus of her chapter, the Committee of Concerned Scientists, helped create the 'circus' atmosphere that Jeri Laber remembered at CSCE meetings such as the follow-up meeting in Madrid.[6] Vezzosi also complicates our understanding of scientists' human rights activism, highlighting the differences among groups; there was not a single response among scientists' organizations to violations of human rights in the Soviet bloc.

Hamit Kaba's chapter addresses the caveat that every scholar must employ when explaining who signed the Helsinki Final Act – thirty-five European and North American states, everyone except Albania. In answering why not Albania, Kaba demonstrates that the Chinese factor was not as prominent as previously imagined. Albania's leadership was well aware of planning for the negotiations and refused to participate based on ideological opposition, pragmatism and a recognition that internal stability required isolation. Its decision, as Kaba shows, did not give the country immunity from the change sweeping Eastern Europe. In 1991, the communist government fell in Albania as well.

Many earlier accounts that examined the CSCE negotiations relied heavily on the memoirs of a small number of participants. In this volume, a number of contributors approach the question of diplomats and their contributions from a more scholarly perspective. Martin D. Brown and Angela Romano, Nicolas Badalassi and Stephan Kieninger all illuminate the non-traditional nature of key CSCE diplomats. The first two adopt what they call 'a prosopographical approach' to understanding CSCE diplomats as a broader community, highlighting their shared characteristics, interests and skills, despite national differences. All four emphasize the creativity of the negotiators and the independence CSCE diplomats were able to exert; in their telling, these were not mere marionettes carrying out orders from their capitals. The authors treat the diplomats as human beings, not just representatives of their governments.

Badalassi's chapter highlights how the CSCE represented a fundamental shift from the earlier Congress of Vienna, which is often invoked as a reference point for the CSCE negotiations; the CSCE talks involved a massive expansion of the number of voices at the negotiating table. His contribution also demonstrates how the process was further transformed in the years that followed, as diplomats, not only NGOs and activists, inspired by the signal of the Prague Spring, sought long-term change in Europe. For Kieninger, US Ambassador Max Kampelman represents a new type of CSCE diplomat because he is deeply enmeshed in the human dimension, focusing on the plight of individuals. Negotiating on their behalf was one of the central efforts of his diplomacy in Madrid.

Connected in some ways with Kieninger's chapter, Maximilian Graf shows Austria's efforts to engage with dissidents in Eastern Europe, even offering asylum to all in 1976. Much later he demonstrates the country's role in facilitating the passage of East Germans out of the Soviet bloc in 1989, which seriously destabilized the GDR in a process that culminated with the opening of the Berlin Wall.

Earlier scholarship, particularly by Svetlana Savranskaya, has demonstrated the unanticipated consequences of the Helsinki Final Act inside the Soviet Union. Contributions to the volume, particularly Carl Bon Tempo's chapter, similarly highlight the unanticipated consequences of the Helsinki Final Act beyond the Soviet Union.[7] His chapter highlights the use of the Helsinki Final Act in advocacy for immigration to the United States, as opposed to on behalf of emigration, on which scholarship has previously focused. Bon Tempo also demonstrates why the human rights elements of the agreement resonated less in the United States than other signatory countries; in this case, human rights violations remained an issue of foreign policy, not one to be addressed domestically.

The preceding chapters highlighted how the Helsinki process unfolded – at multiple sites and on a wide range of issues – and how it shaped the end of the Cold War and the division of Europe. They show that the CSCE was not a simple diplomatic process aimed at sustaining détente in the mid 1970s. On the contrary, the conference and its aftermath enabled diplomats and leaders of Western and neutral countries to address the division of Europe in myriad ways. Their broad provisions established concrete links between diplomatic approach and societal concerns. Better still, the chapters that make up this book reveal how the CSCE succeeded in giving human rights a prominent place in international relations, by allowing Soviet power to recognize the legitimacy of a dialogue on a subject that went against the values and practices of the Eastern bloc. In this sense, the principles of the first basket and the provisions of the third one laid the foundations for new diplomatic practices that enjoyed a boom beginning in 1990–91, marking a shift to approaches that took account of the interests of 'civil societies' in the formulation of foreign policy.

This volume is certainly not the final word on these important questions, but it will contribute to moving the scholarly conversation forward.

Nicolas Badalassi is Associate Professor of Contemporary History at the Institut d'Etudes politiques d'Aix-en-Provence (Sciences-Po Aix). He holds a PhD from the University of Paris – Sorbonne Nouvelle (2011). In 2012–13, he administrated the Sorbonne Cold War Studies Project. He is the author of the award-winning *En finir avec la Guerre froide: La France, l'Europe et le processus d'Helsinki, 1965–1975* (Presses Universitaires de Rennes, 2014). He has published various articles concerning French foreign policy in the Cold War era, the Helsinki process and security in the Mediterranean. He has also co-edited with Houda Ben Hamouda *Les pays d'Europe orientale et la Méditerranée, 1967–1989* (Les Cahiers Irice, 2013).

Sarah B. Snyder teaches at American University's School of International Service. She is the author of *From Selma to Moscow: How Human Rights Activists Transformed US Foreign Policy* (Columbia University Press, 2018) and the award-winning *Human Rights Activism and the End of the Cold War: A Transnational History of the Helsinki Network* (Cambridge University Press, 2011).

Notes

1. M. Kramer, 'Editor's Note', *Journal of Cold War Studies* 18(3) (2016), 1.
2. Ibid., 2.

3. D.C. Thomas, *The Helsinki Effect: International Norms, Human Rights, and the Demise of Communism* (Princeton: Princeton University Press, 2001).
4. Thomas's book is cited in seven of the book's thirteen chapters.
5. One notable exception is P. Rubinson, '"For Our Soviet Colleagues": Scientific Internationalism, Human Rights and the Cold War', in A. Iriye, P. Goedde and W. Hitchcock (eds), *The Human Rights Revolution: An International History* (New York: Oxford University Press, 2012), 245–64.
6. J. Laber, *The Courage of Strangers: Coming of Age with the Human Rights Movement* (New York: Public Affairs, 2012), 120–21.
7. See, for example, S. Savranskaya, 'Unintended Consequences: Soviet Interests, Expectations and Reactions to the Helsinki Final Act', in O. Bange and G. Niedhart (eds), *Helsinki 1975 and the Transformation of Europe* (New York: Berghahn Books, 2008), 175–90.

Bibliography

Kramer, M. 'Editor's Note'. *Journal of Cold War Studies* 18(3) (2016), 1.

Laber, J. *The Courage of Strangers: Coming of Age with the Human Rights Movement*. New York: Public Affairs, 2012.

Rubinson, P. '"For Our Soviet Colleagues": Scientific Internationalism, Human Rights and the Cold War', in A. Iriye, P. Goedde and W. Hitchcock (eds), *The Human Rights Revolution: An International History* (New York: Oxford University Press, 2012), 245–64.

Savranskaya, S. 'Unintended Consequences: Soviet Interests, Expectations and Reactions to the Helsinki Final Act', in O. Bange and G. Niedhart (eds), *Helsinki 1975 and the Transformation of Europe* (New York: Berghahn Books, 2008), 175–90.

Thomas, D.C. *The Helsinki Effect: International Norms, Human Rights, and the Demise of Communism*. Princeton, NJ: Princeton University Press, 2001.

Westad, Odd Arne. *The Cold War: A Global History.* New York: Basic Books, 2017.

# Index

Adamec, Ladislav, 262
Adamkiewicz, Marek, 186
Adelstein, Bob, 134–35, 138
Afghanistan, 100, 106, 130, 140, 154, 163, 213, 216, 234, 275, 279
Albania, 9, 74, 330–44, 351–2
Albania's Labor Party (ALP), 331–33, 338, 346n23, 347n39
Alexeyeva, Lyudmila, 5, 30
Alia, Ramiz, 331–32, 336, 343
Alpert, Yakov, 139
Amalrik, Andrei, 5
American Bar Association (ABA), 236
Amnesty International, 161, 326n47, 343
Anderson, Carol, 231, 242n7
André, Gérard, 78
Andréani, Jacques, 47, 50, 57, 78–81, 83–84, 88, 90
Andropov, Yuri, 90, 162, 215–19, 225n59
Arafat, Yasser, 252
Arms control, 97–99, 101, 103, 105, 154, 159, 167–68, 212, 214, 218–20, 222n23, 276, 291–93, 295, 305–6, 308, 312, 316, 318
Arms race, 99, 155–7, 159, 188, 192, 199n7, 307
Aron, Raymond, 74–75
Austria, 3, 6, 9, 249–65, 353
Auswärtiges Amt, 276, 278–80, 282–83, 287–88, 290, 293, 295
Azbel, Mark, 123–24, 130, 135, 139

Bahr, Egon, 282
Balluku, Beqir, 339
Bartels, Wim, 161, 165, 199n15

Basket Four, 154, 276
Basket One, 3, 76, 81, 87–88, 153, 354
Basket Three, 3, 5, 7, 10, 17, 19–21, 24, 26, 53, 56–58, 60, 75–76, 81–85, 88, 90–91, 120, 132, 183, 211, 215, 218–19, 249, 253, 263, 277, 288, 305–6, 322n1, 343
Basket Two, 134, 140, 254, 282
Batrovin, Sergei, 160–61
Bauer, Friedrich, 257
Belgium, 155, 193
Belgrade CSCE Follow-up Meeting, 4, 11n7, 17, 21–24, 26, 29, 31–32, 37n23, 97, 101–2, 105, 107, 109, 121, 134–35, 137–38, 140, 183, 208, 211–15, 223n25, 262–63, 277–78, 294, 335, 342, 348n62
Berlin Wall, 9–10, 265, 353
Bern Meeting of Experts, 17, 23, 30, 32, 109, 282–83, 288–90, 300n62, 310, 312
Bielka, Erich, 258
Biermann, Wolf, 258, 261
Bindy, Leonid, 162
Birman, Joe, 132, 144n44
Bogoraz, Larisa, 195
Bonner, Yelena, 5, 213
Braithwaite, Rodric, 53–54, 67n48, 68n63
Brandt, Willy, 79, 102, 104, 294, 336–37
Braunmühl, Gerold von, 293
Brezhnev Doctrine, 49, 83, 87–88
Brezhnev, Leonid, 1, 55–56, 62n3, 64n16, 74–75, 84, 91, 101, 107, 129, 139, 160, 277, 294, 307–8, 315, 322n3, 323n6, 333

358 • Index

Brimelow, Thomas, 54, 68n63
Brooklyn Antinuclear Group (BANG), 152, 162–63, 174n38
Brown, George, 53, 68n60
Brzezinski, Zbigniew, 102, 105–6, 132
Bulgaria, 26, 36n8, 263, 285, 287, 317
Bullard, Julian, 54, 68n63
Burns, Andrew, 53
Burt, Richard, 108–9
Bush, George H. W., 99, 281, 319
Butler, Broadus, 233

Callaghan, James, 51
Campaign for Peace and Democracy – East and West (CPDEW), 152, 156, 159–60, 163, 165–66
Canada, 24, 37n8, 153, 284
Carrère d'Encausse, Hélène, 81
Carter, Jimmy, 23–24, 97–98, 100–102, 121, 132, 136, 234, 236, 243n14, 245n36, 277
Ceausescu, Nicolae, 313, 340
Central Intelligence Agency (CIA), 162–63
Conventional Forces in Europe (CFE), 306–7, 318–21, 327n56, 328n68
Chamberlain, Owen, 136
Charter 77, 5, 151, 159–61, 164, 184, 186–88, 190, 192, 195, 197, 201n33, 207, 209–12, 235, 261
Charter of Paris for a New Europe, 10
Chazelle, Jacques, 57–59, 78, 84, 86
Chernenko, Konstantin, 218–19
Chertoff, Lilli S., 120
China, 330–31, 336, 338–42
Chmykhalov Family, 101, 109
civil society, 17–18, 28, 32, 34, 55
Cohen, Jack, 128
Comaneci, Nadia, 236
Commission on Security and Cooperation in Europe, 27, 32, 99, 121, 133–34
Committee for State Security. *See* KGB
Committee for the Defense of the Unjustly Prosecuted (VONS), 212

Committee of Concerned Scientists (CCS), 119–21, 124, 126–40
Committee on the Present Danger, 98–99
Communism, 85, 90, 99, 104, 127, 130, 167, 207, 209, 214, 220, 253, 255, 262, 332, 350–51
Common European Home, 292–94, 301n76
Communist Party of Soviet Union (CPSU), 85–86, 107, 190, 216, 291, 307–8, 310, 312, 322n3
Coordinating Committee on Multilateral Export Controls (COCOM), 292
Conference on Confidence and Security Building Measures and Disarmament in Europe (CDE), 278, 280–81, 306–11
Conference on the Human Dimension (CHD), 20, 25–27, 30, 33–34
Confidence-building measures (CBMs), 105–7, 109, 277–78, 283, 306, 308, 323n6, 323n8
Congress of Vienna, 74, 76, 88–89, 91, 353
Copenhagen Conference on the Human Dimension, 20, 26, 31
Council of Europe (CoE), 19, 27–28
Courcel, Geoffroy de, 82
Crocker, Chester, 233
culture, 5–6, 75, 81, 83, 85–86, 187, 239–40, 282, 286–87
Culture Forum, 285–86
Czechoslovakia, 5, 9, 21, 36n8, 151, 157–59, 166, 184–87, 190, 193, 201n33, 209–10, 212, 249–50, 252, 260–63, 265, 275, 285–86, 289, 332, 335

Danecker, Gail, 160
Dash, Greg, 124
Decalogue of the CSCE first basket, 75, 88–90
De Gaulle, Charles, 55–56, 63n10, 77–78

Dejean, Maurice, 56, 92n7
Denmark, 104, 193
Diehl, Jackson, 192
disarmament, 100, 105–6, 157–58, 161–62, 166, 172n27, 185–88, 190–195, 197, 202n42, 212, 216, 218–20, 222n23, 276, 278, 280–81, 283, 286, 290–95, 306–8, 313, 318, 352
Dizdarević, Raif, 295
dissidents, 5–8, 28–30, 75, 79–80, 82, 90, 105–6, 126–29, 136, 183–87, 189, 194–95, 197, 207–8, 210, 213–14, 235–36, 238, 250, 258, 260–62, 276, 281, 305, 315, 320, 337, 347n36, 353
Dobrynin, Anatoly, 101
Douglas-Home, Alec, 51, 53
Dubinin, Yuri, 58–60, 91
Dufourcq, Bertrand, 57

Eagleburger, Lawrence, 98–100, 107–8
education, 3, 8, 44, 215, 311
Eickhoff, Ekkehard, 284, 288
Esche, Dieter, 191
Euromissiles, 101, 104, 154–55, 171n18, 216–18
European Community (EC), 2–3, 6, 21, 44–46, 49, 51, 56, 59, 61–63, 84, 89, 153, 275, 306
European Court of Human Rights (ECHR), 19, 28, 34
European Disarmament Conference (EDC), 104–7
European Nuclear Disarmament Convention (END), 151–52, 156–59, 163–164, 168n1, 185, 187–88, 199n7, 201n33, 202n39
European Network for East-West Dialogue (ENEWD), 164
European Political Cooperation (EPC), 57,63n10, 287–89
European Union, 44, 306
exit visas, 29, 58, 81, 101, 107, 109, 112n27, 122–24, 129–30, 135, 139, 166, 191–92, 201n33, 237–38, 254–58, 265

Faber, Mient Jan, 158, 186, 199n15, 200n16, 201n33
Falk, Richard, 164
family reunification, 3, 32, 81, 98, 100, 107, 134, 215, 236, 276, 284, 288–89, 299n38, 312
Federal Foreign Office. *See Auswärtiges Amt*
Federal Republic of Germany (FRG), 6, 9, 103, 216, 218, 277, 279–80, 284–86, 288–290, 293, 318, 328n68, 333, 341, 351
Finland, 6, 251
Fischer, Oskar, 258, 316, 326n47
Fleischman, Janet, 192
Flory, Paul J., 137
Foreign and Commonwealth Office (FCO), 50–53, 61, 65n28, 65n31, 67n51
Ford, Gerald, 47, 74, 99, 121, 129, 132
France, 6, 24, 45, 54–56, 60, 63n10, 76–77, 79–80, 83, 85–91, 93n27, 124, 143n19, 216, 225n51, 234, 277, 279, 295, 351
Freedom and Peace Movement, 184, 186–87, 190–91, 193–94, 196–97

Gamsachurdia, Zviad, 195
Gauchet, Marcel, 80
Geneva stage, 46, 48, 50–54, 57, 64n16, 67n49, 78, 81, 83, 85–86, 88, 91
Genscher, Hans-Dietrich, 102, 104, 106–7, 112n27, 276, 278–82, 285, 289–90, 292–95, 351
Georgian Helsinki Group, 195
Geremek, Bronisław, 191, 201n36
German Democratic Republic (GDR), 4, 26, 36n8, 103, 207, 209–12, 215, 218–19, 224n34, 226n65, 250, 252, 257–59, 263–65, 277, 281–82, 284, 294, 305, 307–8, 310–21, 322n5, 326n47, 337, 352–53
German question, 276, 334
German reunification, 293, 306, 319, 321
Ghebali, Victor-Yves, 91

Gilde, Benjamin, 250, 253, 262
Ginzburg, Alexander, 5
Giscard d'Estaing, Valéry, 55–57, 74, 76, 81, 105
Gitterman, Moshe, 123–24, 130
Glucksmann, André, 80
Goldberg, Arthur J., 102, 183
Goldfarb, Alexander, 131
Goma, Paul, 29
Gorbachev, Mikhail, 6, 9, 25, 166–67, 190, 193–95, 197, 214, 219–20, 249, 263, 265, 291–94, 301n76, 301n78, 310, 312–13, 317–19, 321, 324n18, 336, 343
Grass, Günter, 286
Greece, 240
Greenwald, John, 103
Gromyko, Andrei, 1, 64n16, 223n24, 281, 283, 291, 333
Grosser, Pierre, 91

Haig, Alexander, 108, 113n42
Hase, Karl-Günther von, 285–87
Havel, Václav, 5, 159, 195, 260, 262
Heath, Edward, 51
Helsinki Commission. *See* Commission on Security and Cooperation in Europe
Helsinki Consultations. *See* Multilateral Preparatory Talks (MPT)
Helsinki Final Act 2–3, 5–7, 18, 21, 34, 50, 60, 74–75, 77, 86, 91, 101, 103–4, 109, 110n9, 112n27, 119–21, 123–24, 129, 131–37, 140, 151, 163, 165, 183, 184, 187–89, 207, 209–12, 214–15, 223n24, 230–41, 249, 253, 257–58, 261, 275, 279, 282, 284–85, 288, 293, 295, 305, 314, 330, 334, 336–37, 342–43, 351–53. *See also* Basket One, Basket Two, Basket Three, Basket Four
Helsinki monitors, 5, 109, 284
Helsinki network, 5, 99, 207, 211, 214–15, 219
Hirsch, Dorothy, 120

Honecker, Erich, 211–12, 218–19, 224n34, 226n65, 259, 281, 310, 313, 315–16, 322n2, 337
Hooks, Benjamin, 234
Horn, Gyula, 265
Hoxha, Enver, 332–38, 340, 343, 346n23, 347n39
human contacts, 3, 5, 10, 17, 23, 30, 32, 64n16, 102–4, 109, 154, 188, 211, 215, 217, 219, 252, 258, 276, 281, 283, 288, 307–8, 312, 316–17, 352
human rights, 2–5, 7–10, 17–20, 23–35, 76, 79, 81, 86–91, 97–99, 101–7, 109–10, 119–22, 125–27, 129–30, 132–33, 135–37, 139–40, 142n7, 151–54, 156, 158–68, 170n11, 172n27, 183–88, 190–92, 194–97, 198n2, 207–15, 217–19, 230–35, 238–41, 242n7, 244n27, 245n36, 251, 256, 261, 277–78, 281–85, 288–89, 291, 308, 310, 312–13, 317, 321, 331, 334, 337–38, 343, 351–54
Human Dimension Mechanism (HDM), 18, 20, 25–28, 31, 33–35
Human Rights Council (HRC), 19, 28, 33–34
Humphrey, Hubert, 97
Hungary, 9, 25–26, 36n8, 50, 158, 185, 187, 193, 201n33, 214, 219, 249–50, 252, 254–55, 258, 263–65, 285–87, 314, 317, 319
Husák, Gustav, 261, 337

immigration, 9, 141, 231, 235–39, 241, 243n19, 276, 353
information, 3, 8, 17, 19, 57–59, 81, 98, 104–5, 120–22, 132–34, 136, 139–40, 151, 169n2, 183, 188, 196, 283, 308, 315, 317
Initiative for Peace and Human Rights (IFM), 191, 210
Interchurch Peace Council (IKV), 156–60, 186, 201n33
Intermediate-Range Nuclear Forces (INF) missiles, 171n18, 291, 306–7, 310–11, 313

International Helsinki Federation for Human Rights (IHF), 195
International Peace Communication and Coordination Work (IPCCN), 160
inviolability of frontiers, 1, 3, 81, 87
Ionesco, Eugène, 74
Israel, 32, 100, 109, 122–24, 136, 138, 213, 299n38
Italy, 60, 155, 163

Jackson, Henry M., 128–29
Jackson-Vanik Amendment, 80, 127–31, 140
Jao Ven Juan, 341
Jaruzelski Plan, 184, 192, 197, 202n42
Jaruzelski, Wojciech, 193, 217, 279
Jobert, Michel, 55
John Paul II, 186, 192
journalists, 3, 29, 33, 52, 58, 80–81, 207, 209, 212, 311, 315, 317, 326n44

Kac, Marc, 137
Kádár, Janos, 254
Kampelman, Max M., 97–110, 281, 308, 353
Kaplun, Irena, 213, 224n37
Kassof, Allen H., 133
Kastl, Jörg, 108–9
Kavan, Jan, 187, 192
Kemoularia, Claude de, 59
Kennedy, Edward, 138
Kessler, Heinz, 318
Keys, Barbara, 240
KGB, 5, 12n12, 90, 100, 122–25, 136, 139, 208–10, 212–15, 224n37
Khanin, Vladimir, 123
Kirchschläger, Rudolf, 252, 261
Kis, Janos, 192, 201n33
Kislik, Vladimir, 139
Kissinger, Henry, 23, 47, 62n3, 64n16, 80, 98–99, 124, 128–30, 153, 333
Kohl, Helmut, 13n19, 102, 104–5, 280, 294, 301n76, 301n78
Kohout, Pavel, 261
Kondrashev, Sergei, 100–1, 107, 109, 281, 299n38

Korey, William, 129
Kosharovsky, Yuli, 124
Kosygin, Alexei, 342
Kovalev, Anatoly, 82, 91, 107
Kovalev, Sergei, 34
Kramer, Mark, 266n3, 350–51
Kreisky, Bruno, 252–56, 258–62
Kuron, Jacek, 186, 189

Laber, Jeri, 238, 352
Laloy, Jean, 56, 92n7
Lanc, Erwin, 259
Landy, Joanne, 160, 166–67
Lee, Bill, 235
Lerner, Alexander, 124, 139
Levich, Benjamin, 122, 124, 127, 130, 134, 138
Levine, Ruth, 120
Lévy, Bernard-Henry, 80
Liedermann, Helmut, 253
Ligachev, Egor, 312
Litvinov, Maxim, 87
Loginov, Vadim, 312
Lundts, Alexander, 123
Luxembourg, 193

Madrid Concluding Document, 26
Madrid CSCE Review Meeting, 4, 11n7, 17, 22–23, 26, 29–31, 33, 97–99, 101, 103–9, 110n8, 121, 134–35, 137–38, 211–18, 260, 262–63, 276–82, 284, 289–90, 293–95, 307–8, 352–53
Mallaby, Christopher, 53
Malta, 281, 297n12
Manzione, Joseph, 119
Maresca, John J., 102
Marxism-Leninism, 80, 334, 338
Mastnak, Tomas, 192
Mastny, Vojtech, 7
Mazowiecki, Tadeusz, 189
McGovern Amendment, 237–39
McGovern, George, 237
Mediterranean, 6, 12n13, 49, 278, 297n12, 342
Mehlhorn, Ludwig, 210
Meiman, Naum, 138

362 • *Index*

Mellman, Mark, 126, 139
Mendelevich, Lev, 3, 54
Mexico, 235
Meyers, Michael, 234
Michnik, Adam, 189
Mielke, Erich, 208–9, 215, 218, 226n65, 311, 313–14
Ministry for State Security (Mfs). *See* Stasi
Minkiewicz, Jan, 187
Mintoff, Dom, 339
Mitterrand, François, 344
Mlynář, Zdeněk, 261
Mock, Alois, 265
Moscow Helsinki Watch Group, 30, 34, 106, 136, 207, 211, 213, 235
Moscow Trust Group, 152, 155–58, 160–63, 165, 173n29, 201n33
Movement for the Defense of Human and Civil Rights (ROPCiO), 209–10
Multilateral Preparatory Talks (MPT), 2–3, 22, 46–50, 54, 57, 121, 253, 276
Munich Agreements, 75
Mutual and Balanced Force Reductions (MBFR), 51, 53, 66n43, 105, 278, 294–95

Napoleon I, 74
National Association for the Advancement of Colored People (NAACP), 9, 231–35, 239, 241, 242nn6–7, 243n14
National Committee for a Sane Nuclear Policy (SANE), 154, 162, 172n19, 172n27, 173n31
Neither East nor West – NYC (NENWN), 162–63, 176n60
Németh, Micklós, 264
Netherlands, 24, 193, 286
Neutral and Nonaligned States (NNA), 3–4, 6, 9, 21, 24, 45, 48–50, 91, 109, 250–51, 253, 262–65, 277, 284, 287, 289, 310–11, 354
Nimetz, Matthew, 121, 135
Nixon, Richard, 64n16, 98–99, 124, 128, 153, 171n12, 341–42

Non-governmental organizations (NGO), 5–8, 18–19, 26, 28–35, 151, 207, 209, 211–12, 214, 230, 279, 287, 326n47, 351–53
non-intervention in internal affairs, 23–25, 81, 83, 87–88, 343
non-use of force, 87–88, 282–83, 325n37
North Atlantic Treaty Organization (NATO), 2–3, 9–10, 21, 45–46, 48–49, 56, 63n10, 103–9, 154, 171n18, 185–86, 190, 194, 199n7, 213, 218, 223n25, 237, 251, 275, 278–80, 283–89, 293–95, 306–7, 309–12, 318–19, 323n9, 324n21, 330–31, 344
Novak, Michael, 289–90

Orban, Victor, 194
Organization for Security and Cooperation in Europe (OSCE), 10, 18, 23, 28, 35, 52, 62n1, 67n49, 306, 321
Orlov, Yuri, 5, 106–7, 136–37, 146n61, 284
Orzechowski, Marian, 193
Ostpolitik, 79, 103–4, 250, 252, 254, 275, 294, 337
Ottawa Meeting of Experts, 17, 23, 25–26, 29, 31, 109, 282–83, 285, 288, 299n38
Owen, David, 53, 68n60

Pahr, Willibald, 259, 261
Pasch, Johann, 261
Pasolini, Pier Paolo, 3
Peace Activists East and West (PAEW), 160
peaceful change of frontiers, 153, 346n28
peaceful settlement of disputes, 278, 297n12
Pentacostals, 101, 107, 109
Perestroika, 30, 185, 291, 294
Perez de Cuella, Javier, 343
Petrova, Jana, 195
Physicians for Social Responsibility (PSR), 154

Pierret, Alain, 78, 81–82, 91
Pipes, Richard, 125
Plaisant, François, 78, 81
Poland, 4, 9, 11n7, 25–26, 32, 37n8, 50, 103–4, 107, 112n27, 157, 159, 163, 184–87, 189–93, 207, 209–10, 212–14, 216–19, 225n59, 249–50, 252, 254–58, 262, 275, 279, 285, 289, 295, 308, 317, 319–20
Polish Workers' Defense Committee (KOR), 160, 207, 209–12
Political prisoners, 12n12, 27, 100, 197, 343, 347n36
Pollack, Fred, 130
Pomerantz, Mel, 130
Pompidou, Georges, 1, 55–56, 64n16, 76, 78, 85–86, 93n27
Poppe, Gerd, 210
Poppe, Ulbrike, 210
Portugal, 51, 60, 185
Poudade, Paul, 78, 81
Pozsar, Gheza, 236
Prague Spring, 2, 75–76, 78, 87, 251, 260, 353
Press, Frank, 121, 135

Quai d'Orsay, 56–57, 78, 82, 87–88, 93n19

Radio Free Europe, 209
Radio Liberty, 209
Reagan, Ronald, 6, 97–101, 103–9, 114n81, 154, 196, 216, 233, 237, 279–81, 290–91, 308, 322n2
refuseniks, 27, 29, 119, 122–28, 130, 134–39, 142n7
Renard, Pierre-Henri, 78
Renouvin, Pierre, 7
Richard, Robert, 78
Ridgway, Rozanne, 238, 300n60
Robin, Gabriel, 57
Rocard, Michel, 80
Rokita, Jan, 196
Romania, 26, 29, 32, 36n8, 48–49, 97, 167, 219, 226n68, 263–65, 285, 287, 289, 313, 317, 340–41
Rostow, Eugene, 99–100

Rougagnou, Michel, 78
Rubin, Vitaly, 124
Rubinson, Paul, 119
Rumyantsev, Oleg, 30
Ruth, Friedrich, 283

Sakharov, Andrei, 74, 80, 91, 106, 123, 128, 136–38, 213, 284
Salansky, Naum, 139
SALT II, 130, 277, 290
Sauvagnargues, Jean, 55, 59
Schadrin, Vladimir Nikolaevich, 213
Schifter, Richard, 198n2, 284
Schmidt, Helmut, 64n16, 74, 102, 104–5, 277, 280, 294
Schneider, Rolf, 258–59
Schollwer, Wolfgang, 282
Schumann, Maurice, 55
Scientists for Sakharov, Orlov and Shcharansky (SOS), 136–37
self-determination of peoples, 76–77, 88, 187–89, 233, 281–82
Seydoux, Roger, 56
Shanker, Albert, 236
Sharansky, Natan, 5, 109, 136–37
Shcharansky, Anatoly. See Sharansky, Natan
Shehu, Mehmet, 341
Shevardnadze, Eduard, 292
Shinbaum, Myrna, 124
Shulman, Marshall, 102
Shultz, George, 99, 104–5, 108–9, 115n81, 281, 283, 289, 291
Snyder, Sarah B., 7, 211, 214
Socialist Unity Party (SED), 259–60, 282, 305, 307, 311, 313–20, 322n5, 326n47, 337
Solidarity. See Solidarnosc
Solidarnosc, 155, 160, 184, 186, 189, 191, 196, 198, 200n28, 202n44, 213, 225n59, 256, 279–80
Solzhenitsyn, Alexander, 79, 82
South Africa, 232–34, 240
sovereign equality, 87–88
Soviet Academy of Sciences, 122, 138, 161

Soviet Jews, 80, 101, 127–29, 137, 299n38
Soviet Union. *See* Union of Soviet Socialist Republics (USSR)
Spain, 60, 223n25
Staden, Berndt von, 281
Stanley, Eugene, 126,
Stasi, 208–14, 224n34, 311–16, 321
Stern, Edward, 131
Stever, Guyford, 121, 132
Stewart, Michael, 51
Stockholm Conference on Confidence and Security Measures and Disarmament in Europe, 105, 109, 263, 276, 282–85, 288, 290–91, 293, 295, 305–6, 309–11
Stoph, Willi, 258–59
Strategic Arms Reduction Treaty (START), 98
Strategic Defense Initiative (SDI), 292
Strauss, Franz Josef, 260
Strougal, Lubomir, 195
Suslov, Mikhail, 217
Sweden, 3, 6, 263
Swedish Helsinki Committee, 195
Switzerland, 3, 6, 60, 263

Talleyrand, Charles-Maurice de, 74, 76, 91
Templin, Wolfgang, 201n33, 210
Theatre Nuclear Forces (TNF), 277, 279–80
The Netherlands, 24, 193, 286
Thomas, Daniel C., 7, 90, 207, 212, 214–15, 217, 225n51, 230, 350–51, 355n4
Tickell, Crispin, 52–53, 67n52
Timofeyev, Lev, 30, 194–95
Tito, Josip Broz, 340, 342
Tomin, Zdena, 160

U.S. Helsinki Watch Committee, 234
Ukraine, 28, 97, 213
Ukrainian Public Group to Promote the Implementation of the Helsinki Agreements in the USSR, 5
Ulbricht, Walter, 336–37

Ulrich, Maurice, 55
Union of Soviet Socialist Republics (USSR), 1–2, 4–5, 9, 21, 23, 25, 27, 30–34, 36n8, 37n8, 46, 52, 55–56, 77, 79–80, 82–85, 87–88, 90–91, 97–102, 104, 106–7, 109, 112n27, 114n81, 120–40, 153, 155, 157–58, 161–62, 164–65, 168, 173n31, 187–88, 190, 193–95, 207, 209, 211–17, 219, 220, 225n59, 230–31, 234–35, 237–38, 240, 251, 254, 256, 263, 277, 279, 281, 283–86, 289–90, 293, 306–8, 310, 315–18, 320, 330–41, 343, 346n20, 350–51, 353
United Kingdom, 6, 45, 50–51, 54, 60–61, 63n10, 124, 127, 154, 158, 279, 286, 333, 340, 351
United Nations, 52, 88, 128, 143n19, 219, 231, 242n7, 245n36, 316, 331
United Nations Charter, 18, 87–88, 335
United Nations Educational, Scientific and Cultural Organization (UNESCO), 59, 143n19
United Nations Universal Declaration of Human Rights, 18, 126, 233
United States, 2, 5–6, 9, 17, 23–24, 26, 31, 37n8, 55, 62n3, 80, 84, 99, 101, 114n81, 120–21, 124–26, 128–29, 130–33, 135, 138–39, 146n61, 153–57, 159, 165, 167, 171nn18–19, 173n31, 188, 193, 196, 209, 211, 214, 216–17, 219–20, 223n25, 230–41, 242n7, 243n19, 245n36, 277, 280, 286, 292, 299n38, 307, 309, 320, 330–31, 333–36, 338–41, 343, 344n1, 348n64, 352–53
United States Helsinki Watch Group (USHW), 152, 161–62, 166, 170n11
United States State Department, 24, 27, 32, 99, 102, 108, 110n9, 121, 125–26, 132, 135–38, 140, 238
Urban, Jan, 195
Urban, Jerzy, 193, 202n42

Vance, Cyrus R., 102, 106, 136
Vancūra, Jiri, 192
Vanik, Charles A., 128
Vashchenko Family, 101, 109
Vest, George, 54, 99
Veverka, Ota, 195
Vienna Concluding Document, 20, 30, 33, 264, 314–16, 319, 321, 328n68
Vienna CSCE Review Meeting, 4, 6, 8–9, 17, 22–27, 30–31, 33, 36, 51, 64n16, 109, 164–65, 189, 219, 250, 257, 262–64, 281, 283, 287–288, 290, 293, 295, 312–13, 316–21
Vietnam, 2, 84, 216, 218, 240, 342
Voigt, Karsten, 192
Voronel, Alexander, 123–25, 130

Wałęsa, Lech, 186, 189, 201n36
Warsaw Pact, 6, 9, 48, 77, 85, 91, 102, 104, 163, 171n11, 186–87, 189–90, 192–94, 199n7, 207–8, 216–17, 223nn24–25, 275–80, 283–89, 293–95, 305, 309–313, 315–319, 323n9, 324n21, 326n47, 330–34, 346n20
Warsaw Treaty Organization. *See* Warsaw Pact
Western Group of Forces (WGF), 306, 327n63
Westphalian System, 1–2, 4, 9, 88, 90
Wilson, Harold, 51, 64n16
Winzer, Otto, 252
Women's International League for Peace and Freedom (WILPF), 154
World War II, 45, 59, 78–79, 98, 191, 231, 334, 338
Wright, Patrick, 53

Yakunin, Gleb, 195
Yoffe, Alik, 139
Yugoslavia, 234, 334, 338, 340–341

Zhou En Lai, 342
Zhukov, Yuri, 159
Ziman, John, 121
Zimmermann, Warren, 99, 102
Zorin, Valerian, 53, 91

www.ingramcontent.com/pod-product-compliance
Lightning Source LLC
Chambersburg PA
CBHW072142100526
44589CB00015B/2049